EDUCATING PEOPLE OF FAITH

EDUCATING PEOPLE OF FAITH

Exploring the History of
Jewish and Christian Communities

Edited by

John Van Engen

WILLIAM B. EERDMANS PUBLISHING COMPANY
GRAND RAPIDS, MICHIGAN / CAMBRIDGE, U.K.

Wm. B. Eerdmans Publishing Co.
255 Jefferson Ave. S.E., Grand Rapids, Michigan 49503 /
P.O. Box 163, Cambridge CB3 9PU U.K.

Printed in the United States of America

09 08 07 06 05 04   7 6 5 4 3 2 1

Library of Congress Cataloging-in-Publication Data

Educating people of faith: exploring the history of
Jewish and Christian communities / edited by John Van Engen.
p.   cm.
Includes bibliographical references.
ISBN 0-8028-4936-9 (pbk.: alk. paper)
1. Spiritual life — Christianity — History of doctrines.
2. Spiritual life — Judaism — History of doctrines.
I. Van Engen, John H.

BV4490.E38   2004
268'.09 — dc22

2003064207

www.eerdmans.com

Contents

v

THE MIDDLE AGES

THE REFORMATION ERA

Contents

Foreword

"The church is always more than a school," declares historian Jaroslav Pelikan at the beginning of his five-volume history of Christian doctrine. "But the church cannot be less than a school."[1] As time passes and new generations arise, the continuity and integrity of the Christian faith depend upon its transmission to newcomers. A parallel claim can be made regarding Judaism, a tradition that for millennia has observed God's command through Moses to "take care and watch yourselves closely, so as neither to forget the things that your eyes have seen nor to let them slip from your mind all the days of your life; make them known to your children and your children's children" (Deuteronomy 4:9). Teaching and learning have been woven into the fabric of Jewish and Christian communal life across the centuries and in countless social and cultural contexts. In each of these "religions of the book," adherents have educated and formed one another in the tradition's wisdom and way of life through numerous, diverse, and historically changing practices.

In recent decades this perennial necessity has become a matter of acute concern for those who care deeply about these traditions. Even though hunger for things spiritual is strong and widespread, religious groups shaped by centuries of theology, liturgy, and communal life often seem less attractive to contemporary Americans than do spiritual movements that offer newer, more free-floating approaches. The challenges to religious formation presented by an image-laden consumer culture with immense formative power of its own

1. Jaroslav Pelikan, *The Christian Tradition: A History of the Development of Doctrine* (Chicago: University of Chicago, 1971), 1:1.

have also become increasingly evident. Some denominations have experienced decline in the number and commitment of their members, and few are surprised when young people drift away from the religious communities of their birth.

The idea for this book emerged during a conversation among scholars and religious leaders about this concern. One of the scholars was John Van Engen, who calmly called to the attention of those gathered the fact that concern about faith formation was hardly a new thing. Educating people of faith has been not only a necessary goal within each tradition, he pointed out; it has also been a persistent problem. Without diminishing the particular challenges inherent in late modernity, he noted that forming persons and communities into life guided by Torah or into membership in the Body of Christ has always faced resistance. Yet within the ancient and continuing endeavor of forming people of faith, there have been some periods of remarkable creativity when movements or structures have emerged that drew sizable numbers of believers into deeper reflection and greater devotion.

With support from the Valparaiso Project on the Education and Formation of People in Faith, a project of Lilly Endowment located at Valparaiso University, Professor Van Engen gathered a group of outstanding scholars of ancient, medieval, and early modern Christianity and Judaism and asked them to explore important episodes, settings, or issues in faith formation in the areas of their expertise. The results are published here. In richly detailed essays, we see how Jewish and Christian orientations to life took shape both through specialized practices such as catechesis, study of scripture, rituals, and preaching and in the ordinary choices of daily life, such as what and when to eat or not to eat. Together the essays portray religious formation across social levels, from the textual attentiveness of highly literate rabbis and monks to the local experiences of illiterate medieval Christians for whom the veneration of the shrines of saints, street performances of religious dramas, and public sermons by wandering preachers were profoundly formative.

As one reads these essays, it becomes clear that educating people of faith did not in the past (and cannot today) take place only or even primarily in places recognizable as "school." Rather, this process takes place through and within practices — some of them deliberately and intentionally educational, but most pursuing other goods, such as communion with God or love of neighbor. Through worship and study, community governance and catechesis, spiritual direction and household prayer, Jews and Christians over time have been educated and formed within a web of practices transmitted and transformed by the communities that live them out in daily life. Engaging in such practices — whether highly ritualized or thoroughly quotidian — individuals and communities come to know themselves, others, and God in specific ways. Through them, in multiple contexts of inculturation, resistance, and negotiation, basic orientations within the world are both expressed and absorbed.

This book demonstrates that attention to the practices of actual religious communities can open fascinating new insights into specific periods in history and into important themes in religious formation, even when distance in time limits access to sources and necessarily leaves readers with unanswered questions. I am confident that a wide range of readers interested in the practices of Christianity and Judaism will find these essays informative and stimulating. However, I want especially to encourage historians and religious educators to explore the excellent work assembled here.

Historians will note that John Van Engen's introductory chapter places this book in the context of contemporary academic approaches to history and religion. While there is no need for me to reiterate his fine discussion, I do want to add my own commendation of the essays gathered here as exemplary work with rich potential as a model for future research. This volume resists the disciplinary structures that have tended to divide scholars into, say, those who read the works of Calvin and those who study social mobility in sixteenth-century Switzerland. Thus the essays seek to overcome a separation between the "intellectual" and the "social" that has too often restricted historians' understanding of those human communities that were oriented by and to an overarching religious account of themselves and their world. The dynamic intertwining of theological ideas and social forms characteristic of such communities is, it turns out, right at the heart of efforts to form people in religious faith. As a result, the topics taken up in this volume afford remarkable insight into historic Christian and Jewish communities that would not be accessible from other angles of vision. For this reason, this book could serve to very good effect as a classroom text for historical study on the part of ministerial and rabbinical students, as well as for graduate students and advanced undergraduates in history or religious studies.

Those who bear special responsibility for educating others within specific traditions — teachers in churches and synagogues, pastoral leaders in congregations and parishes, scholars in divinity schools and seminaries — will also find much to value here. This book will help these educators to make the resources of the past available to practitioners in the present. This is not to say that premodern methods can or should be lifted out of context and deployed in twenty-first-century congregations. Rather, I would urge contemporary practitioners to allow these essays to stimulate their imaginations and to generate reflection on enduring issues. How have others thought about the relationship between the yearnings of ordinary believers and the articulate faith of religious elites? How do practices born in devotion also become exclusive and even harmful? Is the local congregation necessarily the most important place of religious formation? How do images — not texts, not propositions — form people in faith? Historians are not charged with offering systematic answers to questions like these. However, they can (and here they do) lead readers into the company of other human beings who have responded to these questions, both in words and in the ways in which they lived their lives.

Educating People of Faith belongs to a growing body of literature that focuses on practices as key elements in the education and formation of people in faith. The scholar who has done most to encourage this perspective is the practical theologian Craig Dykstra, who has written the most fully developed argument for a practice-based understanding of Christian education and formation, *Growing in the Life of Faith: Education and Christian Practices.*[2] Dr. Dykstra and I have worked together on scholarly teams that have produced two other books that develop this approach. *Practicing Our Faith: A Way of Life for a Searching People* explores twelve Christian practices — honoring the body, hospitality, household economics, saying yes and saying no, keeping sabbath, discernment, testimony, shaping communities, forgiveness, healing, dying well, and singing our lives — as constituent elements within a way of life that is lived in the light of and in response to God's presence in Christ.[3] *Practicing Theology: Beliefs and Practices in Christian Life,* which explores the implications of this approach for systematic theology, emphasizes attention to practices as a way of bringing theology into closer touch with daily life in the world and enabling it to fulfill its primary purpose of serving Christian living.[4]

Although these previous works have sought primarily to serve Christian readers, I am delighted that the present historical volume includes the work of Jewish scholars and gives attention to the history of Jewish education. This fact greatly enhances the account of the past here set forth. Further, I hope that having portraits of Jewish and Christian education side by side in this context will

2. Louisville: Geneva, 1999. Dykstra is Vice President for Religion, Lilly Endowment Inc.

3. Edited by Dorothy C. Bass (San Francisco: Jossey-Bass, 1997). *Practicing Our Faith* is not so much about faith formation as it is a contribution to it; the book has been studied in hundreds of congregations, retreat centers, and institutions of higher learning. The website www.practicingourfaith.org serves as a hub of reflection on practices and faith formation and will be updated as subsequent publications on this theme appear.

4. Edited by Miroslav Volf and Dorothy C. Bass (Grand Rapids: Wm. B. Eerdmans, 2002). One section of the book addresses the education and formation of ministers and academic theologians.

stimulate fresh reflection on the part of historians, religious educators, and other readers from both traditions.[5]

Dorothy C. Bass

---

5. The Valparaiso Project on the Education and Formation of People in Faith has also sponsored the work of the Catholic-Jewish Colloquium, in which Christian educator Mary C. Boys and Jewish educator Sara Lee worked with scholars and educators from both traditions to develop an approach they call "interreligious learning." See "Religious Traditions in Conversation: The Work of the Catholic-Jewish Colloquium," a special issue of *Religious Education* 91, no. 4 (Fall 1996). The work of Boys and Lee continues in association with the Boston College Center for Christian-Jewish Learning.

Acknowledgments

For help in the initial stage of editing, I owe an enormous debt to Dr. Lisa Wolverton, of the University of Oregon, whose sharp eye and thoughtful mind contributed to better formulations and more accessible essays. She became, virtually, a co-editor. For help with the mechanical labors that come with a manuscript of this size, I am grateful to Abram Van Engen and to Dr. Daniel Hobbins. And I am profoundly grateful to Dr. Dorothy Bass, who encouraged me to undertake this project, supported me throughout, and was gracious and patient in seeing it to completion.

JOHN VAN ENGEN
Notre Dame, Indiana
October 20, 2003

The development of this book was supported by the Valparaiso Project on the Education and Formation of People in Faith, a project of the Lilly Endowment Inc. based at Valparaiso University.

Formative Religious Practices in Premodern European Life

John Van Engen

This is a book about Jewish and Christian beliefs and practices in premodern Europe. Comprised of fifteen historical essays, each written by a professional historian with general readers in mind, the book aims to present studies rigorous in historical method, stimulating for future research, useful to those who live out of these traditions (and those who do not), yet broadly accessible. Each essay asks about a complex of beliefs and practices in a distinct community and era before the year 1600. Each also asks, implicitly or explicitly, how historical work may be done, whether there is indeed a "usable past," whether, to put it simply, we the living have access to the "lived religion" of past ages. This may appear to set up an impossibly strained triangulation: present-day questions, historic sources, methodological queries. But precisely that three-way tension has often generated the most stimulating historical writing. The questions that lie behind this volume were first formulated as part of the Valparaiso Project on the Education and Formation of People in Faith, headed by Dr. Dorothy Bass, a historian of religion in America, the project itself under-written by the Religion Division of the Lilly Endowment under the leadership of Dr. Craig Dykstra. The essays were written independently, though commonly discussed. They propose no one-for-one correspondences between past and present, indeed are careful to respect historical distance and difference. Still, they point toward analogies and materials worthy of deeper consideration by scholars and practitioners alike.

Religion, like politics, is a constant in human affairs. A century ago thinkers in Europe and America might have denied that, or at least queried it, and many would still today. Human society, they might observe, is a constant, and with it politics, economy, gender relations, and much else. But religion is not.

1

Its practice will give way as humans find other means to understand their world, shape communities and identities, make ethical choices, deal with the unknown. The coping mechanism of a prescientific, premodern era, as many came to construe it, religious practice was bound to fade, and did fade. Max Weber put it best a century ago. With modernity comes an ever expanding "rationalization" of the world, hence a "disenchantment," all its enveloping "magic," his German word intimates, escaping into thin air. And yet in the twenty-first century and in observable reality, religion has not faded. "Enchantment," if you like, is still at work all around, even in materialist societies like the United States. In enlightened and post-enlightened lands, new and old forms of religious seeking persist, or flourish anew, some as heterogeneous older practices cultivated in a "new age" mode. In former Soviet lands Christianity, Judaism, and Islam outlasted three generations of overt suppression, as Taoist cults and Buddhist practices did a half-century of government hostility in China. Even among Weber's academic heirs in the humane disciplines (history, literature, sociology), religious subjects enjoy a degree of interest these days that might have astounded scholars two or three generations ago. More noticeably still, over the last generation groups called "fundamentalist" have grown in power and numbers worldwide. For historians, essayists, and journalists, not to say politicians, it is now the fundamentalists, not the secularists, who seem to set the agenda. Not altogether tongue in cheek, we might try reversing Weber: "enchanters," not "disenchanters," are making the future.

This, you object, is hardly the real story of religion in our day, not the fundamentalists, not even those practicing religion. In many places (and perhaps especially in those most familiar to professional historians) the feel of everyday life remains broadly a-religious, and practice continues to decline worldwide. People drift out of practice fully as much as enthusiasts find their way into new or renewed practices. To be clear: my point is not that all people are religious, or that religious practice is inherently intelligible apart from interpretation, though people this past century have often treated "secularizing" tendencies as self-evident and inevitable. My point is to highlight a presence too easily dismissed as foreign to modern life and as thus no longer worthy of independent status or reflection. We slip all too easily into accounts of religious practice that represent it as largely the expression of something else — outdated science or sublimated sex, social resentment or political power, therapeutic need. In effect this tends to perpetuate, perhaps unwittingly, earlier polemics that were once employed, perhaps legitimately, to create breathing space for spheres of life suffocating in a world suffused with the religious. But explaining away religion, in the media or in learned discourse, denies meaningful breathing space to religion itself and leaves vast areas of human existence uninterpreted. We do better to recognize religious expressions as a significant and persistent dimension of human experience and history, in the words of Talal Asad, "a distinctive space of human practice and belief which cannot be reduced to any other."[1]

More, and directly to the purposes of this volume, religious practices and beliefs have exercised formative powers in shaping human lives, inwardly as well as outwardly, in the past as well as the present. Writers and practitioners once took those powers for granted: hence efforts by earlier regimes to regulate them, hence too the stories of people who spent their lives trying to shake off their persistent presence. Today we are quick to register religion in its effects: when practices or beliefs fold a person into a new community or lifestyle, when they put someone at odds with a family or group, when they take hold to elicit a new sense of self or to provoke flash points in public policy, no less when they fail to take hold (endless sociological talk, for instance, about the Boomer generation in America, and their children). But if we react only to observed or presumed effects, we overlook the complexities at work inwardly and outwardly, the nature of religious life itself in experience and performance, those tangled webs alluded to broadly by our title words "formative practices." Trying to get at those connections, to give this grasp of religion in the past its due — that is the object of this book.

Belief and Practice: The Big Picture

Belief and practice interact complexly in human persons and groups, not singularly or simply. Any unilateral notion that belief generates practice, as theologians and church historians seemed once to imply and zealous proponents often still do, or that practice produces belief, as anthropologists and sociologists intimate and anxious religious leaders hope, will not do, even if both observations express real human truths. Aware that this problem has normative overtones, a group of systematic theologians has explored it in a volume on beliefs and practices in Christian life entitled *Practicing Theology,* locating their "focus on practices" in relation to contemporary currents within the academic field of theology.

As modernity gives way to postmodernity, the enduring question of the grounds for Christian believing has taken on fresh urgency. "What Grounds

---

1. Talal Asad, *Genealogies of Religion: Discipline and Reasons of Power in Christianity and Islam* (Baltimore and London, 1993), p. 27. Maureen Miller, "Religion Makes a Difference: Clerical and Lay Cultures in the Courts of Northern Italy, 1000-1300," *American Historical Review* 105 (2000): 1095-1130, has proposed that "religion" be placed alongside the famous triad of the last twenty years, "race, class, and gender," as constants in human life and history.

What?" Miroslav Volf asks in the final chapter of that book. As he notes, contemporary academic and popular culture tends to subordinate beliefs to practices "to the point of completely functionalizing beliefs." At the same time, other academic and popular voices, claiming the mantle of tradition, resist this approach by insisting that the influence goes only in the other direction, from beliefs to practices, with practices being the mere enactments of beliefs. By offering what they call "a more complex response," this group of theologians aimed to develop an approach that would strengthen "the vitality of a living tradition capable of being fully engaged with history and culture without becoming their captive."[2]

How we interpret the complex interplay between beliefs and practices touches on very sensitive matters in our grasp of individuals within groups. These essays take up historic instances of Jews and Christians "educated" or "formed" in the faith life of their communities. In popular conceptions of what is at stake or how it works, contraries come quickly and easily to mind these days: total freedom of association and persuasion among free individuals or heavy-handed coercion, whether individual or group, covert or overt. It is accordingly very easy to misconstrue or misrepresent the past. We imagine enforcement by way of public laws or social controls, and note that when pressures lift, people drift away — observations that are partly true, if one-sided. Past peoples, it is widely assumed, might on occasion choose to believe and practice, but most often were made to believe and practice. All middle ground thereby disappears, all movement between belief and practice, all variations in practice, all the intricate negotiations within a person, also between personal aspirations and group expectations — certainly in our grasp of the past, also in our sense of the present.

A true entering into the life of a religious community, into its practices and beliefs and animating spirit, could rarely be coerced or taken for granted, and mostly was neither. These essays aim to recover some of that middle ground, to recognize enfolding structures without foreclosing the freedom of individuals. This is not easy. It is as much an art as a programmatic stance: how to speak of religion's formative powers and meanings in ways true at once to individual experience and to the larger forces at work in the historic past. We historians have often attempted to do it by focusing on the "great man" or the "big story." We are drawn magnetically to extraordinary figures, an articulate rabbi like Maimonides, an eloquent convert like Augustine, an outspoken reformer like Luther, and we have interpreted each (nearly always a "him" until recently) as

2. Dorothy C. Bass, introduction to *Practicing Theology: Beliefs and Practices in Christian Life*, ed. Miroslav Volf and Dorothy C. Bass (Grand Rapids, 2001), p. 3.

4

standing in for a whole community's movement into or out of beliefs and practices. By contrast we have tended to silence women or to render their experiences extraordinary by comparison, placing them outside or over against the community, as visionaries or prophets, often as figures apart, all too easily demonized in one or another way. If not great figures as our models, we propose instead grand abstractions, our means to render intelligible a complex of historic practices and human acts that must somehow take in countless individual choices and a spectrum of attitudes. So we speak of conversion as well as de-conversion, Christianization as well as secularization, persecution as well as tolerance. Throughout we have found it hard to write and think about "ordinary" Jews or Christians, how they adopted or made their own — entered into — practices animated by religious convictions, how they gained a sense of place as "peoples of faith," how (and in what measure) they acted as agents in their own religious stories. Historians must, I think, imagine afresh all this "becoming," look at its evidences with nuance and richness, if we are to deal fully and honestly with the past — and the present. Movement into religious participation, mysterious though it is, individual though it ultimately is, signals a reality, also a historic reality. It is a reality, true, not finally or fully reducible to a historical text, either in the experience or its interpretation. But it is the moving query that animates the fifteen historical essays that follow.

Religion in History

These essays pursue historical, not polemical or philosophical, ends. The history we write, inevitably, gets informed by present-day perspectives, the distance wrought by time, the knowledge of how things turned out, the sources that have come down to us (or not come down), and much else. For historians these factors raise more hard questions: whether the past is knowable in itself, whether all talk of the past is finally only about the present, whether by research and imagination we can truly reenter other times, cultures, or minds.[3] Some have despaired of the past as a phantasm that is distant, illusory, or simply irrelevant. In extreme form this yields a stark choice: either the past is something truly other and therefore like a foreign country, or it is an extension of the historian's imagination and therefore an alternative conception of the present. Historians of Jewish or Christian communities can appear specially

3. This is an enormous debate with a large specialized literature. For accessible introductions, and contrasting viewpoints, see Richard J. Evans, *In Defense of History* (New York, 1999), and Alun Winslow, *Deconstructing History* (London, 1997).

vulnerable here, since many write or have written with an eye to present-day issues and as, to one or another degree, practitioners. But this tension is nothing new: thoughtful historians have always known and reflected upon it, coming to the past at times as something concretely out there, distinct and knowable, and at other times with supreme awareness that their interpretive acts in some measure help construct that past. Good historians have sensed both and have worked creatively with the tension. Here historians of the Jewish and Christian peoples may derive some advantage from acknowledging their own engagement, their search for discoverable practices or beliefs, for the real lives of real peoples and communities in religion — writing "half-in and half-out," as a recent historian of Pentecostalism put it, "to combine the cool eye of the critic with the warm heart of the believer. . . . I suspect that the posture of being half out and half in, though awkward, defines the fate of many religious historians."[4]

A grasp of religion in history, of recalling the past and living out of it into the future, has animated Jewish and Christian practice from the beginning, indeed was written into the heart of their sacred books. But what of today? After the Holocaust, can Jewish practitioners still think about or enter into, let alone appropriate, the beliefs and practices of those before them, even if they too knew persecution? Writers from Elie Wiesel to Gershom Scholem have movingly confronted this tortured reality. And in a "post-Christian" age, with the public cultures that authorized Christian practice receding or dismantled, do Christian believers have something to gain from the faith and practices of peoples who lived in a different world, in territories and times dominated by the church and churchmen? Writers from Reinhold Niebuhr to John Milbank have reflected upon this quandary. When so much has changed over time, when claims to the "essentials" have proved so divergent and transitory, when so much of the past seems strange, even reprehensible, and when we ourselves harbor so much consciousness of change, does not the past actually become the enemy of the future? That response, though glib, comes easily, even for ardent practitioners, and it is intelligible. But it does not satisfy, and it is not entirely honest. Some working sense of a past, individual and collective, self-conscious or semiconscious, is an integral part of the human condition and will not go away. Appeals to the past never cease, not for any of us, not in our personal lives, not in our social experience. They still shape political rhetoric, as they do legal decision-making and, these days, personal therapy.

This is no less true for religious pasts, collective and individual. In our day

---

4. Grant Wacker, *Heaven Below: Early Pentecostals and American Culture* (Cambridge, 2000), p. x, cited approvingly by Peter Steinfels, *New York Times*, July 7, 2001, p. A9.

queries and claims about those pasts have arisen forcefully in ways that can only be called paradoxical. Those Jewish and Christian communities with arguably the longest ties to the past — groups or denominations that trace a varied history back over centuries, many at one time religious establishments, some still accounted the mainstream — have suffered decline. Though longtime heirs to rich traditions, they have had trouble retaining the loyalty of their young, attracting new members in significant numbers, and exercising the measure of influence in public culture they once enjoyed. Other groups, by contrast, relative newcomers in the eyes of historians but ardent claimants to ancient and authentic tradition in their own, have over the past generation attracted many followers, old and young. Within a public culture they profess partly or wholly to repudiate, these "upstarts" exercise a startling influence, at times revolutionary. Such new groups, "charismatics" a generation ago, now often "fundamentalists" or "new conservatives" (as they are labeled by historians and pundits and sometimes their own adherents), act on a worldwide scale and are by no means limited to Judaism or Christianity. They do so, moreover, with emphatic assertions about their present-day link to the past and the future (think of renewed Hindu claims to sites sacred to Hindus and Muslims alike).

Embedded in fundamentalist stances toward the present is a claim about the past that is crucial to their explosive power: a vociferous insistence that they (alone or uniquely) possess an authentic link to the past, now realized, embodied, recovered, worked out again, in their person or community. So too "Wicca" groups claimed to recover elements of a "Celtic" or "pagan" religious past, as "New Age" adherents, in an eclectic spirit, draw widely and randomly on past materials as integral to informing their present-day practice. All these groups aim somehow to tap a distant spring, to draw today's religious charge and energy from a reappropriated past. And all, in some sense, short-circuit recent history. Reaching back to the past for paradigms and inspiration has venerable precedents in Jewish and Christian traditions as well, usually with the aim of reform or restoration, and there too these rubrics can be invoked too easily or superficially.

The paradoxical relationship of a wide range of religious groups to their past may lead people to suspect that history, in all its movement, may play tricks on them. To put it much too simplistically: Catholic liturgies become ever more low while Presbyterians or Methodists take on "high church" traditions; Catholics form Bible study groups while evangelicals move toward Orthodoxy; assimilated Jews find their way to radical Orthodoxy, or the reverse; and so on. Amidst such "drift," seekers of all stripes see themselves as taking history firmly in hand. The mainline groups, Jewish or Christian, get perceived as treating history too passively, slotting each set of beliefs and practices back

7

into its moment in time. They focus their energy on the present, or an advancing modern time and its pressing issues (gay sexuality, for instance), and allow the past to be the past. This appears to drain the "passing down" of its power, emptying it of any real charge. Even groups committed to the authority of long-term traditions, such as Roman Catholic Christians, bitterly contest the nature of this "passing," whether to live in accord with the "letter" or the "spirit" of Vatican Council II (1960s), for instance, not to speak of Trent (1560s) or Lateran Council IV (1215).

All this has ironic results. Groups that reach back to fixate upon one or another version of past practice or belief, employing it at once to repudiate and to inform their present, appear to flourish, while those that leave the past in the past have trouble sustaining coherent community in the present. Circulating through all these movements are attitudes, implicit or explicit and often unexamined, that manifest a measure of despair in the face of history, which comes then to be treated merely as a giant grab bag: Christians turn to Native American rites or beliefs, Jews become "Jews for Jesus." This is simply, you might say, the cultural and social condition labeled "postmodern," that radically fragmented and ahistorical sense of the human today that conceives present life as a constant and self-conscious constructing of one's self out of disparate pieces from both past and present, from distant cultures as well as near. All this is as true for "fundamentalist" as for "New Age" approaches to religious practice. Yet all these stances, even against their will, implicitly concede the presence of the past, also and emphatically past religion, as a reality to be dealt with, whether perceived as continuous or discontinuous, to be purged or emulated, improved upon or transcended, discarded or restored. Acknowledged as well, however implicitly, are those powers active in the making of practice and belief, whether collectively inherited or personally appropriated. However, few people these days reflect on the significance of these intersections of past and present, of formative powers and personal conviction. Fewer still reflect on the longer history of those intersections.

Notions of "formative powers" are hardly new, even if they have only recently gained more visibility. Many present-day stances seem to presume and to deny those powers all at once, as does, it seems to me, the thinker whose works have resonated so deeply with intellectuals in the last generation, Michel Foucault.[5] He claimed for humans a radical sense of freedom to construct one's own self while acknowledging, with despair and frustration, that larger historic forces go a long way toward conditioning and even limiting that self. He

---

5. See the interesting texts and the introduction in *Religion and Culture: Michel Foucault*, ed. Jeremy R. Carrette (New York, 1999).

touched a nodal point for many by pointing to the powers latent in inheritance (genealogy) and in language (discourse) as generating those "disciplining" structures that frame the lives of "shape-changing" individuals. Others have attempted to integrate the historical more seamlessly: for instance, going back to 1933, Michael Oakeshott's approach to "historical experience."[6] At the moment, theologians (to this historian) seem wary, reluctant to engage, in part because notions like "tradition" have become so politically and personally charged.[7] The writers in this volume are historians. They engage the issues primarily by way of praxis rather than deliberate reflection. The intent is introductory and historical: to take a step back, to ask about access to lived religion in the past, how persons and communities came into practice and belief, from person to person, generation to generation. Is it possible for historians to discern how peoples long ago lived religiously from their past into their present, passed on or transmuted beliefs and practices central to their communities? Was this a manifestly historical process, or is it a retrospective illusion? And if they fostered formative practices, how deliberately, how effectively, how unconsciously?

Writing about Formative Religious Practices in History

Writing religious history goes very far back in European history. Writers recorded and recalled the past to shape their present, in telling the stories of monastic or rabbinic fathers and their sayings, of holy people and their miraculous deeds, of communities and their leaders. Renaissance humanists cultivated new paradigms derived from antiquity and worked with a heightened sense of historical distance, even of loss; but they too aimed at programmatic recovery, whether of antiquity or the early church. During the early modern period industrious collectors assembled enormous repositories of texts and materials, often to serve causes polemical or apologetic, but especially to build up layers of tradition on behalf of a faith community or a special practice or a religious order — often, it should be added, with a joyful zeal for discovery and recording. Endowed with remarkable humanist educations, with an astounding intelligence and curiosity, they could nonetheless barely imagine history without en-

---

6. Michael Oakeshott, *Experience and Its Modes* (Oxford, 1933), esp. pp. 86-168.

7. But see Jaroslav Pelikan, *The Vindication of Tradition* (New Haven, 1983). In addition, several essays in *Practicing Theology* explore the formative power of historic Christian practices even as they are appropriated in new circumstances; see especially Craig Dykstra and Dorothy C. Bass, "A Theological Understanding of Christian Practices"; Sarah Coakley, "Deepening Practices: Perspectives from Ascetical and Mystical Theology"; and Gilbert I. Bond, "Liturgy, Ministry, and the Stranger."

gagement, as a pure exercise in reconstructing the past. Whatever nuance, so-phistication, or critique they might bring to bear, they mostly took larger community purposes for granted. Indeed, Enlightenment historians too, a Vol-taire or a Gibbon, came to the past with a purpose: to bring light and reason, to illumine the antics of human foolishness, to showcase the perils of religious su-perstition.

To write about history "as it really was," to see each epoch and community in its own right, as it existed unmediated in the "eye of God": this was the goal of "scientific" historians in the mid–nineteenth century, a position now often labeled "positivist," its most famous expositor the Berlin historian Leopold von Ranke. Professors were to work toward science and objectivity, to uncover laws or at least patterns, a verifiable reading of past texts and acts within their own meanings and contexts. Above all — this is sometimes forgotten now — they deliberately sought to lift their work above the muck of partisan polemic. So Ranke, a German Protestant, and later Erich Kaspar, a German Jew, wrote books about the Italian papacy that impressed contemporaries with their dis-passionate learning and relative evenhandedness. The ideal they proposed has held among professionals for generations, and fundamentally still does, despite stinging critiques and the full realization that no historian entirely sheds his or her outlook — that Ranke himself, as recent scholars have insisted, remained a German and a Protestant with clear interpretive predilections. It is striking, even ironic, and perhaps deserving of more notice, that this more distanced, more "objective" view of history-writing claimed for itself, in Ranke's words, the "eye of God." Earlier historians had written for centuries in greater or lesser confidence of delivering a "God's-eye" view of their Lutheran or Hasidic com-munity and of making manifest God's repugnance for their rivals.

Reaction to this new history was not long in coming. In 1874 Friedrich Nietzsche, a young professor of classical language and culture, poured out his scorn in the essay "On the Uses and Disadvantages of History for Life." His point, worked out in a many-sided argument, was simple: the past carefully re-constructed by this new historical science *(Wissenschaft)* was useless, a past drained of life. Nietzsche worried mainly about antiquity, specifically a vital life force he perceived there ("Dionysiac") that went missing in prosaic reconstruc-tions. But as the son of a pastor and a determined critic of Christianity, Nietz-sche understood, and occasionally noted, the potential impact of historical sci-ence upon Christian uses of the past as well. The truest followers of Jesus, in Nietzsche's view, had always stood outside its worldly success and its accumu-lated powers and were not consumed, like his contemporaries, by "the process of the Christian idea." Hence they, the "truest," would go unnamed and un-known in any "scientific" historical reconstruction. Any purely historical look at Christian tradition would not yield its "essence" (Harnack's goal a generation later) but only tend to dissolve and destroy. People proud of their new sense of history, their more accurate past, were generating a past of endless detail, of constant "becoming," a past of no use whatsoever, except to produce a "hopeless skeptical sense of endlessness." Should not life animate learning, he countered, rather than to have learning sap life? All this indigestible data only overwhelmed, filling people with irony and cynicism, leaving them with no drive to live or act. Indeed, this approach, he imagined more darkly, actually derived from, and served, the hateful animus of the Christian religion: sapping all things vital and new in the world, subverting this present life-world with an ironic sense of endless, ever shifting becoming, hence turning people toward a lifeless "eternity." Christianity in its critical mode, its attack upon "idols" and infidels, had, after all, always tried to effect this — and now again, but in a more subtle and approved way, in the guise of modern historical science.[8]

We take up historical work a full century later. Despite much sophisticated reflection on the nature of the historical enterprise, these two stances remain broadly with us: efforts to lift history out of the polemical present, to grasp the past accurately and fully in its historical pastness; no less, efforts to discern in and claim from that past some life force, some understanding, for the present. We are today more at ease with acknowledging our motives and aims, not posturing with a false impersonality. But actual practice remains caught somewhere in the middle. And that is not all bad. Most, writers as well as readers, instinctively find it desirable to combine life with history, an intuitive entering-in with critical distance, present concern with past evidence. In practice that middle ground is a shifting and uncertain place; at its best, a terrain worthy of high respect, useful, even powerful — but not easily reduced to a slogan or a method.

For historians of religious communities there is a further twist, a most interesting insight, bringing at once a gain and a complication. During the last generation, and actually going back a century, scholars have discovered that religious phenomena are amazingly revealing of cultural and social life. Several outstanding scholars around the year 1900 perceived in human history deep and broad veins of religious culture and set out to exploit them on behalf of sociological, anthropological, and cultural understanding — thus turning the old religious story to new purposes. This work, impressive and important, turned the inherited insider's story, with all it presumed and purposed, inside out. Religious pasts were called upon not primarily as narratives drawn up to consoli-

8. For the text see, for instance, Friedrich Nietzsche, *Unmodern Observations* (New Haven, 1990), pp. 87-145, with an introduction (pp. 75-86) by Werner Dannhauser.

11

date a contested point or the claims of a community or the validity of a disputed practice, but to elucidate broad cultural and human themes, say, social or gender relations, or the cultivation of the self. Leading theologians, Troeltsch in particular, urged emphatically that scholars undertake a self-conscious and much needed historicizing of their religious traditions. For general historians, with methodological help from sociologists and anthropologists, this approach opened up vast resources in the European and American past, seemingly, or even largely, apart from any confessional predilections or agendas. This approach also effects a reversal, the religious materials subordinated to other historical priorities (rather than the other way round), and this has tended to produce, even to require, an "instrumentalizing" of religious phenomena. So, ironically, "mainstreaming" religious history can make it harder at times to see the religious phenomena in their own right as imbued with their own energies and dynamisms.

For both Weber and Troeltsch, who were colleagues at Heidelberg at the turn of the century, with the differing accents of a sociologist and a theologian, religion in history came down finally to cultural practices in time, belief generating patterns of human action made manifest in distinctive societies. A good example is Weber's proposed link between a system of beliefs and practices peculiar to Calvinists and the coming of capitalist enterprise.[9] Both Weber and Troeltsch saw "life forces" as real in religion and as acted out in, also as yielding, distinct cultures. They proposed to isolate these as a complex series of historical types and to grasp their evolving impact upon world history. Emile Durkheim, by comparison, working in France at the same time, saw the issue revolving rather around the rites that helped mold and shape a social unit: "Religion is an eminently social thing. Religious representations are collective representations that express collective realities; the rites are a manner of acting which take rise in the midst of the assembled groups and which are destined to excite, maintain, or recreate certain mental states in

9. Excellent introductions to these pivotal thinkers are in *Nineteenth Century Religious Thought in the West,* ed. Ninian Smart, John Clayton, Steven Katz, and Patrick Sherry (Cambridge, 1985), here vol. 3: Roland Robertson, "Max Weber and German Sociology of Religion," and Trutz Rendorff and Friedrich Wilhelm Graf, "Ernst Troeltsch," pp. 263-304, 305-32. For representative texts see *From Max Weber: Essays in Sociology,* ed. H. H. Gerth and C. Wright Mills (Oxford, 1946), pp. 267-362, and *Religion in History: Ernst Troeltsch,* trans. James Luther Adams and Walter F. Bense (Minneapolis, 1991). See also Sarah Coakley, *Christ without Absolutes: A Study of the Christology of Ernst Troeltsch* (Oxford, 1988), esp. chap. 1 on the nature of Troeltsch's relativism.

10. Emile Durkheim, *The Elementary Forms of the Religious Life,* trans. Joseph Ward Swain (1915; New York, 1965), p. 23.

those groups."[10] He conceived of ritual practices as persistent in human life, if not unchanged, as transforming themselves rather than disappearing, as the highest expression of the collective consciousness.[11] There are ironies aplenty here. Weber and Troeltsch, Protestant in heritage, idealist in philosophical orientation, looked for religion culturally in ethical acts, in deeds. Durkheim, his father a rabbi, his orientation anthropological and beyond Europe, saw it most fully in the rites that fostered the consolidation of meanings and groups and thereby also distinguished a sacred from a profane world. All these thinkers (and the contemporaries around them) operated with a strong sense of history and of change, even if Weber tended to look for social-religious "types" in the past (around the world), Durkheim for religion first in its most "primitive" manifestations (Australia), and Troeltsch for the outworking of Christian belief in historical cultures (Europe).

These insights and approaches are now taken for granted, or refined, or disputed, but at any rate part of a larger common cultural inheritance, whatever their origins. Still, there is in them something deeply true to Jewish and Christian traditions, religion measured by its social and cultural deeds: "By their fruits shall ye know them" — including their bad fruit, we might add, driving a concomitant impulse for reform or renewal. But for historians, and also practitioners, religious culture as paradigmatic manifestations cannot make up the whole story. Historians ask how people in time acquired and acted upon religious practices or beliefs; they look beyond structural paradigms, whether cultural, sociological, religious, or indeed theological. For historians of formative religious practices, then, the aim is to see all the complex and concrete modes of human experience through which people came into forms of participation, how they shaped and reshaped inherited or invented paradigms for themselves and their needs, even while being shaped by them. If we choose to substitute abstractions or institutions or types for concrete and contingent situations, also on occasion because the evidence in all its human or social or cultural fullness simply has not come down to us, we must at least be aware that we are doing so. Insisting upon this historical dimension is not to reduce human practices to sheer contingency. A refusal to recognize historical contingency is one sort of blind spot, against which scholars have reacted for a long time. Another, however, is to see only contingency, to deny the presence and persistence of deeper patterns, or variations on patterns. Again there must be a middle way. Religious traditions have a life force, a presence, all their own, which is not to deny constant and real change, even from generation to generation. Such traditions en-

11. For representative texts, and a useful introduction, see *Durkheim on Religion,* ed. W. S. F. Pickering (Atlanta, 1994).

tered into the forming of peoples and communities, shaped attitudes and convictions within and actions without, structured communal bonds as well as individual aims and orientations — enabled people, in short, to take on "habits of the heart," to borrow an influential title of fifteen years ago. Still, they did so in time, and with multiple changes over time.[12] All this brings us to the elusive notion of "formation."

Notions of "Formation"

The term "formation" is early modern and Roman Catholic in origin. It refers to the comprehensive preparation of religious men and women, in orders or in seminaries, for the life they will lead, this often begun at a very early age. Such formative practices are old, and not restricted to Christian monks and nuns — think of boys preparing for the rabbinate, or apprentices living in a master's house to prepare themselves for a trade. During the centuries covered by this book, most such practices were local and piecemeal. After the Council of Trent Catholic reformers in the early seventeenth century gave them new and more deliberate attention, to counter charges that clergy were not living up to their way of life, also to rival a newly forming Protestant leadership. Until recently, even if little studied, the reality of formative religious practices was presumed (notably by Foucault, as part of his own upbringing),[13] even their reaching down on occasion to broader levels of the populace. For all this the essential paradigm was monastic: acquiring over time, by practice and self-examination, by self-mortification and applied will, a disciplined way of life, internalizing its expectations, integrating its acts into one's desires consciously and unconsciously — becoming thus at once "sacrificed" to this way of life and personally master of it, even able to stand above it. To see the general significance of this monastic paradigm required the eye of a modern anthropologist. Talal Asad

12. The notion of "habitus," antique in origin, also widely employed by medieval scholastic philosophers and theologians, has gained new currency through the work of the French sociologist Pierre Bourdieu, accessible, say, in his *Outline of a Theory of Practice* (ET, Cambridge, 1977). The difficulty is that contemporary usages (and maybe ancient too) have a powerfully ahistorical and atemporal character. They allow for the molding of internal "habits" or dispositions, especially through practice or repetition, but they foresee little in the way of mechanisms for change or revision, or indeed reversal.

13. Acknowledged in *Religion and Culture*, p. xiv, where Bernauer puts it this way: "Foucault came to esteem and utilise a Christian style of liberty which combined a care of the self with a sacrifice and mortification of that self. . . . [He] was fascinated with Christianity's earliest form of penance . . . drawn to the paradox of a self-revelation that was also a self-destruction."

construed monastic disciplinary practices as "forming and re-forming" the moral dispositions that constitute a human self, and thereby — his emphasis — forming within a will to obey. Obedience emerges, in dialectic with expectations and contrary demands, as a chosen virtue.[14] Asad's is a subtle and balanced account, if somewhat timeless and ahistorical, with evidence drawn mainly from Benedictine sources (where obedience is the key virtue). Franciscans, for instance, worried a great deal more about poverty as crucial to the forming of religious lives and practices, and indeed aroused large followings and provoked severe crises with several popes over the meaning of living out lives of poverty. Pierre Hadot, an important progenitor for Michel Foucault's notion of a "care of the self," argues that the foundations for an understanding of formative practices were laid by Stoic and Epicurean philosophers, Greek and Roman, with notions of "philosophy as a way of life" and especially of "spiritual exercises."[15]

So why have medieval and modern historians largely missed the opportunity to take advantage of this "formation" paradigm? There are several reasons. Most historians of religious orders, until recently, were themselves religious, and took the formative disciplines for granted, as a second nature, not in need of deliberate historical reflection or investigation. Or they took them as practices peculiar to themselves, as that which set them apart as "religious"; or indeed, especially in the last generation, as practices they were anxious to cast off, as often brutal in their manifestations and effects. By contrast historians of religious "peoples" have tended to look for a "lay" stance decidedly opposed to this monastic disciplining, it being perceived as threatening to an indigenous lay culture; or indeed, if enforced by authorities lay or ecclesiastical, as the secular extension of "social control." Historians of education, for their part, often have focused more on cognitive or narrowly pedagogical issues, less the whole person, this fuller shaping of the moral and affective faculties. As historians become ever more fascinated with the whole range of human experience, from the political to the emotive (not to say the sexual), they have also grown more alert to these formative practices in shaping human life. Their reality is certainly undeniable, also in the present. Think of the "formative" exercises under-

14. Talal Asad, "On Discipline and Humility in Medieval Christian Monasticism," in his *Genealogies of Religion*, pp. 125-67, an essay first published in 1987.

15. Pierre Hadot, *Philosophy as a Way of Life: Spiritual Exercises from Socrates to Foucault* (Oxford, 1995), a collection of translated essays going back into the 1970s, with this personal remark about the origins of his antique philosophical investigations: "I received a very intense Catholic religious education. I gradually became detached from it, but it played a considerable role in my formation, both because of the first impressions it made upon me, and because of the problems it raised for me" (p. 276).

gone today by young physicians, lawyers, and professors in residency, prepartner law, and pretenure teaching, or the discipline undertaken by those wishing to become sport or entertainment stars. Not a few medieval and early modern people sought to emulate, as best they could and from a distance, saints or religious as the "stars" of their era (as some have put it), and consequently imposed some of these disciplines upon themselves (fasting, for instance), sometimes with startling, sometimes with disastrous, results. This dynamic is only now coming under the lens of historical investigation.

In medieval Christian history the models were mostly monastic. But such texts spoke not so much of "formation" as of "institution" *(instituere)*, of "instituting mores," the practices that made up a way of life. The significance of this term *(instituere)*, antique and Christian, lies in its multilayered meaning, for it meant "to instruct" fully as much as "to establish" or "to discipline." The introduction to Roman law mandated by Justinian in 534 and the new introduction to the Christian faith written by John Calvin in 1536 were both titled "institutes," that is, manuals to inform the practice of, respectively, legal or godly affairs. Proper training took up the moral, the physical, and the mental all at once, with, obviously, varying emphases among groups and individuals. One early religious manual, eleventh century, later ascribed to Bernard of Clairvaux, aimed to have "good customs (i.e., practices) increase with age," and described the task at hand as to "cast off all sluggishness" and by the grace of Christ "to correct one's life, put in order ('compose') one's *mores,* and improve one's practices in all things." The driving assumption is that the "outer" and the "inner" person hang together, that the spirit *(animus)* is revealed in the "walk" *(incessum),* that the disposition of mind *(habitus mentis)* is perceived in the position of the body *(corporis statu).*[16] This text addressed the training of young men for life in a monastery. Such texts appear to have abounded in the twelfth century; most were for men, a few increasingly for women.[17] A second term, *disciplina,* originally harbored much the same lexical ambiguity, pointing toward instruction (retained in our notion of academic disciplines) as much as conduct. Ancient and medieval education took for granted a physical regime, sometimes fairly harsh, as part of instruction: no master without his cane, no shaping of the mind apart from the body — the patterns found as well among

16. *Tractatus de ordine uitae et morum institutione,* available in *Patrologia Latina,* 184:561-84.

17. Barbara Newman, "Flaws in the Golden Bowl: Gender and Spiritual Formation in the Twelfth Century," in her *From Virile Woman to WomanChrist* (Philadelphia, 1995), pp. 19-45, 313-16, provides a list and an important discussion of them. The same issues inform the essays gathered in Caroline Walker Bynum, *Jesus as Mother: Studies in the Spirituality of the High Middle Ages* (Berkeley, 1982).

boys learning in rabbinic or Muslim circles. This "instituting," it must be added, though sometimes severe, did not aim in principle at pain, as we often imagine today, which is in part our continuing (and now mostly legendary) reaction to this older regime. Tenderness and concern were often manifest as well, along with a real determination to sharpen a person's faculties, mental as well as moral, to hone habits of mind and spirit along with habits of speech and demeanor. At the center remained the created and free soul, finally answerable to God alone, which could (as Foucault emphasized) energize a spirit of liberty, even anarchy.

Practicing Religion?

In the historical profession today, and in this volume, "practicing religion" refers to those approaches that take seriously the integral place of concrete practices in forming a religious self or community. However deeply anchored in religious traditions over centuries, it took the insights and methods of anthropologists to render it historically meaningful, whether the focus fell upon the integrative social functions of religious rites, as with Mary Douglas and others in a Durkheimian mode, or upon integrative meaning systems, as with Clifford Geertz and his heirs. Anthropologists helped students of European Christianity and Judaism look back on their own religious cultures, as it were, from the outside; helped them de-familiarize their sense of an inherited culture, and so better act as observers rather than participants. Since a focus on practices draws attention to specific peoples in specific rites, it could also, at least potentially, help raise questions of social class and gender, of material and political power, in quite specific historical situations. This positive approach also subverted a long-standing critique of religious rites and practices, common among intellectuals, as mainly "externalities," as the stuff of the "simple." Largely unawares, historians were reiterating the stance of numerous medieval reformers and mystics who presented the "interior" life as properly passing through and beyond the routines of ordinary external practice. Sometimes unwittingly still today, with all the extraordinary attention given to reformers and mystics, historians can end up replicating such attitudes, discounting or even disparaging liturgical practices as merely customary or as mindless and meaningless.

Still, "practicing religion," despite the richer grasp of the religious and social meanings of those practices effected by this approach over the last generation or two, has itself come in for severe critique. The anthropological eye cannot be taken naively as external and observant; it is itself caught up in the dynamic of observing. Further, all religious practices do not work the same, not outside Europe, also not inside Europe, and certainly not in different times and places. Rites and practices, quite simply but most importantly, are not self-interpreting. We must indeed ask whether it is historically appropriate, or even possible, to distinguish performance from meaning, outer from inner, body from spirit (and vice versa). This too, it turns out, was discussed with great profundity and subtlety by premodern Jews and Christians, keenly aware of the layers at work in the dynamic between performance and meaning, also between group meaning and individual understanding.

An important improvement — distancing religion from the normative and prescribed, yet not cutting off practice from meaning — may be found in the notion of "lived religion." By this term historians mean the religion people lived and practiced, in all its fullness and variety, as distinguished from that leaders or books may have prescribed. In its actual application thus far, more in France where it originated than in America, this approach can risk replicating or reinforcing notional distinctions between an "elite" and a "popular" practice of religion. This duality, widely diffused since the 1970s,[18] is, most now agree, too stark, misleadingly simplistic, if not entirely wrong. "Lived religion" at its best serves, helpfully, as a middling or mediating concept.[19] Within a dominant or approved cultural expression of religion, even one backed with political or social power, there existed, especially in pretotalitarian times, a broad historical range of subgroups and distinctive combinations, lived out by all differing social groups, sometimes in surprising mixes of peoples.[20] Some, even many, may not have comported exactly or at all to the norms, and yet never intended or perceived themselves as dissenting or even aberrant. Whether a religious group or practice was dominant within society (a preoccupation of recent scholarship: the "persecuting church"), or found itself in a position apart, by choice or by force, is an important question, but not the only question, especially not for a broader understanding of formative practices. Societies without power simply do not exist, also religious societies, and yet power is not all there is to say about society, or about how people came to "live their religion" — which is not to ignore the coercive character of social and spiritual relations in premodern Europe.

---

18. See François-André Isambert, *Le sens du sacré: Fête et religion populaire* (Paris, 1982).

19. Thus, as presented by David Hall, in a volume of essays complementary to this one in origin, *Lived Religion in America: Toward a History of Practice* (Princeton, 1997).

20. I have tried to present such an approach in my essay "The Future of Medieval Church History," *Church History* (2002): 492-523.

Acquiring Faith?

This volume, and the project of which it is a part, asks about "forming" and "educating" peoples of faith. From one perspective it would seem to state what synagogues and churches have always been about, even if, at the moment, this approach has less resonance in the academy (and maybe among people generally). From another, in the light of so much twentieth-century experience and so much coercive use of religious power, it can be taken as referring to some form of ideological indoctrination. This has made it hard for recent historians to talk helpfully about the cognitive and educative dimensions of religious experience and of religious communities. The essays in this volume take "belief" and the "forming of belief" seriously as distinct factors in the making of Jewish and Christian communities.[21] Earlier historians and polemicists took it largely for granted, and for centuries. They expounded belief over time as the defining characteristic of a community, its practices and organization as an expression and amplification of that community's beliefs, even beliefs or a reshaping of beliefs as the major engine in historical change. And still today, when people reach for a study of their own religious tradition, this is usually what they expect to find or to read. A singular emphasis in one direction inevitably elicits its reverse: hence the view that it was not ideas or convictions but material realities or social pressures or political power or cultural predilections that shaped religious life and change.

Lest we all too dismissively assimilate "acquiring faith" to coercive ideology, it is good to remind ourselves of how deeply the "educative" approach is built into historic religious experience, the high premium Jewish and Christian communities have placed upon forming people in the Torah and the faith, a charge grasped as anchored in their sacred writings. So before Moses died, we read, he called the people together one last time to remind them of the day when "God talked to you face to face on the mountain from the midst of fire" (Deut. 5:4), and reiterated the essential provisions of their covenant. These he ordered people to keep in their hearts, to teach diligently to their children, to talk about as they sat in their houses or walked along the way, to bind upon them as a sign and to write upon the doorposts of their houses (Deut. 6:6-8). After the people had taken possession of the Promised Land and fallen on evil times, renewal came when King Josiah rediscovered the Torah and had it read aloud to all the assembled people great and small (2 Kings 23:1-3). And after the destruction

---

21. For a statement of this approach, with an important introduction, see the essays edited and introduced by Thomas Kselman, *Belief in History: Innovative Approaches to European and American Religion* (Notre Dame, Ind., 1991).

and rebuilding of Jerusalem, Ezra had all the people, men and women to the age of understanding, gather for the reading of the Law (Neh. 8:2). And significantly, at the central annual feast, the Passover, recalling the exodus from Egypt, the youngest child is asked to reiterate the liberating events that led to covenant making.

Christians formed their communities around the person of Jesus, acknowledged as the Messiah (Christ), presented in their sacred texts as the image of the invisible God, in whom all the fullness of God was pleased to dwell (Col. 1:15, 19), the exemplar and source of grace and truth (John 1:17). One writer described himself as bearing witness to what he had seen with his eyes and touched with his hands (1 John 1:1). Jesus instituted a meal whereby his own death and rising could be recalled and appropriated each time believers gathered. Further, because Jesus was the Word in the flesh, he was to be imitated. Be perfect, he said, as the Father in heaven is perfect (Matt. 5:48). And those in whom the spirit of Jesus dwelt were themselves accounted worthy of imitation. Paul said the Thessalonians became "imitators" of himself and of the Lord, and thereby examples to all believers in Macedonia and Achaia (1 Thess. 1:6-7).

It might seem a little unusual to insert scriptural texts into a historical discussion. But the point is simple: forming belief and understanding together with practices, also critiquing and reshaping them over time and in time, all spring from the heart of these traditions. We may recognize how time-bound are religious manifestations, also the difficulties that come with trying to put belief at the center of a historical narrative. The "form" of a community does not arise simply from belief or inductively from historical investigation of beliefs and practices. Accounts that put belief at the center have often focused upon their normative instances (teachers, books, rulings, community paradigms), explicitly or implicitly, though they need not do so. What about all the resisters or even the indifferent? One of the more powerful narrative lines of the last generation (actually with deep roots) hinges, perhaps unawares, upon a reversal of an older "faith-forming" narrative, in effect conceding its centrality but casting it in a mostly negative role. "Imposing" thereby becomes, even unawares, the central driver in a story line fully as much as "joining" or "evangelizing" shaped earlier story lines (with both implicitly present in most accounts of "Christianization," construed as positive or negative). The structural analogy is simple. As European or American regimes imposed their way of life upon indigenous peoples elsewhere, for instance, on Native Americans in North America, so religious culture in early Europe came as the foreign imposition of a clerical caste, a kind of internal colonization in the name of religion, often given the anthropological term "acculturation." Even in textbookish accounts, not particularly ideological or thesis-driven, this view is treated as standard; thus recently Hervé Martin's volume in the Nouvelle Clio series: "To return to the term 'acculturation' may seem a little too systematic [in approach], but it allows one to underline that religious teaching descends from the summit to the base, that clerics pursue ideological ends that are very precise, and they employ, depending upon the case, a certain measure of coercion."[22] In this, as in its earlier reversed forms, there is an oddly unilateral dynamic, not very helpful to understanding the actual historical give-and-take of individuals associated with religious communities, not at all subtle about the nature of belief, or the mix of belief and practice at the heart of most Jewish and Christian discussions. This draconian vision imagines powers of coercion virtually no premodern society could achieve — which is not to dismiss the real and brutal effects of coercive measures undertaken by religious leaders blinded by the conviction of their own rightness. Further, it fails to account for the inner resistances, so powerful precisely in the realm of religious conviction and animation, of acting on their own beliefs or desires or needs, which so often propelled people in their own directions or caused reformers to turn on the very society that had coddled their privileged estate.

Approaching Formative Practices in History

Practices are not generic, not in real historical time. We may recognize patterns or structures in retrospect, also try to learn from them, but we do so in distinct environments, as historians or practitioners. This is a reality manifest in the Jewish and Christian sacred writings, where the stories and their meanings always come down to cases, evident in Talmudic teaching as it is in Christian ethics (think of all the attention paid to the details in penance). Clear as the injunctions are that people be formed in Torah or the person of Jesus, the writings offer relatively few specifics on how exactly this "forming" is to be carried out. Perhaps that is why groups often fix on one or another item that seems clear and occasionally make a fetish of it — certain precepts in the Hebrew Bible which Orthodox Jews mean to implement literally, items in the New Testament which certain Christian groups insist upon (veiling or silencing of women, for instance). In practice formation is intricately bound up with historic cultural acts. Still, not every generation has started over, and valued experience persists, sometimes for generations. Scholars are right to see some patterns become deep traditions, central to group and individual forms of believing and practicing, while others pass quickly out of practice or belief.

22. Hervé Martin, *Mentalités Médiévales, XIe-XVe siècle* (Paris, 1996), p. 218.

Even in their cultural contingency, moreover, practices come with a presumed divine charge, a claim to live out of the strength of the sacred, enabling people to understand themselves as formed into something larger than themselves, this larger reality also integrated into themselves.

History presumes change, as well as tradition or deep structures. Both for individuals and for these overarching inherited structures, that change may come suddenly, unexpectedly, and with lasting results. We speak of "revolutions" or "reforms" or "restorations" throughout the centuries of Jewish and Christian communities. In this volume David Steinmetz has reflected thoughtfully and innovatively on just such change, and its impact upon Reformation-era actors. The spiritual guidance of individuals, their internal change, draws upon traditions that are very old, yet this phenomenon is not commonly recognized until the early modern period, as Lawrence Cunningham sets out. In trying to comprehend historical change, both personal and structural, analogies, however rough, sometimes help. Some readers of this volume will have experienced "the '60s" and may wonder in retrospect at the rapidity and breadth of change, the degree of individual choice (and the implications for families or careers), the sense of being swept up in something larger, the time lag until the full implications are realized and reflected upon pro and con.

These essays will have done their job if they deepen readers' sense of the past, its complexities and potentialities, but also awaken in them sensitivity to this matter of religious "formation," personal and collective. Historical work can hardly define "formation," but it can alert sensitive readers to a range of operative elements: unconscious inheritance and conscious decisions, overarching structures and individual initiatives, society and person, body and spirit, the affective and the cognitive. Without attempting to summarize the fifteen essays, each to be read in its own right, I do wish to point toward a few of the various possibilities and questions that arise from them.

The guiding purposes of formative practices cannot be presumed or cloaked in generalities. To what end were people being formed: spiritual salvation, social liberation, personal well-being (moral or social), ethical action, inner contemplation, community solidarity? Not every age treated Torah in the same way, or envisioned its application uniformly. Robert Goldenberg makes clear that at the very outset of postbiblical history Jewish leaders foresaw quite distinct modes of living out the precepts of Torah. Similarly, not every group of Christians had the same vision of "following Christ," or even spoke of "imitating Christ." Robert Wilken shows early Christian leaders anxious to enable persons as moral agents and to do so by imparting the stories that informed their community, holding up the model of exemplary lives, no less by training the passions of the soul and thus creating internal "habits" through repetition —

22

all this beginning in the familial household. Striking in both cases is the degree to which Jewish or Christian leaders presumed the social and cultural features of their "antique" world, Philo as fully as Christian bishops, and yet sought to bend its presumptions and methods to their ends, ends drawn from a reading of their sacred writings.

Both Judaism and Christianity are book religions, and questions of purpose cannot meaningfully be separated from reading, understanding, and intellectual inquiry. Blake Leyerle's masterful exposition of the conjunction between word and body, mind and ascesis, in the sayings of early Christian monks illumines one innovative form of their "consumption" of the book. John Cavadini argues that Augustine, an intellectual, the bishop of a Roman city, preached sermons that raised substantive theological matters and tried to carry his often unruly audiences with him. By contrast, such ambitious passages tended to get left out, or were not attempted, by the bishops a century or two later who passed Augustine's heritage on to the world of early Europe. Their aims were other, perhaps more moral or social. So distinctions must be made in our approach to the book and to exegesis, distinctions about communities, times, and places. Was it matters derived from the book, or from culturally or socially dominant concerns, or some mix between the two that church or synagogue adjudged crucial? Who decided? How was it transmitted? Can we measure as historians what got transmitted?

In historical practice the first stage in being formed in the Law or in Christ, outside the household, usually eventuated in public ritual expressions: preparing people for baptism, for first communion, for confirmation, for bar mitzvah. The baptismal ritual reached its most elaborate stage of development — an appeal to the senses in ritual, to the mind in teaching, to the moral person in demands for fasting and change of life — just when Christianity emerged as the favored religion of the Roman Empire. It is fair for us to step back and ask how a ritual embodied its purpose, or indeed whether a ritual expression (this one eventually practiced on infants) itself became an end as well as a means.

In both Judaism and Christianity a periodic change of heart and mind — atonement, penance, remorse, confession — is central to the communal and individual understanding of what it means to make one's own Torah or faith in the Christ. What the heart and mind were to be changed to, what it was that a person was to acquire, speaks directly to the perceived purposes of educating and forming. That periodic change of heart and mind, moreover, nearly always proved crucial to community rituals such as the Day of Atonement or Shrove Tuesday. Stanley Harakas sets out with great clarity how late antique practices surrounding baptism and especially the Lenten fast proved constitutive for Byzantine and Orthodox practices of periodic renewal. The rites, also the presence of the divine by way of icons, collapsed time and made worshipers partici-pants in the divine economy. Do all practices of religious renewal tend to draw people into sacred time and in some sense out of their own time? Or do some forms of renewal aim precisely to "incarnate" sacred time in historical time and practice? And why the differences in dynamic?

Practices, whether ritual, ethical, or devotional, became closely linked with, and indeed were encouraged within, sacred spaces. Both Jewish and Christian leaders were exceedingly protective of their sacred spaces, synagogues or churches, and wanted their people to associate them with the deity and divine teaching. Perhaps this states the obvious. But human beings in premodern Eu-rope knew multiple sites — homes, shrines, houses of holy people — where they could encounter the sacred. Religious leaders might recognize those and still work to direct religious experience, practice, and teaching toward the sa-cred space of church and synagogue. Michael Signer sets out the ways in which this gradually transformed the character and purposes of the synagogue in me-dieval Europe, a place not only of prayer but of teaching and of adjudicating community life. Joseph Goering shows how the parish, perhaps only truly in the thirteenth century, emerged as the focal point of local Christian life, from baptism to burial, in thousands of villages across Europe. Still, opportunities for religious practice beyond the parish never ceased, even increased, a dynamic which I pointed toward in later medieval and Philip Soergel in early modern Europe. Such practices may well threaten the monopolistic claims of the parish, and yet ironically deepen devotion.

Considerations of purpose and of place serve "framing" roles. Key to under-standing formative practices — at least from the perspective of historical dis-tance — is the conception of the human person being formed. Is this person a "blank slate" or predisposed to sin? willful or rational? child or adult? woman or man? priest or layperson? Within a person or set of persons, which aspects most needed forming, and by what practices? It might be the cognitive aspect of an in-dividual, his or her knowledge and understanding of a faith tradition — cer-tainly evident in rabbinic training, also in Reformation emphases upon cateche-sis and preaching. At other times the affective aspect of humans was lifted out, the shaping of desires and emotive responses, which was a very powerful dimen-sion of later medieval practices, both devotional and iconic. This also took place by way of song, in chants and in hymns, one aspect sadly missing in this selec-tion of essays. Or it might come down to social or ethical practices. For both Jews and Christians, nearly everything pivoted on the makeup of an individual — conduct in community and in the world at large, also conduct, so to speak, within. This could take quite surprising turns. Anne Clark sets out beautifully the impact of a new Marian modeling during the high Middle Ages, in practices of prayer and also in matters of lifestyle. Elliot Wolfson shows with sophistication how in Jewish mystic circles, at roughly the same time, adherents were drawn toward a knowing of the divine name beyond knowing through practices fostered by oral teachings, which nonetheless presupposed written texts.

Historically the ends envisioned for the forming of religious professionals, pastors or rabbis, monks or nuns, often overshadowed those foreseen for the people as a whole. The education of "professionals" might be conceived as a more intense and refined form of that which all people should acquire, given time and means. Or was it? At issue in this volume are the people encompassing a whole community of faith. Did the education of the priest, pastor, or rabbi and of the people, the congregation, aim finally at the same ends? Lee Palmer Wandel raises the question thoughtfully about Zwingli and the early Reformed community at Zürich: Is this a humanist Reformer attempting to draw an entire community into his new educated worldview? Or in this intense, "stripped-down" set of ritual practices, do we gain access to the formative impulses at work in an entire community? So too, in Robert Kingdon's remarkable study of consistory records in Geneva, do we see pastors imposing their practices on people or an entire community remaking its own practices and expecting everyone to conform? We should separate out educational materials and practices intended for the community at large from others designed to form professional leaders. Still, the transference from one to the other and back again was hardly conscious, even if at times the chasm between the two appeared nearly unbridgeable.

The ultimate object of these essays is a better historical understanding of religious practices. In human history practices — which may seem on first glance to be the means of formation — come deeply to influence and even to drive its purpose and substance, as is evident here with respect to institutions (Kingdon's Genevan consistory), devotions (Clark's Marian paradigm), and experience (Wolfson's mystics). Perduring though they may appear, however, practices will nearly always be peculiar to epochs and therefore not easy to generalize about, though ironically they may also gain their own momentum (like those noted) to spread across times and spaces and peoples. We must allow for great differences in premodern European communities: people who were mostly literate or nonliterate, communities emphasizing or de-emphasizing ritual worship, churches or synagogues supplied or not supplied with well-educated leaders. Spaces also differed vastly: the home, the church or synagogue, the school, a shrine, a pilgrimage route, preaching in a public square. A church, to take that case, might be bare and spare in design or filled with a plethora of images, windows, stations, and altars, a veritable repository of teaching tools. Indeed, spareness itself might offer a powerful form of teaching, as in many synagogues and Reformed churches. In a household (about which we know far too little), was religious experience delimited to a certain time or space (i.e., before an icon)? When and how was the sacred associated with schools as such? Or was most religious formation in fact "absorbed," so to speak, by the larger, ongoing functions of the community, in customs, in ritual worship, in sermons, and the like? What of the differences between the literate and the nonliterate, manuscript culture and print culture? Did practices and materials appeal to the eye, as in images, stained glass windows, and icons? Or to the ear, as in sung prayers, preached sermons, and hymns? Or to the mind by way of printed instructions, catechisms, devotional books? Can these different appeals be so neatly separated out? Was not the liturgy learned by memory and by doing, heard as well as read out of those books of hours so popular at the end of the Middle Ages? Was not the catechism taught and learned by heart as well as read out of a book? Was not the Torah or Scriptures learned as much (or more) through public hearing as through private reading? The questions about historic practices of formation are difficult, complex, and are just now being asked with increasing sophistication.

Quite apart from the broader dilemmas that come with writing about the past, historians of religious communities have struggled to find a conceptual language that is not merely a reflex of that community's theological or political program. General historians have felt more confident talking about how people over the last century or two moved away from religious practices, communities, or identities. But in this "postsecular" age, as one journalist recently dubbed it, even that discussion has come in for severe scrutiny, as self-defining, self-justifying, as begging all the hard conceptual and perceptual issues — just what people earlier accused church historians or Jewish historians of doing. Can we talk with greater care about matters of participation in historic religious communities, about "formative practices" in the experience of peoples and communities? The basic intent is clear enough, and historically manifest: distinct communities of belief and practice animated by transcendent allegiances, and the assimilation of peoples over time into that collective life. It is the assimilative movement that is historically at stake here, poorly understood, too easily imagined as religious participation that was absorptive and almost unconscious ("practicing religion"), as personal and purposeful ("converting"), or as imposed and coercive ("forming faith"). Each, in these crude definitions, is presumed more or less to exclude the other, without differentiations in time and space, in persons and groups, in age or gender or class. But it need not be so. One purpose of these essays is to help historians and practitioners alike think their way beyond these disjunctive dead ends, to imagine middle-ground positions that are truer to historic and personal experience, that can enter into historical narratives.

EARLY SYNAGOGUE AND CHURCH

Religious Formation in Ancient Judaism

Robert Goldenberg

This essay will largely be concerned with elite groups of Jews, or in one case an elite individual, rather than the mass of ancient Jewry. It cannot pretend to cover all Jews or even all types of Jews who lived in the ancient world, and in any case very little is known about the inner lives of ordinary Jewish people in antiquity. Surviving sources are not particularly interested in the religious experience of such individuals and make little effort to understand or describe them. Available materials speak for and from within specific groups of Jews, people who were convinced that their manner of leading a Jewish life was worth describing or propagating. The inner lives of only these groups and their members emerge with any fullness from the ancient Jewish texts available today.

This essay will focus on the three largest surviving bodies of ancient Jewish literature, each of which reflects a particular conception of the meaning and character of the Jewish religion. It will seek to answer a series of questions for the varieties of ancient Judaism to be surveyed: (1) According to this view of Judaism, what is the summum bonum, the ultimate goal which a religious education should prepare one to achieve? (2) What conceptions of the person and of community are implied by this understanding of the highest good? (3) How does one achieve the summum bonum? What materials, and what types of personal discipline, are useful or necessary? (4) Can one help others achieve this end, and how important is it to devote one's own energies to such assistance of other people? After exploring the varieties of religious formation — here defined as the preparation of individuals for the ideal religious life — that underlie those conceptions, the chapter will conclude by tracing the development of Judaism in its familiar "traditional" form out of its ancient roots.

Philo of Alexandria

It is extremely difficult to know which Jews, and how many Jews, are reflected in the voluminous writings of Philo of Alexandria.[1] Philo often portrays Jewish life as undifferentiated, as though he speaks for all Jews everywhere: he will say the Jews celebrate their Sabbaths in a certain way, or the law of the Jews demands a certain level of ethical sensitivity, and so on. At other times, however, Philo clearly indicates that in his own city of Alexandria there lived other Jews whose understanding of Judaism was quite different from his. Some "literalists," as he occasionally calls them, were openly scornful of his elaborate allegorical readings of the Torah with their emphasis on spiritual and intellectual experience; these Jews were interested only in the proper execution of the Law, which Philo likened to caring only for the body and forgetting the soul.[2] Conversely, other Jews carried Philo's allegorizing further than he himself thought suitable, disregarding the literal meaning of Scripture altogether and disdaining to carry out the Law at all. Philo likened these people to those who would cultivate the soul while forgetting to feed the body.[3] This essay will sidestep the question of whether Philo's description of Judaism spoke for the bulk of his contemporaries, or a sizable minority, or only for himself and a handful of similar eccentrics. Philo's writings will simply provide one model of what Jewish religious life could involve.

Philo's writings draw a rich picture of a particular kind of spiritual experience and provide detailed information about the intellectual training he considered necessary for those who hoped to achieve it. For Philo the ultimate goal of religious life is to achieve a kind of beatific ecstasy, a "sober intoxication"[4] that comes to those who are filled with divine grace and spirit. Broadly speaking, this goal is achieved through scrupulous adherence to the laws of Moses, not merely as a behavioral discipline (though the laws provide that as well), but through recognition of the perfection of these laws in contrast to all others[5]

1. Beginning readers of Philo may wish to consult Erwin Goodenough, *An Introduction to Philo Judaeus* (New York, 1963); Harry A. Wolfson, *Philo* (Cambridge, Mass., 1982); Ronald Williamson, *Jews in the Hellenistic World: Philo* (Cambridge, 1989); Alan Mendelson, *Philo's Jewish Identity* (Atlanta, 1988); Naomi G. Cohen, *Philo Judaeus: His Universe of Discourse* (New York, 1995). A complete English translation of Philo's works can be found in the Loeb Classical Library.

2. In his *Questions and Answers* on Genesis and Exodus, Philo frequently contrasts the "literal" meaning of the text with the deeper meaning he is concerned to propound.

3. See *On the Migration of Abraham* 89-91.

4. *Every Good Man Is Free* 13; see also *On the Allegory of the Law* 3.82.

5. If only the material situation of Israel could be improved, "each nation would abandon its peculiar ways, and, throwing overboard their ancestral customs, turn to honoring our laws

and in full awareness of the ethical and philosophical lessons implied by these laws and by the stories that accompany them in Israel's sacred Scriptures. The key to achieving this ecstasy is to understand that the true meaning of these texts and rites is not apparent on the surface; Jewish life and Jewish tradition embody a rich allegory which must be carefully decoded before their full significance can be captured. This decoding requires a full Greek education,[6] ending with the study of philosophy and the cultivation of contemplative skills.

Philo's ultimate religious goal was thus shaped for him by the world of Greek philosophical-contemplative piety. Those aspiring to his "sober intoxication" must have two sorts of training: the best Greek education available, and also a strong acculturation into — formation in — the Jewish community and its way of life. The necessary mental skills include intimate familiarity with Scripture, or at least the writings attributed to Moses; solid preparation in the dominant philosophical notions of the time; and a strong orientation toward solitary contemplation. The necessary behavioral skills include familiarity with the rituals and the rules of Judaism and willingness to be bound by these. The necessary social skill is the readiness to sacrifice one's contemplative ecstasy when one's cousins in the covenant need attention and support.

With respect to this last, Philo in a well-known passage speaks with poignant nostalgia for the days of his youth:

> There was a time when I had leisure for philosophy and for the contemplation of the universe and its contents, when I made its spirit my own in all its beauty and loveliness and true blessedness, when my constant companions were divine themes and verities, wherein I rejoiced with a joy that never cloyed or sated. I . . . seemed always to be borne aloft into the heights with a soul possessed by some God-sent inspiration, a fellow-traveler with the sun and moon and the whole heaven and universe. . . . I blessed my lot in that I had escaped by main force from the plagues of mortal life.[7]

But alas, he had to give this up: "My steps were dogged by . . . envy, which suddenly set upon me and ceased not to pull me down with violence till it had

---

alone" (*The Life of Moses* 2.44). This proud tribute to Jewish law does not necessarily imply, as J. J. Collins thought it did, that "Philo envisaged the conversion of the gentiles." See *Between Athens and Jerusalem: Jewish Identity in the Hellenistic Diaspora* (New York, 1983), p. 115; similarly Wolfson, 1:187; 2:415. Philo engages here in hypothetical boasting from which concrete implications cannot safely be drawn. See also the comments of M. Goodman, *Mission and Conversion: Proselytizing in the Religious History of the Roman Empire* (Oxford, 1994), pp. 68, 75 (and cf. p. 55, with reference to Tob. 14:6).

6. See Alan Mendelson, *Secular Education in Philo of Alexandria* (Cincinnati, 1982).

7. This and the next two quotations form a single extract from *On the Special Laws* 3.1-6.

plunged me in the ocean of civil cares, in which I am swept away, unable even to raise my head above the water." Scholars have not agreed on the cause or the nature of this terrible misfortune. Whatever the details, however, Philo reports that he was pulled from his study by some social responsibility which only he could meet; he had to enter the world of affairs.

Fortunately he kept sight of the higher good even while pursuing the lower:

Amid my groans I hold my own, for planted in my soul . . . I keep the yearning for culture *(paideia)* which ever has pity and compassion for me, lifts me up and relieves my pain. . . .

It is well for me to give thanks to God even for this, that though submerged I am not sucked down into the depths, but can also open the soul's eyes, which in my despair of comforting hope I thought had now lost their sight, and am irradiated by the light of wisdom, and am not given over to lifelong darkness.

So behold me daring, not only to read the sacred messages of Moses, but also in my love of knowledge to peer into each of them and unfold and reveal what is not known to the multitude.

For Philo, then, the highest good is to extract hitherto unknown lessons from the teachings of Moses, that is, from Scripture. These lessons are not suitable for that same "multitude" whose concerns have pulled him away from his studies; he sees to their needs when this becomes necessary, but his first love remains his private spiritual quest, and his favorite public service remains the propagation of his teachings to those select few who are able to receive them. He remains grateful to God that even while neglecting his studies he can resume them from time to time; he has not forgotten how to do this, nor has he lost the deep fulfillment this activity provides. In Philo's own moving phrase, his inner eyes have not lost their sight.

The quest for fulfillment that emerges here is a solitary quest, to be carried out by a solitary individual, isolated to the greatest possible degree from the distractions of the world. Even such a solitary, to be sure, is a social being, under strong obligation to abandon this isolation when the community requires aid: the hierarchy of intermediate ethical values thus serves the summum bonum at some times but undermines it at others. As strongly as he feels his social obligations, Philo does not clearly indicate their ground. They seem to arise in part out of gratitude for (and dependency on) the practical benefits that social organization provides, but Philo also reveals an intuitive solidarity with his fellow Jews that is so strong he does not stop to analyze or account for it at all.

Still, while community provides the framework within which educational and other institutions can be established, it functions ultimately as a distraction. The highest fulfillment of individual existence is not of a sort to be shared with others, except indirectly through the training of disciples by personal or written instruction and example. That sort of sharing was the driving force of Philo's life, but it is very hard to determine whether it was really a broadly social sharing or the interpersonal bond among a small self-selected elite. For Philo religious formation is ultimately the individual's own responsibility, pursued by himself and for his own sake,[8] with the occasional help of those teachers the individual can find. Those teachers' main responsibility, in turn, is to their chosen disciples; to use a recently fashionable phrase, the rest of the world just won't get it.

The Qumran Community (Dead Sea Scrolls)

The second group of writings is found in the so-called Dead Sea Scrolls.[9] Here too it will be best to disregard current controversies over the identity of the people who composed these texts and over the relation of the texts and their authors to the people buried at Qumran; as with Philo, the scrolls will simply be allowed to disclose the religious ideas of a group of Jews who seem to have set themselves up as a sect apart from the rest of Israel and declared themselves the only righteous remnant of an otherwise corrupt and doomed people. The task here will be to examine the conceptions of religious life that underlie the scrolls, and more particularly to see what these documents teach about the way their authors believed a person might prepare (or be prepared) for such a life.

The Qumran community apparently maintained itself more through recruitment than through biological continuity, so that its members took no direct responsibility for guiding the spiritual development of the young: people grew up elsewhere, and in a sense the very act of requesting admittance into the group was a sign that one considered one's own essential formation complete. What then led people to reach that conclusion? How did the writers of these texts imagine that such formation went on? In a key passage one hears echoes of the idea Christians later called predestination:

---

8. Philo knows of Jewish women who have devoted themselves to lives of exemplary piety (see *On the Contemplative Life* 32-33), but he shared the common ancient presumption that females are not suited for advanced intellectual training.

9. Useful background to the Dead Sea Scrolls can be found in two works by Joseph Fitzmyer: *The Dead Sea Scrolls: Major Publications and Tools for Study* (Atlanta, 1990) and *Responses to 101 Questions about the Dead Sea Scrolls* (New York, 1992). The scrolls themselves have been translated in numerous editions.

The God of Knowledge . . . has created man to govern the world, and has appointed for him two spirits in which to walk until the time of his visitation: the spirits of truth and falsehood. Those born of truth spring from a fountain of light, but those born of falsehood spring from a source of darkness. All the children of righteousness are ruled by the Prince of Light and walk in the ways of light, but all the children of falsehood are ruled by the Angel of Darkness and walk in the ways of darkness.

The Angel of Darkness leads all the children of righteousness astray, and until his end, all their sin, iniquities, wickedness, and all their unlawful deeds are caused by his dominion in accordance with the mysteries of God. . . . But the God of Israel and his Angel of Truth will succour all the sons of light. For it is he who created the spirits of Light and Darkness and founded every action upon them and established every deed upon their ways. . . .

And as for the visitation of all who walk in this spirit, it shall be healing, great peace in a long life, and fruitfulness, together with everlasting blessing and eternal joy in life without end, a crown of glory and a garment of majesty in unending light. . . .

The nature of all the children of the men [sic] is ruled by these [two spirits], and during their life all the hosts of men . . . walk in [both] their ways. And the whole reward for their deeds shall be . . . according to whether each man's portion in their two divisions is great or small. For God has established the spirits in equal measure until the final age. . . . He has allotted them to the children of men that they may know good and evil, and that the destiny of all the living may be according to the spirit within them at the time of the visitation.[10]

Having completed this rather imposing introduction, the author proceeds without further ado to lay out the working rules of the group: "And this is the rule for the men of the community who have freely pledged themselves to be converted from all evil and to cling to all his commandments according to his will."[11] The author devotes no space at all to examining why these people have made such a pledge. The existence within the people Israel of a smaller group of individuals marked for righteousness is at every point simply taken for granted in these documents. The texts are written by and for and about such people.

A very different sense of human nature and of religious community thus emerges from this text than from Philo, and with it a dramatically different implied conception of religious formation. Where Philo envisions a life of con-

---

10. The Qumran Manual of Discipline or Community Rule: 1QS 3.15–4.26, in the Pelican translation by Geza Vermes; editorial restorations are not indicated.

11. 1QS 5.1.

stant striving for improvement (to be sure, not everyone can improve to the same degree), the picture from Qumran suggests that the world is divided between the doomed and the saved. You cannot struggle to move yourself from one camp to the other, but only hope to discover that the "God of Knowledge" has placed you in the camp of the blessed.

In actual lived experience, therefore, adults already educated elsewhere somehow became convinced that they wanted to join this self-constituted spiritual elite, so they arrived on their own and petitioned for membership.[12] How did such individuals reach such a conviction? Did existing members of the sect work in any way to encourage or facilitate such an outcome?[13] A passage like the one just quoted evokes a classic pattern of conversion: certain susceptible individuals, on hearing such ideas, entered into a lengthy process of introspection and eventually reached the conclusion that heaven had assigned them to the children of light. Such persons then did what the children of light were expected to do: they abandoned their current way of life, collected what movable property they had, and went off into the desert to join the settlement at Qumran, or more precisely, they petitioned the settlement at Qumran to admit them. Once admitted, they entered by stages into the spiritual discipline of the group: acceptance of rank, rigorous control of behavior, participation in night-long sessions of Torah study, and so on. Acculturation into this way of life constituted the final stage of their "religious formation"; a radical break with their previous lives, it was at the same time the fruit of all their previous experience.

Given that it prepared them for the momentous steps just described, this previous experience must have been quite remarkable; the modern reader, unfortunately, can say very little about it. The sect's documents seem uninterested in the past lives of its members,[14] or perhaps they discreetly turn aside from such past lives as of no further consequence.[15] Postulants appear in the Manual

12. Scrutiny of petitioners and novices takes up a considerable portion of the Manual of Discipline, while the education of children receives no attention at all. In modern terms, the Dead Sea community was a huge mutual education project for adults.

13. It may seem obvious that the very production of the Dead Sea Scrolls was undertaken as a means of propagating the teachings of the sect, but these documents were just as likely written for internal consumption, as a means of reinforcing members' loyalty or conviction. Much of Jewish-Hellenistic literature, even documents that directly address Gentile readers, was apparently aimed at Jewish audiences. The literary form was no more than a possibly transparent fiction.

14. The Qumran hymn scroll (1QH) is full of expressions of gratitude to God for having brought the writer from his previous way of life to the life of the children of light, but these expressions tend to be highly stylized, in the manner of the biblical psalms they imitate. No useful biographical information can be extracted from them.

15. The Talmud (*Bava Meṣia* 58b, 59b) contains a similar warning that converts to Judaism should be protected from reminders of their previous state.

of Discipline as though they had simply wandered in from the desert (and in a sense they had). The Dead Sea texts have no rules at all for training or supervising emissaries or "missionaries" from the sect to the larger society. The social self-image of the group was one of exile and isolation from that society, and the sect waited in the desert for others to come to it on their own accord. One cannot even be sure that copies of the sectarian documents found at Qumran were in wider circulation; aside from a copy of the Damascus Covenant found in Cairo a hundred years ago, none of these texts has ever been found, so far as I know, in another location, nor is any of them cited in any other Jewish or Christian document from antiquity.[16]

How then did outsiders ever even find out about the group and its ideas? Groups of this sort tend to arouse interest and provoke gossip, and those who lived anywhere nearby could not help but notice them. Many outsiders, to be sure, probably had a profoundly distorted conception of what the Qumran people were trying to do, but certain individuals took the trouble to examine them more closely and more carefully, and some of those were drawn in. That is the process implied by the texts themselves, and there is no reason to doubt that something of this sort went on.

For the authors of the Dead Sea Scrolls, then, the summum bonum is to belong to the children of light; this is experienced, however, not as an achievement but as a gift from heaven or the "God of Knowledge." One apparently discovered (after the fact, as it were) that one's lot had been placed among the blessed from the time of one's birth. No conscious preparation for achieving this summum bonum could be imagined, but much unconscious preparation no doubt went on. Recruits must have imagined that their entire lives had led up to the moment when they left behind their previous lives and headed out into the desert. Such people must have received a particular kind of education and psychological formation, or they would never have been open to the Qumran message (as most people were not); there are no signs, however, in the scrolls or elsewhere of a formal educational program aimed at preparing its recipients for that message or for entry into the sect. People in the cities and towns of Judea no doubt spent time discussing the religious fanatics (as we might say) of Qumran. Probably most outsiders found those people scary and repellent, an attitude the Qumran texts warmly reciprocated, but some were drawn closer and closer until they crossed over the line and joined the sect.

Perceptions of person and community are reflected in the implied sequence of stages by which members of the Qumran community hoped to fulfill

16. There may be minor exceptions, but this general impression was confirmed in a private communication from Prof. L. H. Schiffman dated January 4, 1996.

their religious destiny. In the sect's view, one did not strive in advance to qualify for admittance to the group; applicants were not admitted to full membership until after a long period of gradual incorporation into the community, and no applicants could be judged truly worthy until their years of testing had run their course. In other words, the hallmark of belonging to the "children of light" was a lifetime of disciplined perfection, but the law of the sect could properly be fulfilled only after admittance; such fulfillment was thus not even possible until after one had already joined the group. In contrast to Philo, therefore, all striving took place only after the summum bonum had already been attained, but from that point on a life of unremitting attention to every detail of the community's rules became urgently necessary.

The community thus provided the indispensable vehicle for individual fulfillment: without the embodiment of divine will that the life of the community provided, the life of the individual could have no satisfying meaning whatever. Outside the community were only the children of darkness. Within the community, among the children of light, religious formation was by implication complete from the very beginning and at the same time never fully accomplished. Members lived their lives in the tension between those two poles.

Early Rabbinic Texts

The third group of writings, the vast corpus of rabbinic literature and in particular the Babylonian Talmud,[17] eventually became the foundational literature of Jewish life. In antiquity, to be sure, while these documents were first being assembled, rabbinic literature seems to have been chiefly an internal literature, intended for use primarily by those already participating in the rabbinic movement; most Jews in antiquity probably had no familiarity at all with these soon-to-be-canonical texts. By processes that can no longer be traced, however, the early Middle Ages saw the persistent spread of rabbinic influence throughout the Jewish world, until finally virtually all Jews everywhere lived under the guidance of these texts and of teachers who had mastered them. The significance of this development will be briefly examined in the next section of this chapter.

17. The scholarly bibliography on ancient rabbinic literature is enormous. A useful introduction can be found in *The Study of Ancient Judaism*, ed. J. Neusner (New York, 1981), which conveniently reprints a number of comprehensive bibliographies that first appeared in *Aufstieg und Niedergang der römischen Welt* II.19.2. See also H. L. Strack and G. Stemberger, *Introduction to the Talmud and Midrash* (Edinburgh, 1994), and the present author's own chapter on the Talmud in *Back to the Sources*, ed. B. W. Holtz (New York, 1984), pp. 129-75.

As in the case of Philo, it is very difficult to measure what percentage of, say, fourth-century Jews were interested in rabbinic ideas about religious formation. For the vast reaches of the western diaspora, an immense area containing many Jews, there is almost no indication of rabbinic presence at all. The synagogues of late antiquity, in all parts of the Jewish world, do not seem to have functioned under rabbinic supervision: archeologists have uncovered numerous synagogues that do not seem to have been built according to talmudic norms,[18] and nothing anywhere in rabbinic literature would have prepared us for the pictorial splendor of the famous third-century synagogue at Dura-Europus in present-day Syria.[19] Even in the rabbinic heartlands of Babylonia (now Iraq) and the land of Israel, however, places where rabbis' public roles made them unavoidable, it is hard to tell whether Jews voluntarily submitted their own religious formation (or that of their children) to the rabbinic lawyer-clerks who governed so much of their communal life. Rabbis are not often described as teaching children,[20] and even with adults one generally finds rabbis in conversation with their own disciples rather than with ordinary Jews off the street. No doubt some individual rabbis attracted a more widespread following as preachers or sages or wonder-workers, but as in the previous sections of this chapter, it is better here to leave aside the question of numbers and mine rabbinic literature for the particular conceptions of a specific group of Jews who were more or less distinct from the masses of Jewry.

The main venues of rabbinic activity in antiquity were the school and the court; neither of those terms, however, means quite what the modern reader first imagines. Rabbinic courts apparently did have some recognized jurisdic-

18. This is equally true for the numerous synagogues located in territories where rabbis were active, particularly the Galilee in late antiquity. See now L. I. Levine, "The Sages and the Synagogue in Late Antiquity: The Evidence of the Galilee," in *The Galilee in Late Antiquity*, ed. L. I. Levine (New York and Jerusalem: Jewish Theological Seminary of America, 1992), pp. 201-22.

19. On the Dura paintings see E. R. Goodenough, *Jewish Symbols in the Greco-Roman Period* (New York, 1953-68), vols. 9-11; also Emil Kraeling, *The Synagogue*, rev. ed. (1979).

20. Modern writers frequently assume that rabbinic discussions of the importance of teaching, proper techniques of teaching, honor due the teacher, and so forth have to do with primary education, but in fact this is rarely the case; the rabbinic teacher was almost always the teacher of adult disciples. One previous writer has laid proper stress on this important distinction; see Eliezer Ebner, *Elementary Education in Ancient Israel* (New York, 1956), pp. 58-60 and 109 n. 44.

One important talmudic sage, the early third-century R. Hiyya, is sometimes described as having engaged in the education of children. The talmudic reference usually cited in this connection, however, *Ketubot* 103b (= *Bava Meṣia* 85b), refers to his organizing such activity, not actually engaging in it. Moreover, that text reports a schematic boast rather than solid biographical information.

tion, and the Talmud suggests such courts were endowed with all the trappings of modern courts (bailiffs, archives, and the like); even so, an ancient rabbinic court may have had much less in common with a modern courtroom than with the living room of a modern village justice of the peace. Surely rabbis' judicial power was limited: there is no sign they tried capital cases, and they may have lacked criminal jurisdiction altogether. Rabbis seem primarily to have adjudicated Jewish matrimonial cases as well as property and loss claims among Jews.[21]

As for rabbinic "schools," modern writers often go so far as to call them yeshivoth, or academies, and often identify the semilegendary gathering of first-century sages at Yavneh/Jamnia near the Judean coast as the first in a long line of distinguished institutions of advanced rabbinic learning, but again the reality may have been far less imposing. A famous sage allowing several chosen followers to live in or near his house and follow him around all day while they discussed any questions of law or lore that arose may be closer to the truth.[22]

Unlike philosophers after the model of Philo or the sectarians gathered at Qumran, ancient rabbis had no social ethic of isolation. Rabbis strove (often with limited success, to be sure) for maximum involvement in, and control over, the life of the community.[23] On the other hand, rabbis seem to have avoided the direct instruction of children; by their own choice, therefore, rabbis had no direct impact on the crucial early stages of the religious formation of young Jews. They quite willingly left that task to others, people to whom no special recognition was granted because they had assumed this responsibility: rabbis saw their own mission as a higher one, and considered the teaching of children a menial task. Rabbis did, however, strive to attract adult disciples. A slogan attributed to the earliest forerunners of their movement, the so-called Men of the Great Assembly, mandated that they do so.[24] The study of Torah, which rabbis considered the essence of their calling, consisted largely of endless discussions with those disciples about every imaginable question. "Religious formation" is our name for what they would have called study of Torah: it was a lifelong task, a perpetual campaign to narrow the gap between themselves and an unattainable ideal. With respect to religious formation, therefore, any dis-

---

21. A general portrait of the rabbinate in ancient Babylonia emerges from Jacob Neusner's *History of the Jews in Babylonia*, 5 vols. (Leiden, 1964-70); see also Shaye J. D. Cohen, "The Place of the Rabbi in Jewish Society of the Second Century," in *The Galilee in Late Antiquity*, pp. 157-73.

22. See David Goodblatt, *Rabbinic Instruction in Sassanian Babylonia* (Leiden, 1975). Goodblatt prefers the term "disciple-circle" to "school."

23. But see Shaye J. D. Cohen's commments cited in n. 21.

24. Mishnah *Avot* (the "Ethics of the Fathers") 1.1.

cussion of early rabbinic Judaism must focus on a later stage of personal development.

Once other persons had taught a young adult the basic skills of literacy, and had introduced that person to the study of Scripture and the fundamentals of Jewish tradition, what led him to seek to become a "disciple of the sages"? Remarkably little is said about this in the texts: in spite of the ancient exhortation just cited, rabbinic masters, like the people of Qumran, seem to have waited for would-be disciples to come to them. In those areas where their movement had established itself, however, rabbis were highly visible people. They presided over courts and held other official positions. They cultivated a striking public image by engaging in activities that were designed to attract maximum attention: muttering Torah as they walked along the street, dressing differently from other people, conversing and debating in public. Stories constantly circulated about the powers of rabbis — they would have said, of the Torah — to achieve miracles, to prolong life, and so on.[25] Certain individuals will have been caught up in all this, and will have sought to take part in those activities and to obtain a share in those powers by becoming a sage. Such persons will have sought out a nearby rabbinic sage and asked to become his disciple. If the petitioner was found worthy, a new stage in his "religious formation" will have begun.

That stage consisted of learning what his teacher knew and learning how his teacher thought and acted in every imaginable circumstance. This process amounted, as Jacob Neusner has written, to a kind of apprenticeship: the goal in rabbinic discipleship was to turn oneself into a close replica of one's teacher. A famous talmudic story tells of a disciple who followed his master into the privy and one who hid under his teacher's marital bed; when rebuked for such egregious violations of their teachers' dignity and privacy, they responded, "But this is Torah, and I must learn!"[26] This was "formation" of a most intensive kind.

The great texts of ancient rabbinic Judaism can most easily be understood as compendia of information assembled to serve this enormous project of formation. To start with the earliest extant document, the Mishnah is often called an early rabbinic law code because it is constructed, as a code of law might be, out of sections pertaining to a topic of law, each divided in turn into numbered chapters and paragraphs. Indeed, someone who wanted to teach the rules of the Sabbath might very well generate a text resembling the Mishnaic tractate *Shabbat* as his instrument; one might do the same for the rules of marriage, of property damage, of menstrual purity and impurity, of Levitical tithes, and the

---

25. All this is described in Neusner's *History of the Jews in Babylonia*.
26. *Berakhot* 62a.

many other topics the Mishnah embraces. While one might generate texts resembling the Mishnah, however, one would not likely generate the Mishnah itself: that document is too full of apparently irrelevant stories, unresolved disputes, unhelpful exegeses of Scripture, and the like to meet the need that codes of law are designed to answer. If the Mishnah is designed to tell us the law, why does it contain so much nonlegal material, and why does it so frequently leave the law itself unclarified?

The Mishnah more likely has another purpose entirely: it was produced to help disciples learn to think like rabbis, on the assumption that once they were trained they would be perfectly capable of determining on their own, without further recourse to books, the actual law in any situation that might arise. From the stories disciples learned what rabbinic exemplars had done in previous situations. From the exegeses they learned how to elicit hints from Scripture about questions that Scripture seems not to be addressing. From the unresolved disputes they learned the range of acceptable options in different cases, and they began to understand why the range in some instances is quite large while on other matters single opinions are simply recorded without dispute. By the end the disciple was "formed": he could pronounce "oral Torah" on his own.

Formation was never complete, however, because one always had more to learn: that is why the Talmud presently came to dwarf the Mishnah with its own immensely larger collection of teachings and analyses, and that is why the rabbinic tradition overall has remained as relentlessly textual and interpretive as it has. The rabbinic ideal is the sage, not the saint. Saints may be born, but sages are made: that is the key to understanding the summum bonum of rabbinic Judaism.

The rabbis actually developed a kind of two-layered summum bonum, one for themselves and one for the mass of Jewry. According to rabbinic teaching, the highest goal for the community is to shape itself according to the teachings of the sages; this entails accepting rabbinic authority over its public life. For individuals the corresponding highest goal is to open up their private lives to rabbinic teachings in every way: to sit at the feet of scholars and absorb their wisdom, to consult them as to the proper action in every situation, to learn from them the general meaning of human life and the particular hope and destiny of the covenant people. When the community has thus been properly shaped, it will become the "kingdom of priests" of which Scripture speaks (see Exod. 19:6). When individuals have submitted themselves to the discipline of rabbinic teaching, they will have become what their Creator intended for them to be.

For the rabbis themselves, however, the summum bonum was dramatically different from the one just described. The term "oral Torah" is the key: rabbis designated their ordinary daily teachings, their quotidian legal rulings and their matter-of-fact pragmatic and ethical counsels, by the same term that Israel had used for centuries to designate the sacred "Book of the Teaching of Moses [through which] God had commanded Israel" (Neh. 8:1). The word "Torah" denotes divine revelation; Moses gave Torah in his day, rabbis give Torah in theirs, in ours.[27] Each time a rabbi — any rabbi — speaks, that speech gives sound to the voice that spoke at Sinai: it brings Torah into the world and provides sacred guidance to the people of the covenant. For rabbis, therefore, the teaching of Torah did more than bring them closer to God: it made them more like God, it confirmed their holiness in the midst of the people. This was the highest of all possible ends. A holy life was a life guided by Torah. Rabbis, and only rabbis, could lead others toward such a life: this was true for both other individuals and the community as a whole. Rabbis could learn to exercise such leadership through submission to, and close imitation of, those elders who had already learned to do this from others senior even to them. The sacred heritage passed in this way from one generation to the next, and the rabbinic sage was the indispensable agent of this transmission.

Ancient or "Traditional" Judaism?

The modern forms of Jewish religion engage in constant debate on the question of continuity and change in the history of the tradition.[28] Those contemporary movements dedicated to resisting change naturally contend that previous ages held the same attitude, that "traditional" Judaism now is what it has always been. Contemporary movements more open to change naturally contend the reverse: in their view Judaism has always been fluid and responsive to changes in its environment and must maintain this flexibility in the modern world. This is the wrong place to enter that debate, but it will still be useful to examine the contribution to later ages of the three varieties of ancient Judaism just examined.

Of two, little can be said. The sectarians of Qumran disappeared virtually without a trace, and their voluminous writings were almost entirely forgotten for nearly two thousand years. The writings of Philo were preserved by Christians and indeed may have influenced such Church Fathers as Origen, but again

27. This is the import of a statement attributed to R. Dosa b. Harkinas that "any three persons [of recognized authority?] who constitute a court are the equivalent of the court of Moses" (Mishnah *Rosh Hashanah* 2.9), or of the talmudic elaboration that Jephthah, not an admirable man in the rabbis' view, was in his generation as Samuel was in his (*Rosh Hashanah* 25b).

28. A useful, though slightly dated, introduction to this matter is J. L. Blau, *Modern Varieties of Judaism* (New York and London, 1966).

the Jews forgot him completely. The reason may be that Philo wrote in Greek, a language Jewish religious thought ceased to use, or it may be that rabbinic Judaism developed along lines that left no room for Philo's style of thinking. In any case, Philo and his teachings completely disappeared; no surviving Jewish text from his own time until the Renaissance so much as mentions his name. Even the great Maimonides, whose conception of Judaism was strikingly like Philo's, seems not to have heard of him; the two thinkers over a thousand years apart seem to have drawn from common Greek sources to reach common conclusions, but the later writer's life and thought would have been no different had Philo never lived.

There was, however, one important difference between Philo and Maimonides: Maimonides was a rabbi. While Philo was read largely by Christians and the dissidents of Qumran sank into oblivion, rabbinic leadership steadily widened its range until its orbit embraced virtually every Jew in the world. To ask about the connection between ancient Judaism and "the Jewish tradition" is to ask how the Talmud shaped nearly all of Jewish life through the Middle Ages and beyond.

Because of the limitations of this chapter, certain brief remarks will have to suffice. It has already been noted that emergent rabbinic Judaism had a "relentlessly textual" character. This is not surprising: the earliest rabbis were legal experts who spent their time learning and applying legal texts. This textual character was inherited by medieval Judaism, but by the Middle Ages the texts in question were no longer collections of "oral Torah" set to memory, they were books: at the close of antiquity, for reasons which have not yet been determined, the vast body of ancient rabbinic teaching was reduced to writing in authoritative documents.[29] To be a rabbi, or to be a Jew under rabbinic tutelage, was to study holy books, the books of Scripture in one's childhood and the growing library of rabbinic writings as one grew to maturity. Most Jews throughout history were too poor to pursue this course of study very far beyond its elementary stages, and for most of history women were excluded from it more or less completely,[30] but studiousness has been a prized virtue among all Jews who have looked to the rabbis and their teachings for religious formation.

Talmudic literature, however, has a definite character and a specific range of interests. The Talmud is not the work of contemplative mystics or systematic

---

29. Rabbinic traditions had existed all along in written form, but now these books replaced the official memorizer as the recognized medium for preserving and transmitting rabbinic teachings. A useful discussion of this still obscure transformation can be found in Strack and Stemberger, *Introduction to the Talmud and Midrash*.

30. Over the past generation, the exclusion of women from rabbinic study has ended in all non-Orthodox forms of American Judaism.

philosophers: it was produced by expert practitioners of the law, and under its influence Judaism became the sort of religion lawyers might produce. Rabbis saw the Torah as a God-given code of law, and saw Jews' highest obligations as to learn that code and follow its instructions. Clear argumentation won rabbis' admiration more readily than passionate eloquence; rabbis cared more about action and its results, things which could be seen and measured, than about intention or motive.[31] All these preferences[32] shaped the emerging Jewish way of life, and supplied the framework within which Jews of later ages received their religious formation. Some Jews, philosophers or mystics or poets, were not content within this argumentative framework, but it dominated Jewish life for over a thousand years.

Many particular features of traditional Jewish religion seem to have been contributed by the early rabbis. Many now-familiar ceremonies, for example, the Habdalah ritual that ends the Sabbath, make their first appearance in the pages of the Talmud. The prayer book used in later ages was first standardized in those same pages. The Torah commentary of Rashi,[33] the gateway to Bible study for centuries of Jewish children, is essentially a compendium of earlier rabbinic midrash. In later centuries rabbinic texts governed the training of Jewish leaders, and rabbinic teachings shaped the lives of the Jewish masses. The religious formation of Jews in the Middle Ages and beyond was a legacy of the ancient rabbis.

Concluding Remarks

The three configurations of ancient Judaism just surveyed can profitably be compared and contrasted on their conceptions of religious formation. Depending on the criterion one adopts, they fall into different groupings.

Despite Philo's powerful sense of civic obligation, and for all his courageous willingness to risk his life in defense of his community's needs and interests,[34] he saw religious fulfillment as ultimately a matter of personal experience.

---

31. These are generalizations, of course, and very many exceptions could be found. As generalizations, however, they point into the heart of rabbinic Judaism as a lived religion.

32. One might also mention, perhaps, a tendency toward an argumentative intellectual style, but such general cultural tendencies lie beyond the concerns of this volume.

33. Rabbi Solomon b. Isaac (1040-1105), the most important rabbinic commentator of all time. Virtually every Hebrew edition of the Pentateuch or the Talmud that has ever been published has included Rashi's commentary in the margins of its pages.

34. In the year 41 Philo led a delegation to Rome to petition the emperor for relief from harassment and oppression in Alexandria. See his memoir of that trip, *The Embassy to Gaius*.

Groups might exist for the purpose of encouraging and assisting such experience (Philo names the Therapeutae in Egypt and the Essenes in Judea as examples), but Philo himself belonged to no such organization, and he nowhere expresses a sense of loss or deprivation on that account. Perhaps the quasi-monastic groups he praises existed for those who could not afford the leisure and private instruction made possible by Philo's enormous wealth, but Philo never discusses this question. For people like himself, communal life provided the necessary background — it might now be called the infrastructure — for an essentially private quest. His own religious formation was largely a matter of private education, book learning in its earlier stages and then a training of the mind to discover those truths that books can never teach. He never shows any doubt that this model would also be ideal for others.

In sharp contrast, both the early rabbis and the authors of the Dead Sea Scrolls took for granted that religious fulfillment is the direct consequence of membership in a holy community. The rabbis identified that community with the entire people of Israel, while the sectarians at Qumran distinguished themselves from the bulk of Jewry in the most emphatic manner possible. This distinction implies a further difference between the two groups in their conception of the social setting of religious formation. Postulants approached the group at Qumran after being formed in the outside community, presumably without direct exposure to the desert community and its way of life, while rabbis moved in the wider Jewish society and were a constantly visible model to children growing up, even if they took little direct part in training them.

Secondly, Philo saw religious formation as essentially a training of the mind: he was openly hostile to the view that one might be satisfied to learn all the Jewish rules of behavior without also cultivating a proper understanding of the lessons those rules teach. For the other two models, however, following the rules was far closer to the heart of the matter: religious formation meant instilling in people the necessary knowledge of the rules, together with the willingness and the ability to follow them. The rabbis knew well that one had to learn a lot to follow the rules correctly, but they balanced Philo's intellectualism with a corresponding hostility toward those who learn without the intention of doing. To them, such people are like trees with many branches but few roots: they look impressive, but at the first wind they blow over and are gone.[35] As for the people at Qumran, the very desire to follow the rules was a token of belonging to the children of light, but in the long run, actual ability to follow them was the

---

35. See Mishnah *Avot* 3.22, also 1.17: "the main thing is not study, but action." Both these statements are ascribed to specific masters, but they express widely held values.

only thing that mattered. People who meant well but could not maintain the discipline were quickly ejected from the community.

On yet another matter, however, the grouping shifts: both the Dead Sea Scrolls and the writings of Philo envision a religious formation that ends by isolating its recipients, whether through personal seclusion or group secession, from the mass of Israel. For the rabbis, however, the same *Ethics of the Fathers* also contains the famous admonition of Hillel, "Do not withdraw from the community."[36] The Torah had originally been given to the entire nation, and in the rabbinic view only the entire nation could properly fulfill it.

All three conceptions of Judaism, however, share certain important features. All essentially address adults: the widespread modern assumption that the really important "formation" takes place in childhood is not so much denied in these texts as ignored. All address individuals who have learned the basic skills of literacy; all address individuals who know and accept the basic requirements of Jewish law; none is especially interested in children or especially concerned about directing the formation of that basic foundational layer which modern theories of education consistently emphasize.

For related reasons, all three seem ready to wait and let the world come to them. In every case, to be sure, the situation contains ambiguities. In theory rabbis sought disciples, but talmudic literature contains little record of rabbinic outreach. Rabbis mostly taught their own students and cultivated their own learning, though from time to time outsiders did approach them with private questions or public lawsuits of some kind. The Qumran people might have been more energetic about attracting followers, but after all, they were already in the desert because their vehement opposition to the Jerusalem regime had put their lives in danger: they had no choice but to wait. Philo for his part wrote many books, and he must have expected people to read them, but in the many autobiographical remarks scattered throughout his writings he never refers to himself as a teacher with actual students or a preacher facing an actual audience. In fact, almost nothing is known about Philo's own educational activities, even whether he engaged in any such activity at all beyond his voluminous writing. He apparently just expected that his books would find their own way into the right hands.

And finally, it is important again to note that all three bodies of literature examined here were written by people who emphatically distinguished themselves from the common masses of Jews in their day. None of these writers claim to speak for the ordinary Jews of antiquity; in fact, none express much respect for the lives such Jews must have led nor take any responsibility at all for

36. *Ethics of the Fathers* 2.4.

the religious formation such Jews must have undergone in and after childhood. About such Jews we know almost nothing, just odds and ends of information from excavations, papyri, references in Gentile writings, and the like.

It is clear, however, that such ordinary Jews did undergo a very strong formation. The Jewish tradition could not otherwise have survived at all; and in the end it did better than survive, it flourished throughout the Roman Empire and beyond. Jews who never heard of Philo, never read the Dead Sea Scrolls, and never met a rabbi lived their lives, raised their children, and made their contribution to the survival of Judaism for another generation. Without such Jews the nascent rabbinic tradition could not have taken root and prospered.

Christian Formation in the Early Church

Robert Louis Wilken

"Be ye therefore perfect, even as your Father which is in heaven is perfect" (Matt. 5:48 KJV). These words of Jesus are echoed throughout the New Testament, in the writings of Paul (2 Cor. 7:1), in the epistle to the Hebrews (12:14), and in 1 Peter: "As he who called you is holy, be holy yourselves in all your conduct; since it is written, 'You shall be holy, for I am holy'" (1:15-16 RSV). Whether the term is "perfection" or "holiness," the New Testament presents Christian faith as a life oriented toward an end, toward a goal, what in the language of the early church and ancient moral philosophy was called the "final good," the summum bonum. In the passage from the Sermon on the Mount, the term used in Greek for "perfect" derives from the word for goal, *telos*. Human actions are understood in relation to ends, an understanding inherited from the Greeks.

In the ancient world all thinking about the moral life was teleological. In his *Nichomachean Ethics,* Aristotle observed that every activity or undertaking is directed at some good or end, and that end we desire for its own sake, for which all other things are done, is the "supreme good."[1] Echoing Aristotle, Cicero, the Roman statesman and philosopher, gave his treatise on ethics the title "On ends" *(De finibus),* and in it he argued that human actions are praiseworthy only if they are directed toward the summum bonum, the highest good, that end which is not itself a means to something else.[2] Augustine adopted this same vocabulary to speak about the goal of human life. The "final good," he writes, is that which is desired for its own sake.

---

1. *Nichomachean Ethics* 1.1.
2. *De finibus* 1.42.

It is that end whereby the good "is brought to final perfection and fulfilment."[3]

The Classical Inheritance

When Christianity came on the scene, there was already in place a well-developed system of moral formation in the Greco-Roman world.[4] Its aim was to lead people toward a "happy life," that is, a life directed toward those ends appropriate for human beings. In practice this meant training in the virtues. The writings we have from antiquity are often organized around the virtues, in particular the cardinal virtues of prudence, justice, courage (or fortitude), and temperance (or self-control). Virtue was not given by nature; it had to be learned, and it was best learned by practice. Moral philosophy was a practical undertaking directed at doing something, not at knowing something. Ethics had to do with the formation of character, the making of a certain kind of virtuous person. To form men and women in lives of virtue, the ancients therefore placed a high premium on example, acting on the basis of simple moral maxims, habit, and discipline.

Formation usually took place in a one-to-one relation, between parent and child, tutor and student, master and disciple. The best-documented example in antiquity can be found in the letters of Seneca to his disciple Lucilius. In them Seneca offers concrete suggestions that are tailored to the unique personality of Lucilius. He gives Lucilius advice on which books to read; he cites proverbs and axioms to direct his thoughts; he discusses Lucilius's particular temptations and fears. He urges him to use each day as an opportunity to cultivate a specific action or thought or feeling: "Each day acquire something that will fortify you against poverty, against death, indeed against other misfortunes as well; and after you have run over many thoughts, select one to be thoroughly digested that day. This is my own custom; from the many things which I have read, I claim some part for myself. The thought for today is one which I discovered in Epicurus. . . . He says: 'Contented poverty is an honorable estate.'"[5]

---

3. *De civitate Dei* 19.1.

4. See in particular Paul Rabbow, *Seelenführung: Methodik der Exerzitien in der Antike* (Munich, 1954), and Pierre Hadot, *Philosophy as a Way of Life* (Oxford and Cambridge, Mass., 1995). For a survey of classical ethics, see Alasdair MacIntyre, *A Short History of Ethics* (New York, 1966). For the affections and the moral life in the Hellenistic period, see Martha Nussbaum, *The Therapy of Desire* (Princeton, 1994). For education see Henri Marrou, *A History of Education in Antiquity* (London, 1956).

5. *Epistulae morales* 2.5-6.

Although the ancients use the language of moral philosophy to speak of formation, it is clear that they were not concerned with ethics in the narrow sense of the term. Their business was how one should live, what they called happiness *(eudaimonia)*, a term best translated "human flourishing." Moral philosophy focused on the person, the agent, not on general principles of right and wrong. Nor was formation a matter simply of the will or the intellect; it was also an affair of the heart or soul. In the words of Cicero: "There is, I assure you, a medical art for the soul. It is philosophy, whose aid need not be sought, as in bodily diseases, from outside ourselves. We must endeavor with all our re-sources and all our strength to become capable of doctoring ourselves."[6] In many ways the closest analogy to the moral philosopher was the physician.

The Jewish Inheritance

Christianity was heir to this Greek and Roman tradition of moral formation, but the first Christians were Jews, and Christianity was heir to the Jewish Bible and to distinctively Jewish ways of understanding the religious life. The words of Jesus cited at the beginning of this essay — "Be ye therefore perfect, even as your Father which is in heaven is perfect" (Matt. 5:48) — are based on the pas-sage from Leviticus, "You shall be holy; for I the LORD your God am holy" (Lev. 19:2 RSV). Elsewhere in the Gospels, in answer to the question "which com-mandment is first?" Jesus says: "The first is, 'Hear, O Israel: The Lord our God, the Lord is one; and you shall love the Lord your God with all your heart, and with all your soul, and with all your mind, and with all your strength.' The sec-ond is this, 'You shall love your neighbor as yourself'" (Mark 12:29-31 RSV; cf. Matt. 22:37-39). Jesus is simply citing the Shema (Deut. 6:4-5), which is recited daily by observant Jews.

The father was primarily responsible for the child's education, which be-gan in the home. It was believed that if a person studies the Scriptures and the Mishnah, attends to those who are wise, is honest in dealing with others, and speaks gently, then it will be said of him: "Happy the father who taught him To-rah, happy the teacher who taught him Torah" (*b. Yoma* 86a). For the Jew the home was the center of religious life. The regular rhythm of Sabbath and the calendar of festivals — Passover, Weeks, Sukkoth — was observed and cele-

---

6. *Tusculan Disputations* 3.6. This does not mean that ethics was simply an applied science. How one thought about the human person, about the freedom of the will (what the ancients called "choice," that which is within one's own power), about the unity of the virtues, about ex-pediency — all was part of the staple of moral treatises. As Sextus Empiricus put it: "Philosophy is an activity that secures the flourishing *(eudaimon)* life by arguments and reasonings."

brated in the home; this was the context for the formation of the young and the ongoing nurture of adults.

Like the Greeks and Romans, the Jews in antiquity also had in place a well-developed educational system.[7] Its goal was to form people so that all their words, deeds, work, and study were seen as service to God. It consisted primarily of the study of Torah, but integral to it was the performance of mitzvoth, ritual actions such as reciting the Shema, putting on the tallith (prayer shawl with tassels on the corners), or shaking the *lulav* (small palm branch) on the festival of Sukkoth.[8] "Let all your actions be for the sake of heaven," in the words of an ancient Jewish sage.[9] Early on the child was sent to a small school not unlike our early one-room schools, where he was put under the tutelage of a teacher who guided his spiritual and intellectual formation. Like the Greeks and Romans, Jews knew that education in the things that mattered most was best done in a one-to-one relation. Besides the school, the synagogue — with its reading of the Torah (and Prophets), sermon, and fixed forms of prayer — offered a less individual but nevertheless intimate setting for moral and spiritual formation.

Judaism's greatest contribution to Christianity's understanding of moral and spiritual formation was not institutional but theological. The Jewish Bible recorded the creation of human beings in the image of God. For Jews the end of human life was set by its beginning. Because we are made in God's image, the only telos appropriate for human beings is fellowship with God. Only in loving and serving God will we find fulfillment, that supreme good in which good is brought to perfection. Christian themes such as *imitatio Dei* or "holiness" have their origins in Judaism. Citing Leviticus 19, "You shall be holy for I am holy," an ancient rabbi said: "Ye shall be holy, and why? Because I am holy, for I have attached you to me, as it is said, 'For as the girdle cleaves to the loins of a man, so I have caused the whole house of Israel to cleave to me.'"[10] From Jewish tradition Christians learned that human beings were called to be "like God," to "cleave to God," to walk in God's ways, to imitate the divine qualities of mercy and compassion.

---

7. See S. Safrai, "Education and the Study of the Torah," in *The Jewish People in the First Century,* ed. S. Safrai and M. Stern (Philadelphia, 1976), pp. 945-70; also Yehuda Moriel, in *Encyclopaedia Judaica* (Jerusalem, 1972), 6:398-403.

8. See Tosepta, *Ḥagiga* 1.2.

9. Avot. 2.12.

10. Solomon Schechter, *Some Aspects of Rabbinic Theology* (New York, 1909), pp. 199-218.

Christian Masters and Disciples

Christians then were heirs of a dual tradition, the one coming from the Jews, the other from the Greeks and Romans. They would make the love of Christ and communion with the triune God their end. But they shared with the world in which they lived an essential technique of ethical formation, the teaching of a disciple by his master. The third-century Christian author Gregory Thaumaturgus wrote a treatise in appreciation of his teacher, Origen, the Christian philosopher and biblical scholar from Alexandria.[11] Gregory's little essay was designed to give readers a sense of what it was like to be a student in the school of Origen. Origen's "school" was not an institution in the conventional sense but a group of disciples gathered about a master. According to Gregory, some of the subjects taught were logic, natural philosophy, cosmology, and sacred science; but the reason he went to Palestine was to "have fellowship with this man and through him to be led to salvation." Like others, Gregory was attracted by Origen's learning and his fame as an interpreter of the Scriptures. Yet in his essay he dwells on Origen's moral and spiritual qualities. "From the time I became a student," writes Gregory, Origen urged him "to adopt a philosophical [i.e., virtuous] life," for he said, "only those who live a life truly fitting reasonable creatures and seek to live uprightly . . . are lovers of philosophy [a virtuous life]."

When students came under his tutelage, Origen expected them to adopt a new way of life. In the language of Origen's day "philosophize" did not mean discussion of moral questions, but changing one's life, being "transformed," learning to live virtuously. Entering on the philosophical life created an inner struggle between one's former life and the new life to which one aspired.[12] At first Gregory preferred spending his time "in arguments and intellectual debate" and "held back from practicing philosophy." But in time Origen's "words struck like an arrow," and he gave himself to a life of virtue. A student who listened to Origen's lectures and was not changed missed the whole point of his teaching. In Gregory's nice phrase: he "taught us to *practice* justice and prudence."

---

11. Text can be found in H. Crouzel, *Grégoire le Thaumaturge: Remerciement à Origéne suivi de la Lettre d'Origène à Grégoire*, Sources Chrétiennes 148 (Paris, 1969). For discussion see Robert L. Wilken, "Alexandria: A School for Training in Virtue," in *Schools of Thought in the Christian Tradition*, ed. Patrick Henry (Philadelphia, 1984), pp. 15-30.

12. On this point see Augustine: "Although virtue claims the topmost place among human good, what is its activity in this world but unceasing warfare with vices, and those not external vices but internal, not other people's vices but quite clearly our own, our very own?" (*De civitate Dei* 19.4).

The key factor in helping students live virtuously was not a set of precepts but the personal guidance of the teacher, what we would today call "spiritual direction"; Gregory's term for it is "friendship." Friendship, he says, "is not something one can easily resist, it is piercing and penetrating, it is an affable and affectionate disposition shown in the [teacher's] words and achieved by his association with us." Origen "ignited in him love for the divine Word who is most lovable." Gregory also came to love Origen as well. Smitten by these two loves, he was persuaded to give up those things that stood in the way of "living virtuously."

Gregory compares his relationship with Origen to the friendship between David and Jonathan. "I was joined to Origen," he writes, "as the soul of Jonathan was attached to David." The love was reciprocal: "This David of ours [Origen] holds us," writes Gregory, "binding us to him now and from the time we met him." Origen's love for his students was part of the process of moral formation. The master had first to know and love his disciple before he could cultivate the soul of the disciple, just as a "skilled husbandman" had first to prepare an "uncultivated field" before it could bear fruit. To correct, reprove, exhort, and encourage, the master had to know the habits and attitudes of the student. This Origen did by "digging deeply and examining what is most inward, asking questions, setting forth ideas, listening to the responses of his students." When he found anything "unfruitful and without profit in us," he set about clearing the soil, turning it over, watering it, and using all his "skill and concern" that the students might bring forth good fruit.

Finally Origen taught by example. In the moral life (and in matters of the spirit) the teacher can only lead the student on a path he or she has already traversed. Origen taught his students, says Gregory, by "his own virtuous life," for he was himself an "example of the wise man." Virtue is best learned by imitation. In his effort to teach his students to "gain control over [their] inclinations," Origen taught them "not only by words but also by his actions." While other people might try to teach virtue by precept or by lecturing on the meaning of the virtues, Origen "exhorted us by his actions and incited us more by what he did than by what he said."[13]

The Formation of Children

In the family of Basil the Great, it was his grandmother, Macrina, to whom he attributed his initial formation in the faith: "What could be clearer proof of our

13. *Panegyric* 6.83-84; 6.93-95; 9.123, 126.

faith than that we were brought up by a grandmother, a blessed woman." She taught the children "sayings" she had learned from Gregory, the same Gregory Thaumaturgus. As a young girl she had learned these sayings by heart, "holding them in her memory," and, says Basil, "she molded and formed us while still young in the teachings that lead to a godly life."[14] The sayings were probably based on verses from Scripture, short pithy aphorisms from the Psalms, Proverbs, Sirach, or Wisdom (part of the Bible of the early church). Gregory of Nyssa, Basil's younger brother, says in their home the children were instructed in "passages from the inspired Scriptures adaptable to the early years," especially the Wisdom of Solomon, and other books that lead to a "moral life." The Psalms were also part of early formation; Gregory says his older sister, also named Macrina, read psalms before and after meals, when she rose in the morning and retired in the evening. The psalms, he writes, "were like a good and faithful traveling companion" that accompanied her wherever she went and whatever she did.[15]

Teaching the young was the responsibility of parents, not the clergy or tutors. Writing to a young widow, John Chrysostom gave advice on how she should bring up her children. "Bringing up children," notes John, is the first thing Paul mentions in 1 Timothy 5:10: "one who has brought up children, shown hospitality, washed the feet of the saints, relieved the afflicted, and devoted herself to doing good in every way" (RSV). He is not speaking of providing food or the necessities of life; parents do not need a command to know this. Paul is speaking about justice and religious devotion, about the moral and spiritual life. For education of the young has to do with the "beauty of the soul" and with "virtue," with piety, and with morality.[16]

Commenting on Colossians 3:16, "teach and admonish one another in all wisdom" (RSV), John says parents should teach their children "to sing those psalms that are full of love of wisdom," as for example, "Blessed is the man who walks not in the counsel of the ungodly" or "In God's sight a wicked doer is condemned, God honors those that fear the Lord" (Ps. 26:4).[17] The Psalms and the Wisdom Literature were the backbone of the formation of the young. Besides teaching children sayings from the Psalms and Wisdom Books, parents

14. *Epistle* 104.

15. *Life of Macrina,* in *Patrologia Graeca* (hereafter *PG*), 46:961d. John Chrysostom says the young were taught psalms that urged them to restrain their desires, to avoid taking things in excess, not to be greedy about money (*Hom. in Colossians* 9.2); *PG*, 52:362-63.

16. *PG*, 51:327. For another example of advice on how to raise a child, in this case for the religious life, see Jerome's letter to Laeta (*Epistle* 107).

17. *Hom. 9.2 on Colossians 3:16* (*PG*, 62:362c); see also *Hom. 59.7 on Matthew 18:7* (*PG*, 58:582).

should monitor their comings and goings, listen to their conversation, take note of their circle of friends. Parents, writes John, are the child's first teachers and guides. They are given charge of the young when they are soft and malleable and receptive to formation. Only in their early years can one train children to love that which is good and hate that which is evil. John cites Sirach 7:23: "Make them obedient from their youth."[18]

Christian leaders recognized the importance of repetition and memorization, hence they encouraged the use of memorable sayings and axioms from the Psalms and Wisdom Books that would stay with the child into adulthood. The Church Fathers also knew the importance of stories in the education of children. The most extended discussion of the pedagogical use of stories can be found in a little treatise by John Chrysostom on instructing the young. The first story he mentions is that of Cain and Abel in Genesis. In telling the story, says John, parents should make it interesting so that the child will delight in it and not grow bored. John presents the story as a tale of two sons, each of whom gave an offering to God. One gave God his best and the other held back the best for himself, offering God only second-best. John recommends that the parent rephrase the biblical language in words that the child can easily understand. In other words, the story is to be told, not read from the Bible. The same story should be repeated often so that after it has been told a few times the child will ask: "Tell me the story." Repetition helps the child memorize the story. Teaching children biblical stories has an additional benefit. When the child comes to church and hears the story read aloud, he will leap with pleasure because he knows what other children do not know, remembers what happens, anticipates the ending, and in that way gets more from the story than the child who hears it for the first time.

Once the first story is fixed in the memory, parents should teach the child another story. John's second illustration is the story of Jacob and Esau. This is a deeper story, he observes, because "the reversal of fortune is greater." After the child has learned this story, the parent should say: tell me the story of the two brothers. If he begins to tell the story of Cain and Abel, he should stop him and say: No, it is not that one I want, but the other one about the two brothers (without mentioning their names), in which the father gives his blessing. In these examples we can see not only the centrality of the Scriptures in Christian education, but the application of sound educational principles, in this case repetition.[19]

As is clear from these few illustrations, early Christian formation rested not

18. See *Hom. 7*, in *PG*, 51:327-28.
19. M. L. W. Laistner, *Christianity and Pagan Culture* (Ithaca, N.Y., 1951), pp. 102ff.

only on a firm biblical foundation, it was also informed by sound psychological and educational principles. Formation began when the child was malleable, and its goal was to teach a few simple and elementary truths, for instance, to restrain one's desires and appetites, to love that which is good. The parents were not only the child's first teachers but also the first examples of the Christian life. Without the testimony of life, exhortations are only "empty words."[20] The use of stories for moral and spiritual instruction is based on the principle that children (as well as grown-ups) learn best by example. Before we can become doers, we first must be spectators. As Origen put it: "Genuine transformation of life comes from reading the ancient Scriptures, learning who the just were and *imitating* them," to which he shrewdly appended the caveat, and "learning who were reproved and guarding against falling under the same censure."[21]

Models for the Christian Life

As important as the biblical stories were for moral instruction, over time they tended to function more as types, that is, more as instances of particular virtues than as iridescent models. Abraham illustrates faith, Susanna modesty, David courage, Job patience. Christians also began to compose new stories based on the lives of holy men and women. The first lives offered accounts of the heroic deaths of martyrs. As Pontius says of Cyprian, this holy man "had much to teach, independently of his martyrdom; what he did while he lived should not be hidden from the world."[22] Thus began the practice of writing *lives,* not simply martyr accounts of exemplary men and women.[23] One characteristic of these early lives is that they are composed about people from the community, the local church, if you will, noteworthy persons of recent memory.

The lives from Christian antiquity are many and varied, but all intend to teach Christians how to live by example. For example, in the *Life of Antony,* the most famous of ancient lives, Athanasius writes: "Simply by seeing Antony's conduct many desired to become imitators." Theodoret of Cyrus, who wrote about the holy men and women from his region, Syria, said he was writing

20. Laistner, p. 95.

21. *Homilies on Jeremiah* 4.6, ed. P. Nautin and P. Hussou, Sources Chrétiennes 232 (Paris, 1976), pp. 274-76.

22. Pontius, *Vita et passio Cypriani,* ed. A. von Harnack, Texte und Untersuchungen 39.3 (Leipzig, 1913).

23. On the lives as a means of moral formation, see Robert L. Wilken, "The Lives of the Saints and the Pursuit of Virtue," in *Remembering the Christian Past* (Grand Rapids, 1995), pp. 121-44.

down their lives so that others may "imitate" them. The proper subjects of these lives are deeds, not sayings, though they include sayings. In a letter placed at the beginning of his *Lausiac History,* Palladius writes: "Words and syllables do not constitute teaching. . . . Teaching consists of virtuous acts of conduct. This is how Jesus taught. . . . He did not use fine language . . . he required the formation of character."[24] Once one ventures on this path of moral formation, narrating deeds or telling a story, the means of moral formation become varied and subtle. For one thing, the account of a person's life allows one to exploit the passage of time. No one becomes virtuous in a few weeks or months; holiness is learned only gradually over a long period of time. Saint Antony lived alone for twenty years, and only at the end of this time, when his soul had achieved "utter equilibrium," was he ready to accept disciples. This is of course a sound Aristotelian principle from the *Nichomachean Ethics.* The lives of the saints accentuate repetition, the constant performance of good deeds as the way to progress in virtue. Another word for this is habit, a necessary feature of moral formation.

Stories were narrated through words, but they were really a form of seeing. They did not portray ideas, but deeds, the actions of individual human beings. Hence they could also be told through pictures, and much early Christian art has a didactic purpose. The most impressive evidence comes from the use of icons in Eastern Christianity. Icons not only depicted scenes from the Old Testament — for example, the visit of the mysterious three men to Abraham and Sarah — and from the Gospels, they also portrayed holy men and women, the martyrs and saints. Icons were displayed in prominent places within the churches so that the faithful would be reminded of biblical stories and the exploits of the saints. They served as a permanent open book, as one writer observed: "There are times when the reading of Scriptures is lacking in churches, but the presence of icons in them evening, morning and midday narrates to us the truth of what has taken place."[25] Icons, then, are another way stories were employed in moral formation. The ancient sources describe icons in the same terms used for written lives. They portrayed "the performance of good deeds" and served as "models of virtues and of a God-pleasing way of life." The icon was a "brief narrative" that excited the faithful to imitate the saint who was portrayed.[26]

24. For references see Wilken, "Lives of the Saints," n. 17.
25. *Sacrorum conciliorum nova et amplissima collectio,* ed. J. D. Mansi (1757-98, 1901-27; reprint, 1960-61), 13.316a.
26. Germanus, *Dogmatic Epistle 4 to Thomas of Claudiopolis* (*PG*, 98:172cd).

Community Worship

The most obvious vehicles for teaching in worship were the biblical readings, the sermon, and the singing of hymns and psalms. The use of antiphons (a psalm verse repeated in alternation with the other verses) in the singing of psalms was introduced for the express purpose of helping people focus on the meaning of the texts.[27] Preaching in antiquity was the exposition of a text read in the church. Its task was edification, to promote spiritual growth and moral zeal. In a sermon on Leviticus Origen says there would be no purpose in reading these things "in the Church unless some edification was supplied to the hearers from them."[28]

The techniques that appear in sermons are the same that we have seen in the home and in the lives, namely, exhortation and example, often in conjunction with one another. In his exposition of the two men possessed by demons in Matthew 8, John Chrysostom uses the story as a way of teaching the commandment "You shall not covet." The covetous person, he writes, is like someone who is overcome by demons. Shunning the company of other human beings, he spurns all counsel, like someone who lives in a desert outside of the city. He cares only for possessions and wants to possess all things, a man whose imagination is obsessed with what belongs to others.[29] Earlier Origen had used Abraham in the story of the sacrifice of Isaac as an example for fathers in his congregation: "Many of you who hear these words are fathers in the Church of God. Do you think any one of you from the mere relating of the story acquires so much steadfastness, so much strength of soul, that, when a son perhaps is lost by a death that is common and due to all, even if he be an only son, even if he be a beloved son, might bring in Abraham as an example for himself and set his magnanimity before his eyes."[30]

Preachers in the early church, like preachers in every age, also used what might be called negative sanctions. They knew the Scriptures also spoke of judgment and divine wrath, and that fear could also move people to change their lives. Just as they appealed to positive examples as models to imitate, so homilists also appealed to negative examples, such as Judas or Ananias, persons in the Bible who exhibit how one ought *not* to live. They also warned the faithful of the torments of eternal damnation. John Chrysostom, for example, citing

27. Basil, *Epistle* 107.
28. Origen, *Homilies on Leviticus* 5.12.6, trans. Gary Wayne Barkley, Fathers of the Church 83 (Washington, D.C., 1990), 1:113.
29. Chrysostom, *Hom. 28.4-5 on Matthew 8:23-24*, in *PG*, 57:555-57.
30. Origen, *Homilies on Genesis* 8.7, trans. Ronald Heine, Fathers of the Church 71 (Washington, D.C., 1981), p. 142.

Isaiah 13:9, "The day of the Lord comes . . . with wrath and fierce anger," describes in vivid detail the "fire that is not consumed." No words, he writes, can describe the "piercing pains of those who suffer in that place."[31]

Worship was not just words, it was also ritual, indeed public ritual. One ritual key to moral formation was the public act of penance. This rite, called *exomologesis* in Greek, was used for major sins such as adultery or apostasy. The early Christians took the passage in Hebrews, "It is impossible to restore again to repentance those who have once been enlightened," to mean that there could be no repentance after baptism. The baptized person, it was thought, "should sin no more." Sin is understood here as a flagrant transgression of the divine law, the kind that should not occur in the life of a Christian.[32] If, however, a serious sin was committed after baptism, the church allowed for one, but only one, repentance. To undertake the regime of penance for such sins, the penitent must first request permission and demonstrate his or her intention by evidence of sincerity. Once accepted as a penitent, the person was excluded from the Eucharist and sat in a section in the back of the church set off from the congregation. Penitents also wore special dress, and in some cases had their hair cropped. During the period of penance (the length being determined by the bishop), penitents fasted, prayed regularly, gave alms, and were expected to abstain from sexual intercourse. On feast days they kneeled as the congregation stood. They engaged in public acts of self-accusation and had to stand at the church doors pleading with the faithful to intercede on their behalf. Finally came the rite of reconciliation in which the congregation prayed for the sinner, and the bishop received him or her back into the church through the laying on of hands. The penitent was, however, never restored fully. A person who had sinned gravely remained a Christian of inferior status his or her entire life, barred from holding public office or serving in the military or entering one of the clerical orders.

Baptism too was an elaborate public ritual that extended over two years, forming the attitudes and behavior not only of the catechumens but also of the faithful. In the early church, it must be remembered, baptism was always by immersion, and one can see to this day the pools that were used. They were deep enough for a person to stand in; water came up to the breast, and on either end there were stairs to go down into and come up out of the water. The *competentes* were baptized naked, and when they came up out of the font they were clothed in white with a linen head cover. At their first Eucharist they re-

---

31. Chrysostom, *Hom. 43.4 on Matthew 12:38-39* (*PG*, 57:402a-b); see also *Hom. 12.5 on Matthew 3:13* (*PG*, 57:207-8).

32. Augustine, *De symbolo ad catechumenos* 7.15 (*Patrologia Latina*, 40:636); *Sermon* 351.4.7.

ceived a cup of milk and honey. Easter week they attended services in their white garments. Each year Christians had the pleasure of seeing family members, neighbors, and friends undergo an unforgettable drama. When Victorinus, a well-known philosopher, was baptized, people could not keep their eyes off him: "When he mounted the steps to affirm the confession of faith, there was a murmur of delighted talk as all the people who knew him spoke his name to one another. And who there did not know him? A suppressed sound came from the lips of all as they rejoiced, 'Victorinus, Victorinus!' As soon as they saw him, they suddenly murmured in exaltation and equally suddenly were silent in concentration to hear him."[33]

The rite of public confession and the catechumenate shows vividly that formation in the early church was carried out not only by words or precepts, not only by the telling of stories, but also by ritual. As a recent student of the rite put it: "[T]he ritual drama of baptism and its Lenten preparations were the *spectacula christiana* — the new theatre, the new racetrack, and the new boxing ring. It is difficult to overestimate the impact of this extended ritual drama on convert and community alike."[34] The catechumenate led people through an experience that was itself transformative, renewing the mind and the will and also the heart.

Conclusion

This essay has reviewed four central aspects of the moral formation of Christians in antiquity: home and family, preaching, lives of the saints, and communal ritual. Many early Christian Fathers wrote treatises on ethics and the Christian life: Clement of Alexandria's *Instructor;* Lactantius's *Divine Institutes;* Ambrose's *On Duties (De officiis);* Basil's *To Youths (Ad adolescentes),* an exhortation telling youths how they shall best profit by the writings of pagan authors; Augustine's *On the Morals of the Catholic Church (De moribus catholicae ecclesiae);* and not least, Gregory the Great's *Pastoral Rule.*

These treatises help us understand the theological and philosophical conceptions supporting the practices I have described. In them we can see how early Christian moral thinking was influenced by the classical tradition of the virtues. Ambrose's treatise, *De officiis,* was modeled on a treatise of Cicero by

---

33. Augustine, *Confessions* 8.2.5.

34. Thomas Finn, "It Happened One Saturday Night: Ritual and Conversion in Augustine's North Africa," *Journal of the American Academy of Religion* 58 (1990): 589-616. For fuller discussion see his *From Death to Rebirth: Ritual and Conversion in Antiquity* (New York, 1997), pp. 212-38.

the same name, and like Cicero, Ambrose structured his discussion around the four cardinal virtues: prudence, justice, temperance, fortitude. Ambrose, however, illustrates the cardinal virtues with biblical examples, and he redefines the virtues in accord with biblical language and ideas. Prudence, for example, becomes a form of faith. Christian thinkers also expanded the list of virtues. Tertullian wrote an essay on patience (as did Cyprian and Augustine), a virtue that was not celebrated in antiquity but is central in the Scriptures. Through these treatises the tradition of the virtues was passed on to later generations of Christians.

But thinking about the virtues was not only a matter of philosophy, it was also theological. For Christians the end toward which one aspired, the summum bonum, was not virtue or wisdom as such, but cleaving to God. This could only be done, says Augustine, by "affection, desire and love."[35] Jesus had taught: "You shall love the Lord your God with all your heart, with all your soul, and with all your mind, and with all your strength." In his treatise *On the Morals of the Catholic Church*, Augustine interpreted the words of Jesus to mean that "virtue" is nothing other than the perfect love of God. For that reason he redefined the four cardinal virtues as four forms of love: temperance is love giving itself entirely to that which is loved; fortitude is love bearing all things for the sake of that which is loved; justice is love serving only that which is loved; and prudence is love distinguishing between what helps and what hinders love. "The object of this love is nothing other than God, the chief good, the highest wisdom, the perfect harmony."[36]

By making love of God central to the moral life, Christian thinkers gave a much larger place to the affections than had classical thinkers. Indeed, one of the most distinctive features of early moral teaching is that Christian thinkers defended the role of the passions in the virtuous life. It is not enough to know what we are to do; there must be something that draws us to the good. Without affections like desire and fear, there can be no movement toward the good or aversion to evil. In the same way, without desire for God, without love, there can be no movement toward God and no ongoing fellowship with God. "If love is taken way," writes Gregory of Nyssa, "how will we be joined to God?"[37] If there is nothing that holds us to God, and this can only be love, we will drift away. This is why Paul said: "Love never ceases."

Formation in the early church, in practice and in theory, was first and foremost a matter of training of the affections — in a word, the education of desire.

---

35. *On the Morals of the Catholic Church* 13.23.
36. *On the Morals of the Catholic Church* 15.25.
37. Gregory of Nyssa, *On the Soul and Resurrection;* in *PG*, 46:65b.

Whether it be the telling of stories, the memorization of verses from Proverbs, or the elaborate ritual of the catechumenate, each in its own way served to train the soul to desire the right things, to delight in what is good and to feel anger in the face of evil. Moral formation is as much a matter of the heart as of the mind or the will. In the words of the psalm: "I incline my heart to do your statutes" (Ps. 119:112). Maximus the Confessor spoke of "loving God with a holy passion," and Augustine said, "the whole life of a good Christian is a holy desire."[38]

It is this understanding of the Christian life that John Chrysostom had in mind when he instructed parents how to teach the stories of the Bible, and it is this that Basil was thinking of when he spoke about what he had learned from his grandmother. This is what Abba Poemen, a monk of the desert, meant when he responded to the question of a younger brother who asked: "What is the meaning of 'See that none of you repays evil for evil'?" Abba Poemen said to him: "Passions work in four stages — first in the heart; secondly in the face; thirdly in words; and fourthly, in deeds — deeds that do not repay evil for evil."[39]

What gave Christian formation its power and tenacity was that it was carried out within the context of a coherent theological framework. It was also thoroughly biblical and philosophically astute. People knew why they did what they did. In its simplest form, what they thought can be stated in the words of Jesus cited at the beginning: Be ye perfect as your father in heaven is perfect. The Christian life was oriented toward a goal, toward life in fellowship with God. Its end was to know and love God as we have been known and loved by God, for only in knowing and loving God and sharing in God's life would human beings find happiness.[40]

---

38. Maximus, *Four Hundred Chapters on Love* 3.66-67; Augustine, *Tractates on the First Epistle of John* 4.6. For discussion see Robert Louis Wilken, *The Spirit of Early Christian Thought* (New Haven, 2003), pp. 291-311.

39. *PG,* 65:332a-b. On this point see Douglas Burton-Christie, *The Word in the Desert: Scripture and the Quest for Holiness in Early Christian Monasticism* (New York, 1993).

40. Origen, *Contra Celsum* 4.6, trans. Henry Chadwick (Cambridge, 1953), p. 188.

Simplifying Augustine

John C. Cavadini

[T]he very desire with which you want to understand is itself a prayer to God.

Augustine, *Sermon* 152.1

E arly in the year 800 Alcuin of York received a letter from two nuns, Gisela and Rotruda (daughter and sister of Charlemagne), asking him for an exposition of the Gospel of John. Styling Alcuin as their teacher, they explain that they have in mind something which would "lay open the venerable opinions of the holy Fathers." They have Augustine's expositions on the Gospel, but complain that these are at points "very obscure" and too stylistically complex.[1] Alcuin's *Commentary on John,* completed in response to their request and based on Augustine's *Tractates on the Gospel of John,* can thus be thought of as a simplified presentation of Augustine's tractates, which Alcuin largely follows both in content and sequence.[2] Alcuin's procedure for simplification is easily summarized: he quotes verbatim the passages he wants (without attribution),

---

1. *Monumenta Germaniae Historica,* Ep. 4:196, p. 324. All citations of Augustine's sermons are from the Nuova Biblioteca Agostiniana edition, which presents the best edition available for any given sermon: Sant'Agostino, *Discorsi,* Nuova Biblioteca Agostiniana, vols. 29, 30.1, 30.2, 31.1, 31.2, 32.1, 32.2, 33, 34 (Rome: Città Nuova Editrice, 1979-89). All translations are from Augustine, *Sermons,* pt. III, vols. 1-10 of *The Works of St. Augustine: A Translation for the Twenty-First Century* (New York: New City Press, 1990-95).

2. See Donald A. Bullough, "Alcuin and the Kingdom of Heaven," in *Carolingian Essays,* ed. Uta-Renate Blumenthal (Washington, D.C.: Catholic University of America Press, 1983), pp. 16, 60-62; and John J. Contreni, "Carolingian Biblical Studies," in *Carolingian Essays,* pp. 90-92.

sometimes paraphrasing but generally omitting the rest, or else replacing it with easier material from Bede or Gregory the Great. Much of the material omitted even we might consider difficult or esoteric — broadly speaking, "philosophical" and Neoplatonic, concerning such topics as incorporeal substances, ascents to spiritual vision, and the character of God's eternal Word. This sort of material, very common in Augustine's text, is almost completely eliminated in Alcuin's. Indeed, such a huge proportion of the first eleven tractates is so preoccupied with philosophical issues that Alcuin, seemingly in desperation, omits them altogether and turns to other sources instead.[3]

How Alcuin "simplifies" Augustine raises the interesting question of what this material is doing in Augustine's text in the first place, since Augustine's tractates are themselves a series of homilies and thus presumably to some degree accessible, or exoteric. These tractates are among the most carefully planned and retouched of Augustine's homilies. Though in their present form they were meant more to be read than heard, probably all of them, and at least the first fifty-four, were originally preached. It is hard to believe that these philosophical themes were not originally present in some form, especially in the first few tractates.[4] Nor does it appear that such themes would, in themselves, have been any easier for most of Augustine's North African contemporaries to grasp than for Gisela and Rotruda.[5]

Thus arises the interesting question of the relation between the "esoteric" and the "exoteric" in Augustine's work itself. We have noted how Alcuin simplifies Augustine, and we will briefly examine below how Caesarius of Arles simplified Augustine for his own congregation. The question here is how does *Augustine* simplify Augustine? Or is this even the correct question? More neutrally posed, what is the relation between Augustine's work in the more esoteric genres of commentary and treatise to that in the more exoteric genre of sermon and preaching?[6]

A note on terminology: I am not using the word "esoteric" in its more tech-

3. For more on this topic, see John Cavadini, "Alcuin and Augustine on John," *Augustinian Studies* (forthcoming).

4. The discussion, and the bibliography, is summarized by John Rettig, in the introduction to his translation: Augustine, *Tractates on the Gospel of John* 1–12 (Washington, D.C.: Catholic University of America Press, 1988).

5. On this point see Roland J. Teske, S.J., "Spirituals and Spiritual Interpretation in Augustine," *Augustinian Studies* 15 (1984): 65-81.

6. For an essay asking a similar question of Origen's work and specifically using the language of "esoteric" and "exoteric," see Eric Junod, "Wodurch unterscheiden sich die Homilien des Origenes von seinen Kommentaren," in *Predigt in der alten Kirche,* ed. E. Mühlenberg and J. van Oort (Kampen: Pharos, 1994), pp. 50-81.

nical sense of "secret," as describing teachings that are intentionally veiled from the public at large and revealed only to a few worthy initiates. In this sense the gnostics advocated esoteric teachings, sometimes with more "exoteric" versions designed expressly to entice potential insiders without actually revealing any hidden teachings.[7] Augustine did not have "esoteric" teachings or genres in this sense, but as a professional rhetor he had a keen sense of audience, and he made distinctions among his own works regarding their appropriateness for a particular audience, in some cases explicitly. For example, in *Retractationes* he notes that he wrote *Psalmus contra partem Donati* specifically for the "most lowly mass of people," which he characterizes as "uneducated and unlearned."[8] It is surely appropriate to call this an "exoteric" work, precisely as something meant to be accessible to the "uneducated" as opposed to the educated, but not as an attempt to hide secret doctrines specifically reserved for elect initiates. Nevertheless, even this weaker sense of the contrast between "exoteric" and "esoteric" should not be underestimated, especially in late antiquity. The acquisition of a liberal education, of literary culture, could itself be likened to an initiation, or else to a process of transformation that, in the view of the educated, made them "as superior to the uneducated as they were to cattle."[9] An expensive literary education defined one as part of an elite. It was a mark of noble birth, and only very rarely an avenue of social advancement. As such it was a "means of expressing social distance,"[10] and the cultural forms and practices associated with it are not inappropriately characterized as "esoteric."

To examine the question at hand, it is my intention to compare *De Trinitate* with *Sermones ad populum*. *De Trinitate* is arguably one of the most difficult or

7. See, for example, Harold W. Attridge, "The 'Gospel of Truth' as an Exoteric Text," in *Nag Hammadi, Gnosticism, and Early Christianity*, ed. Charles W. Hedrick and Robert Hodgson, Jr. (Peabody, Mass.: Hendrickson, 1986), pp. 239-55.

8. "Volens etiam causam Donatistarum ad ipsius humillimi vulgi et omnino imperitorum atque idiotarum notitiam pervenire . . . ," *Retractationes* 1.20.1, Corpus Christianorum, Series Latina (hereafter CCSL), 57:61.1-2. Augustine's style reflects this intention; not only is the "psalm" itself abecedarian, but its rhythm explicitly avoids classical meters which might force Augustine to use a word unfamiliar to the uneducated: "Ideo autem non aliquo carminis genere id fieri volui, ne me necessitas metrica ad aliqua verba quae vulgo minus sunt usitata conpelleret" (ll. 10-13). See also Augustine's comments about his *De agone Christiano*: "Liber de agone christiano fratribus in eloquio Latino ineruditis humili sermone conscriptus est . . ." (*Retractationes* 2.3.1, CCSL, 57:91.2-3). *De catechizandis rudibus* 1.8.12–1.9.13 shows Augustine giving instructions for adapting one's discourse to the educational level of the audience.

9. See Robert A. Kaster, *Guardians of Language: The Grammarian and Society in Late Antiquity* (Berkeley: University of California Press, 1988), pp. 16-17. The quotation is from the grammarian Diomedes, cited by Kaster on p. 17.

10. Peter Brown, *Power and Persuasion in Late Antiquity: Toward a Christian Empire* (Madison: University of Wisconsin Press, 1992), p. 39.

"esoteric" works Augustine ever wrote. He himself remarked repeatedly that he expected it to be understood only by "few";[11] presumably this means "few" among those who could read, already few enough in late antiquity.[12] The second half of *De Trinitate* assumes familiarity with the liberal arts and presupposes skills in philosophical thinking, while books 5-7 require a facility with dialectic almost unique in the Augustinian corpus.[13]

On the other hand, the nearly 550 *Sermones ad populum*[14] verifiable as genuinely Augustinian are some of the most accessible or exoteric[15] works we have

---

11. ". . . libros de trinitate . . . nimis operosi sunt et a paucis eos intellegi posse arbitror" (*Epistula* 169.1.1, Corpus Scriptorum Ecclesiasticorum Latinorum [hereafter CSEL], 44:612.6-9, ca. 415, to Evodius); cf. *Epistula* 120.3.13, CSEL, 34:715.18-21, on the extreme difficulty of the subject of the Trinity as discussed in *De Trinitate* (hereafter *Trin.*), then in progress.

12. See Kaster, pp. 35-48, based largely on the work of R. P. Duncan-Jones, "Age-Rounding, Illiteracy, and Social Differentiation in the Roman Empire," *Chiron* 7 (1977): 333-53. "We must imagine a state of very sparse literacy at best," Kaster writes (p. 39), with the literate concentrated among the upper classes but found throughout the whole social pyramid. An even smaller proportion of the population would have been educated in liberal studies. Arguments for somewhat higher rates are advanced by E. A. Meyer in her 1989 Yale dissertation, "Literacy, Literate Practice, and the Law in the Roman Empire, A.D. 100-600"; lower estimates are defended by W. V. Harris, *Ancient Literacy* (Cambridge: Harvard University Press, 1989), pp. 285-322. Harry Y. Gamble, *Books and Readers in the Early Church* (New Haven: Yale University Press, 1995), pp. 2-10, is a good summary. He assesses literacy, i.e., "the ability to read, criticize, and interpret" Christian literature, at "not more than about 10 percent in any given setting" (p. 5), although he argues that this does not mean only a small percentage of Christians knew Scripture, since they heard it read regularly (p. 141).

13. *Retractationes* 1.5.1, CCSL, 57:16.

14. This is Augustine's own designation for them at *Retractationes* 2.Epilogus, CCSL, 57:143.5 (also see *Epistula* 234.2, where he refers to them as *tractatus populares, quos Graeci homelias vocabant*). On the signification of the word *sermo* and its relation to *populus* or *popularis* in the sense of something directed to the "people" assembled in church, see Christine Mohrmann, *Etudes sur le Latin des Chrétiens* (Rome: Edizioni di Storia e Letteratura, 1961), 2:71-72; also Maurice Pontet, *L'Exégèse de S. Augustin Prédicateur* ([Paris]: Aubier, [1944]), pp. 51-52. See also Pontet on the connection between *sermo* and *tractatus*, and Mohrmann, 2:63-72; André Mandouze, *Saint Augustin: L'Aventure de la raison et de la grâce* (Paris: Etudes Augustiniennes, 1968), pp. 599-615. On the number of authentic Augustinian sermons, see Pierre-Patrick Verbraken, *Etudes critiques sur les sermons authentiques de Saint Augustin* (Steenbrugis: Martinus Nijhoff, 1976), p. 18, although this will have to be adjusted in the light of recent discoveries of about twenty-six more sermons (see Henry Chadwick, "New Sermons of St. Augustine," *Journal of Theological Studies*, n.s., 47 [1996]: 69-91).

15. In book 4 of *De doctrina Christiana* (hereafter *Doct. Chr.*), contemporaneous with *Retractationes*, Augustine clearly marks out discourse addressed to the "people" as appropriately different from that found in books: "There are some things which with their full implications are not understood or are hardly understood, no matter how eloquently they are spoken. . . . And these things should never, or only rarely on account of some necessity, be set before an au-

from Augustine, most of them neither written down nor dictated but preached extemporaneously, recorded by notaries or others and for the most part not significantly revised or retouched.[16] Augustine's audience varied with time and place, but generally included both educated and uneducated, literate and illiterate members,[17] and he developed a homiletic style that was intentionally sim-

dience of the people *(in populi audientiam)*. In books, however — which, when they are understood, hold the readers to them in a certain way, and, when they are not understood, are not troublesome to those not wishing to read — and in conversations *(conlocutionibus)* the duty should not be neglected of bringing the truth which we have perceived, no matter how difficult it may be to comprehend *(quamvis ad intellegendum difficillima)* or how much labor may be involved, to the understanding of others, provided that the listener or disputant wishes to learn and has the capapcity to do so *(nec mentis capacitas desit)* no matter how the material is presented" (4.9.23, CCSL, 32:132, trans. D. W. Robertson, Jr. [Indianapolis and New York: Bobbs-Merrill, 1958]). That is, with a large crowd of listeners, some or many of whom may not have the "capacity" to understand intricate points, and none of whom can ask questions on the spot (cf. 4.10.25), some topics are inappropriate not because they are secret but because they will not be understood. This corresponds roughly to the distinction between "esoteric" and "exoteric" I intend in this paper.

16. Possidius, *Vita Augustini* 7.3; cf. *Enarrationes in Psalmos* 51.1; *Epistula* 213.2. See Michele Cardinal Pellegrino's excellent general introduction to *The Works of St. Augustine*, pt. III, *Sermons*, 1:13-137, at 15-19. Also Mandouze, pp. 591-663, esp. 595-98. Stephen M. Oberhelman, *Rhetoric and Homiletics in Fourth-Century Christian Literature*, American Philological Association American Classical Studies, no. 26 (Atlanta, 1991), studies the prose rhythms across the genres in which Augustine wrote; he concludes: "Augustine's sermons were spontaneous creations that entered unplanned territory as the bishop extemporized" (p. 89).

17. There has never been a thorough study of the audience of the homilies of Augustine. Van der Meer assumes a highly variegated audience but without much evidence (*Augustine the Bishop*, trans. Brian Battershaw and G. R. Lamb [New York: Harper and Row, 1961], "A Sunday in Hippo," pp. 388-402, esp. 389, and "The Servant of the Word," pp. 412-52; cf. P. R. L. Brown, *Augustine of Hippo* [Berkeley: University of California Press, 1967], p. 252). Ramsay MacMullen assumes a homogeneous audience of the educated property-owning aristocracy (with their slaves) on the basis of equally slender evidence: "The Preacher's Audience (AD 350-400)," *Journal of Theological Studies*, n.s., 40 (1989): 503-11, devotes less than a page to Augustine (p. 509); the article is seemingly a retraction of his earlier "A Note on *Sermo Humilis*," *Journal of Theological Studies*, n.s., 17 (1966): 108-12. Kaster's statement that Augustine's audience was "largely uneducated" (Kaster, p. 84) references only this earlier article of MacMullen, but MacMullen's later article rightly points out that we cannot necessarily take references to the "poor" or other classes in the congregation at face value, for the "poor" sometimes turn out to have substantial property. Pontet (pp. 55-61) provides a slightly fuller documentation for a mixed crowd of educated and uneducated, men and women, rich and poor, and analyzes in good detail the differences in audience based on the place Augustine is preaching (pp. 72-91; see also A. Becker, *L'appel des beatitudes* [Paris, 1977]). Alexandre Olivar, *La Predicación Cristiana Antigua* (Barcelona: Editorial Herder, 1991), pp. 761-70, adds no new evidence on this point. Pellegrino's discussion (1:84-93) is a good basis for further inquiry, although the worries of MacMullen need to be considered more fully. What seems beyond doubt, however, is that the congregation to which Augustine

ple, shorn of rhetorical intricacy, plain and vivid, specially created to reach just such a heterogeneous group.[18] Augustine's renunciation of the intricate, jew-

---

preached was usually a mixture of the educated and uneducated though in varying proportions, and that Augustine was explicitly concerned to address both: see, e.g., *Sermones* 131.9; 241.5 (most of Augustine's audience knows the *Aeneid* from the theater, not from having read it); 247.1; 264.4; 299M.3; 277.13; 313B.3; etc. Cf. 352.4, which distinguishes between the *veloces* and the *tardos* among the listeners and directs the exposition to the latter. By contrast *Sermo* 52 may be directed only at the literate (see 52.10), and at *Sermo* 150.3 Augustine remarks that since he is preaching in Carthage, he can expect some of the congregation to know the difference between Stoic and Epicurean, although some will not. This concern to appeal to a heterogeneous audience including the uneducated captures the sense of "exoteric" as I am applying it to the sermons; cf. Junod's characterization of Origen's struggle to appeal to a similarly "heterogeneous" audience (p. 80). Note: hereafter *S.* will refer to both *Sermo* and *Sermones*.

18. Augustine himself provides the theory for a style that emphasizes clarity over ornamentation (*Doct. Chr.* 4.8.22), and editors since Erasmus have commented on it (see the preface to his Basel edition of Augustine's *Opera*, 1529, cited by van der Meer, p. 417). For an evocation of Augustine's preaching style in English, see van der Meer, pp. 412-52; Brown, *Augustine of Hippo*, pp. 244-58. Fundamental is Erich Auerbach, *Literary Language and Its Public in Late Latin Antiquity and in the Middle Ages*, trans. Ralph Manheim (London, 1965), pp. 1-66, "Sermo Humilis." Peter Auksi, *Christian Plain Style: The Evolution of a Spiritual Ideal* (Montreal and Kingston: McGill–Queen's University Press, 1995), pp. 110-26, summarizes and provides basic bibliography; see also Pellegrino, 1:111-31. Michael Banniard, *Viva Voce: Communication écrite et communication orale du IVe au IXe siècle en Occident latin* (Paris: Institut des Etudes Augustiniennes, 1992), describes the style and its connection to a mixed audience of literate and illiterate, and documents the connections to Augustine's theory in *Doct. Chr.* 4 and *De catechizandis rudibus* (65-104). Mohrmann's work on Augustine's style is foundational. She shows that Augustine's use of puns in his sermons is more indebteded to Plautus and the popular speech he reflects than to Cicero and the rhetoric of the schools ("Das Wortspiel in den Augustinischen sermones," *Mnemosyne* 3 [1932]: 33-61, reprinted at Mohrmann, *Etudes*, 1:323-49). She shows how Augustine invented a new style, based on popular speech and the Bible, which he used to modify the eloquence taught by the schools of rhetoric ("Augustine and the 'Eloquentia,'" trans. Mary Hedlund, in Mohrmann, *Etudes*, 1:351-70), and demostrates how this style is especially characteristic of his sermons: "Augustin a consciemment créé un style homilétique qui devait répondre aux besoins de la prédication populaire. . . . La langue de la prédication augustinienne n'est pas le latin vulgaire de son époque, c'est plutôt une forme très stylisée du latin tel qu'il se parlait dans un milieu cultivé, mais qui était, dans sa simplicité, facile à comprendre, même par l'homme du peuple. Sans descendre au niveau du peuple, il parle une langue qui lui reste accessible" ("Augustin Prédicateur," *La Maison-Dieu* 39 [1954]: 83-96, reprinted in Mohrmann, *Etudes*, 1:391-402, quotation from p. 396, partly reversing the earlier 1931 judgment of Ferdinand Lot ["A quelle époque a-t-on cessé de parler Latin?" in *Recueil des travaux historiques de Ferdinand Lot*, vol. 1 (Geneva: Librairie Droz, 1968), pp. 440-42], fully refuted by Banniard [pp. 98-101]). Mohrmann also shows that this lively, direct style was not a feature of Augustine's earliest sermons, but developed as Augustine learned to speak directly to his hearers ("Saint Augustin Ecrivain," *Recherches Augustiniennes* 1 [1958]: 43-66, reprinted at Mohrmann, *Etudes*, 2:246-75; this study also calls attention to the predominance of rhyme as a feature of the popular

eled rhetorical style meant forgoing a traditional, identifying characteristic of the elite, so that such a rhetorical posturing was itself a kind of social statement.[19] Apart from the very early sermons from the period of Augustine's presbyterate, a reading of the *Sermones ad populum* betrays not the slightest hint that there ever was a "second sophistic";[20] Augustine has nothing to offer comparable to the funeral orations of Ambrose or the Eastern homilists.

"Faith Seeking Understanding"

Turning now to a comparison between *De Trinitate* and the *Sermones*, perhaps the most salient feature is that Augustine does not "simplify" his own work by omitting particular topics of discussion, or at least not in any way easy to describe. Nearly all the topics taken up in *De Trinitate* are well represented in the sermons, and some qualify as homiletic preoccupations. The theophanies in the Pentateuch, with special reference to the question of who appeared and how;[21]

---

style of the sermons). See also her "Considerazioni sulle 'Confessioni' di Sant'Agostino," *Convivium* 25 (1957): 257-67; and 27 (1959): 1-12, 129-39; reprinted as a whole at Mohrmann, *Etudes*, 2:277-323. Mohrmann's emphasis on the Bible as a formative influence in the style of Augustine's preaching is corroborated by the work of Karl-Heinz Uthemann, "Bemerkungen zu Augustins Auffassung der Predigt," *Augustinianum* 36 (1996): 147-81.

19. "The style was . . . a subtle form of episcopal discipline. Implicitly discounting the distinctions and prestige of the traditional literary culture . . . his style . . . was another continuing form of self-restraint"; "his language . . . a unifying force, moving downward to instruct the simple, reaching upward to set the *docti* an example" (Kaster, p. 84). William Klingshirn points out the struggle Caesarius of Arles, admirer and imitator of Augustine's style, had in persuading aristocratic bishops to give up the ornamented style, a traditional mark of prestige and status, in favor of plain speech: see his *Caesarius of Arles: The Making of a Christian Community in Late Antique Gaul*, Cambridge Studies in Medieval Life and Thought, no. 22 (Cambridge: Cambridge University Press, 1994), pp. 81-82, 146-51. Sarah Spence also comments that Augustine's rhetorical practice involved a shift in the relationship between audience and orator: "Instead of insisting on the absolute power and verity of language and reason, the Christian persuader must remain part of the audience even while assuming temporarily what is objectively the role of teacher. There is consequently a reorganization of the hierarchy implicit in classical rhetoric, for no matter how much the Christian teacher or preacher is like the classical orator, he is also like the Ciceronian audience. Such power as the classical orator has over his audience — a power possible only if a distance exists between them — is thus denied. . . . The shift in pragmatics is thus a shift in underlying assumptions: the Christian orator must persuade laterally, not from on high, and all that he says is subject to a higher authority" (*Rhetorics of Reason and Desire* [Ithaca, N.Y.: Cornell University Press, 1988], p. 76).

20. See Mohrmann, *Etudes*, 1:396.

21. See, e.g., two homilies on the burning bush: 6 (esp. 6.2, with its discussion of the manner in which God appeared — through an angel, not in his unchangeable essence) and 7 (esp.

trinitarian relations;[22] rules for the interpretation of Scripture;[23] soteriology;[24] detailed anti-Arian polemic;[25] the human soul as trinitarian image of God;[26] discussions of love similar to that in book 8 of *De Trinitate*;[27] and above all the question of "seeing" God, the character and quality of an incorporeal substance, and Neoplatonic "ascents" to contemplation[28] — each the subject of Alcuin's particular editorial censorship — are all taken into the *Sermones* with relish.[29]

7.3-7, with discussion of which person of the Trinity appeared to Moses and later to Abraham); cf. *Trin.* 2.19-22; 3.22-27; and *S.* 23.14.

22. E.g., *S.* 71.18 (an "improvement" on *De Trinitate?* — see Edmund Hill's comments on sermon 71, in *The Works of Saint Augustine: A Translation for the 21st Century*, gen. ed. John E. Rotelle, O.S.A., Part III, *Sermons on the New Testament*, trans. Edmund Hill, O.P. [Brooklyn, NY: New City Press, 1991], vol. 3, p. 271, n. 1) and *S.* 25-27 (cf. *Trin.* 1.7, 25; 2.3 on the inseparability of the works of the Trinity, also the subject of *S.* 135) and 28-33 on the Holy Spirit (cf. material in *Trin.* 15.27-49); *S.* 103.4 (cf. *Trin.* 5.11, etc.); 117.7 (cf. *Trin.* 1.1 on not applying characteristics of creatures to God); 118; 126.11 (cf. *Trin.* 12.6); 127.4-5; 195.1; 196.1; 212; 213.7; 214.5-6, 10; 215.3-4, 8 (a series of homilies on the creed); 229G; and 288.5 (cf. in both cases *Trin.* 1.17); etc.

23. *S.* 89.4; 341.10-12 (cf. *Trin.* 1.14; 2.2-3; note also that *S.* 186.2-3 uses Phil. 2:6-7 as a rule for interpreting John 14:28 and 10:30, etc., without actually calling it a rule, as also at *S.* 229G.3 and other places).

24. Most extended treatment at *S.* 80.

25. *S.* 7.4; 117.6-16; 126.7-9; 139.3; 229G.4-5; 244.3-4; 341; etc.

26. Esp. at *S.* 52, but this seems directed to a more educated audience (see 52.10).

27. *S.* 21.5; 23.13; 34.4-5; cf. 90.10, where growth in love is the renewal of the image of God.

28. One theme especially worth noting in this regard is the ubiquity of the comparison between God's Word and our words. Ascent from consideration of our own words, both exterior and especially interior, to God's Word is a pivotal theme in *De Trinitate* (see, e.g., 9.12-15; 14.10; 15.19-20, 22-25, 50): see *S.* 28.4-5; 119.7; 120; 179.6; 187; 223A; 225.3; 288.3-4; etc. On seeing God in general see esp. 68-69; 179.6; 362.3-4. Excellent, fully explicit ascent, very reminiscent of *Confessions* 10, at *S.* 293.5 and 52.7; see also 43.3; 68.6; 369.2.

29. The presence of Augustine's favorite theological themes in his sermons is frequently noted: "One could briefly describe the essential character of the content of his sermons by saying that they contain the sum of his profoundest spiritual knowledge and experience adapted to the pattern of everyday practical life. . . . That which he had stated in his great works in packed and highly articulated form he gave bit by bit in his sermon, never giving too much at once, but giving what he did give without adulteration" (van der Meer, pp. 433-34; cf. Pellegrino, 1:56-70; and H. Rondet, "La théologie de S. Augustin prédicateur," *Bulletin de Litterature Ecclesiastique* 72 [1971]: 81-105, 241-57). Mohrmann comments, "C'est un fait remarquable que ce prédicateur qui s'efforce de parler une langue simple et compréhensible, qui fait des concessions à ses auditerus en ce qui concerne la forme extérieure de sa prédication, ne leur relâche rien quand il s'agit de la doctrine. La prédication augustinienne revêt un caractère nettement théologique et spéculatif. Il donne dans ses semons la plénitude de ses connaissances théologiques et de ses expériences spirituelles" (*Etudes*, 1:402). See also Ekkehard Mühlenberg, "Augustins Predigen," in *Predigt in der Alten Kirche*, pp. 9-24, who points out that "Augustin bringt für sein Predigen die ganze Theologie mit" (p. 17). But the question I have posed is not simply whether Augustine incorporates theology into his sermons, but more precisely *how*. How does he adapt his theol-

In fact, there is a striking continuity in tone between *De Trinitate* and the *Sermones ad populum*. It is true that in the sermons there are no passages of sustained dialectic, such as book 6 of *De Trinitate;* there are no summaries of philosophical jargon, such as the review of Aristotle's categories in *De Trinitate* 5.7.8. Nor is there any sustained argument based on Augustine's own jargon, such as the distinction between *scientia* and *sapientia* developed in book 12, or the lengthy discussion of substantial versus relational predicates from book 5. Extensive discussions of technical trinitarian terms, such as that of the word *persona,* do not figure largely in the sermons.[30] And there are very few citations of classical authors comparable to the sustained consideration of passages from Cicero extending over books 13 and 14 or the steady peppering of intertextual allusions to other authors there.[31] Nor is the concerted reference to the process of acquiring a liberal education[32] duplicated in the sermons. In short, what is missing from the sermons is any concerted appeal to the common culture of the educated elite, any sense that the discussion is among persons who know the repository of texts and skills that would characterize those educated in the liberal arts.

Yet the two genres of work appear finally as variations on a common endeavor of inquiry, which Augustine explicitly structures as such, and in particular, as "faith seeking understanding." It is certainly nothing new to use this phrase as a way of describing Augustinian theology, but a close reading of the homilies reveals that "faith seeking understanding" is as much a homiletic principle in Augustine as it is a theological principle. What emerges from a comparison of the homilies with *De Trinitate* is not that Augustine is popularizing, or "exotericizing," the *results* of inquiry when he preaches, but that he recontextualizes inquiry itself for the people.[33] In his homilies such inquiry is

---

ogy for a mixed audience of educated and uneducated, literate and illiterate people? Mühlenberg's conclusion is that Augustine's theology is present in his sermons as that which serves to bind together his biblical citations, a kind of "coordinate system" both governing and explaining the extent of his citations (p. 19), an excellent conclusion, although to my mind the result is more than a "lay dogmatic" ("Laiendogmatik," p. 19), the summary results of Augustine's inquiries, but rather a new context for inquiry itself.

30. There are a few exceptions, e.g., the discussion of "consubstantial" at *S.* 139.2-3.

31. See, e.g., citations of Ennius (*Trin.* 13.6), Terrence (*Trin.* 13.10), Virgil (*Trin.* 14.14,18; 15.25). One exception is Augustine's defense of the *Christiana tempora* against charges that they have been the destruction of the empire: *S.* 81.9, where Augustine cites both Virgil and Sallust against claims that "Christian times" have resulted in the fall of Rome; but here he is careful to explain what "penates" means and to retell the story of the fall of Troy. Also, in the same context, *S.* 105.10.

32. As at *Trin.* 9.15, 18; 10.1-4, 7; 12.23; 14.9, 11; etc.; in fact, many of the "trinities" that image God in the senses and mind are actually analyses of *learning.*

33. "Exotericizing," while awkward enough, is better than "popularizing," both because "popularizing" implies watering down and also because of what Arnaldo Momigliano called

no longer the exclusive province of the liberally educated elites. And *De Trinitate*, which explicitly styles itself as a defense of the "starting point of faith"[34] for those desiring understanding, becomes the theoretical justification of this recontextualization. If *De Trinitate* succeeds, it succeeds only as a defense of a requirement before and beneath the sheer dint of educated expertise employed therein, detaching inquiry from any essential connection with that expertise and attaching it to the sort of seeking which faith in itself represents.[35]

In the first place, Augustine repeatedly and consistently styles his sermons

---

"the Christian abolition of the internal frontiers between the learned and the vulgar," noting that "Christian intellectuals succeeded where pagan intellectuals had failed for centuries, both in transmitting their theories to the masses and in sharing the beliefs of the masses" ("Popular Religious Beliefs and the Late Roman Historians," in *Popular Belief and Practice*, ed. G. J. Cuming and Derek Baker [Cambridge: Cambridge University Press, 1972], pp. 1-18, at 17), continuing, "However divided they were, the Christians were not divided culturally in the upper and lower strata. . . . Indeed I do not know of any ecclesiastical historian who condemns a Christian practice simply as being vulgar" (p. 19). As such there were no "popular" beliefs strictly speaking, i.e., beliefs discredited because they were characteristic of the masses. A comment such as this, however, begs for clarification, since distinctions between educated and noneducated certainly persisted. I am suggesting that instead of focusing on the communication of "theories," i.e., the *results* of inquiry to the "masses," although that surely must be considered, there is the additional focus of recontextualizing the process of inquiry itself, making the homilies of Augustine in some sense themselves an educational venue. Brown comments that "Fourth-century Christianity, in fact, was far from being a 'popular' movement," and that this image of it is a function of Christian self-representation on the part of highly cultivated, educated bishops whose very education (*paideia, Power and Persuasion*, passim) continued to mark them as members of the elite (pp. 75-76). But to the extent that inquiry itself is recontextualized in Augustine's rhetoric as something available to all people of faith, it is not only represented as such but actually, in the delivery of the homilies, "exotericized," thus vindicating to some extent Momigliano's insight. On this topic see also Norbert Brox, "Der Einfache Glaube und die Theologie: Zur altkirchlichen Geschichte eines Dauerproblems," *Kairos* 14 (1972): 161-87; H. J. Carpenter, "Popular Christianity and the Theologians in the Early Centuries," *Journal of Theological Studies*, n.s., 14 (1963): 294-310; W. H. C. Frend, "Popular Religion and Christological Controversy in the Fifth Century," in *Popular Belief and Practice*, pp. 19-29.

34. *Trin.* 1.4; see J. Cavadini, "The Structure and Intention of Augustine's *De Trinitate*," *Augustinian Studies* 23 (1992): 103-23, at 107. See also J. Cavadini, "Augustine's *De Trinitate* and the Quest for Truth," *Theological Studies* 58 (1997): 429-40.

35. It is faith, not the liberal arts, which purifies the heart for the happy life of understanding (*Trin.* 13.25), a reversal of Augustine's position in the Cassiciacum Dialogues; see my discussion at "The Sweetness of the Word: Salvation and Rhetoric in Augustine's *De Doctrina Christiana*," in *"De Doctrina Christiana": A Classic of Western Culture*, ed. Duane W. H. Arnold and Pamela Bright (Notre Dame, Ind.: University of Notre Dame Press, 1995), pp. 164-81, at 167-68 and nn. 40-43, though I believe that in that discussion I underestimated the role that faith, hope, and love played even in the dialogues, especially *Soliloquia*.

as acts of inquiry, as instances of seeking understanding of Scripture.[36] Seeking for understanding, we are to look "in the books of the Lord" and knock on the Lord's door for understanding by praying.[37] Scripture, or the church in which Scripture is read, is styled as a "school," and those who come to hear Scripture read are "students of divine letters." They will know what the titles of the psalms mean;[38] those who have been "well educated" in the "school of Christ" will know that Jacob and Israel are the same person.[39] Biblical miracles are meant to enrich those who are in the school of Christ with understanding, not simply to strike them with wonder.[40] Among the hearers of Sermon 133 are both educated and uneducated people, but Augustine refers to both groups as those who have been "brought up in the church, educated in the Scriptures of the Lord." As for those who have not been schooled in the liberal arts, they are nevertheless not uneducated since they have been raised "on the word of God."[41]

---

36. *S.* 32.7. The idea is not only to hear Augustine's "discussions" *(tractatus)*, but to understand the Scripture which Augustine's treatment is meant to clarify: ". . . non solum ad audiendos tractatus nostros, sed etiam ad intellegendas ipsas Scripturas, de quibus vobis ista tractamus." At 36.1 it is not only Augustine who will investigate the text in the hopes of understanding it, but the audience as well: "Sancta Scriptura quae modo in auribus vestris lecta est admonuit nos . . . quaerere vobiscum et pertractare quid sit et quid sibi velit quod lectum est. . . ."

37. "Et ubi quaeras? Ubi, nisi in dominicis libris" (*S.* 105.3).

38. Augustine singles out those who pay attention and come frequently as those "Qui rudes non sunt in Scripturis divinis, qui amant frequentare istam scholam, qui non oderunt magistrum sicut pueri desperati, et intentam aurem praebent in ecclesia lectoribus atque exceptorium cordis sui in fluentia Scripturae divinae patefaciunt . . ." (32.2), but the sermon is explicitly addressed to those who are not regulars, not "usitata intentis et studiosis litterarum divinarum" as well. These latter will need to be told the story of David and Goliath before it can be expounded (32.2).

39. ". . . in schola Christi eruditi estis" (*S.* 122.3). At 74.1 Augustine admonishes his hearers not to come to school unprepared, so that they will not understand the Scriptures properly when heard, but understand the words according to "worldly" usage: "Debemus enim non frustra intrare scholam, sed nosse in qua significatione Scripturarum verba teneamus; ne cum aliquid de Scripturis sonuerit, quod in alio saeculari usu intellegi solet, aberret auditor. . . ." In 399 Augustine talks about "what is to be learned [*discatur*] here," i.e., in church, and goes on to compare the process of learning that goes on when the Scriptures are read and expounded to secular education (399.11-12); Christ is the teacher, his school *(schola)* is on earth, his school is his body, the Head is teaching the members (399.15); his house is a house of "discipline" because it is a house of learning, as *disciplina* comes from *discendo* (399.1).

40. "With regard to miracles, some saw them and also understood them, and of such sort should we be who are in the school of Christ" ("tales nos in schola Christi esse debemus") (*S.* 98.3).

41. "Videte, fratres mei, distinguite nutriti in Ecclesia, eruditi in Scripturis dominicis, non rudes, non rustici, non idiotae. Sunt enim inter vos docti et eruditi viri et quibuscumque litteris non mediocriter instructi: et qui illas litteras quae liberales vocantur, non didicistis, plus est quod in sermone Dei nutriti estis" (*S.* 133.4).

Further, Augustine always postures himself as essentially and primarily a listener to the Scriptures: "Don't listen to me, but together with me. There's someone, you see, who says to us, 'Come, children, listen to me' (Ps. 34.11). And let's all come running, and stand there, and prick up our ears."[42] Augustine notes explicitly that the preacher is above all a listener. It is Augustine's duty to speak, but "it's a futile preacher outwardly of God's word, who isn't also inwardly a listener."[43] Augustine is very careful not to posture himself as the teacher in this school, but as a fellow inquirer, someone who is seeking for understanding just as much as other students in the school of Scripture:

> Your graces know that all of us have one teacher, and that under him we are fellow disciples, fellow pupils [condiscipulos]. And the fact that we bishops speak to you from a higher place does not make us your teachers; but it's the one who dwells in all of us that is the teacher of us all. He was talking to all of us just now in the Gospel, and saying to us what I am also saying to you; he says it, though about us, about both me and you: "If you remain in my word" — not mine, of course, not Augustine's, now speaking, but his, who was speaking just now from the Gospel.[44]

In another place Augustine notes that "We bishops are called teachers [doctores], but in many matters we seek a teacher ourselves, and we certainly don't want to be regarded as masters [magistros]. That is dangerous, and forbidden by the Lord himself, who says 'Do not wish to be called masters; you have one master, the Christ' (Mt. 23.10). So the magisterium is dangerous, the state of disciple safe."[45] Augustine expects to be judged, and not only by God but by his listeners; "You are listening as judges," he tells them.[46] He speaks from a higher place in church, but it is the hearers' office to pass judgment on

42. "Audite non a me, sed mecum simul. Ait enim nobis quidam: *Venite, filii, audite me.* Et concurramus, et stemus, et aures arrigamus, et corde intellegamus Patrem qui dixit: *Venite, filii, audite me*" (S. 108.6). Cf. 60.6, "I have spoken, and you have listened — or rather he has spoken and we have all listened together" ("Nos diximus et vos audistis, immo ille [Christus] dixit et simul audivimus").

43. "Intus auditor" (S. 179.1).

44. S. 134.1; cf. 23.2; 16A.1.

45. S. 23.1. Note that at 213.11, a sermon for handing the creed over to the catechumens, Augustine tells the catechumens not to be afraid if in eight days they have not memorized the creed perfectly, for "we [clergy?] are your fathers, we aren't carrying the canes and switches of schoolteachers [grammaticorum]." In other words, unlike the grammaticus, he is not concerned with exact wording, but with the faith underlying it: "Si quis in verbo erraverit, in fide non erret" (cf. *Ennarationes in Psalmos* 138.20, where he explains he would rather offend the grammatici than speak in a way the people could not understand).

46. "Iudices auditis" (S. 52.8).

what he says.[47] They too may consult the inner teacher: "inwardly, we are all hearers"; the inner teacher can prompt applause if the hearer is delighted with the truth spoken, or accusation: "'I would like to know if this guy who's speaking to me does all the things that he hears himself or says to others.'"[48] "In this way, for whatever we say that is true (since everything true is from Truth) you will praise not us but him, and wherever being human we slip up, you will pray to the same him for us."[49]

Augustine rhetorically positions himself and his audience as embarked upon a joint venture of inquiry.[50] His choice of topic, therefore, was sometimes based on his listeners' interests. In *Sermo* 362 he focused on a particular verse because of his congregation's vocal reaction to it when read (362.1). He also shaped his expositions around questions which his fellow seekers had asked, or which he imagined them asking. "'Amen and Alleluia,'" they say, "'we're going to say that forever and ever? Who will be able to endure it?'" (362.29). Augustine responds with an inquiry about the resurrected life in the hereafter "according to the Scriptures."[51]

When Augustine treats the scriptural passage read by the lector as a "problem" *(quaestio)* that challenges the inquiry and study of all its hearers, he is most effective rhetorically in posturing himself and his hearers as fellow seekers. Augustine sets out a passage of Scripture as presenting a dilemma, and says to his hearers that he will "seek with [them]" what it means. Another text presents a "problem which really must be solved."[52] Faced with Matthew 12:32, the

47. ". . . adiuvet [Dominus] nos misericordia et gratia sua me loquentem, vos iudicantes. Quamquam enim propter commoditatem depromendae vocis altiore loco stare videamur, tamen in ipso altiore loco vos iudicatis, et nos iudicamur" (*S.* 23.1).

48. "Intus autem . . . omnes auditores sumus" (stated twice in *S.* 179.7); "'Vellem scire, si iste qui mihi loquitur, omnia facit quae vel ipse audit, vel ceteris dicit'" (179.10, note 355 and 356 as defenses against just such a question, and note at 180.10 Augustine's admission that he still swears ["For all that, I'm not telling you that I don't swear. I mean, if I do say that, I'm lying"]).

49. ". . . ut in eo quod verum dicimus — quoniam omne verum a veritate est — non nos, sed ipsum laudetis; ubi autem sicut homines offendimus, eumdem ipsum pro nobis oretis" (*S.* 23.2).

50. Perhaps best summed up at 379.4: "Try and understand, my brothers and sisters, recall the saving mystery, have a hunger for the Word of God, grasp what I am proclaiming [*praedicamus*], and let us together find joy in the truth."

51. ". . . secundum Scripturas quaereremus, qualis in resurrectione futura sit vita iustorum" (362.1). On the way in which Augustine's sermons respond to concerns of the people, see Eric Rebillard, "Contexte local et prédication: Augustin et le détresse des mourants," in *Cristianesimo e specificità regionali nel Mediterraneo latino (sec. IV-VI)*, Studia Ephemerides Augustinianum 46 (Rome: Institutum Patristicum Augustinianum, 1994), pp. 179-87.

52. "Oritur quaestio profecto solvenda" and "videtis certe profunditatem quaestionis" (*S.* 99.4), followed by "Iam nunc quia ut potuimus, quaestionem profundam in tantilla temporis brevitate solvimus; aut si nondum solvimus debitores, ut dixi, teneamur" (99.7). Cf. 52.6-8.

passage about the sin against the Holy Spirit, Augustine notes: "It's a real problem that we are faced with, in this passage read just now from the Gospel" (*S.* 71.1). He draws out his exposition to heighten the sense of the difficulty of the problem and the desire for a solution, noting, after the resolution of some antecedent difficulties, that the passage is a "colossal problem," that "there is probably no greater problem to be found in all the holy Scriptures," and that he himself had avoided speaking about it, although not "seeking, asking, knocking" about it (71.7-8).[53] Passages such as this are specifically meant to prompt the reader or hearer to inquiry, for upon inquiry he or she may discover more than one "right meaning."[54] There is a real pleasure in the discovery of meaning in a text which had been obscure. In this sermon Augustine heightens the sense of the problem so much and delays his answer so skillfully that he almost teases his hearers into seeking and appreciating that pleasure (71.13, 18). In another sermon on John 7:2-10, where Jesus says he is not going up to the feast but then goes, Augustine poses the problem plainly in order to "engage [his hearers'] interest."[55] In another sermon he speaks of the enthusiasm of the audience when he "sets some problems before [them] to be solved," and how it has prompted him to set even further inquiry before them.[56]

The sermons consistently present faith as the sine qua non for understanding,[57] but even more importantly they style the faith of the hearers as a posture of inquiry or seeking. Not everyone may understand at present, but the sermons direct everyone's faith, preacher as well as hearers, toward understanding. This occurs eschatologically, to be sure, but also in the present, in the time that

53. Cf. 362.1, where the subject for discussion is called a *questio.*

54. See n. 69 below.

55. "But let me tell you briefly where the problem [*quaestionis*] lies in this reading [*lectio*], and then, when your interest is engaged by the problem we have been set [*facti intenti per propositam quaestionem*], pray that I may be enabled to solve it" (*S.* 133.1).

56. "Cum quaedam solvenda proponerem, studium vestrum me fecit et aliud poponere, quod forte non quaereretis" (*S.* 352.4). At other places he comments on the pleasure of discovery in a way reminiscent of *De doctrina Christiana.* On the figurative meaning of the bodily death of Moses: "O mira mysteria! Hoc certe expositum et intellectum, quanto dulcius quam manna?" (352.5), and again later, "Non ad fraudem, sed ad iucunditatem clausa erant. Neque enim tam dulciter caperentur, si prompta vilescerent." The obscurity of passages is a source of "fun" for the inquirer. At 71.11 Augustine points out that we are nourished by the clear passages in Scripture, and exercised by the obscure or difficult ones, which serve to save us from boredom ("pascimur apertis, exercemur obscuris; illic fames pellitur, hic fastidium"); cf. 8.18 on the pleasure generated by the successful search for the meaning of a text. See *Doct. Chr.* 2.6.7-8.

57. *S.* 43, an exegesis of Isa. 7:9, glossed with Mark 9:24, "Help my unbelief," is one of the best expositions of this principle, especially because, like *De Trinitate* (or at least, like Augustine in a letter referring its reader to *De Trinitate* [*Epistula* 120.3, CSEL, 34:707.2-5]), it concedes that some measure of understanding must come before faith.

the sermon is delivered and over the long term of attendance at the "school" of divine Scripture. Thus faith is the basis for the joint venture of inquiry described above: "Let's be companions in believing. What am I saying? Let's be companions in seeking" (*S.* 53.13). Augustine remarks: "Faith is a step towards understanding"; faith is entitled to understanding.[58] For some, understanding may have to be postponed, but not necessarily for long, even for a difficult verse like John 5:19, "The Son cannot do anything of himself, except what he sees the Father doing." Augustine proceeds immediately to an exhortation to understand, despite the presence of a large number of people whom he does not expect to understand immediately: "God gave you eyes in your head, reason in your heart. Arouse the reason in your heart, get the inner inhabitant behind your inner eyes on his feet, let him take to his windows, let him inspect God's creation."[59] Augustine is admonishing his hearers to a Neoplatonic ascent to interior or spiritual vision: "Look at the facts, the things made, and seek the underlying factor, the maker. Observe what you see, and seek what you cannot see. Believe in the one whom you cannot see, on account of these things which you can" (126.3). It is the faith of the hearers that here is presented as an orientation, indeed almost an imperative, to make the ascent to spiritual vision, which alone can provide understanding of a difficult trinitarian verse like John 5:19. If Augustine exhorts his hearers to faith, it is *so that* their minds might be capable of understanding, since the mind imbued with faith becomes capable of understanding *(intellectus capax)*. Apart from eschatological vision, Augustine means "understanding" with regard to what he has just said, that is, the very words of his sermon.[60]

Since anyone can have faith, even those uneducated in the liberal arts, and

58. "Fides enim gradus est intellegendi; intellectus autem meritum fidei" (*S.* 126.1).

59. *S.* 126.8, where he addresses both groups, apologizing if what he says appears to be a waste of time to those who will not immediately understand, yet going on to give the explanation which the text (John 5:19) as he sees it demands. There is no hiding of "esoteric" material here.

60. "In his enim quae supra diximus hortantes ad fidem, ut animus imbutus fide sit intellectus capax, ea quae dicta sunt, festiva, laeta, facilia, sonuerunt, exhilaraverunt mentes vestras, secuti estis, intellixistis quae dixi" (126.8). Augustine's exhortation to faith is a stimulus to understanding. The same progression is evident in *S.* 127: "'I've never seen this,' you will say, 'someone begetting, and the one he has begotten always with him. . . .' You're quite right; I've never seen this, because it belongs to *what the eye has not seen*. . . . It is to be believed, and cultivated. When it is believed it is cultivated; when cultivated, it grows; when it grows, it is grasped" ("Credatur, et colatur. Cum creditur, colitur; cum colitur, crescitur; cum crescitur, capitur" [I have modified Hill's translation]). Faith here *is* the cultivation of understanding, and it bears at least partial fruit (or at least could bear partial fruit) now, in the course of this sermon. For the theme of faith seeking understanding in the sermons, see Pontet, pp. 113-15.

since faith is an orientation to understanding, in the rhetoric of Augustine faith could be said to "exotericize" the esoteric Neoplatonic quest for spiritual vision.[61] This is what permits Augustine to tackle John 1:1 in a sermon. It is one of the most difficult passages of Scripture — one which, in the *Confessions*, he singles out as something the Neoplatonists had understood. It cannot be understood without some sort of ascent to spiritual vision, and in a homily for Easter Sunday, preached to a packed house in Hippo, Augustine exhorts his hearers to "lift up [their] hearts, reject anything bodily from the imagination," and to "think of the Word as being everywhere whole and entire."[62] This is an undiluted teaching of Plotinus, the philosophical master, presented to the masses as something which they, and in particular those who have just been "enlightened" (120.3) by baptism, can understand. It is not that Plotinian doctrine has been simplified for the masses but that inquiry, the quest for spiritual vision, has been recontextualized by faith. And thus the rest of this brief homily is a kind of guided ascent to vision. In another Easter homily on the same text, Augustine admonishes, "If you understand, rejoice; if you don't understand, believe. Because the word of the prophet cannot be nullified, 'Unless you believe, you shall not understand' (Is. 7.9)." The exhortation to faith is an exhortation to that which will permit understanding, to some degree even in the present (118.2). In another homily on the same text Augustine exhorts his audience to the understanding of the Word of God conceived in strictly Platonic fashion as "a kind of form, a form that has not been formed, but is the form of all things that have been formed, an unchangeable form, that has neither fault nor failing, beyond time, beyond space, standing apart as at once the foundation for all things to stand on."[63] Later in the homily (117.17) he describes the slow growth

---

61. Note that the issue of rhetorical posturing does not mean that this is *merely* a rhetorical device, that it is *mere* rhetoric. Peter Brown has shown that by representing reality in a certain way, it *made* reality — the rhetors evoked a set of classical expectations for deportment that was, as he puts it, the "only effective constitution" that the empire ever knew (*Power and Persuasion,* p. 59). And Maude Gleason, in somewhat the same vein, has recently shown how the eunuch Favorinus "made" himself a man by his rhetorical practice (*Making Men: Sophists and Self-Presentation in Ancient Rome* [Princeton: Princeton University Press, 1995]).

62. *S.* 120.2; cf. 52.15. On the Easter homilies of Augustine, see Suzanne Poque, in Sources chrétiennes (hereafter SC), 116:9-153; see esp. at 119: ". . . parmi les *Sermones ad populum,* la prédication de la Pâque est certainement celle qui met l'orateur en présance de son public le moins cultivé, non le petit noyau des fidèles assidus mais le peuple accouru en raison de la solennité, avec au premier rang, adultes et enfants, les derniers catéchisés" (cf. Pontet, p. 61). This makes the similarity of theme between *S.* 120, preached in Hippo on Easter, and *S.* 52, preached in Carthage to what is perhaps a more select audience, very significant.

63. The text shows the power of Augustine's preaching, "simple" though its style may be: "Est enim forma quaedam, forma non formata, sed forma omnium formatorum: forma

of understanding from faith, and the reason faith has this capacity to beget understanding. Faith is the indwelling of Christ, who is the loftiness of God made lowly, the indwelling of God's "instruction" *(praeceptio Dei)* begetting the charity that cleanses the inner vision. It is the incarnation that is God's teaching, which is, in a way, the exotericizing of teaching itself, and it dwells in our hearts through faith.

Finally, this means that Augustine's homiletic discussions of "mystery" are not exhortations to blind faith, but precisely the opposite. Faith is the healing of the eye of the mind and, as such, a capacity for understanding or "penetrating" mystery.[64] Having faith in Christ, whom we can see temporally, Augustine preaches, we come to understand the divinity we cannot perceive, and not simply in the eschaton but even now, in the course of a sermon: "How, then, are our eyes healed? Just as it's by faith that we perceive Christ passing by in his temporal activities, so we have to understand him stopping and standing still, as Christ in his unchanging eternity. The eye is healed, you see, when it understands Christ's divinity. Your graces must try to grasp this; pay attention to the sublime mystery [*grande sacramentum*] I am speaking of" (*S.* 88.14). On the other hand, the mysteries of faith are such that no one, no matter how educated, can completely grasp them in this life; before them, all, preacher and hearer, are "little ones to be educated."[65] Speaking about John 1:1-2, Augustine says, "Who can work it out? Who can observe it, who contemplate it, who think fitting thoughts about it? Nobody" (229E.4). In another homily on the same verse he remarks, "And I know, I'm telling you, that not even I who am speaking to you, not even I understand."[66] The continuing and permanent need for faith in face of the mystery of the Trinity is the source of the preacher's posturing of himself (and his rhetoric) as seeking, and as doing so on essentially the same

---

incommutabilis, sine lapsu, sine defectu, sine tempore, sine loco, superans omnia, existens omnibus et fundamentum quoddam in quo sint, et fastigium sub quo sint" (117.3, compare to *Trin.* 5.1-2, and even to the prologue of the *Confessions*). Note also *S.* 53 as explicitly taking the faith of a "carnal" believer — one who interprets Isa. 66:1 and 40:12 to mean that God has a body — and leading that faith, through a course of reasoning, to understanding.

64. "Videamus ergo, et adhuc quantum possumus conemur penetrare mysterium" (*S.* 352.4).

65. "Erudiendos nos parvulos," *S.* 88.14; cf. 117.16, where Augustine styles himself a *parvulos* along with the audience, "lacte parvuli nutriremur"; cf. 127.5, where it is the milk of faith that nourishes "us *infantes*" until the solid food of sight.

66. "Et ego scio, inquam, qui tecum loquor; nec ego comprehendo" (*S.* 225.3). Augustine goes on to point out that thinking about these things stretches our capacity to understand, but that even the enlarged capacity which results will not enable us to understand completely: "cogitatio facit nos extendi, extensio dilatat nos, dilatatio nos capaces facit. Nec facti capaces totum comprehendere poterimus."

level as those to whom he speaks.[67] And if Scripture is, for now, "the face of God" for us,[68] we are always rendered seekers by the inexhaustible variety and depth of meaning which presents that face to us.

Turning to *De Trinitate* from the sermons, one finds the same rhetoric, equally insistent, of a discourse shared between writer and reader as coseekers on a joint project of inquiry.[69] Augustine does not expect simply to be believed, and expects to be corrected if he is wrong. He gives readers the wherewithal to see for themselves, even if only in the distorted "mirror" of their own souls, the long, drawn-out series of Neoplatonic-like interior ascents of the second half of the treatise. *De Trinitate,* however, is not addressed simply to persons of faith, a point Augustine makes after a lengthy citation of one of his own homilies[70] (to my

67. Ultimately the mystery of the Trinity and its unfathomableness is for Augustine not simply the mystery of a divine nature, a divine puzzle to try our wits, but the mystery of God's love as displayed in the economy of salvation, i.e., the mystery of the incarnation, "this stupendous gift of God" (*S.* 215.3), before which all our intellects are humbled and all our speech insufficient, itself definitive of God's greatness (see the whole of 215.3).

68. "Ergo pro facie Dei, tibi pone interim Scripturam Dei" (*S.* 22.7). Not only does this mean that the same passage can have different, legitimate interpretations, but that it is impossible to codify figurative or allegorical meanings of *res* because these meanings shift and are determined by context (32.6). Yet some meanings are consistent enough so that those who come to the *schola* of Scripture regularly can learn them, and understand even before Augustine speaks, for example, that the "valiant woman" of Prov. 31:10 is the church (37.1). It is the possibility of figurative meaning that keeps those who already understand something seeking more: "Ne forte et ibi aliqua figura expressa sit, et innuerit intellegenti, et ad inquirendum commoverit et provocaverit animum." The text can have an indefinite quality, open to the discovery of more than one true meaning, and that invites and even impels continuing inquiry; see, e.g., 71.10, regarding the blasphemy against the Holy Spirit, the nature of which is left indeterminate in the text, as Augustine points out: "Exercere quippe nos voluit [Dominus] difficultate quaestionis. . . . Quaeri, inquam, voluit. . . . Quia ergo nec universaliter nec particulariter enuntiata sententia est . . . sed indefinite. . . . Id exprimere noluerit, ut petendo, quaerendo, pulsando, si quid recti intellectus acceperimus, non viliter habeamus." The passage implies that more than one right meaning may be found (on this see *Doct. Chr.* 3.27.38, with regard to possible multiplicity of figurative meanings, and *De Genesi ad litteram* 1.20-21 on the fruitful difficulty of establishing even the correct literal interpretation of many passages).

69. See, e.g., *Trin.* 1.5; 2.1; 3.2; 5.1. In a more general way, Auerbach comments on the stylistic connection between the sermons and a treatise like *De Trinitate:* "[T]he *sermo humilis* . . . has other features besides vulgarisms and the like; one is its implication of direct human contact between you and me, a note that was lacking in the sublime style of Roman antiquity; another is its power to express human brotherhood, an immediate bond between men: all of us here and now. . . . My primary purpose in quoting the passage from the *De Trinitate* was to show precisely that this style also pervaded the most speculative and least popular writing" (Auerbach, pp. 56-57). Banniard (pp. 83, 94) also comments on the presence of such a style in the treatises, precisely, in part, as an appeal to the illiterate, who could not read but certainly could be read to.

70. *Tractatus in Johannis evangelium* 99.8-9, at *Trin.* 15.48.

knowledge the only time he cites one of his homilies in a treatise). The citation underscores the kinship between these two parts of Augustine's oeuvre, but it also underscores the difference. *De Trinitate* has as at least part of its agenda the defense of starting with faith if one is to attain understanding. The tone in this treatise, suggesting dialogue, is not necessarily predicated on shared faith, but on a shared educational tradition, that of the liberal arts.[71] If the emphasis in the sermons is to propose faith as an orientation to understanding, as an inquiry, the emphasis in *De Trinitate* is to demonstrate that inquiry can come to fruition only if founded on faith. Here the rhetoric shapes the inquiry, or more particularly, the dialogic rhetoric of philosophical inquiry is itself being employed as the dialectic of faith, enjoined to "seek God's face evermore" (Ps. 105:3).[72] The shared, conversational ascent to the vision of truth, in Augustine's dialogues the prerogative of the liberally educated, has been transformed in the sermons to become the dialectic of faith seeking understanding, available to all. *De Trinitate* can be imagined as the place where Augustine works out the theory behind the shift of the ancient, dialogic quest for wisdom to the exoteric provenance of the sermon.[73]

71. The sermons, too, with their stylized give-and-take, where the audience sometimes speaks out but more often is presented as giving voice to questions, can themselves be imagined as a reincarnation or recasting of the dialogue form Augustine tried out early on and then abandoned. This feature of the sermons as in some sense "dialogic" is commented on frequently. Mandouze, *Saint Augustin,* entitles his chapter on the sermons "Dialogues avec la foule" (p. 591), insists on the "real" character of the dialogue with the audience (pp. 641-42), and also compares them to the *Soliloquies* (p. 663). Note too the characterization of Augustine's rhetoric at Spence, p. 82, as one that allows "an increase in the participation and power of the audience" (cf. p. 72, where "the audience, who, at least theoretically, had no voice, now has, at least in part, the voice of the orator, since the orator is always part of the audience"). See also Poque, in SC, 116:121-23, on the relation between Augustine's style and the technique of diatribe; and M. I. Barry, *St. Augustine the Orator: A Study of the Rhetorical Qualities of St. Augustine's "Sermones ad Populum"* (Washington, D.C.: Catholic University of America Press, 1924), pp. 149-51. More recently Mark Vessey has commented on the "conference"-style mode of exegesis developed by Augustine in the *Confessions* ("Conference and Confession: Literary Pragmatics in Augustine's 'Apologia contra Hieronymum,'" *Journal of Early Christian Studies* 1 [1993]: 175-213), although I would argue for more continuity between the *Sermones ad populum* and the theory behind them in *Doct. Chr.* 4 on the one hand and *Confessions* 11-13 on the other, than the contrast on p. 209 implies (but see above, n. 15, where *De doctrina Christiana* does distinguish between a sermon and an actual conversation; yet the same would apply to *Confessions* 11-13, itself part of a book and not an actual conversation).

72. *Trin.* 15.1. I have argued elsewhere that *De Trinitate,* complete with its dialogic tone of a shared endeavor of seeking, is a kind of avatar or transmogrification of the early dialogues ("The Structure and Intention," pp. 109-10).

73. It may well be that one of the most abstruse parts of *De Trinitate* — the teaching on the "inner word" — is a teaching that very closely links it with the sermons, and it may be an example of a teaching that went from the sermons to the treatise rather than the other way around (see n. 28 above for some examples).

From Augustine to Caesarius

The effect of Augustine's work, presenting faith in his sermons as an orienta-tion to understanding, can be underscored by a comparison with the sermons of another "simplifier" of his work, the sixth-century bishop of Arles, Caesarius. Caesarius admired Augustine's plain style and imitated it.[74] In many cases he took over parts of Augustine's sermons verbatim.[75] But he never takes over the rhetoric of "faith seeking understanding" (Isa. 7:9).[76] There is not, as far as I have been able to determine, a single reference to this verse.

Caesarius lays out at length the various figures and "mysteries" of Scripture in homily after homily, but it is almost as though he is merely reading a code which has long ago been cracked. In Caesarius, as in Alcuin, the results have, in principle, already been discovered by the Fathers. For him the idea of preaching (or in Alcuin's case, writing a commentary) is to convey the results in a simpli-fied form, not to engage in a search together with the hearer or reader. Caesarius explicitly styles himself as presenting the results of the learned in-quiry of the "holy fathers" in simplified form:

> If we wanted to make known to the ears of your charity an explanation [*eloquio*] of Sacred Scripture in the same order and language in which the holy fathers expressed it, the food of doctrine [*doctrinae*] could reach only a few scholarly souls [*paucos scolasticos*], while the remaining crowd of people would remain hungry. For this reason I humbly beg you that learned ears [*eruditae aures*] be content to hear with patience these simple words [*verba rustica*]. . . . Since inexperienced, simple souls cannot rise to the height of scholars, the learned [*eruditi*] should deign to bend down to their ignorance. What is said to simple souls can, indeed, be understood by the educated [*scolastici*], but what is preached to the learned cannot be grasped at all by the simple.[77]

74. On Caesarius's style and its relation to Augustine's, see Klingshirn, pp. 148-51.

75. See the discussion of Marie-José Delage at SC, 175:101-10.

76. Note in particular Caesarius's long S. 12 on faith. The absence of any reference to "seek-ing understanding" or any hint that faith is even related to understanding is glaring for a reader used to Augustine. See also S. 82.1, where Caesarius describes those who believe in the Trinity as "carnal" and "spiritual," which in Augustine generally leads to a description of some who can "see" or "understand" while some, the carnal, cannot, although by believing they will come to understand. For Caesarius "carnal" merely means those who do not avoid sins and vices that the "spiritual" do in fact avoid.

77. S. 86.1, trans. M. M. Mueller, O.S.F., Fathers of the Church 31. The source for this pas-sage is probably Augustine, but not a sermon; see *De Genesi contra Manichaeos* 1.1.1, cited by Banniard, p. 83.

This passage is the virtual unsaying of Augustine's most treasured homiletic principles. The faith of the simple is an absolute; it is not imagined or employed as an orientation to inquiry or study. If there is any need for the Christian people to seek, they do it only by asking questions "of the priests who reveal the secrets of Holy Scripture," like calves going after the udders of their mothers: "so also the Christian people should continually appeal to their priests, as the udders of holy church, by devout questions."[78] In Augustine the "milk" for babes is prepared by the Word in being made flesh, not by Augustine;[79] Augustine is perfectly ready to characterize himself as an infant, or *parvulus*, who is the recipient of the Word's milk.[80] On the other hand, there is a strict division of labor envisioned in Caesarius's analogy. There is no sense in which preacher and hearers are embarked on a common inquiry. In his remake of Augustine's Sermon 8, Caesarius (*S.* 100) omits Augustine's approach to the sermon as "walking together on the way to [God's] truth" (8.1). And despite Caesarius's insistent recommendation that Christians read the Bible, or have it read to them, for three hours every day,[81] in none of his sermons is there a reference to the pleasure associated with the discovery of meaning in obscure texts. It goes almost without saying that hearers of Caesarius's preaching are never construed as people who might be in a position to judge the truth of what is said.

The "low" or "simple" rhetorical style, for which Caesarius argues so strongly in two key sermons (1 and 86), when divorced from the Augustinian rhetoric of "faith seeking understanding," becomes not a way of "exotericizing" inquiry but of distinguishing the hearers precisely *as* an exoteric, "simple" class, who have only to memorize the results of someone else's inquiry, conducted long ago and mediated by Caesarius. Caesarius implies that his hearers are children,[82] and he their father, as Augustine never does. In a way, what Caesarius has done is to "esotericize" the Fathers, and with them, the preachers who dole

78. *S.* 4.4. Earlier in this section the comparison had been slightly different: the priests were instructed to gather flowers from Holy Scripture and so offer spiritual milk to them, feeding the Christian people with their two udders, the Old and New Testaments, just as cows eat grasses and leaves and feed their calves with the milk prepared from them.

79. Although Augustine is perfectly ready to describe the preacher's task as offering, more generically, "nourishment" ("alimentum," *S.* 8.1; etc.).

80. See *S.* 229E.4. Also at Augustine *S.* 10.8 the church, schismatic communions included, offers the milk (compare Caesarius's *S.* 123 to Augustine's *S.* 10, both on the story of Solomon's judgment over the two women claiming the same baby).

81. *S.* 6–8. The reading of Scripture is to replace long meals leading to drunkenness, especially in winter.

82. *S.* 6.1, remarking on how glad he is to see the people, "Quis enim pater est, qui filios suos, et praecipue fideles et bonos, non frequenter videre desideret?" (SC, 175:320).

out "crumbs" from the loaves of Scripture.[83] Finally, if *De Trinitate* has any relevance to the world of Caesarius's sermons, it is only as supplying the odd passage handy in the refutation of Arians.[84] Setting *De Trinitate* next to the sermons of Caesarius only underscores the complementarity of Augustine's treatise with his own homiletic oeuvre. In a famous passage introducing his classic biography of Augustine, Peter Brown notes that he will steer a middle course along a cliff face, "above the plains of Augustine's routine duties as a bishop, and far below the heights of his speculations on the Trinity."[85] Perhaps, at least if preaching is one of the most salient elements of Augustine's routine pastoral duties, these two loci of Augustinian geography are not quite so far apart.

83. *S.* 93.1, said, however, with a note of self-deprecation, as though he should be able to dole out more; and in general, one must finally not underestimate Caesarius's achievements as a preacher. He could raise and answer, based on his readings in the Fathers, awkward objections to the faith (such as why did God force the Canaanites out of their land [*S.* 114.1-2, against the Manichees], or if the devil is bound, why is he so powerful? [121.6]) in a way that listeners could easily grasp and repeat; he consistently presented biblical figures as exemplars of virtue (such as the series on the patriarch Joseph [90–93]) and hammered away unceasingly at the typological connections between the two Testaments; preached a program of Scripture reading, almsgiving, chastity, which was easily summed up (at 6.8 Caesarius calls upon his congregation to try to remember parts of what he had said so that in conversation later they could piece together the whole program); inveighed against pagan religious practices and practices he considered holdovers from paganism; etc. Perhaps Caesarius's congregations were less well educated than Augustine's, but it is hard to tell, especially since Caesarius worked very hard to remove from his homilies all place and time references so that they could be easily preached anywhere at anytime by anyone (see Delage, in SC, 175:67-69). He certainly indicates the presence of both where any reference is made (as at *S.* 86, cited above). It is true that he "uniformly gave preference to the least well-educated members of the audience" (Klingshirn, p. 149), while Augustine did not observe this preference and sometimes warns that the unlearned may not be able to follow certain points, and yet there is also a cost to Caesarius's practice. In Augustine's practice the faith of all present, learned and unlearned, becomes styled as an orientation to inquiry in which all are *condiscipulos*, whereas in Caesarius's case no one's faith is styled that way, faith becomes not the doorway to understanding but a kind of closure to it, and the conceptual possibilities for any theory of *condiscipuli* seem obliterated. One might be able to compare this to the "dumbing down" of preaching and political rhetoric sometimes noted as a characteristic of our own time.

84. As, perhaps, at *S.* 212–13, but even here the Augustinian teaching is mediated through Faustus of Riez.

85. Brown, *Augustine of Hippo*, p. 9.

Monastic Formation and Christian Practice: Food in the Desert

Blake Leyerle

W ithin decades of the emperor Constantine's own momentous shift in religious allegiance (312 C.E.), the language of conversion was itself transformed. No longer indicating an abandonment of a prior faith in favor of
Christianity, "conversion" now meant a turn toward a more radical commitment to the Christian life: the adoption of a monastic vocation. From this linguistic shift we can know that by the late fourth century it was the monk who
bodied forth most clearly the lineament of a truly Christian life.[1] This was a life
that was subject from its outset to the most meticulous scrutiny: even the simplest gesture was understood to manifest virtue — or its lack.

Monasticism as a kind of formation is peculiarly bodily; its aim is to
shape the individual body into conformity with a communally determined
ideal. In response to the Gospel teachings, much of this formation is deliberately negative, consisting of a program of silence, fasting, celibacy, and paci-
fism — representing a steadfast refusal to engage in the social spheres of influence, material inducement, kinship obligations, and power brokerage.[2] Yet
the monastic tradition insists that this negative work represents only the first
step in the slow revelation of a positive identity. "Give the body discipline,"
said a Christian to a Manichean, "and you will see that the body is for him

---

1. Peter Brown, "Aspects of the Christianization of the Roman Aristocracy," *Journal of Ro-
man Studies* 51 (1961): 1-11, esp. 5-7; Brown, "The Challenge of the Desert," in *A History of Private
Life*, vol. 1, *From Pagan Rome to Byzantium*, ed. Paul Veyne (Cambridge: Harvard University
Press, Belknap Press, 1987), pp. 287-95.

2. Bruce Malina, *Christian Origins and Cultural Anthropology* (Atlanta: John Knox, 1986),
pp. 185-204.

who made it."[3] Bodies, like arable land, are understood as sites for labor-intensive cultivation.[4] This study will concentrate on only one aspect of this program: matters of orality. I choose the term "orality" because I will argue, among other things, for a link between the refusal to ingest food and drink (i.e., fasting) and the slow incorporation of Scripture.

Monasticism encompasses an enormous range of periods and texts. My attention here will be confined to two early and central monastic groups and bodies of texts: the Egyptian solitaries of Lower Egypt (Nitria, Scetis, and the Cells) and the first generations of the communal monasteries established by Pachomius in Upper Egypt. Whereas the solitaries lived in scattered groupings under no direction other than the informal guidance of the Abbas or "old men," the lives of the Pachomian monks were highly centralized and structured by a growing complex of rules. Despite these obvious social differences, however, the *Sayings* of the solitaries and the *Rules* of the communal monks share a common origin: both textual collections stem from Egypt in the late fourth and fifth centuries. This geographical and temporal proximity lends a richness and balance to the developed model, which can then be extended, with some modification, to other times, places, and institutions.

Focusing on Food

It is difficult to focus on food. We tend to dismiss it as neutral, as simply a matter of fuel, and therefore of trivial importance. Unlike our commitments, which we accept as shaping the persons we are, food seems essentially nondefining.[5]

---

3. Theodora 4, *Apophthegmata Patrum,* in *Patrologia Graeca* (hereafter *PG*), 65:204, translated in Benedicta Ward, *The Sayings of the Desert Fathers* (New York: Macmillan, 1975), p. 83. Cf. Poemen 184, *PG,* 65:568, Ward, p. 193.

4. "This body that God has afforded me," confided Horsiesios, "[is] a field to cultivate, where I might work and become rich." See *Instructions of Horsiesios* 1.6, translated in *Pachomian Koinonia 1-3,* ed. Armand Veilleux (Kalamazoo: Cistercian Publications, 1981-82), 3.138, hereafter *Koinonia.* See the remarks of Peter Brown, *The Body and Society: Men, Women, and Sexual Renunciation in Early Christianity* (New York: Columbia University Press, 1988), pp. 235-40.

5. Roland Barthes, "Toward a Psychosociology of Contemporary Food Consumption," in *Food and Drink in History: Selections from the Annales Economies, Sociétés, Civilisations,* ed. R. Forster and O. Ranum (Baltimore: Johns Hopkins University Press, 1979), 5:167; Deane W. Curtain, "Food/Body/Person," in *Cooking, Eating, Thinking: Transformative Philosophies of Food,* ed. Deane W. Curtain and Lisa M. Heldka (Bloomington: Indiana University Press, 1992), pp. 2-22, esp. 12-13. As Mary Douglas observes, "food is a blinding fetish in our culture." See "Food as a System of Communication," in her *In the Active Voice* (London: Routledge and Kegan Paul, 1982), p. 123.

The antithesis between thinking and eating, in fact, goes back to Plato, who considered it as seemly for a philosopher to be concerned with food and drink as with cobbling.[6] Fasting, however, quite marvelously concentrates one's attention on this neglected subject. And for this reason every monastic tradition lavishes attention on the issue. What kinds of foods one can eat, when, how, and with whom, are all matters of, shall we say, consuming interest.

Beyond such discussions of actual eating practice, early monastic texts often use food as a metaphor for sins seemingly unrelated to the alimentary canal. Consider, for example, Abba Macarius's vision of the devil on his way "to stir up the memories of the brethren." Satan had dressed for the occasion, we are told, in a cotton garment full of holes, from each of which hung a small flask. When Macarius asked the reason for this outfit, Satan replied, "'I am delivering tasty treats to the brethren.' The old man said, 'All those kinds?' He replied, 'Yes, for if a brother does not like one, I offer him another, and if he does not like the second any better, I offer him a third; and of all these varieties he will like one at least.'"[7] Macarius later pays a pastoral call on the lone monk who received Satan gladly. We discover that his favorite flask was that of fornication: hardly an expected foodstuff. If the basic nature of sin is defined as appetitiveness, food is crucial. As something we voluntarily take into ourselves which in turn changes us systemically, food is a particularly apt metaphor for sin: it is not only "good to eat" but also "good to think."[8]

When we turn to the communal literature of Upper Egypt, we are initially tempted to understand the monks' abstinence in primarily economic terms: that they ate simply to husband their resources for works of charity. Certainly some rules explicitly condemn any waste of supplies.[9] But this theory cannot

6. *Gorgias* 462b-465e; cf. *Phaedo* 64a-67b; *Republic* 585a-e. Lisa M. Heldke, "Foodmaking as a Thoughtful Practice" and "Food Politics, Political Food," in *Cooking, Eating, Thinking*, pp. 203-29, 301-27.

7. Macarius 3, *PG*, 65:26, my translation; compare Ward, p. 126. Satan "supplies nourishment to the passion which he sees the soul is slipping toward." See Matoes 4, *PG*, 65:289, Ward, p. 143.

8. A phrase coined by Claude Lévi-Strauss in his *The Savage Mind* (London: Weidenfeld and Nicolson, 1966); it has become a major premise of all structuralist approaches to eating, which have yielded compelling analyses of meal practices. See Roy C. Wood, *The Sociology of the Meal* (Edinburgh: Edinburgh University Press, 1995), esp. pp. 1-45, 112-26. Mary Douglas and Baron Isherwood, *The World of Goods* (New York: Basic Books, 1979), esp. pp. 56-70.

9. Compare the saying of Megethius when asked, "If some cooked food remains over for the next day, do you recommend the brethren eat it? The old man said to them, If this food is bad, it is not right to compel the brethren to eat it, in case it makes them ill, but it should be thrown away. But if it is still good and is thrown away through extravagance in order to prepare more that is wrong." See Megethius 3, *PG*, 65:301, Ward, p. 149. For a series of injunctions against waste, see *Regulations of Horsiesios* 22, *Koinonia*, 2.205. Palladius tells us that monasteries even

adequately explain instances in which a waste of food is consciously mandated. Pachomius, for example, was returning to his home monastery after a round of pastoral visits when he was met by a boy complaining that "from the time you left to visit the brothers until now, they have not cooked either vegetables or porridge for us." The cook, confronted by Pachomius, agrees that he has not prepared any cooked food for two months. After noticing that none of these dishes were eaten, he stopped cooking them so that the monastery should not suffer the unnecessary expense of preparing food simply to be thrown out. Forty measures of oil, apparently, went into the ordinary cooked food of the brothers every month. Reasoning that "one man was sufficient in the kitchen to prepare the small dishes for the brothers, that is, mustard greens with vinegar and oil, garlic and fine herbs," the cook had occupied his time profitably in weaving mats. Pachomius, however, was far from pleased. He took the five hundred mats the cook had made and burned them before his eyes, saying, "Do you not know that when a man has the possibility of looking for something and he abstains from it for God's sake, he will receive a great reward from God; but if he has not such power over a thing and is forced by necessity to abstain from it because he does not have it, he will seek a reward for this in vain? . . . For the sake of eighty measures of oil you have cut off so great a harvest of virtues! . . . Truly I want food cooked every day and set before the brothers in abundance."[10] Even in the frugal communal tradition, the cook's action is seen as a false economy. A certain amount of discarded food is not a waste; instead, it signals the self-mastery of the monks, which is a more important virtue. In similar fashion the solitaries praise occasional indulgence in food when it signals a renunciation of a personal desire to fast: humility is a greater good. But before examining how both eating and not eating articulated communally held values, and so promoted individual and group formation in early monasticism, we must consider the prosaic questions of what particular foods were eaten, as well as with whom, when, and how.

Good to Eat: The Daily Regime

The desert solitaries typically ate once a day, toward evening. Their basic fare was bread, salt, and water, and some took nothing else.[11] Even this simple food

---

raised swine, precisely so that leftovers would not be wasted. See *Lausiac History* 32.10; *Koinonia*, 2.128.

10. *Paralipomena* 15-16, *Koinonia*, 2.36-38.

11. Eulogius 1, *PG*, 65:169-71, Ward, pp. 60-61; Heladius 2, *PG*, 65:173, Ward, pp. 62-63. *Vita Antonii* 7. Sisoes distinguished himself by refusing to eat bread. See Sisoes 52, *PG*, 65:408, Ward,

was eaten in great moderation. Abba Daniel records how every year he took Arsenius a single basket of bread; when he returned a year later, he would be of-fered some of that same bread.[12] Other monastics supplemented their diet with seasonal vegetables and fruit, as well as thin soups made of grains, lentils, or other legumes.[13] Although some practiced extended fasting, the ideal was regu-larity: it was preferable to eat one loaf every day than to fast for two days and then eat two loaves at a sitting.[14] It was by this "quality of balance" that Amma Syncletica could distinguish true asceticism from demonic self-punishment.[15] Everyone accepted, however, that growth in holiness was signaled by an increas-ing desire to fast.[16] Some days were kept as communal fast days.[17] These proba-bly included, but were not confined to, the weekly Friday and Wednesday fasts observed throughout the early church.

As we have seen, an important distinction existed between "cooked" food and all other foods. As a gesture toward greater asceticism, a person might tem-porarily or altogether forgo cooked food.[18] In seeking a reason behind this

---

p. 221; cf. John Colobos 29, *PG,* 65:213, Ward, p. 91. Even this meager diet, however, replicates the binary system of all meals in antiquity, which consisted of grain *(sitos)* and flavoring or sauce *(opson).* See James Davidson, "Opsophagia: Revolutionary Eating at Athens," in *Food in Antiq-uity,* ed. John Wilkins, David Harvey, and Mike Dobson (Exeter: University of Exeter Press, 1995), pp. 204-13. R. J. Forbes, *Studies in Ancient Technology,* 2nd ed. (Leiden: Brill, 1955), 3:98-104. Gildas Hamel, *Poverty and Charity in Roman Palestine, First Three Centuries* C.E. (Berkeley: University of California Press, 1990), pp. 8-56.

12. Arsenius 17, *PG,* 65:92, Ward, p. 11.

13. Soup at the ninth hour, see Macarius 33, *PG,* 65:276, Ward, p. 135; bread and vegetables or foraged green matter, see Arsenius 22, *PG,* 65:93, Ward, p. 12; Dioscurus 1, *PG,* 65:160, Ward, p. 55; Gelasius 6, *PG,* 65:152, Ward, p. 49; Poemen 186, *PG,* 65:568, Ward, p. 193; Abba of Rome/ Arsenius 1, *PG,* 65:588, Ward, p. 209; F. Nau, "Histoires des solitaires Egyptiens (MS Coislin 126, fol. 158 sqq.)," *Revue de l'Orient Chrétien* (hereafter *ROC*) 17 (1912), #343, p. 296, a translation from the Latin text may be found in Helen Waddell, *The Desert Fathers* (Ann Arbor: University of Michigan Press, 1977), pp. 132-33, saying number 22 (hereafter Waddell); lentils, see Dioscurus 1, *PG,* 65:160, Ward, p. 55; Isaiah 6, *PG,* 65:181, Ward, p. 70; Moses 13, *PG,* 65:288, Ward, p. 141; Paul the Great 3, *PG,* 65:381, Ward, p. 205; chickpeas, see Theodore of Pherme 7, *PG,* 65:189, Ward, p. 74; fruit, see Arsenius 16, *PG,* 65:92, Ward, p. 11; Isaac 10, *PG,* 65:225, Ward, p. 101; Joseph of Panephysis 5, *PG,* 65:229, Ward, p. 103; Sarah 8, *PG,* 65:421, Ward, p. 230.

14. The ideal was "a dry and even diet." See *Anonymous Sayings* 1.4, Sources chrétiennes (hereafter SC), 387.102, Waddell, 62.4; cf. Evagrius 6, *PG,* 65:176, Ward, p. 64; Megethius 2, *PG,* 65:301, Ward, p. 149; Pambo 2-3, *PG,* 65:368-69, Ward, p. 196; Poemen 31, *PG,* 65:329, Ward, p. 171.

15. Syncletica 15, *PG,* 65:426, Ward, pp. 233-34.

16. Ares 1, *PG,* 65:132-33, Ward, p. 34; Dioscorus 1, *PG,* 65:160, Ward, p. 55; Serapion 1, *PG,* 65:413-16, Ward, p. 227. An inability to fast is a sign of demonic possession (Nau 354, *ROC* 17.300).

17. Sisoes 15, *PG,* 65:396-97, Ward, p. 215; Silvanus 1, *PG,* 65:408, Ward, p. 222.

18. *Anonymous Sayings* 8.26, SC, 387:416, Waddell, 137.54. "Macarius heard from some that the Tabennesiots eat their food uncooked throughout Lent, so he decided that for seven years he

practice, we might initially suppose it to be an endorsement of rawness: a refusal to utilize the cultural apparatus for processing food. Upon inspection,
however, "cooked food" emerges as a conceptual category rather than a
straightforward description,[19] for bread, despite its method of preparation,
does not fall under this heading. The operative distinction may have been one
of warmth, since bread was not only eaten cold but often at such remove from
its baking that it required "softening" in water before it could be eaten.[20] Unlike
the application of heat, softening through immersion in water or brine was acceptable; pickles were an important foodstuff in the communal monasteries.[21]
Some of the solitaries, however, took a stern view even of this kind of juicing up
of dry food. Abba Isaiah was publicly shamed for moistening his heel of bread
with water by Achilles, who called to everyone, "Come, see Isaiah eating sauce
in Scetis."[22] It was, we gather, an unconscionable luxury. But here we move away
from the issue of heat to the more fundamental issue of dryness.

The limitation of fluids emerges as a major preoccupation of this desert literature. Reasons for this range from the philosophical association of dryness
with lightness and spirituality to the more pragmatic concern to minimize the
occurrence of nocturnal emissions.[23] This preference for dryness gave a certain
urgency to any discussion of wine. The solitaries did not drink wine, except on
occasions of illness, travel, or hospitality. Even in these situations, when wine
was not only tolerated but expected, drinking might nevertheless be cause for
later penance. When dining with others, Abba Macarius made a rule for himself
that he would drink for the sake of conviviality, but "for each cup of wine,

---

would eat no food that had passed through fire. He ate nothing except for raw vegetables, if they
could be found, and soaked pulse." See *Lausiac History* 18.1b, *Koinonia*, 2.123.

19. On this topic see Anne Murcott, "Cooking and the Cooked: A Note on the Domestic
Preparation of Meals," in *The Sociology of Food and Eating*, ed. Anne Murcott (Farnborough:
Gower Publishing, 1983), pp. 178-85.

20. *Anonymous Sayings* 4.69, SC, 387:218, Waddell, 72-73.56. Hamel, pp. 12-15.

21. *A Letter of Bishop Ammon* 24, *Koinonia*, 2.93; *Rules* 80, *Koinonia*, 2.159. Theodoret describes the preparation process: they collected vegetables that were growing wild and, putting
them in pots, covered them with as much brine as was sufficient. See *Historia religiosa* 2.4, SC,
234:200.

22. Achilles 3, *PG*, 65:124, Ward, p. 29.

23. *Historia monachorum in Aegypto* 20.2-3, 16. Ps-Aristotle, *De physiognomia* 29, in
Scriptores physiognomic: graeci et latini, ed. Rirch Förster (Leipzig: Teubner, 1893), 1.36; Brown,
The Body and Society, pp. 238-39. "Virtue is noble, dry and hard — sunburnt, with roughened
hands." See Catharine Edwards, *The Politics of Immorality in Ancient Rome* (Cambridge: University Press, 1993), p. 174, cf. 173-206. Hippocratic medicine, to the contrary, stressed the benefits
of moist food; see Elizabeth Craik, "Hippokratic Diaita," in *Food in Antiquity*, esp. pp. 344-45.
David Brakke, "The Problematization of Nocturnal Emissions in Early Christian Syria, Egypt,
and Gaul," *Journal of Early Christian Studies* 3 (1995): 419-60, esp. 439-41 and n. 143.

spend a day without drinking water." He drank so happily that the brothers urged more wine upon him until his disciple pleaded with them, "In the name of God, do not give him any; if you do, he will go and do violence to himself in his cell."[24] The intensity of the old man's pleasure arose, no doubt, from the co-alescence of two goods: the giving up of his own will for the sake of others (which is the essential definition of humility) and the prospect of increased as-ceticism.[25] In general, however, wine was not for monks.[26] This proscription seems to be associated less with our own understanding of alcohol as relaxing than with the perception that it was strong and stimulating: for these very properties, it was suitable for those undertaking a journey or recovering from an illness.[27] Dryness was also prized in communal monasticism, where the brothers were promised that "God will not forget even the saliva that has dried in your mouth as a result of fasting."[28]

Food was more plentiful in the communal monasteries, as apparently every-one knew. A saying attributed to the solitary Poemen records his conversation with the head of a monastery who came asking how he could acquire "the fear of God." Abba Poemen replied laconically, "How can we acquire the fear of God when our belly is full of cheese and preserved foods?"[29] In the *cenobium* the brothers ate their midday meal together; there was also a communal supper, but some either skipped this second meal altogether or made do with some bread in their cells.[30] A typical midday meal might consist of "pickled mustard greens, ol-

---

24. Macarius 10, *PG*, 65:268, Ward, p. 129; while Abba Eulogius had a small bottle of wine to share with visitors, he and his disciples normally drank water mixed with salt water. See Eulogius 1, *PG*, 65:169-72, Ward, pp. 60-61; Abba Isaac mixed ashes into his bread. See Isaac 6, *PG*, 65:225, Ward, p. 100.

25. By doing much the same, Paphnutius converted a whole band of robbers. See Paphnutius 2, *PG*, 65:377-80, Ward, p. 202.

26. Poemen 19, *PG*, 65:325, Ward, p. 169; Peter the Pionite 1, *PG*, 65:376, Ward, p. 200; Xoius 1, *PG*, 65:312, Ward, p. 158; *Anonymous Sayings* 4.63, 4.79, SC, 387:216, 226.

27. For a journey see Xanthias 2, *PG*, 65:313, Ward, p. 159; for sickness see Abba of Rome 1, *PG*, 65:588, Ward, p. 209.

28. *Instructions* 1.16, *Koinonia*, 3.18; "Let those who practise ascesis labor all the more in their way of life, even to abstaining from drinking water, which the dogs enjoy." See *Instruction on the Six Days of the Passover* 4, *Koinonia*, 3.48.

29. Poemen 181, *PG*, 65:365, Ward, p. 192. When Macarius tried to join the *koinonia*, he was at first rebuffed by Pachomius, who said, "you are an old man and cannot practise ascesis!" But when the brothers saw his way of life, they quarreled with the superior, saying, "Where did you get this fleshless man for our condemnation? Either cast him out or know that we are all with-drawing from you." See *Lausiac History*, 18.13-15, *Koinonia*, 2.124-25.

30. *Rules* 79, *Koinonia*, 2.159. "On other days those who want to do so eat after noon and the table is set again at dinner time on account of those who are tired, the old, and the boys, and on account of the very severe heat. There are some who eat a little the second time, others who are

91

ives, cheese made of cow's milk . . . and small vegetables."[31] According to the *Regulations of Horsiesios*, "even if all the brothers need a bit of beer . . . the superior of the community will grant this to them generously and gladly."[32] The brothers also received a three-day ration of sweets as they left the refectory.[33]

The use of oil in the cooked food of the monasteries is particularly striking. Ancient cuisine valued fat. In Diocletian's Price Edict of 301, the most expensive meat is pork, but even its cost is surpassed by lard and grease.[34] Seneca registered, even while ridiculing, this taste when he commented on the pleasure afforded by dishes of meat so fatty that "they almost melt and can hardly retain their own grease."[35] Even the gods shared this preference; had they not, they never would have fallen for Prometheus's deceptive offering of bones wrapped in a thick layer of fat.[36] The Pachomian use of oil thus marks a concession to the taste of the age, all the more striking in view of the extreme aversion to fat evinced by the solitaries. When Abba Benjamin, for example, discovered that he alone of the brethren had extracted "a few drops" of oil from the pint he had received a year ago, he felt, he said, "as ashamed as though I had committed fornication."[37] Pachomius's early formation, indeed, had been with the solitary Palamon, who had an almost pathological reaction to fat. When he saw the special meal Pachomius, at his request, had prepared for Easter, he noticed "a bit of oil" that Pachomius had put into the salt. Thereupon "he struck his face and

---

satisfied with one meal, either at noon or in the evening; and some taste a little bread and then go out. All eat together. Anyone who does not want to go to table receives in his cell only bread with water and salt, either daily or every other day, as he wishes." See *Rules* 5, *Koinonia*, 2.143. Each one is to be permitted to eat and drink "according to his strength." See *Lausiac History* 32.2, *Koinonia*, 2.126. The brothers knew when to come to table by the letter their house was assigned: a particular letter might come at the sixth, seventh, eighth, ninth, or eleventh hour, others in the late evening, and still others only once every other day. See *Lausiac History* 32.11, *Koinonia*, 2.128.

31. *Lausiac History* 32.11, *Koinonia*, 2.128 (accepting Norman Russell's emendation of "pickled" for "mixed" [*The Lives of the Desert Fathers* (Kalamazoo: Cistercian Publications, 1980), p. 128 n. 3]). Missing from this list is "animals' feet"; these are problematic as most testimony asserts the vegetarianism of the community. The same list, without the feet, appears elsewhere. See *Bohairic Life* 59, *First Greek Life* 55, *Koinonia*, 1.78, 335.

32. *Regulations of Horsiesios* 49, *Koinonia*, 2.215.

33. *korsenelia* (*Rules* 37, *Koinonia*, 2.151; *First Greek Life* 25, *Koinonia*, 1.374).

34. *Corpus inscriptionum latinarum* 3.806, translated in *An Economic Survey of Ancient Rome*, ed. Tenney Frank (Baltimore: Johns Hopkins University Press, 1940), 5.307-421.

35. *Moral Epistles* 110.13, trans. Richard Gummere, Loeb Classical Library 273 (adapted). See Mireille Corbier, "The Ambiguous Status of Meat in Ancient Rome," *Food and Foodways* 3 (1989): 234-37.

36. Hesiod, *Theogony* 538-41, with thanks to Andrew McGowan for reminding me of this episode and its relevance.

37. Benjamin 1, *PG*, 65:144, Ward, p. 43.

said, 'My Lord was crucified for me and am I to eat that which would give strength to my flesh! . . . but for the holy sanctuary lamp and the work with bristles, I would not have tolerated that creature, oil, in my cell.'"[38] Although Pachomius later endorsed, as we have seen, the use of oil in the preparation of his community's food, he himself seems to have spurned it. Even in his final sickness, when Theodore brought him some "very good [i.e., fatty] broth" so that he might eat it, he asked for a jug of water. "When it was brought to him, he poured some water into [the broth] which he stirred with his hand until the oil that was in it was emptied out."[39]

Manners and Hospitality

On how to eat, the solitary ascetics are reticent, perhaps not surprisingly, since the question of manners is a social one. Where we read of rituals of deference and sharing, it is in the context of communal gatherings. Apparently when they gathered to eat, some order of seniority or importance was observed. Peter the Pionite tells of a time he was invited to "go to the table of the senior brethren."[40] It was also customary for a junior monk to serve the elders. The old men praised Alonius for getting up to serve, but scolded John Colobos for allowing an elder to serve him.[41] Common meals, however, were not to become an occasion for strife. In this case this prohibition was directed against attempts not to grab more or better food but to use the meal as a showcase for one's ascetic restraint, as when one abstemious brother refused to share in the common soup, pointedly chewing a single dried chickpea.[42]

Proper decorum demanded a soberness of demeanor: laughter and smiling were inappropriate.[43] Theodore, however, provides us with the only real instruction on manners: "One day Abba Theodore was entertaining himself with the brethren. While they were eating, they drank their cups with respect, but in silence, without even saying, 'Pardon.' So Abba Theodore said, 'The monks have

---

38. *Bohairic Life* 11, *Koinonia*, 1.33-34; "eating oil, drinking wine, eating cooked meats are something quite unknown among us [monks]." See *Bohairic Life* 10, *Koinonia*, 1.31. Like strengthening wine, oil was appropriate for the sick; see *Bohairic Life* 44, *Koinonia*, 1.68.

39. *The Life of Saint Pachomius and His Disciples* 61, *Koinonia*, 1.81.

40. Peter the Pionite 3, *PG*, 65:377, Ward, p. 201.

41. Poemen 55, *PG*, 65:336, Ward, p. 174; John Colobos 7, *PG*, 65:205, Ward, pp. 86-87.

42. *Anonymous Sayings* 8.27, SC, 387:418, Waddell, 95.22; "Do not make a name for yourself by saying, 'I do not participate in the assembly' or 'I do not eat the common meal *(agape)*.'" See *Anonymous Sayings* 8.14, SC, 387:410, Waddell, 94.11.

43. *Anonymous Sayings* 3.16, 3.41, 3.51, SC, 387:156, 174, 178.

lost their manners and do not say "Pardon."'"[44] It is hard to understand the rationale for this custom. It may be that they felt a need to apologize for drinking at all, even as we would apologize for some lapse in bodily decorum, like sneezing. While occasionally unavoidable, it nevertheless signals an embarrassing failure of control. Other sayings support a concern for even pale impressions of greediness or need.[45]

If manners, as a topic, are in short supply, there is no dearth of information about hospitality. Indeed, a willingness to share food marks the boundary of the community.[46] When one old man received a few dried figs, he sent them to another brother, who in turn sent them to another, until they had gone around all of Scetis. But because they were poor specimens, no one took them to Abba Arsenius, who had once lived very luxuriously. When he learned how he had been excluded, however, Arsenius refused to join the brothers at prayer, saying, "You have cast me out by not giving me a share of the blessing which God had given the brethren and which I was not worthy to receive."[47] The obligation to share one's food could be carried to extremes: during a famine, when Abba Sisoes found a couple grains of barley in a lump of camel dung, "he ate a grain and put the other into his hand. His brother came and saw him in the act of eating and said to him, 'Is this charity, to find food and to eat it alone without having called me?' Abba Sisoes said to him, 'I have not wronged you, brother, here is your share which I have kept in my hand.'"[48] Many sayings speak against judging a brother's regime by the kind of food and drink he sets before his guests. When monks ate together, their fare was usually superior to their daily food. Others, like Abba Sisoes, were vigilant that outsiders not be deceived. When some visitors excused his unwelcoming silence on the grounds of prolonged fasting, he immediately replied that he ate when the need arose.[49]

The celebration of community through eating was reinforced ritually in a common meal held weekly after the Sunday prayer service. In this agape, at

44. Theodore 6, *PG*, 65:188, Ward, p. 74.

45. Visitors from Egypt were scandalized at the voracity of the monks after fasting. See Nau 242, *ROC* 14.363; cf. Simon 2, *PG*, 65:412-13, Ward, p. 225.

46. Wood, esp. pp. 46-79.

47. Arsenius 16, *PG*, 65:92, Ward, p. 11. Food given to one monk would be shared with the others; it could also be left at the church. See Achilles 2, *PG*, 65:124, Ward, p. 29; John Colobos 1, *PG*, 65:204, Ward, p. 86. Zeno recycled the gifts he received. See Zeno 2, *PG*, 65:176, Ward, pp. 65-66.

48. Sisoes 31, *PG*, 65:401, Ward, pp. 218-19.

49. Sisoes 21, *PG*, 65:400, Ward, p. 217; cf. 16, *PG*, 65:397, Ward, p. 215; Theodore of Pherme 28, *PG*, 65:196, Ward, p. 78.

least a piece of bread and a cup of wine were distributed to each of the brethren.[50] Communal fasting also reinforced group solidarity. When an order had gone out into Scetis to "Fast this week," the brothers were scandalized to see smoke rising from Abba Moses's cooking fire. Later they were edified to discover that he had had company: even on fast days, hospitality took priority over individual asceticism.[51]

In the communal tradition, where the regular practice of eating together marks the shift from solitary to communal life, we discover an abundance of material on manners.[52] Table manners were to be taught by the housemasters. No one was to talk or laugh while eating; a system of signs alerted the server to whatever was required. The use of a hood assured the privacy of each eater. "While eating they shall cover their heads with their hoods, so that a brother may not see his brother chewing. Nor shall one talk while eating or cast his eyes anywhere besides his own plate or table."[53] This discreet covering allowed monks to mime eating without being detected.[54] Regardless of whether one intended to eat or abstain, one's presence was required: arriving late for a meal was grounds for punishment.[55] No one, moreover, was ever to help himself to food or drink: food was always to be received from another, as a gift.[56] Other rules detail how a monk should dress for table: "He shall sit with all modesty and meekness, tucking under his buttocks the lower edge of the goat skin which hangs over his shoulder down his side, and carefully girding up his garment — that is, the linen tunic without sleeves called *lebitonarium* — in such a way that

50. Isaac the Theban 2, *PG*, 65:241, Ward, p. 110; Isaiah 4, *PG*, 65:181, Ward, p. 69. Cf. C. Donahue, "The Agape of the Hermits of Scete," *Studia Monastica* 1 (1959): 97-114. For an overview of community issues, see Graham Gould, *The Desert Fathers on Monastic Community* (Oxford: Clarendon, 1993).

51. Moses 5, *PG*, 65:284, Ward, p. 139. Cf. Matoes 6, *PG*, 65:292, Ward, p. 143; Sisoes 15, *PG*, 65:396-97, Ward, p. 215; *Anonymous Sayings* 4.77, SC, 387:224, Waddell, 73.64. Nau 284-85, 288, *ROC* 14.374, 375. Arsenius punished himself for failure in hospitality. See Arsenius 34, *PG*, 65:101, Ward, p. 16.

52. Philip Rousseau, *Pachomius: The Making of a Community in Fourth-Century Egypt* (Berkeley: University of California Press, 1985), p. 60. As Brown comments, "By the end of the fifth century, ascetic literature had developed a code of deportment for novices that was quite as meticulous as had been the code once propounded to young Christians by Clement of Alexandria" (*The Body and Society*, p. 249).

53. *Lausiac History* 32.6, *Koinonia*, 2.127. Cf. *History of the Monks in Egypt* 3.2, *Koinonia*, 2.121; *Rules* 29-30, *Koinonia*, 2.150.

54. *History of the Monks in Egypt* 3.1, *Koinonia*, 2.121.

55. *Rules* 30-34, *Koinonia*, 2.150.

56. *Rules* 38, *Koinonia*, 2.151; of ministers: *Rules* 35, 41, 53, *Koinonia*, 2.151, 155; of cooks: *Rules* 44, *Koinonia*, 2.152; of agricultural laborers: *Rules* 71, 73-77, *Koinonia*, 2.158-59; of travelers: *Rules* 64, *Koinonia*, 2.157.

it covers his knees."[57] Sitting on one's goatskin may have reduced wear on the tunics, and since the monks wore nothing beneath the tunic, modesty may inform the prescription that tunics not ride up above one's knees. Uniformity, however, may have been an equally important goal. Each monk went with his "house" to table; no monk was to go in to eat before the signal was given.[58] Within the houses a strict order of precedence reigned: whoever had first entered religious life would also be the first to "stretch out his hand at table" and to take Communion in church.[59] This general arrangement, however, was subject to rearrangement by the housemaster, who enjoyed precedence by virtue of his authority.

When Abba Anoub decided to live a common monastic life with his brothers, his first administrative act was to appoint one brother to make and serve all the meals, while simultaneously forbidding the others to say, "Bring us something else another time" or "We do not want to eat this."[60] When Theodore responded to a housemaster, who was urging him to take some more cheese, by saying, "I will not," Pachomius protested: "What is this word you have said . . . ? Even if you do not wish to take some, say, 'I wish none now' but take some and lay it down."[61] How and where a monk should sit, and how he should make his needs known, are all specified. Meals emerge from Pachomius's *Rules* as a primary location for instilling the corporate sense that marks organized monasticism.

Unlike the solitaries, who were hospitable, the communal monks did not permit strangers to the community to eat with them. If there were guests, they took their meals separately at the guest house.[62] Even foodstuffs from outside the monastery were treated with circumspection. If a visitor brought a gift of food for a particular brother, it was to be received by the porter, who would see that the brother for whom it was intended got a single portion.[63] If some family emergency compelled a monk to return to his village, he was to take his own provisions. If circumstances compelled him to share in meals outside the monastery, he was "by no means . . . [to] do this in the house of his parents or relatives."[64]

---

57. *Rules* 2, *Koinonia*, 2.145.

58. *Rules* 90, *Koinonia*, 2.161.

59. *Rules* 3, *Koinonia*, 2.142; cf. *Rules* 1, 30, 130, *Koinonia*, 2.145, 150, 165.

60. Anoub 1, *PG*, 65:129, Ward, p. 33.

61. *Tenth Sahidic Life*, frag. 3, *Koinonia*, 1.452.

62. *Rules* 50, *Koinonia*, 2.153.

63. *Rules* 53, *Koinonia*, 2.154-55.

64. In part, this regulation aimed at the same regularity of food praised by the solitaries. See *Rules* 54, 64, *Koinonia*, 2.155, 157.

Among the solitaries the substances consumed were the focus; among communal groups, as is evident from these regulations, style is what counted. Pierre Bourdieu argues that codes of manners correlate closely with people's relationship to animal nature and their primary needs. A commitment to stylization represents a denial of "the crudely material reality of the act of eating and of the things consumed" as well as of "the basely material vulgarity of those who indulge in the immediate satisfactions of food and drink."[65] In their own way, therefore, the Pachomian rules bespeak an asceticism as austere as that of the solitaries. Instead of limiting specific foodstuffs, they impose drastic restraints on the structure of the meal. Their code insists simultaneously on conformity to, and order within, the group, and the isolation of that group from surrounding society. These monks express their asceticism in their disposition rather than in their meal. In both solitary and communal monastic traditions, food provides a way of expressing group belonging. In this sense it is "good to think." But there is more to be said about the moral formation involved in eating and not eating. Why did monastic formation center so firmly on food?

Good to Think: Autonomy

As a substance that passes through the barrier of our bodies not once but twice, food threatens to erode the boundaries of an autonomous self. Orifices, as points of vulnerability, demand vigilance.[66] Brothers who seemed to exercise no control over their mouths were described as houses lacking doors: open to plunderers.[67] Indeed, the monastic regime can be understood as a systematic attempt to master oneself and secure these "doors." When Pambo asked Anthony for a rule of life, he was told simply, "control your tongue and your stomach."[68] Images of warfare convey the intensity of this effort.

To fast is to struggle. As a choice made over and over again, fasting, how-

---

65. Pierre Bourdieu, *Distinction: A Social Critique of the Judgement of Taste,* trans. Richard Nice (Cambridge: Harvard University Press, 1984), p. 196.

66. Mary Douglas, *Natural Symbols: Explorations in Cosmology,* 2nd ed. (New York: Pantheon Books, 1982).

67. Anthony 18, *PG,* 65:81, Ward, p. 5; Nau 270 (*ROC* 14.371), Waddell, 110.43. "A brother asked Abba Tithoes, 'How should I guard my heart?' The old man said to him, 'How can we guard our hearts when our mouths and our stomachs are open?'" See Tithoes 3, *PG,* 65:428, Ward, p. 236. During Lent, Poemen said one should close not "the wooden door but the door of our tongues." See Poemen 58, *PG,* 65:336, Ward, p. 175.

68. Anthony 6, *PG,* 65:77, Ward, p. 2; cf. Poemen 62, 178, *PG,* 65:337, 365, Ward, pp. 175, 191.

ever rigorous, is quite distinct from starvation. Unavoidable deprivation cannot express the triumph of one's will. Whenever Arsenius learned that a variety of fruit was ripe, he would ask for some to be brought to him; after tasting the smallest piece, we are told, he gave thanks to God and put it away.[69] This behavior is noteworthy on at least two counts. First, his abstinence is not rooted in any denigration of the goodness of creation: following the scriptural injunction of 1 Timothy 4:3, everything is to be eaten with thanksgiving. Second, his abstinence is not a matter of dull habituation: he exercises his taste only to deny it satisfaction. Real asceticism depends upon the presence of desire. The same triumph of control, of dictating the shape of one's body, is expressed in our own day by both the bodybuilder and the anorexic.[70] The two are more similar than we believe. Despite the actual peril to health posed by the prolonged fasting of anorexia, the dominant reported experience is one of a sense of strength, even invulnerability. The ascetics of the desert expressed a similar self-perception in metaphors of transformation. They spoke longingly of "becoming flame." As a light, hot element, fire is a suitable metaphor for matters of the spirit, but fire is also a devouring substance. Those who achieve this transformation are often described as having fire pouring from their mouths.[71] It is hard to imagine a purer image for the triumph over hunger.

Modern studies on the effects of famine, as well as anorexia, have drawn our attention to the close physiological connection between eating and sexuality. Below a certain caloric intake, sexual desire decreases dramatically.[72] This

69. Arsenius 19, *PG*, 65:92, Ward, p. 11.

70. Susan Bordo, "Anorexia Nervosa: Psychopathology as the Crystallization of Culture," in *Cooking, Eating, Thinking*, pp. 39-40. On the monastic desire for self-control, see Aline Rouselle, *Porneia: On Desire and the Body in Antiquity*, trans. Felicia Pheasant (Oxford: Basil Blackwell, 1988), pp. 160-78, esp. 163-64.

71. Macarius 33, *PG*, 65:277, Ward, p. 135; Isaiah 4, *PG*, 65:181, Ward, p. 69. From the fingertips: Joseph 6, 7, *PG*, 65:229, Ward, p. 103; in general: Arsenius 27, *PG*, 65:96, Ward, p. 13; John Colobos 14, *PG*, 65:208, Ward, p. 88; Mark the Egyptian 1, *PG*, 65:304, Ward, pp. 150-51; Sisoes 9, *PG*, 65:393, Ward, p. 214; Theodore of Pherme 25, *PG*, 65:193, Ward, p. 77; *Anonymous Sayings*, 135, 211, 254, 622; *Vita Antonii* 82. In community matters, however, the goal was to become stone (Anoub 1, *PG*, 65:129, Ward, p. 33; Poemen 198, Ward, p. 194, Greek text in J.-C. Guy, *Récherches sur la tradition grècque des Apophthegmata Patrum*, Subsidia Hagiographica 36 [Brussels, 1962], 30.11), or iron (Euprepius 4, *PG*, 65:172, Ward, p. 62), or like the dead (Macarius 23, *PG*, 65:272, Ward, p. 132; Nau 384, *ROC* 18.143). There is some suggestion that monks might engage in fasting in order to see visions: Doulas said privation of food, if combined with silence, "makes the interior vision keen." See Doulas 1, *PG*, 65:161, Ward, p. 55; cf. Macarius 33, *PG*, 65:276-77, Ward, p. 135. But to the pagan priest's question, "Since you live like this, do you not receive any visions from your God?" Olympius answered, "No." See Olympius 1, *PG*, 65:313, Ward, p. 160; cf. Poemen 132, *PG*, 65:356, Ward, p. 186.

72. A. Keys, J. Broněk, et al., *The Biology of Human Starvation* (Minneapolis: University of Minnesota Press, 1950), 2:839-53, cf. 905-18.

fact was well appreciated by the desert solitaries, who valued diminished desire as a palpable sign of their reclamation of a prefall innocence. When a brother was scandalized to hear one of the old men say that he was never troubled by sexual fantasies, the old man explained: "Since the time that I became a monk, I have not satisfied my desire for bread, water, or sleep; and the yearning that pestered me for these things did not allow me to feel the war of which you speak."[73] The young Pachomius was pestered by demons "in the form of naked women" only when he sat down to eat his bread.[74] Years later, when he heard about the well-appointed tables of the urban anchorites in Alexandria, Pachomius knew with abundant clarity that it was only a matter of time before their sexual impurity would be revealed.[75]

Fasting also puts food firmly in its place. In monasticism this place is peripheral. When Abba Pior was asked why he always walked while eating, he said, "I do not want to make eating an occupation, but something accessory."[76] A certain forgetfulness thus marks the true ascetic. To his disciple's invitation, "Abba, get up, and let us eat," Sisoes replied, "Have we not eaten, my child? . . . If not, bring the food, and we will eat."[77] In the subsistence economy of ancient Egypt, this is striking behavior. While supermarkets facilitate our alienation from the fact that eating, like sowing and reaping, is an agricultural act and food the result of a labor-intensive process,[78] the rural environment of the desert Christians would have kept these facts before their eyes. By choosing to live on as little food as possible, they attenuated their connection — their responsibility, as they would have seen it — to those who made the food possible. Their fasting marks a rejection of surrounding society or, more precisely, of the bonds of reciprocity that bind others, in a particularly obvious way, in an agricultural, subsistence economy.[79] Self-sufficiency is a strong motif among the sayings. Even adventitious provisions are to be rejected, as we gather from the

---

73. *Anonymous Sayings* 5.36, SC, 387:274-76, Waddell, 80.31. Put most succinctly: "gluttony is the mother of fornication." See *Anonymous Sayings* 4.80, SC, 387:226; cf. Daniel 2, *PG*, 65:153, Ward, p. 51; John Colobos 4, *PG*, 65:205, Ward, p. 86; Benjamin 1, *PG*, 65:144, Ward, p. 43. Lustful monks could be described as "drunk": *Anonymous Sayings* 5.4, SC, 387:244.38-41, Waddell, 74-75.4. For early ascetic thought on sexuality and its relationship to food, see Theresa M. Shaw, *The Burden of the Flesh: Fasting and Sexuality in Early Christianity* (Minneapolis: Fortress, 1998), pp. 53-78; Brown, *The Body and Society*, pp. 213-40; Rouselle, pp. 160-78.

74. *Bohairic Life* 21, *Koinonia*, 1.45.

75. *Bohairic Life* 89, *Koinonia*, 1.119-20.

76. Pior 2, *PG*, 65:373, Ward, p. 199; cf. Nau 146 (*ROC* 13.50).

77. Sisoes 4, *PG*, 65:392, Ward, p. 213.

78. Wendell Berry, "The Pleasures of Eating," in *Cooking, Eating, Thinking*, p. 374.

79. Peter Brown takes a somewhat different view, stressing the ongoing temptation of food; he agrees, however, that food is central in this literature. See *The Body and Society*, esp. 218-21.

story of a disciple finding a small green pea on the road. He wondered aloud whether to pick it up. But the old man, "looking at him with astonishment, merely asked, 'Was it you who put it there?'"[80] Other sayings voice the principle of autonomy even more tersely: Abba Nisterus declared forthrightly, "I would not ask anyone for anything."[81]

In their business practices they adamantly refuse not only to engage in the process of bargaining, but also to allow anyone to purchase things they do not need. When Poemen, for example, discovered that a merchant had purchased his ropes simply in order to do him a favor, he was outraged. He ordered his servant to hire a camel and bring back the work of his hands. For, the saying explains, Abba Poemen "did not want to receive anything from anyone ever, on account of the trouble it causes." When, after great labor, the ropes were returned to him, Poemen "rejoiced as though he had found a great treasure."[82] This treasure was, of course, his own autonomy. In contrast to this assertion of radical separation from surrounding society, the desert fathers' willingness to accept food from one another strikingly underscores their commitment to their own community.

The Morality of Meat

No society treats food as mere nutritional matter. This is an issue of morality: we ourselves claim that it is "not right" to eat dogs, rats, grubs, and a host of other substances. They are not "food" for us; they cannot properly become part of who we are.[83] Those who violate these taboos place themselves outside our

---

80. Agathon 11, *PG*, 65:112, Ward, p. 22. Cf. Abba Zeno punishing himself for rationalizing his desire to take a cucumber by saying, "Truly it is only a little thing." See Zeno 6, *PG*, 65:177, Ward, p. 66. A brother astonished a farmer by asking if he could eat an ear of wheat while harvesting the field. See Isaac 4, *PG*, 65:225, Ward, p. 100. Macarius grieved over the memory of having eaten a fallen fig as a child. See Macarius 37, *PG*, 65:297-80, Ward, p. 136. On the related issue of finding a lost coin: John the Persian 2, *PG*, 65:237, Ward, p. 108.

81. Nisterus 4, *PG*, 65:308, Ward, p. 155; Pambo claimed, "Since I came to this place of the desert and built my cell and dwelt here, I do not remember having eaten bread which was not the fruit of my hands." See Pambo, *PG*, 65:369, Ward, p. 197. To a monk who had traveled far to fetch fresh bread for a sick brother, the old man said, "It is my brother's blood," and refused to eat it. See *Anonymous Sayings* 348 (*ROC* 17.298). Anthony rejoiced that with his own garden "he would be annoying no one" to bring him provisions. See *Vita Antonii* 50.

82. *Anonymous Sayings* 6.15, SC, 387:324, Waddell, 84-85.11. Poemen 10, *PG*, 65:324, Ward, p. 168 ("lampwicks" according to Gould). No bargaining when selling goods, see Agathon 16, *PG*, 65:192, Ward, p. 77.

83. See Curtain, p. 9.

society and are subject to gestures of revulsion and avoidance. Antiquity was particularly attuned to the moral qualities of certain foodstuffs. An anonymous Jewish author living in Alexandria in the first century before our era expatiated upon the moral qualities of animals. He considered that the book of Leviticus, by proscribing certain animals, was protecting the Jews from acquiring undesirable character traits. Whoever ate a weasel, for example, was ingesting the essence of malicious, backbiting slander.[84]

The desert fathers are known for their scrupulous avoidance of meat. Nowhere is this more patent than in its breach: several sayings describe monks in the awkward social position of either being offered meat or of discovering that a dish they had already eaten contained meat.[85] Whether they eat it out of respect for hospitality or reject it on principle, the clear message is that monks differ from other people in their choice of vegetarianism. Outside of cities, eating meat in antiquity was a rare luxury for all but the very wealthy.[86] For most people the consumption of meat was limited to those few festive occasions when cautious private restraint was dropped in favor of communal celebration. Where eating meat celebrates group bondedness, any refusal to join in marks a pointed rejection of not only the festivities but also any ties to that community.

Eating meat was also, in a way we must struggle to recall, intimately and unavoidably connected with violence.[87] To eat meat was to participate in this violence, as Hilarion knew when he refused some chicken with the words, "Forgive me, but since I received the habit, I have not eaten meat that has been killed." Epiphanius, however, quickly countered, "Since I took the habit, I have not al-

---

84. *Letter of Aristeas* 165-66; cf. Plato, *Phaedo* 81e-82a; Aristotle, *Hist. Animal.* 71.588a; Galen, *On Hygiene* 6.664; Vivian Nutton, "Galen and the Traveller's Fare," in *Food in Antiquity,* pp. 359-70. For patristic examples, see the work of Patricia Cox Miller, "'Adam Ate from the Animal Tree': A Bestial Poetry of the Soul," "Origen on the Bestial Soul: A Poetics of Nature," and "The Physiologus: A Poesis of Nature," in her *The Poetry of Thought in Late Antiquity: Essays in Imagination and Religion* (Aldershot, England: Ashgate, 2001), pp. 23-25, 35-59, 61-73.

85. Epiphanius 4, *PG*, 65:164, Ward, p. 57; Theophilus 3, *PG*, 65:200, Ward, p. 81; Poemen 170, *PG*, 65:364, Ward, p. 190. While rejecting meat, they might occasionally eat fish. See Gelasius 3, *PG*, 65:148-49, Ward, p. 47; Pistus 1, *PG*, 65:372-73, Ward, p. 198.

86. Hamel, pp. 9, 19-21. Within cities "cookshops," taverns, and even wandering vendors might provide poorer people with the opportunity of eating meat. See Corbier, esp. pp. 224-34; Justin J. Meggitt, "Meat Consumption and Social Conflict in Corinth," *Journal of Theological Studies,* n.s., 45 (1994): 137-41.

87. This, of course, remains the case. See Peter Singer, "Becoming Vegetarian . . . ," in *Cooking, Eating, Thinking,* pp. 172-93; Julia Twigg, "Vegetarianism and the Meanings of Meat," in *The Sociology of Food and Eating,* pp. 18-30; Catherine Osborne, "Ancient Vegetarianism," in *Food in Antiquity,* pp. 214-24. For a discussion of the ancient philosophical objections to meat-eating, see Johannes Haussleiter, *Der Vegetarismus in der Antike,* Religionsgeschichte Versuche und Vorarbeiten 24 (Berlin: Alfred Toepelmann, 1935).

lowed anyone to go to sleep with a complaint against me, and I have not gone to rest with a complaint against anyone."[88] The effectiveness of his point, which Hilarion acknowledged, lies in its extension of the avoidance of oral violence: Epiphanius's mouth is innocent of causing harm not only to animals but also to humans. Hurtful words could indeed be seen as a kind of cannibalism, as in Abba Hyperechius's striking advice that it is "better to eat meat . . . [than] to eat the flesh of one's brothers through slander."[89] When Achilles was found spitting blood out of his mouth, we discover that its source was an angry word against a brother that "became like blood" in his mouth.[90] The avoidance of meat, therefore, is in service of a wider formation in nonviolent behavior. Meat in its origin is connected with violence, and as a foodstuff, it feeds the passions particularly.[91]

By rejecting meat, monastics not only separate themselves from villagers who eat meat when they can, but they express their understanding of commonality with the animals. Anthony spoke reasonably to some wild beasts and persuaded them to stop devastating his garden; Amoun enlisted the help of some serpents; Helle that of a crocodile; and yet other animals came to the holy men for healing.[92] These stories suggest an attempt to recapture a time before hu-

88. Epiphanius 4, *PG*, 65:164, Ward, p. 57. Real fasting is to cease slandering or condemning others. See J 741, Lucien Regnault, trans., *Les Sentences des pères du désert* (Sablé-sur-Sarthe: Solesmes, 1985), p. 317; cf. *Bohairic Life* 116, *Koinonia*, 1.170-71. No mortification is more difficult than "to get up from the table when still hungry, and to do our hearts violence so as not to say a disagreeable word to a brother." See *Ethiopian Collection* 14.17, *Sentences des pères du désert: nouveau recueil*, trans. L. Regnault (Sablé-sur-Sarthe: Solesmes, 1970), p. 317. On the competitive aspect of this exchange, see Maud Gleason, "Visiting and News: Gossip and Reputation-Management in the Desert," *Journal of Early Christian Studies* (1998): 501-21.

89. Hyperechius 4, *PG*, 65:429, Ward, p. 238. It is better to eat meat than to be inflated with pride. See Isidore 4, *PG*, 65:236, Ward, pp. 106-7; *Anonymous Sayings* 8.26, SC, 387:416, Waddell, 137.54. Pachomius receives an angelic vision that good men sometimes die suffering, because "they resemble cooked meat that still needs to be cooked a little longer before it is eaten." See *Bohairic Life* 82, *Koinonia*, 1.109; he later tells a parable likening scurrilous speech to ill-mannered guests breaking dishes and eating with ingratitude at a banquet. See *Bohairic Life* 105, *Koinonia*, 1.147. In Artemidorus's second-century dream book, analysis of dreams of meat eating merges imperceptibly into dreams of cannibalism. See *Oneirocritica* 1.70, in Robert J. White, trans., *The Interpretation of Dreams* (Park Ridge, N.J.: Noyes Press, 1975), pp. 52-53.

90. Achilles 4, *PG*, 65:125, Ward, p. 29. Also described as "smoke." See Nau 372 (*ROC* 18.140). Taking advantage of another brother's labor could also be described as eating "his blood." See Nau 348 (*ROC* 17.298).

91. Porphyry, *On Abstinence* 1.31-38.

92. *Vita Antonii* 50. Nau 333, *ROC* 17.210; Amoun and Helle, *History of the Monks in Egypt* 9.5; 12.5, 7; Abba Bes similarly persuaded a hippopotamus and crocodile. See *History of the Monks in Egypt* 4.3. Antelope, wild asses, gazelles, and other animals delighted in Abba Theon. See *History of the Monks in Egypt* 4.6. Macarius healed the blind cubs of a hyena. See *History of the Monks in Egypt* 21.16; cf. Bessarion 12, *PG*, 65:141-43, Ward, p. 42; Paul 1, *PG*, 65:380-81, Ward, p. 204.

man beings were alienated from the animals: a regression that was also an anticipation of a new Eden. The desert Christians rejected the categories of their contemporaries (which are also our own). These relegate animals under the heading of essentially other and therefore suitable for our use, indeed exploitation.[93] The wider social ramifications of this conceptual view are clear in Aristotle, who, when thinking schematically, could consider an ox the same as a slave.[94] Such casual exploitation of animals bespeaks a deep acceptance of hierarchy, that the strong are right, simply because of their strength, to make use of the weak however they see fit. In contrast, the desert Christians align themselves voluntarily with the weak: for them, animals are not "good to eat."[95] Their relationship to animals is deliberately nonhierarchical; like secular people, animals are different but not other.

Reasons for controlling one's mouth in the ingestion of food, however, cannot finally be divorced from the other principal use of the mouth: to speak.[96] How does language figure into the monastic concern over orality?

Eating the Word

Carolyn Bynum has recently drawn scholarly attention to medieval women ascetics, some of whom practiced extraordinary, nearly unbelievable, feats of fasting. She has pointed out that the miraculous closure of their bodies was often accompanied by equally miraculous exusions of oil or milk.[97] The early desert ascetics also understood themselves to be sources of nourishment. "Open your

93. Shaw, *Burden of the Flesh*, pp. 161-219. See also my forthcoming essay, "Monks and Other Animals," in the Festschrift for Elizabeth A. Clark.

94. *Politics* 1252b.

95. See the comments of Hamel, pp. 44-52; implicitly, Rouselle, pp. 160-78, esp. 163-64. Pachomius fasted in solidarity with those suffering from famine. See *Bohairic Life* 100, *Koinonia*, 1.137. If indeed the Pachomian monastics occasionally ate meat (see n. 31), it would be in keeping with their pervasive commitment to hierarchy.

96. Jerome H. Neyrey, "Ceremonies in Luke-Acts: The Case of Meals and Table Fellowship," in his *The Social World of Luke-Acts: Models for Interpretation* (Peabody, Mass.: Hendrickson, 1991), esp. pp. 368-71.

97. Carolyn Walker Bynum, *Holy Feast and Holy Fast: The Religious Significance of Food to Medieval Women* (Berkeley: University of California Press, 1987), esp. pp. 260-77. Like the medieval women, some of the desert Christians were widely known for their curative powers. These were not accessed through bodily fluids, but sometimes involved their food. One particularly fascinating story describes how a demon-possessed boy was healed by eating some of the monastic bread. The demon showed great perspicacity in discerning fragments of the bread hidden in dates, cheese, or ordinary bread, and carefully picked them out; eventually he was fooled by porridge made out of its crumbs. See *Bohairic Life* 44, *First Greek Life* 44, *Koinonia*, 1.68, 328-29.

mouth," Poemen invited, "and I will fill it with good things."[98] The food they had to offer, however, was metaphorical, as Ephrem's dream clarifies, in which he saw a vine "laden with beautiful fruit" growing out of his tongue.[99] What did they mean by this language?

While Scripture occasionally describes the word of God as something to be eaten and as tasting sweet (Pss. 34:8; 119:103; Ezek. 3:1-4), it was the Greco-Roman tradition that elaborated this metaphor until every aspect of literary endeavor, from composition to delivery and reception, could be described in alimentary terms. So widely was education accepted as "a process of nourishment and assimilation"[100] that Philo, a first-century Alexandrian Jew, could move easily from the dietary code of Leviticus privileging ruminant animals to an endorsement of students diligently repeating their lessons.[101] The same associative transition occurs in one of the anonymous sayings of the desert: "'The clean animal has a cloven hoof and chews the cud' (Lv. 11:3). We then who have truly believed and received the two Testaments ought to chew good food and not bad. Beneficial food consists of the good thoughts supplied by the tradition of the holy fathers and the reading of Scripture. On these the soul of one who loves God must continually meditate. Bad food, on the other hand, consists of the impure thoughts inspired by demonic attacks."[102] If this emphasis on the orality of the acquisition of knowledge seems strange to us, we must recall that reading in late antiquity was always done aloud: the difference between reading to oneself and to others was simply a matter of projection. Only the realization that reading, like eating, was an action done visibly with the mouth makes sense of Pachomius's otherwise bizarre advice to his monks: "Open your mouth . . . so that your eyes see and you read the characters well."[103] Unlike the eating of

---

98. Poemen 8, *PG,* 65:324, Ward, p. 167; cf. Rufus 2, *PG,* 65:392, Ward, p. 211. For fascinating parallels with the black church's use of food metaphors for preaching, see Jualynne E. Dodson and Cheryl Townsend Gilkes, "There's Nothing Like Church Food," *Journal of the American Academy of Religion* 63 (1995): 534-35.

99. Ephrem 1, *PG,* 65:168, Ward, p. 59; cf. *Vita Antonii* 54; *Historica monachorum in Aegypto* 7, *Patrologia Latina,* 21:416BC.

100. Emily Gowers, *The Loaded Table: Representations of Food in Roman Literature* (Oxford: Clarendon, 1993), pp. 41-42. Quintilian, for example, recommended that readers assimilate texts in the same way they chew and digest food. See *Institutio oratoria* 10.1.19. Further citations in J. C. Bramble, *Persius and the Programmatic Satire* (Cambridge: Cambridge University Press, 1974), pp. 45-59. Michel Jeanneret, *A Feast of Words: Banquets and Table Talk in the Renaissance* (Chicago: University of Chicago Press, 1991), pp. 131-39.

101. *The Special Laws* 4.100-115, esp. 106-7; cf. *Letter of Aristeas* 153-55.

102. *Anonymous Sayings* J 676 N 645, *Les Sentences des pères,* p. 289.

103. Pachomius, *Letter* 2.3, *Koinonia,* 3.52. Harry Y. Gamble, *Books and Readers in the Early Church* (New Haven: Yale University Press, 1995), pp. 203-4.

food, however, the ingestion of Scripture was an unambiguous good. Abba Titoue deserves only praise for being "fattened like suet on the mercies of God."[104]

This understanding that Scripture should be taken internally appears most clearly, if also paradoxically, in what seems initially to be a rejection of Scripture. In a number of sayings, elders reprimand brothers for possessing Bibles.[105] The reason given is sometimes one of expense. Books in antiquity were valuable and therefore open to criticism as the kind of possessions a true monk should sell in order to follow the Gospel.[106] But expense is not the whole story. More often the owning of books is rejected on the basis of exteriority. Real scriptural knowledge is a matter of possessing the word inwardly rather than keeping it bound on a shelf.[107] Even demons, after all, can recite Scripture.[108] Living out of Scripture is the issue, as Abba Gelasius demonstrated when his expensive, leather-bound Bible was stolen. The dealer to whom the thief presented the book brought it back to Gelasius for an estimate of its worth. Handling the familiar volume, he simply averred that it was indeed beautiful and well worth the price. When the thief heard that Gelasius had seen the Bible and not betrayed him, he was filled with compunction and tried to return it. The old man, however, would not take it back. He was persuaded to do so only when the thief begged him, saying that otherwise he would have no peace.[109] Gathered into this brief story is the complex relationship of the solitaries to Scripture. It is prized by them, but not as an object. In an oral culture such as theirs, spoken words, which remain "evanescent, powerful, and free," have clear priority over the inert "thingness" of the written

---

104. *First Greek Life* 79, *Koinonia*, 1.351.

105. Possession of books: a leather book worth eighteen pieces of silver which was kept in the church for common use, see Gelasius 1, *PG*, 65:145, Ward, p. 46; books of parchment, see Ammoes 5, *PG*, 65:128 Ward, p. 31; "three good books," see Theodore 1, *PG*, 65:188, Ward, p. 73; a Psalter and a copy of the New Testament epistles, see Serapion 1, *PG*, 65:413-16, Ward, pp. 226-27; a copy of Genesis, see Agathon 22, *PG*, 65:116, Ward, p. 23; the "reading of books" as desirable, see Bessarion 12, *PG*, 65:144, Ward, p. 42; cf. Epiphanius 8, *PG*, 65:165, Ward, p. 58.

106. *Anonymous Sayings* 6.6-7, SC, 387:318, Waddell, 140.70; Nau 392 (*ROC* 18.144), Waddell, 106.94; Nau 385 (*ROC* 18.143); N541, *Sentences des pères*, 199; Serapion 2, *PG*, 65:416, Ward, p. 227, Nau 228 (*ROC* 14.361).

107. Nau 228, *ROC* 14.228. Douglas Burton-Christie, *The Word in the Desert: Scripture and the Quest for Holiness in Early Christian Monasticism* (New York: Oxford University Press, 1993), pp. 111-16. Antiquity in general understood a reliance on books as gravely inferior to memorized knowledge; see Mary Carruthers, *The Book of Memory: A Study of Memory in Medieval Culture* (Cambridge: Cambridge University Press, 1990), esp. pp. 16-45. For Anthony, "memory took the place of books" (*Vita Antonii* 3).

108. *Vita Antonii* 25.

109. Gelasius 1, *PG*, 65:145-48, Ward, p. 46.

word.[110] Gelasius needs no text to tell him to forgive someone who has wronged him; because he has made Scripture his own, he has no need of a book.[111]

Only long apprenticeship could drive this kind of knowledge deep into one's body.[112] Since instruction, like other forms of overt discipline, belongs to the cenobitic and hierarchical way of life, teaching among the solitaries is by example.[113] Even in the most provocative situations, the old men seldom allow themselves more than a terse "Watch yourself."[114] Monks learned by watching and then internalizing the "enscriptured" way of life of the Abba. It was a kind of reading. Abba John summed up the pedagogical ideal in his deathbed reflection that he had never taught anything which he had not previously carried out.[115] Some disciples, however, found the lack of explicit instruction extremely frustrating:

> Abba Isaac said, "When I was younger, I lived with Abba Cronius. He would never tell me to do any work, although he was old and tremulous; but he

110. Walter Ong, *Orality and Literacy: The Technologizing of the Word* (London and New York: Methuen, 1982), esp. pp. 31-77.

111. Since true knowledge was embodied, Anthony knew immediately that a woman claiming to have learned both the New and the Old Testament by heart was lying, since she could not admit that honor and shame, loss and gain, her parents and strangers, poverty and abundance were all alike to her. See N 518, *Sentences des pères*, pp. 189-90. When a brother was upset to discover that his newly copied book had omissions, the scribe responded by telling him, "Go and practise first that which is written, then come back and I will write the rest." See Abraham 3, *PG*, 65:132, Ward, p. 34. Cf. Arsenius 6, *PG*, 65:89, Ward, p. 10.

112. Ong, p. 9. Cf. Burton-Christie, pp. 77-95.

113. "To instruct your neighbor is the same thing as reproving him," see Poemen 157, *PG*, 65:360, Ward, p. 189; "Be their example, not their legislator," see Poemen 174, *PG*, 65:364, Ward, p. 191. Speaking Scripture, of course, also implied authority, as when a secular, asked to "say a word" to the brothers, replied, "I do not know how to speak of the Scriptures; so I will tell you a parable." See Poemen 109, *PG*, 65:348-49, Ward, p. 182; cf. *First Greek Life* 118, *Koinonia*, 1.380. Peter Nagel, "Action-Parables in Earliest Monasticism: An Examination of the *Apophthegmata Patrum*," *Hallel* 5 (1977-78): 251-61 (which is not, however, as helpful as one would hope). Teaching by example was also prized in the monasteries. Of Pachomius it was said that "even when he kept silent, [the brothers] saw his conduct and it was for them a word." See *First Greek Life* 25, *Koinonia*, 1.312. See the comments of Claudia Rapp, "Story-Telling as Spiritual Communication in Early Greek Hagiography: The Use of Diegesis," *Journal of Early Christian Studies* 6 (1998): 431-48.

114. Ammonas 10, *PG*, 65:121-24, Ward, p. 28; Waddell, 103.44, *Anonymous Sayings* 5.43, SC, 387:288.48-50, Waddell, 82-83.38.

115. Cassian 5, *PG*, 65:245, Ward, p. 114; cf. Pambo 197, *PG*, 65:440, Ward, p. 194; Psenthaisius 1, *PG*, 65:436-37, Ward, p. 245; Syncletica 12, *PG*, 65:425, Ward, p. 233; Or 7, *PG*, 65:440, Ward, p. 247. Burton-Christie, esp. pp. 150-60.

himself got up and offered food to me and to everyone. Then I lived with Abba Theodore of Pherme and he did not tell me to do anything either, but he himself set the table and said to me, 'Brother, if you want to, come and eat.' I replied, 'I have come to you to help you, why do you never tell me to do anything?' But the old man gave me no reply whatever. So I sent to tell the old men. They came and said to him, 'Abba, the brother has come to your holiness in order to help you. Why do you never tell him to do anything?' The old man said to them, 'Am I a cenobite [official] that I should give him orders? As far as I am concerned, I do not tell him anything, but if he wishes he can do what he sees me doing.' From that moment I took the initiative and did what the old man was about to do."[116]

Like the food itself, Cronius and Theodore set the Gospel action of serving others before their disciple; it is then up to him to take and "eat" it as needed.[117]

It was not always possible, however, to avoid instruction. Fellow monks as well as outsiders came asking the holy men and women, "What shall I do?" But even when asked directly "for a word," they rarely quote Scripture.[118] Instead, they prefer to speak in parables of their own making. Poemen thus replied to a question "on the subject of impure thoughts" by saying, "It is like having a chest full of clothes, if one leaves them in disorder they are spoiled in the course of time."[119] Occasionally these comparisons are strikingly close to Scripture, as when one brother complained to Poemen about the misdeeds of another. "The old man looked at the ground and picked up a small piece of chaff. 'What is this?' he asked him. 'Chaff,' said the brother. Then directing his attention to the roof of the cell, the old man said to the brother, 'Concentrate on the fact that your sins are like this beam, while those of your brother are like this bit of chaff.'"[120] At other times elders prompt scriptural memory by acting out a Gospel moral.[121] Abba Zacharias responded to Moses' question, "What should I do?" by taking off his hood and trampling it under his feet, commenting that "the man who does not let himself be treated thus, cannot become a monk."[122] These gestures could be even more elaborate. When Abba Moses was invited to

---

116. Isaac, Priest of the Cells 2, *PG*, 65:224, Ward, pp. 99-100; cf. "Is it not enough simply to have seen the fire?" See Isaiah 6, *PG*, 65:181, Ward, p. 70.

117. To listen was thus to "feed oneself through the ears." See Zeno 8, *PG*, 65:177, Ward, p. 67; Theodore was "thirsty" for Pachomius's words and "fed eagerly" on the words of God. See *Bohairic Life* 91, *First Greek Life* 50, *Koinonia*, 1.122, 331; cf. *Fragments from Pachomius* 4.2, *Koinonia*, 3.88.

118. *Pace* Burton-Christie, pp. 107-9.

119. Poemen 20, *PG*, 65:328, Ward, p. 169; cf. Anthony 21, *PG*, 65:81-84, Ward, p. 6.

120. Nau 391, *ROC* 18.144, my translation; compare Waddell, 102.37.

121. On the visual aspect of memory in antiquity, see Carruthers, pp. 16-45.

122. Zacharias 3, *PG*, 65:180, Ward, p. 68.

a council convened to condemn a brother, he first refused to go. When sent for again, he went, but not unprepared. "Taking a round loosely plaited basket, he filled it with sand and lifted it onto his back. Those who had come out to meet him asked, 'What is this, Father?' The old man said to them, 'My sins are running out behind me and I do not see them; yet today I have come to judge the shortcomings of another.'"[123] On other occasions they prefer to prescribe actions reminiscent of a parable. When an old man of Scetis, who was "very austere of body, but not very clear in his thoughts," stopped coming to Abba John Colobos because he was ashamed of repeatedly forgetting his advice, John said to him: "'Go and light a lamp.' He lit it. [John] said to him, 'Bring some more lamps and light them from the first.' He did so. Then Abba John said to the old man, 'Has the first lamp suffered any loss from the fact that other lamps have been lit from it?' He said, 'No.' The old man continued, 'So it is with John; even if the whole of Scetis came to see me, they would not separate me from the love of Christ.'"[124] None of these teachings are without scriptural parallel, and, as Douglas Burton-Christie has so clearly shown, these monks were far from ignorant of Scripture. Why then does Poemen not simply quote Jesus' words about the speck of dust and the beam (Matt. 7:3)? Why does Moses not repeat the scriptural injunction against judging? Why do they prefer this indirect mode of instruction?

A reverence for Scripture, to be sure, makes them cautious. Moses and Poemen may well have recognized the culpable irony of quoting "Judge not," even while passing judgment. Scripture was not to be bandied about lightly. If younger monks had to talk, they were advised that it was safer for them to confine their remarks to the sayings of the Fathers.[125] But the elders took a different position on Scripture. For them the ability to adapt a message to an occasion, visible in this production of "alternative" parables, testifies to the degree to which they have made Scripture their own. Like food, written words only become useful once they have been metabolized, that is to say, memorized. In antiquity memorization meant more than a simple facility in retrieval, but an active ability to rearrange and adapt the material learned.[126] By

---

123. Moses 2, *PG*, 65:281-84, my translation; compare Ward, pp. 138-39. Cf. Anthony 21, 29, *PG*, 65:81-84, 85, Ward, pp. 6, 7; Bessarion 7, *PG*, 65:141, Ward, p. 42; Joseph 2, *PG*, 65:228, Ward, p. 102; Pior 3, *PG*, 65:373-76, Ward, p. 199; *Draguet fragment* 1.3, *Koinonia*, 2.111. Ong comments that knowledge in oral cultures tends to be, among other things, "close to the human lifeworld," "agonistic," "empathetic and participatory rather than objectively distanced," "situational rather than abstract," and has "a high somatic content." See Ong, pp. 42-67.

124. John Colobos 18, *PG*, 65:209-12, Ward, p. 89 (altered).

125. Amoun 2, *PG*, 65:128, Ward, pp. 31-32; cf. Poemen 8, *PG*, 65:321-24, Ward, p. 167.

126. Carruthers, pp. 24-31. Macarius 3, *PG*, 65:261. Sexual thoughts could be compared to a

taking the leaking basket on his shoulder, Moses is not only prompting the brethren's memory of Gospel lessons about forgiveness but he is also demonstrating the extent to which he has taken to heart the example of Jesus. By having the old man light many lamps from a single lamp, Abba John not only reminds him about patience and loving-kindness, he makes visible the welcoming Christ. Such parabolic actions are, therefore, not only gestures of humility but also assertions of authority. By this internalized command of Scripture, the elders are embodying Abba Paul's recommendation: "Keep close to Jesus."[127]

This language of "command of Scripture," however, needs further modulation, again based upon the analogy between eating food and "eating" Scripture. While it may appear that the task of a monk is to take Scripture in by mouth and break it down so that it becomes part of himself, the reality is the opposite. It is the word that grasps the monastic, breaks her down and makes her part of Scripture. This process of incorporation is startlingly similar to a contemporary theory of the Eucharist: unlike ordinary food consumed to become part of one's own flesh, when one eats the Eucharist, one is broken down to become part of the body of Christ. In similar fashion, these sayings suggest that the solitary ascetics understood themselves not as consuming, but rather as consumed by, Scripture. Rather than consuming, the solitary ascetic is ideally consumed by Scripture.[128]

In the communal monastic tradition, the role played by Scripture is less nuanced and complex than among the solitaries. Unlike the Abbas who fret over the cost of Bibles and the concept of any monk's "ownership" of Scripture, in Pachomian monasticism books occupy an accepted and unambiguously good position. The *Rules* indeed mandate that all monks be literate. If anyone enters not knowing how to read, he is to receive instruction three times a day, "very studiously" and "with all gratitude."[129] Books are available from the li-

---

book that when willingly taken into oneself became indelibly fixed. See *Anonymous Sayings* 5.38, SC, 387:278.

127. Guy, p. 32, Ward, p. 205; cf. *Anonymous Sayings* 2.31, SC, 387:140.

128. Ambrose, *Concerning the Christian Faith* 4.118-35; *Concerning the Mysteries* 9.50-58. The Torah is often identified with bread. See Peder Borgen, *Bread from Heaven* (Leiden: Brill, 1965), pp. 99-114, 127-30. Compare the angel's promise to Abba John that he will receive abundantly "the bread of heaven, that is [Jesus'] word and wisdom." See *History of the Monks in Egypt*, Rufinus's addition, 13.7-8. Burton-Christie draws attention to a parallel in modern theological studies that "we not only read a text but 'are read' by it" (see Burton-Christie, pp. 23, 258), but does not note that this is taken directly from the literary theorist Stanley Fish. See *Is There a Text in This Class: The Authority of Interpretive Communities* (Cambridge: Harvard University Press, 1980), esp. pp. 21-67.

129. *Precepts and Institutes* 139-40, *Koinonia*, 2.166; Rousseau, *Pachomius*, p. 81.

brary in each house, and are supplied upon request.[130] In turn, the brothers are to look after their books, remembering to fasten them shut after use and return them to their proper shelf.[131] This positive stress on reading, however, remains ultimately in the service of memorization. The precept stating that "there shall be no one whatever in the monastery who does not learn to read" continues, "and does not memorize something of the Scriptures."[132] Memorization was valued for allowing Scripture to be constantly to hand and heart; while monks went about their communal work, the word of God was to occupy their mouths.[133] Behind this program lies, in part, the same hope of transformation celebrated by the solitaries,[134] but now wedded to the distinctively Pachomian concern with the creation of disciplined bodies. By describing the "word of God" as the "food of life," the *Rules* ensure that a monk would no more chatter while meditating than talk at table with his mouth full.[135] When Pachomius wanted, accordingly, to ensure "silence" at the kneading troughs, he enjoined that "no man should speak in the bakery, but all should recite God's word together."[136]

Scripture and food, therefore, both play an important role in communal self-definition. Among the Pachomian monks Scripture, like food, was much more plentiful. Perhaps for this very reason the relationship between Scripture and food seems less inflected than among the solitaries. Only, it would seem, in situations of relative deprivation in which eating becomes a preoccupation, can an understanding of Scripture as a type of food develop. If it is true, moreover, that, in Mary Douglas's words, "gastronomy flourishes best where food carries the lightest load of spiritual meanings," the spare and monotonous diet of the solitaries provided a perfect environment for symbolic elaboration. Thus from the Pachomian monasteries we have a relatively rich literary record: several *Lives* of Pachomius and his successors, letters, *Rules,* and *Precepts.* Such unproblematic abundance seems entirely in keeping with the more plentiful

130. *Precepts and Institutes* 2, *Koinonia,* 2.170. Monks were not to borrow books from other houses without permission. See *Precepts and Laws* 7, *Koinonia,* 2.182.

131. *Rules* 100-101, *Koinonia,* 2.162; *Rules* 25, *Koinonia,* 2.149.

132. *Rules* 140, *Koinonia,* 2.166; *Regulations of Horsiesios* 16, *Koinonia,* 2.202. Ong points out, however, that even small acquaintance with literacy makes a tremendous difference in thought processes. See Ong, pp. 50-57, 78-116.

133. *Rules* 3, 28, 60, 116, 142, *Koinonia,* 2.145, 150, 156, 163, 166; *Lausiac History* 32.12, *Koinonia,* 2.129; *Fragments* 2.2, *Koinonia,* 3.86; Rousseau, pp. 87-104, esp. 103.

134. Pachomius claimed that his monks were to be like grapevines, which when afflicted yield "only the sweetness of the word of God written in the Scriptures." See *Bohairic Life* 187, *Koinonia,* 1.228; *First Greek Life* 140, *Koinonia,* 1.397. See also Rousseau, *Pachomius,* pp. 103-4.

135. *Regulations of Horsiesios* 15, *Koinonia,* 2.202; *Fragments* 4.2, *Koinonia,* 3.88.

136. *Bohairic Life* 77, *Koinonia,* 1.100; *Regulations of Horsiesios* 44-47, *Koinonia,* 2.212-14.

and varied food of these communal monasteries. From the solitaries, however, we have only a scattering of unelaborated *Sayings,* many of which themselves explicitly counsel silence. Yet the symbolic freight of these words is much greater. The terse genre appears to reproduce in small their meager but sustaining fare.[137] In this way attitudes toward food have formed not simply bodies or even entire communities, but actually types of literature.

Conclusion

In conclusion, matters of orality — both food and words — play a central role in early monastic formation. Through fasting, individual monks laid claim to a holiness that depended, in part, upon visible control. We see this equation of holiness and abstinence in a story told of Abba Simon, who, when he wanted to be left in peace by a visiting magistrate, grabbed a hunk of bread and cheese and sat in the doorway gnawing it. Such undisciplined indulgence had the intended effect: the magistrate took one look and turned on his heel, saying in disgust, "Is this the anchorite of whom we have heard so much?"[138] Reputation demanded abstinence.

Abstinence from meat, however, carried additional meaning. For meat, in a subsistence economy, marked not only a rare departure from grain-based nutrition, but also an inevitable connection with violence. The monastic refusal to eat meat proclaimed a commitment to oral nonviolence. As monks would not place the result of violence in their mouths, so they also avoided wounding words: eschewing a rebuke, an Abba might find himself spitting blood from his mouth.

The ascetic commitment to such forms of fasting set the monks apart from their surrounding society, which was, like all agrarian societies, tied to the rhythms of the land. Among the villagers periods of fasting were imposed from without and, if prolonged, were a matter of dread and despair; the abundance of harvesttime, on the other hand, was cause for feasting and celebration. In this context the voluntary seasonless fasting of the monks proclaimed their self-sufficiency from the land and from the village. At the same time, it strengthened the cohesiveness of their own group, a cohesiveness they celebrated in gestures of hospitality, all the more gracious for the typical meagerness of fare. No matter how austere the regular regime, when monastic guests came, each monk

---

137. On the connection between the slender table *(mensa tenuis)* and the slender style *(genus tenue)* of Latin authors like Horace, see Gowers, pp. 42-44.

138. Simon 2, *PG,* 65:412-13, Ward, p. 225.

would set forth the best he had, dressing his lentils with oil, soaking additional loaves and setting forth a beaker of thin wine.

In the communal monasteries the use of food was rather different. In these large collectivities food was plentiful. The discipline of the *Rules* focused not on individual self-transcendence but rather on the formation of a disciplined society. Assertions of individualism were punished. Among these men and women, the act of eating received new value. Every fold of cloth and gesture at table was carefully scrutinized. A style of commensality served to mark identity. Rank at table also affirmed group hierarchy and status. Yet for all this stress on solidarity, abstention from food remained such a good that, we gather, an overabundance of cooked food was regularly set before the Pachomian monks so that they might demonstrate a mastery over desire.

Among both the solitaries and the communal monks, the sustained practice of fasting liberated their mouths to recite Scripture, which they understood as a kind of eating. Like food, Scripture was to be internalized once ingested. Written words — even those of Scripture — were only useful once they had been metabolized. Proof of this process was evident in the production of "alternative" parables in which the Abbas adapted the scriptural message to a particular situation. But if like food in the manner of acquisition, Scripture is unlike food in its metabolism. Whereas ordinary food, once eaten, becomes the flesh of the eater, ingested Scripture reverses this process: as the monk takes in Scripture, it gradually assimilates the body of the monk to its own essence. Solitaries celebrated this ideal by praising those who had made their inside exactly like their outside.[139] While a similar goal animates the communal rules, it is subdued to the all-consuming pursuit of discipline.

Transformation remains the goal of all monastic formation. Thus despite the harsh deprivations to which monastics subjected their bodies, we would be mistaken to see this program as entirely negative. Ideally in this tradition the body forms a privileged vehicle for the slow revelation of a positive identity.[140] It is, indeed, only this optimism about the body's capacity for holiness that separates orthodox fasting from heretical self-hatred. As the Christian said to the Manichean: "Give the body discipline, and you will see that the body is for him who made it."

---

139. Poemen 63, *PG*, 65:337, Ward, p. 175; cf. Poemen 164, *PG*, 65:361, Ward, p. 189; Anthony 15, *PG*, 65:80, Ward, p. 4.

140. Brown, *The Body and Society*, pp. 223-37.

THE MIDDLE AGES

Faith Formation in Byzantium

Stanley Samuel Harakas

O ne of the most influential dimensions of Eastern Christianity was its incarnational ethos. This concrete yet universal vision meant that Eastern Christianity sought to incarnate its universal message and way of life in the specific realities of language, thought, architecture, art, literature, and law. So also, the approach to the education and formation of people of faith within the Eastern Orthodox Christian tradition is essentially incarnational in character, expressing itself in a wide range of means and methods. The present study will select several aspects of the formation of Christian persons and highlight one in each of four different historical periods. The first section will provide a brief description of formal education and religious instruction. The second section will trace the development of worship by examining a series of services designed to incorporate the young into the Christian community. The third section, which primarily focuses on the issues raised in the iconoclastic controversies from 725 to 842, will examine the role of ecclesial architecture and of the icon. The fourth section will treat those practices and teachings related to the formation of the spiritual and moral life, using the Lenten and Holy Week services to highlight formative practices related to the Bible, monastic and ascetic life, fasting, prayer, and liturgical participation.

Formal Education and Religious Instruction
(Fourth and Fifth Centuries)

Historically and theologically the church was ambivalent about secular knowledge and its relationship to the Christian faith. Knowledge that drew on ancient philosophers, historians, scientists, language studies, and above all rhetoric was described as "foreign" or "Hellene," i.e., classical pagan culture. The culture identified itself as Christian, so that education was based on the Scriptures. The ongoing Christian tradition is often referred to in the sources as "our *paideia*," in other words, Christian learning. Elementary education, called *propaideia* (i.e., preliminary learning) or sometimes "elementary education," focused on the learning of letters *(grammata)*, that is, reading and writing. The instructors were called *didaskaloi* or pedagogues, while the institutions themselves were known as "schools of letters" or "places for the formation of children" *(paideutēria)*. They were all private in character and could be located in the homes of rich and aristocratic families. This formal education began anywhere between six and nine years of age. Elementary or preliminary education in reading and writing the Greek language was accompanied by instruction in "the precepts of piety." In Christian circles pagan texts were replaced by scriptural texts and hymns.

Secondary education was known simply as *paideia*. The full course, called "general" or *engyklios paideusis*, was studied from ages ten to eighteen, though not all pupils with elementary education completed it. There was apparently a distinction between general knowledge and higher religious studies, but both were taught to young people. A phrase used by one of the patriarchs of Constantinople speaks of "the study of the divine words and sharing in the learning from without." This "external" education was characterized as "Hellenic wisdom." It consisted of studies in grammar, rhetoric, logic, philosophy, ethics, and the four mathematical disciplines of arithmetic, geometry, music (harmonics), and astronomy. To these might be added shorthand, calligraphy, and poetry.

This system of education proved effective, for an enormous literature was produced in Byzantium. For most of its history this literature was almost exclusively Christian in content and purpose; "Hellenic learning" was at the service of the Christian ethos. Only during the final days of the empire, in the fourteenth century, was there a renewal of what could genuinely be called "secular" learning. For the vast Byzantine period, learning was inspired and formed by Christian beliefs and values.

Liturgical Services of Initiation
(Sixth to Seventh Centuries)

The standard in the pre-Constantinian church was adult baptism, preceded by formal programs of instruction *(katechesis)* and followed by liturgical training in the meaning and significance of baptism, chrismation, and Eucharist. The practice of baptizing the children of Christian parents was not unknown in the earlier period; there is at least circumstantial evidence that children may have been baptized during early New Testament times, in the references to the baptism of whole households.[1] With the Edict of Milan in 313 and the legitimization of Christianity, the older practice of adult baptism and its concomitant adult instruction and formation continued for several centuries but was eventually supplanted by infant baptism.

The assumption in early Christian communities was that a baptized infant or small child would be educated and formed for Christian living in the home. For example, in his "Address on Vainglory and the Right Way for Parents to Bring Up Their Children," John Chrysostom compares the fashioning of the spiritual and moral life of the child to artists who fashion paintings and statues: "To each of you fathers and mothers I say, just as we see artists fashioning their paintings and statues with great precision, so we must care for these wondrous statues of ours."[2] Using the image of the child's soul as a city which must be protected from evil influence and filled with good and upbuilding influences, Chrysostom addresses the various senses of sight, hearing, and taste, describing them as "gates" to the city of the child's soul. For example, speaking of speech, Chrysostom instructs: "Thus this gate will have been made worthy of the Lord, when no word that is shameful or flippant or foolish or the like is spoken, but all beseems the Master. If those who give military training teach their sons from the first to be soldiers and to shoot and to put on military dress and to ride, and their tender years are no hindrance, how much more should those who are soldiers of God assume all this royal discipline? So let him learn to sing hymns to God that he may not spend his leisure on shameful songs and ill-timed tales."[3]

This home-based religious instruction continued to be practiced in Christian homes through subsequent centuries. But religious education and formation in Byzantium were augmented by a socialization process expressed liturgically and sacramentally. The development over many centuries of a series of rites incorporated newborns and infants into the life of the church through a process of liturgical "socialization." Begun modestly and simply — as is the case with nearly all the liturgical forms of the church — over the centuries the rites

---

1. Among the references to baptized households that could be understood as referring to children are the passages dealing with the belief and baptism of Cornelius in Jerusalem (Acts 11:13-18); Lydia in Philippi (16:14-15); the Philippian jailer (16:27-33); the Corinthian ruler of the synagogue, Crispus (18:8); and the household of Stephanus (1 Cor. 1:16).

2. The work was first translated into English as an appendix to M. L. Laistner, *Christianity and Pagan Culture in the Later Roman Empire* (Ithaca, N.Y.: Cornell University Press, 1951). See p. 96 for quote.

3. Laistner, pp. 100-101.

were expanded and "filled in." Ultimately the series consisted of a short service at the bedside of mother and child on the day of birth.[4] On the eighth day following birth, a brief service at the doors of the church was conducted, to give the child his or her Christian name.[5] On the fortieth day the mother and child were "presented to the Lord" through a service reminiscent of the presentation of Jesus at the temple.[6]

The rite at the fortieth day (also known as *Sarantismos*), consisting at present of four prayers, is itself quite old. The oldest textual witness appears in the eighth-century Barberini Codex, which of course represents compilations of earlier texts. This manuscript is the earliest extant Euchologion, or service book, in the Constantinopolitan liturgical tradition. It contains one prayer only for the rite of the forty-day churching. In time the rite was expanded to contain the present form of four prayers, consisting of a couplet of two, the first emphasizing the cleansing of the mother and the second the churching of the infant. The prayer of the Barberini Codex is the third prayer in the present rite. The prayers were said in the narthex of the church, and then the priest took the infant from the hands of the mother and processed into the sanctuary. Three times the priest raised the child up above his head while saying the formula "The servant of God is churched in the name of the Father, the Son, and the Holy Spirit" as the priest proceeded toward the altar area. The child was then brought into the altar area behind the altar screen, around the altar table. Standing before the altar table, with the child lifted up in dedication, the priest recited the closing prayer, Nunc Dimittis. The child was then returned to the mother and father. As an ecclesial act, it was a striking incorporation of the infant child into the social fabric of the worshiping community.[7]

This process of integrating the newborn child was fulfilled in the rites of baptism, chrismation, and first Communion. The rite of baptism in the Eastern Orthodox tradition requires full bodily immersion in a baptismal font. It was,

4. See the liturgical service, "*Euchai eis Gynaika Lecho, te 40e hemera tes gennesews tou paidiou authes.*" *Euchologion to Mega tes Kata Anatolas Orthodoxou Katholikes Ekklesias* (Athens: Astir Publications, Al. & E. Papademetriou, n.d.), pp. 119ff.

5. "*Euche eis to katasphragesai paidion, lambanon onoma, te 8e hemera tes gennevseos autou,*" in "*Euchai eis Gynaika Lecho, te 40e hemera tes gennesews tou paidiou authes,*" p. 121.

6. Luke 2:27. "*Euche eis Gynaika Lecho,*" in "*Euchai eis Gynaika Lecho, te 40e hemera tes gennesews tou paidiou autes,*" p. 122.

7. See J. Goar, *Euchologion Sive Rituale Graecorum*, reproduction of Graz edition (1960), pp. 267-69; Panagiotes Trembelas, *Mikron Euchologian* (Athens, 1950), pp. 266-71; Ioannis Fountoulis, *Apanteseis eis Leitourgikas Aporias* (Thessalonike: Pournaras Publications, 1982), 4.225-36. I am indebted to my colleague on the faculty of Holy Cross Greek Orthodox School of Theology, Rev. Dr. Alkiviadis Calivas, for the above-noted information and references.

and still is, preceded by a service of exorcism and catechesis, in which the sponsor of the child — most often not a relative but a person of the larger ecclesial community — "speaks" for the child in rejecting evil and accepting Christ. The existence of sponsors for persons being baptized is an ancient tradition in the church. In contrast to the sponsor of an adult candidate for baptism, sponsors of infants about to be baptized "spoke for" the candidate, in addition to assuming responsibility as a personal guide in the Christian life.

> *Priest:* "Do you renounce Satan, and all his works, and all his worship, and all his angels, and all his pomp?" (Repeated in the present, then past, tenses.)
> *Response by Sponsor on behalf of child:* "I do reject him." (Repeated in the present, then past, tenses.)[8]

And in an affirmation of commitment to Christ, the following dialogue is likewise repeated in the present, then past, tenses.

> *Priest:* "Do you join Christ?"
> *Response by Sponsor on behalf of child:* "I do join Him."[9]

Variations of this liturgical rite existed in the West also, such as the seventh-century Gelasian Sacramentary, which included texts from much earlier periods.[10] Simply put, the sacrament of baptism "transfers" the new Christian from the dominion of sin, evil, "the Devil and all his angels," to membership in the kingdom of God, where Christ is acknowledged as king and lord. The sacrament of chrismation is the anointing with the Holy Spirit, which looks toward the development of the newly baptized person in the Christian life. A portion of the Orthodox Byzantine prayer at the anointing with the oils of chrismation reads as follows: "keep him/her in your sanctification; confirm him/her in the Orthodox faith; deliver him/her from the evil one and all his devices; preserve his/her soul through your saving fear, in purity and righteousness, that in every work and word, being acceptable before you, *he/she may become a child and heir of your heavenly kingdom.*"[11] There is a future orientation

---

8. *An Orthodox Prayer Book,* ed. N. M. Vaporis (Brookline, Mass.: Holy Cross Orthodox Press, 1977).

9. The Greek is *Syntassei to Cristo,* literally, "Do you place yourself on the side of Christ?" or in military terms, "Do you enlist (to serve) Christ?"

10. See Thomas Finn, *Early Christian Baptism and the Catechumenate: Italy, North Africa, and Egypt* (Collegeville, Minn.: Liturgical Press, 1992), pp. 91ff., esp. 110.

11. *An Orthodox Prayer Book,* pp. 64-65, emphasis mine.

to this prayer that implies development and growth, in accord with the teaching of Orthodox Christianity that the Christian life is growth toward being "God-like" *(theosis)*.

What impact could such rites have on an infant? In what way could these liturgical practices impact on spiritual and moral formation at such an early age? The earliest experiences and memories of the child were inextricably bound with Christian rites, symbols, sounds, taste, smells, and most importantly, with the ecclesial reality. There was no time in the child's memory or experience when he or she was anything but a participating and communicating member of the church. To this day children are incorporated into the baptismal service by participating in the threefold circling around the baptismal font, holding lit candles as the hymn "As many as have been baptized in Christ, have put on Christ" (Gal. 3:27) is sung. As the child matured, he or she became part of that same faith community while observing the priest at the bedside of the mother and the newborn on the day of birth. The growing child in Byzantium saw the midwife bring the eight-day-old infant to the church door for naming,[12] and was itself part of the worshiping community when an infant just a few years younger than himself or herself was brought by its parents to the church for the forty-day public churching.

Along with parental instruction and the special relationship with the sponsor, this full participation in the eucharistic liturgy and dawning recognition of inclusion in the life of the faith community from the first day of life had a deep and abiding formative influence on the child. The child received an identity that in most cases was accepted, adopted as his or her own in an almost unconscious process of integration and socialization into the faith community. To reject such an identification, replete as it was with powerful influences rooted in practically every sense experience, would have demanded for most a radical reversal of character and loyalties.[13] When such profound personal experiences are accompanied by teaching and study about the faith as the child matures, he or she becomes more fully conscious and can reach a level of a more full and willed affirmation. Such faith was affirmed on a regular basis through the inclusion of the creed in the divine liturgy. Just as significantly, nearly every Byzantine liturgical service included a liturgical call for recommitment to

12. John Fountoulis, *Apanteseis eis Leitourgiks Aporias* (Athens: Publications of the Periodical *Ekklesia*, 1967), question 30, 1.63-66.

13. The concepts presented in this section are treated more fully in the context of the "passages of life" in part IV of my book, *Health and Medicine in the Eastern Orthodox Tradition: Faith, Liturgy, and Wholeness* (New York: Crossroad, 1990), with special reference to chap. 11, to which the reader is referred for more discussion, especially regarding the contemporary situation.

Christ: "Let us commit ourselves and one another and our whole life to Christ our God. . . ."

Icons in Worship and Formation
(Seventh to Tenth Centuries)

The setting for Orthodox worship in its corporate dimension is the temple, or church building. Based on the model of the Church of the Holy Wisdom (Hagia Sophia) in Constantinople, built by Emperor Justinian in the sixth century, the dominant architectural style in all of Eastern Orthodox Christianity over the centuries is a domed building whose floor plan is divided into three parts: the narthex or entranceway, the sanctuary where the congregation worships, and the altar area with a screen on which icons are placed — the iconostasis. The Byzantine-style church structure is capped with domes, and the whole is an architectural representation of the Christian understanding of the universe. The great central dome represents heaven; the traditional icon in the dome is Christ the King *(Pantokrator)* looking down upon his people in the sanctuary. The narthex represents those who are not yet believers but are in the antechamber of faith; in monastic churches the traditional icon in the narthex is of the last judgment. On the back wall of the church, behind the altar table, is an apse that serves as a connecting link between heaven and earth (the dome above and the floor below); the traditional icon in the apse is the Mother of Christ holding the Christ child on her lap. This last, an iconic depiction of the Chalcedonian doctrine of the incarnation, proclaims the coming together of the divine and the human. On the iconostasis are icons of Jesus Christ, the Mother of God *(Theotokos)*, John the Baptist, and the patron saint of the church. All these serve to unite heaven and earth, shaping the consciousness and the spiritual state of the worshiping Christians. They bring the world of heaven to the worshiper, and they transport the believer into the realm of the eternal.

In 726, however, Emperor Leo III condemned the use of icons, already widespread in Christian churches; supporters of the icons from Greece then led an attack on this policy in the city of Constantinople. The controversy became a major test of power, authority, and will between the Orthodox Church and the Byzantine state. Powerful support for the place of icons in the church came especially from monks, from the provinces in the western part of the empire, and from the church of Rome. Known as the Iconoclastic Controversy, this struggle about the place of icons in the Christian life lasted until March 1, 843, when a council in Constantinople ended the controversy and affirmed the decisions of the Seventh Ecumenical Council supporting the use and veneration of icons, held in Nicea in 786-87. Subsequently icons were embedded irrevocably in the ethos and life of the church in Byzantium and are inseparably identified with the liturgical life of the Orthodox Church.[14]

The Seventh Ecumenical Council teaches that icons have concurrently an educational and inspirational purpose; they serve both as teaching devices for the unlettered and as "windows on heaven." They are concrete embodiments of the incarnational and transfiguring truths of the Christian faith. In honoring the icon, the honor is passed on to the prototype, that is, to Christ, Mary, or the represented saint. In Byzantine iconography the style does not seek to re-present empirical reality in its this-worldly, fallen, and distorted forms. The goal is to express the fulfilled and transfigured eschatological reality of the heavenly kingdom. This explains the unusual draftsmanship, such as the inverted perspective, the prominence of the open eyes in saintly figures, the lavish use of gold and other precious metals, and a stylized method of depiction. The Acts of the Seventh Ecumenical Council affirm the use and veneration of the icons, "so that through their representations we may be able to be led back in memory and recollection to the prototype, and have a share in the holiness of some one of them."[15]

The dominant approach to icons was expressed most fully by Theodore the Studite (759-826). In his three *Refutations of the Iconoclasts*,[16] the Studite, proceeding from a theologico-philosophical perspective, said little specifically about the formation of a Christian believer. He was concerned with the issue of incarnation and the "Godward" dimension of icons. He emphasized the function of the icon as pointing heavenward, as a "window on heaven," and as a vehicle of transcendent experience. Such an understanding of icons, one that sought to draw the worshiper into a heavenly and transcendent experience, was nonetheless formative, drawing believers into communion with divine realities.

Other supporters of icons drew on a tradition in the church that affirmed their "human-centered," didactic, and instructive potential. John of Damascus (675-749), for example, expressed the view that the icon is the "book of the illiterate,"[17] an aspect of the patristic affirmation of the icon as having didactic pur-

---

14. This paragraph is based on the chronology of church history in Basileios K. Stefanides, *Ekklesiastike Istoria Ap' Arches Mechri Semeron* (Athens: Astir Publishing House, Al. & E. Papademetriou, 1948), pp. 720-21.

15. "The Seventh Ecumenical Council," in *The Seven Ecumenical Councils*, ed. Philip Schaff and Henry Wace, Nicene and Post-Nicene Fathers, 2nd ser., vol. 14 (Peabody, Mass.: Hendrickson, 1994), p. 541.

16. Theodore the Studite, *On the Holy Icons*, trans. Catharine P. Roth (Crestwood, N.Y.: St. Vladimir's Seminary Press, 1981).

17. John of Damascus, *On the Divine Images: Three Apologies against Those Who Attack the Divine Images*, trans. David Anderson (Crestwood, N.Y.: St. Vladimir's Seminary Press, 1980), p. 28.

pose. It is what might be called the "humanward" movement of the icon.[18] It is analogous to the instructive character of the Gospel, especially for those who could not read, as John of Damascus wrote in his *Exposition of the Orthodox Faith:* "The Fathers gave their sanction to depicting these events on images as being acts of great heroism, in order that they should form a concise memorial of them."[19] Similarly the Sixth Ecumenical Council canon required that the full human icon (but not the symbolic representation of Christ as a lamb) be henceforth used "in order to expose to the sight of all, at least with the help of painting, that which is perfect."[20] This view further holds that the icon not only provides instruction and knowledge; it also provokes a human response to the divine, in particular a response of imitation. One purpose of the icon, according to John of Damascus, is to elicit imitation by the viewer of what is pictured in the icon. Referring to the example of the saints, he writes, "Let us raise monuments to them and visible images, and let us ourselves become, through imitation of their virtues, living monuments and images of them."[21] The painted icon can help the human being — the living icon of God — to respond in life and behavior by imitating Christ and the saints whom the painted icon presents.

In his homily "On the Forty Holy Martyrs," the church father Basil compared painting to the persuasive function of rhetoric: "The brave deeds accomplished in time of war are celebrated by both orators and artists. Orators remember them with decorous words; artists with paintbrush and canvas, and both inspire everyone with valor. That which words are to the ear, silent pictures reveal for imitation."[22] In his sermon on the martyr Barlaam, Basil records his personal experience of this impact of the icon. After comparing the feebleness of his own writing with the power of the icon in depicting the courage of a saint, he exclaims, "Would that I may be included in this image, and be united with Christ, the judge of the contest. To him be glory unto ages of ages."[23] Similarly Patriarch Nicephoros of Constantinople (758-829), a defender of the icons, wrote: "[The icon] leads us to the evangelical vision and memory of those things characterized as honorable and venerable." Further, "iconogra-

---

18. See Stanley S. Harakas, "Icon and Ethics," *Orthodoxisches Forum* 4, no. 2 (Munich, 1990): 195-214; Harakas, "Icon and Ethics," *One World* 131 (1987): 12-14.

19. John of Damascus, *Exposition of the Orthodox Faith* 4.16, in Nicene and Post-Nicene Fathers, 2nd ser., 9:88.

20. Canon 82, quoted in John Meyendorff, *Byzantine Theology* (New York: Fordham University Press, 1974), p. 45.

21. John of Damascus, *Exposition of the Orthodox Faith* 15, p. 87. See also chap. 16, "Concerning Images," where he again refers to the emulation and imitation of the saints (p. 38).

22. Quoted in John of Damascus, *On the Divine Images* 1.13, p. 21.

23. John of Damascus, *On the Divine Images* 1.13, pp. 35-36.

phy is functionally instructive"; it is an "educational visual aid."[24] Christians, according to Patriarch Nicephoros, "by looking at the painted images, bring to mind the valiant deeds of those who served God with all sincerity and [are thus] incited to rival the glorious and ever-memorable exploits, through which they exchanged earth for heaven."[25]

In his three *Homilies on the Divine Images*, John of Damascus also high-lights the role of the icon in eliciting imitation toward virtue. He writes: "Things which have already taken place are remembered by means of images, whether for the purpose of inspiring wonder, or honor, or shame, or to encourage those who look upon them to practice good and avoid evil."[26] In a striking personal passage, the Damascene gave witness to the impact of icons on his own formation: "I bow down before the images of Christ, the incarnate God; of our Lady, the Theotokos and Mother of the Son of God; and of the saints, who are God's friends. In struggling against evil they have shed their blood; they have imitated Christ who shed his blood for them by shedding their blood for him. I make a record of the prowess and sufferings of those who have walked in his footsteps, that I may be sanctified and set on fire to imitate them zealously."[27] In another passage the Damascene affirms the formative and educative value of icons: "[Icons] are a source of profit, help, and salvation for all, since they make things so obviously manifest, enabling us to perceive hidden things. Thus, we are encouraged to desire and imitate what is good and to shun and hate what is evil."[28]

Russian Orthodox theologian Leonide Ouspensky has specially emphasized the formative dimension of the icon. He holds that the theology of the icon presents it as incarnating divine and spiritual realities in wood, paint, color, line, and form.[29] This "Godward" dimension of the icon also becomes, for Ouspensky, "a correct guide for our senses." The icon "is an important educational source." Herein," he says, "lies the essential goal of sacred art. Its constructive role lies not only in the teaching of the truths of the Christian faith, but in the education of the entire man. . . . The content of the icon is, therefore, a true spiritual guide for Christian life and, in particular, for prayer."[30]

24. See John Travis, *In Defense of the Faith: The Theology of Patriarch Nikephoros of Constantinople* (Brookline, Mass.: Holy Cross Orthodox Press, 1984), p. 48.

25. Travis, p. 58, n. 25.

26. John of Damascus, *On the Divine Images* 1.13, p. 21.

27. John of Damascus, *On the Divine Images* 1.21, p. 29 (translation slightly modified).

28. John of Damascus, *On the Divine Images* 3.17, p. 74.

29. Leonide Ouspensky, *Theology of the Icon* (Crestwood, N.Y.: St. Vladimir's Seminary Press, 1978).

30. Ouspensky, p. 53.

"Great Lent" in the Fostering of Spiritual and Moral Life

The final period of Byzantium was marked by a long slow decline, with some bright flashings of learning, spiritual revival, iconographic brilliance, and a flowering of monasticism. Yet the forming of Christian life went forward. Here it is illustrated by Lenten worship, which in crucial ways impresses on believers the essential truths, acts, and attitudes of a believer. The long process of developing liturgically the Lenten worship services in the Orthodox Church was not completed until the end of the empire. This section presents the liturgical book that, to the end of Byzantium, governed the way Orthodox Christians observed and lived the period of preparation for Pascha — the celebration of the resurrection of Jesus Christ. The book containing the liturgical calendar, rituals, practices, observances, spiritual directions, hymns, and prayers for six weeks of public worship during Great Lent is known simply as the *Triodion*. The book takes its name from the unusual number of "odes" in the weekday hymn-canon of the Orthros service (Matins) for the Lenten period, namely, three rather than nine. The purpose of the entire period known as Great Lent is to set a tone of self-examination, repentance, participation in the sacrament of confession, more frequent worship and eucharistic participation, prayer, fasting, spiritual discipline, and liturgical reenactment of the events of the passion and death of Jesus, leading to liturgical participation in Christ's life-giving resurrection. More than any other time of the ecclesiastical year, the *Triodion*'s planned movement and rhythm, its hymnology and the iconography associated with each of the observances, its dramatic services and liturgical reenactments of the passion and death of Jesus Christ contribute to the sense of the organic wholeness of the Lenten season, pointing to the celebration of the victory of Jesus Christ over death, sin, and evil in his resurrection. This essay permits only the most cursory description of Great Lent and Holy Week as it is currently conducted, which is essentially the way it was finally formed by the end of the Byzantine Empire in the fifteenth century. Needless to say, all development has not stopped, but the publication of the Slavic text in Krakow in 1491 and the Greek text in Venice in 1522[31] served to stabilize and form the text.

The *Triodion* begins with four pre-Lenten Sundays oriented around biblical passages, which encourage the faithful to prepare for the beginning of Great Lent. Each has a distinct spiritual theme: the Sunday of the Pharisee and the Publican points toward humility; the Sunday of the Prodigal Son toward repentance; Meatfare Sunday toward remembrance of the last judgment; and

---

31. See entry "Triodion," in Θρησκευτικὴ καὶ Ἠθικὴ Ἐγκυκλοπαιδεία (Athens: Martinos Press, 1967), vol. 11, col. 864.

Cheesefare Sunday toward forgiveness of others, fasting, and accumulating spiritual treasure (Matt. 6:14-21). Abstinence from certain foods leading to the forty-day fast[32] begins with the day after Meatfare Sunday, marking the last day meat is eaten. The following Sunday marks the last day dairy products are to be eaten, hence "Cheesefare Sunday." The next day is "Clean Monday," which begins the Lenten fast. In descending order of severity, to "fast" means abstinence from meat, alcoholic beverages, eggs, milk and cheese, foods prepared with oil, vegetables, and salads. As a spiritual discipline, abstinence from these foods is a means of controlling desires and focusing upon spiritual realities, not an end in itself. The strictest abstinence, which is observed in parish situations only on Clean Monday and in Holy Week, allows for only water and bread. It is an almost total abstinence from food, except for nuts and fruits and water-boiled vegetables (no oil or butter). Clean Monday is also a day of prayer, worship, and quiet reflection. In parish life, especially outside traditionally Orthodox countries, clergy and laity make adaptations based on their various circumstances,[33] but the change in diet is real and it affects the consciousness of parishioners as a constant reminder of the Lenten season of preparation for Pascha.

The Sundays of Great Lent commemorate varied events and lift up varied themes. The first Sunday is the Sunday of Orthodoxy. Ending a week of the very strictest fasting, it is a triumphant celebration of the restoration of the icons following the Iconoclastic Controversy. In contemporary times it has become the custom for the Vespers of the Sunday of Orthodoxy to be a pan-Orthodox observance, thus teaching empirically the unity of the Orthodox Church and expanding the horizons of peoples of diverse ethnic and cultural backgrounds, in addition to inspiring loyalty and commitment to the Church.

The second Sunday of Great Lent is dedicated to Saint Gregory Palamas, the fourteenth-century archbishop of Thessalonica, whose teaching on the "Jesus Prayer" is highlighted. This prayer has been cultivated for centuries in Eastern Christianity. It consists of the continuous repetition of the name of Jesus in a short, easily remembered prayer. One of its more well known forms is "Lord Jesus Christ, Son of God, have mercy on me, a sinner." In the monastic tradition

32. The Orthodox use the word "fast," which literally means "not eating" νηστεία, in the sense of abstaining from certain kinds of foods, depending on the severity of the fast.

33. Timothy Ware points out that "in practice . . . many Orthodox — particularly in the diaspora — find that under the conditions of modern life it is no longer practicable to follow exactly the traditional rules, devised with a very different outward situation in mind; and so certain dispensations are granted. Yet even so the Great Lent — especially the first week and Holy Week itself — is still, for devout Orthodox, a period of genuine austerity and serious physical hardship." See *The Orthodox Church* (New York: Penguin Books, 1980), pp. 306-7.

the goal is for the prayer to "pray itself" in the heart of the believer. It is an Eastern Christian application of the biblical injunction to "pray constantly" (1 Thess. 5:17).[34]

The midpoint of Great Lent comes on the third Sunday with a service called the "Adoration of the Holy Cross." As the people kneel, the priest comes forth from the altar area, preceded by robed acolytes bearing candles, the processional cross, and processional fans. The priest holds above his head a tray full of flowers, in the midst of which is the precious cross. As the choir sings the doxology, ending with the words "Holy God, Holy Mighty One, Holy Immortal One, have mercy on us," the priest stands in front of a table set before the entrance gates of the iconostasis and adores the cross, singing, "We reverence your Cross, O Master, and we glorify your holy resurrection." This is repeated three times by the choir and congregation. At the end of the service, the faithful reverence the cross and, as they leave the church, receive from the priest a flower from the tray that has been blessed. Clearly there are multiple forms of participation in this service (kneeling, singing, kissing the cross, making the sign of the cross, receiving the flower), all of which stand as an encouragement for Christians at the midpoint of their Lenten journey to Pascha.

The fourth Sunday of Lent is dedicated to Saint John Climacus (570-649), author of *The Ladder of Divine Ascent*. This work, a guide to growth in the spiritual and moral life, consists of thirty brief chapters, each dealing with some vice or virtue and how the Christian is to avoid the vices and live the virtues. For example, "Step 9," entitled "On the Remembrance of Wrongs," begins:

> The holy virtues are like Jacob's ladder, and the unholy vices are like the chains that fell from the chief apostle, Peter. For the virtues, leading from one to another, bear him who chooses them up to heaven; but the vices by their nature beget and stifle one another. And as we have just heard senseless anger calling remembrance of wrongs its own offspring, it is appropriate that we should now say something about this. Remembrance of wrongs is the consummation of anger, the keeper of sins, hatred of righteousness, ruin of virtues, poison of the soul, worm of the mind, shame of prayer, stopping of supplication, estrangement of love, a nail stuck in the soul, pleasureless feeling beloved in the sweetness of bitterness, continuous sin, unsleeping transgression, hourly malice.[35]

---

34. For an introductory discussion of the Jesus Prayer, also known as "The Prayer of the Heart," see A Monk of the Eastern Church [Lev Gillet], *The Prayer of Jesus* (New York, 1967).

35. St. John Climacus, *The Ladder of Divine Ascent*, trans. Lazarus Moore (New York: Harper Bros., n.d.), 9.1-2, 129-30.

Needless to say, passages such as this also form excellent texts for preaching on this Sunday, as all of its teachings are useful for spiritual growth and moral development as Christians move closer to the paschal celebration.

The fifth week of Great Lent commemorates Saint Mary of Egypt. It tells the story of a former prostitute who made a pilgrimage to the Holy Land but was prevented from entering the sacred Church of the Holy Sepulcher in Jerusalem by an invisible hand. In response she repented and lived a life of severe asceticism in the Palestinian desert for forty-seven years. At the end of her life she received Communion from a priest, Zosimas. The brief description of her life in the Synaxarion of the Orthros service concludes by giving the reason she is remembered at this point during Great Lent: "The memory of this holy ascetic is commemorated on the first of April. However, it was also placed for remembrance today, since the end of Great Lent is approaching, so as to arouse the slothful and sinners to repentance, having as an example the celebrated saint."[36] Telling the stories of the saints of the church was in itself an important traditional form of teaching and formation in Byzantium.

In the services of Vespers and Orthros for each of the five Sundays of Great Lent, as well as for each day of each preceding week, there are scores of hymns on the Sunday theme. Two examples of the tone and style of these hymns, illustrating their formative and educative intent, are here taken from the fifth Sunday of Lent. The first is from the Vespers and the second from the Orthros service:

> You severed with the sword of abstinence the snares of the soul and the passion of the body, O righteous one. And by the silence of asceticism you choked the sins of thought. And by the stream of your tears you watered the whole wilderness, bringing forth for us the fruits of repentance. Wherefore, we celebrate your memory.

> Having taken you, O righteous Mary, as an exemplar of repentance, implore Christ to grant the same to us in this period of the fast, so that in faith and longing we may praise you with songs.[37]

Holy Week in the Orthodox Church, especially Holy Thursday, Great Friday, Holy Saturday, and Pascha, consists of a series of services lasting throughout the day, which can properly be described as liturgical passion plays, in

---

36. *Triodion Katanyktikon*, p. 338, translation mine.

37. Modified translation into a contemporary idiom, from *Divine Prayers and Services of the Catholic Orthodox Church of Christ*, ed. Seraphim Nassar (Englewood, N.J.: Antiochian Orthodox Christian Archdiocese, 1979), p. 720.

which the dramatic events of the passion and resurrection of Jesus Christ are reenacted. Thus the services are more than just *about* the events; they are opportunities for emotional, physical, and spiritual *sharing* and participating in the events. For example, on Great Friday a funeral bier, bedecked with flowers, holds an icon of the dead Christ. On Great Friday evening the congregation gathers around it and sings three sets of rhythmic hymns, known as the "Lamentations," as if the congregation were at the "wake" or "viewing" of the deceased Christ. Toward the end of the service the funeral bier, in many congregations, is carried in procession outside and around the church building as if to a place of burial. Upon return from the funeral procession, the congregation pays its "last respects" just as they do for their deceased relatives and friends before the coffin. The icon of the dead Christ is then brought in procession to the altar table and placed upon it; the altar table thus "becomes" the tomb of Christ.

It is from there on Holy Saturday at midnight, as the paschal Sunday dawns, that the priest comes forth into the darkened church, holding a lighted paschal candle to announce to the congregation in the darkened church: "Come ye, receive light from the unwaning Light, and glorify Christ, who arose from the dead."[38] The paschal light is then passed to all of the congregants, and soon the whole church is alight with the light of the resurrection. A procession follows to the center of the church and the Gospel of the resurrection is read (Mark 16:1-8), followed by the repeated triumphal singing of the central paschal hymn: "Christ has risen from the dead, by death trampling upon Death, and has bestowed life to those in the tombs."[39]

The whole experience of Great Lent, Holy Week, and Pascha can be understood as a vast liturgical, biblical, hymnological, ascetic, and prayerful process of education and formation, which includes theological, doctrinal, spiritual, moral, historical, personal, corporate, and aesthetic experiences addressing the whole psychosomatic spiritual life of the believer. Depending on the level of involvement by each worshiper, Great Lent, Holy Week, and Pascha provide an atmosphere and ethos of formation and education that transcends exclusively rational instruction, capturing the heart, the mind, the spirit, the body, and the creation within its purview.

---

38. *Greek Orthodox Holy Week and Easter Services,* ed. George L. Papadeas (Daytona Beach, Fla., 1977), p. 448.

39. *Greek Orthodox Holy Week and Easter Services,* p. 450.

Conclusion: Tradition and Formation

At the heart of this continuity in the Byzantine religious experience is its incarnational ethos, which has embodied the Eastern Orthodox Christian faith in various interpenetrating expressions and is intimately connected with a sense of the continuity of Holy Tradition central to the Orthodox theological mind-set. Doctrinally, Holy Tradition in Orthodox theology understands continuity from the time of Jesus Christ through the apostles and subsequent generations as a continuous presence of the Holy Spirit in the life of the church. This theological presupposition of the Eastern Orthodox mind-set places great store in the maintenance of the spirit of ongoing continuity with the sources of the faith, though not in a slavish repetition of the past for its own sake. As Jaroslav Pelikan puts it: "Tradition is the living faith of the dead, traditionalism is the dead faith of the living. And, I suppose I should add, it is traditionalism that gives tradition such a bad name."[40] This sense of living continuity with the Orthodox Byzantine past, made present by a wide range of diverse formative and educational practices, is one of the essential characteristics of tradition as understood in the Eastern Orthodox way of thinking and living.[41]

The teaching of the catechists, the rites of initiation of infants into the Christian community, the role of the architecture of the church building and the icon, and the profound participatory liturgical experiences of Great Lent, Holy Week, and Pascha all embody a tradition of faith that seeks to bring people into contact with the ecclesial tradition of Byzantium and its Orthodox Church, that is, with the "living faith" of those who have peopled the past and those who live in the present. Ultimately it is the power of sharing personally and corporately in the living experience of the past, making it one's own, living it out for the present and for the generations to come — this crosses the barriers of time and the periods of history. It is a commonplace in Orthodox worship, for instance, to present the salvation events not merely as past events to be remembered but as current experiences in which believers participate. Thus, at Christmas, the hymns have the worshipers say, "Today, the Virgin gives birth to the creator of all";[42] at the commemoration of Christ's baptism (Epiphany in the Orthodox Church), it is proclaimed that "Today the nature of water is sanctified";[43] at the feast of the transfiguration the hymn proclaims, "Today you

---

40. Jaroslav Pelikan, *The Vindication of Tradition* (New Haven: Yale University Press, 1984), p. 64.

41. For more on this perspective of lived tradition, see Stanley Samuel Harakas, "'Tradition' in Eastern Orthodox Thought," *Christian Scholar's Review* 22, no. 2 (December 1992): 144-65.

42. *Divine Prayers and Services*, December 25, Vespers, p. 401.

43. *Divine Prayers and Services*, January 6, the Great Hours, p. 438.

have manifested on Mount Tabor, O Lord, the glory of your divine image";[44] on Holy Thursday night, as he carries the crucifix in solemn procession commemorating the crucifixion of Christ, the priest proclaims before the kneeling congregation, "Today he is suspended on a tree who suspended the earth over the waters";[45] on Holy Saturday a hymn declares, "Today, he who holds the creation in the hollow of his hand is contained in a tomb";[46] and at the paschal resurrection service the church sings triumphantly: "Today is the day of resurrection! O nations, let us shine forth; for the passover is the passover of the Lord, in that Christ did make us pass from death to life and from earth to heaven, who now sing the song of victory and triumph."[47] The past is made present. Two thousand years are transcended. The tradition forms the consciousness of the believers and worshipers, as if they are present in the past. The key to the Byzantine approach to education and formation of the Christian consciousness and lifestyle is, then, its adherence to and identity with Holy Tradition.[48]

44. *Divine Prayers and Services,* August 6, Vespers, p. 575.

45. *Divine Prayers and Services,* Great Friday Orthros, sung by anticipation, p. 825.

46. *Divine Prayers and Services,* Orthros, p. 904, translation slightly modified.

47. *Divine Prayers and Services,* 922.

48. In another essay I have given a more technical, theological definition of Holy Tradition: Harakas, "'Tradition' in Eastern Orthodox Thought," p. 165.

Community and Education
in Premodern Judaism

Michael A. Signer

E lements of continuity and discontinuity characterize any description of the
contemporary Jewish community and its antecedents. The premodern
Jewish community has roots which reach back to the biblical period, formulated during the era of Hellenism and late antique civilization, developed
through the high Middle Ages into the eighteenth century in western Europe,
and reaching almost into the twentieth century in many parts of eastern Europe
and the Ottoman Empire. Before the eighteenth century, Jewish communities
stretching from western Europe to India bore a remarkable resemblance to one
another. Allowing for some individual variations in self-governing practice,
there were elements of similarity if not identity in modes of worship, organization of family life, and commercial practices.

What provided the homogenizing elements among these communities dis-
persed through space and time? Jewish communities shared the common foundation of their Scripture (written law) augmented by rabbinic writings (oral
law). They participated in the liturgical life within the synagogue where every
male could lead the prayers and read from the sacred writings as part of the
weekly Sabbath observance. Their religious leadership derived from a group of
men who were trained in a hermeneutical tradition that applied the classical
texts of both written and oral law to the exigencies of contemporary life. Ideal-
izations of piety, role models for proper conduct, and even appropriate occasions for communal gathering and feasting derived from genres of literature
that were grounded in expounding Scripture and called Halakah, which means
"the Path" or simply "Law."

To participate in the life of the Jewish community required some degree
of literacy, a literacy that would at minimum allow members to participate ap-

propriately in worship. It would provide access to the religious authorities, rabbis and their courts, for the negotiations of marriages and divorces. Moreover, as we shall see, this literacy formed the foundation for the ideal male within the Jewish community. Access to the literary sources of the Jewish tradition could, in some cases, provide social and economic upward mobility for young men to advance as rabbis, experts in applying the rabbinic law. The premodern Jewish community's leadership was charged with all important aspects of governance. The leadership of the local community adjudicated disputes between members of the community and those Jews who traveled from distant communities to engage in local commerce. They raised taxes to sustain communal institutions for charitable purposes, maintaining funds for orphans, widows, and indigent visitors. In addition, they represented the community in negotiations with the non-Jewish governing powers.

Education and community, then, for premodern Jewry were almost synonymous. The observation of a twelfth-century Christian about Jewish zeal for education may be exaggerated, but it is congruent with the realities we have tried to portray:

> If the Christians educate their sons, they do so not for God but for gain, in order that the one brother, if he be a clerk, may help his father and mother and his other brothers. They say that a clerk will have no heir and whatever he has will be ours and our brothers. A black cloak and hood to go to church in, and his surplice, will be enough for *him*. But the Jews out of a zeal for God and love of the law put as many sons as they have to letters, that each may understand God's law. . . . A Jew, however poor, if he had ten sons would put them all to letters, not for gain, as the Christians do, but for the understanding of God's law, and not only his sons, but his daughters.[1]

Even if we allow for some rhetorical overstatement to provoke his Christian readers with a contrast between Jewish and Christian attitudes toward education, we would maintain that the formation of Jewish community life, in its leadership and ideals, required, if not a real level of literacy in Torah, at least an idealization of education.

In this paper we shall first examine two foundational Jewish locations for education: the assembly and the family. We shall then survey some aspects of the core curriculum within the Jewish communities, and the variety of approaches to its pedagogy. This essay takes up, finally, issues of gender and edu-

---

1. Beryl Smalley, *The Study of the Bible in the Middle Ages* (Notre Dame, Ind., 1952), p. 78, quoting the *Commentarius Cantabrigiensis in Epistolas Pauli e Schola Petri Abaelardi*, ed. A. Landgraf (Notre Dame, Ind., 1937), ii, 434.

cation in the premodern Jewish community, as well as the question of Hebrew and vernacular learning.

Foundations of Jewish Education: Community and Family

Literacy is the point of entry into the Jewish community. Jewish religious life, which is guided by the commandments of God, requires continuous exposure to learning during the entire lifetime of the Jew. Therefore education is more than pedagogy within the Jewish community. It is a continuous process. An examination of the voluminous literary creativity of the early rabbis (third to sixth centuries) indicates that they depicted Jewish life as a constant balance between study (Talmud and Torah) and a livelihood for providing material sustenance. However, they affirmed that pursuit of learning was always the ideal.[2]

From the perspective of rabbinic Judaism, the collective memory of the Jewish people is embedded in Scripture. The significant moments of Scripture for the rabbis were moments when the people of Israel stood together in assembly assenting either to obey or to learn the word of God. Such moments of assembly were incorporated by the rabbis into the festival lectionaries. Our focus in this paper turns to the synagogue lectionary for two significant religious festivals in the Jewish cycle of holy days. First, we shall analyze the Pentateuch lection for the Pentecost (Shavuot), Exodus 19–20:26, and the prophetic reading for the New Year (Rosh Hashanah), Nehemiah 8.

The rabbis celebrated Pentecost as the feast of God's revelation of Torah to Israel. Therefore the reading of the Decalogue and the chapter preceding it provides images of the moment when Israel entered into its unique covenant with God, with Moses acting as messenger both for the assembled Israelites and for God's words to Israel. What is of significance in chapter 19 is the multiple dimensions involved in explaining the nature of divine revelation. God expresses the divine benefice to Israel in visual terms: "You have seen what I did to the Egyptians, how I bore you on eagles' wings and brought you to me. Now then, if you will obey Me faithfully and keep My covenant you shall be My treasured possession among all the peoples" (Exod. 19:4-5). The visual images continue: "On the third day, as morning dawned there was thunder and lightning and a dense cloud upon the mountain and a very loud blast of the horn and all the people who were in the camp trembled. . . . Now Mount Sinai was all in smoke, for the Lord had come down upon it in fire; the smoke rose like the smoke of a

---

2. For an articulate statement on the place of a Torah-educated life in Judaism, see Jacob Neusner, *Judaism's Theological Voice: The Melody of the Talmud* (Chicago, 1995).

kiln, and the whole mountain trembled violently. The blare of the horn grew louder. As Moses spoke, God answered him in thunder" (Exod. 19:16, 18-19). In these passages the divine revelation is mediated through bombastic visual and auditory media. The people during the entire transmission of revelation are, as it were, transfixed, absorbing the events. There is no direct explication of their reaction at the moment of wonder.

However, Exodus 19 also contains a series of transactions between Moses, the people assembled, the elders, and the priests. The people assent to obey the divine commandments prior to the thunder and lightning: "All that the Lord has spoken we will do" (19:8). Moses provides the people with instructions preparing and purifying them for the moment of revelation (19:10-13). The priests are also instructed by Moses, and Aaron is given special dispensation (19:20-24). It is Moses who becomes the mediating figure between the elders, the priests, and the people assembled.

From Exodus 19 we gain some insight into the elements of what constituted the Jewish people as a community: their assembly, their common purification, their witness to the events at Sinai, and their assent to obey God whose beneficence had brought them to the mountain. The inclusive nature of the revelation, the entire people — men and women — is also mediated by a hierarchy: women, men, elders, priests, Moses. Therefore the community who stood at the foot of the mountain were depicted as those who would instruct *and* those who would receive instruction.

From the hierarchy of those assembled at Sinai, we may now turn our attention to the prophetic reading for New Year's Day. For the rabbis the New Year festival was a time of reflection upon divine judgment. It was the beginning of a ten-day penitential period culminating in the Day of Atonement, when Israel was forgiven its sins. Nehemiah 8 recounts the gathering of the community in Jerusalem on the New Year, all those who had returned. Both the timing of the assembly and its activities constitute another important layer of memory about the nature of the Jewish community and its task of education.

When the seventh month arrived — the Israelites being [settled] in their towns — the entire people assembled as one in the square before the Water Gate, and they asked Ezra the scribe to bring the scroll of the Teaching of Moses with which the Lord had charged Israel. On the first day of the seventh month, Ezra the priest brought the Teaching before the congregation, men and women and all who could listen with understanding. He read from it, facing the square before the Water Gate, from the first light until midday, to the men and the women and who could understand; the ears of all the people were given to the scroll of the Teaching.

This assembly is a gathering of people from nearby towns who come together in Jerusalem. They have asked Ezra, who is designated as a scribe, a professional teacher of wisdom, to bring a scroll of the teaching of Moses *(Sefer Torat Moshe)*. Men, women, and all who could understand listen. There is no theophany at this assembly, no transformation of natural forces before the "eyes" of Israel. There is no direct sound of the divine word. Instead there is a public reading. As the narrative continues, the text describes the process of reading, teaching, and learning. "Ezra the Scribe stood upon a wooden tower made for the purpose and beside him stood Mattithiah, Shema, Anaiah, Uriah, Hilkiah, and Maaseiah at his right, and at his left Pedaiah, Mishael, Malchijah, Hashum, Hashbaddanah, Zechariah, Meshullam" (Neh. 8:4-5). Ezra is surrounded by a group of elders on a platform, and is thus visible. When the scroll is opened, the biblical text describes a moment of affirmation by the people. "Ezra opened the scroll in the sight of all the people, for he was above all the people; as he opened it, all the people stood up. Ezra blessed the Lord, the great God, and all the people answered, 'Amen, Amen,' with hands upraised. Then they bowed their heads and prostrated themselves before the Lord with their faces to the ground" (vv. 5-6). The gesture of opening the book evokes the response. Reading from the written word is part of a liturgical assembly. It is one of several gatherings that are recounted in the book of Nehemiah. In these assemblies the exiles renew their commitment to the covenant of their ancestors. The distinguishing feature of assembly in chapter 8, and the reason for its inclusion here, is that it evokes a method of study which will characterize the Jewish community henceforth. "Jeshua, Bani, Sherebiah, Jamin, Akkub, Shabbethai, Hodiah, Maaseiah, Kelita, Azariah, Jozabad, Hanan, Pelaiah and the Levites explained the Teaching to the people while the people stood in their places. They read from the scroll of the Teaching of God, translating it and giving the sense; so they understood the reading" (vv. 7-8). The elders who stood with Ezra and those named in this passage, together with the Levites, engage in the process of instruction. They explain the teaching to the people *(mevinim)*. They read it *(qr')*, translate it *(prsh)*, and give the sense *(som sekhel)*. The result is that the people understand the reading *(yavinu bamiqr'a)*.

In this postexilic assembly there are teachers whose goal is to bring the people to an understanding of the written text of Scripture. The revealed word of God has now been transformed into a written document. It has become a "scroll of the teaching of Moses." The explication of the written text is performed in public assembly by designated elders and members of the Levitical tribe. The visual and auditory predominance of the Sinai assembly has become the orality and textuality of a group of teachers.[3] When the rabbis, teachers of

---

3. Cf. Michael Fishbane, *Biblical Interpretation in Ancient Israel* (Oxford, 1985), which de-

the oral law, later provide their lineage of authority linking them back to Scripture, they will feature "the elders" and the "men of the great assembly" as joining them to the prophets, Joshua, and Moses.[4]

If the community as an assembly is a significant locus for instruction, the Hebrew Bible also emphasizes the family and its home as a place for learning. Deuteronomy 6:4-9 (and the parallel passage, 11:18-21) obliges parents to instruct their children. "Take to heart these instructions with which I charge you this day. Impress them upon your children. Recite them when you stay at home and when you are away, when you lie down and when you get up. Bind them as a sign upon your hand and let them serve as a symbol on your forehead, inscribe them on the doorposts of your house and upon your gates." Parents are to internalize the words of divine instruction and repeat them to their children (NJV, "impress"; Heb. *shnn*). This would seem to imply oral instruction. The words of Torah are objects of continuous thought either at home or away, both in rising and going to sleep. Gestures and rituals such as the phylacteries (as the rabbis would later interpret *totafot*) indicate that the words of Torah served as a source of protection as well as commemoration. Each of the actions described in this passage from Scripture reinforces the home and family as a place of instruction.

A ritual from twelfth-century northern France indicates how firmly Scripture as word and object became embedded in Jewish communal life. It is recorded in *Mahzor Vitry,* a liturgical compendium that contains the customs and practices of Jewish communities in France and the Rhineland. A careful reading of these rituals will demonstrate the continuity between the idealized community and family as the preferred locus of instruction in Scripture to Jews living in another land in another millennium. "It is a custom that a short time after the ceremony of circumcision, ten men should gather. The child should be in its crib dressed in the fine garments as it was on the day of the rite of circumcision. They should take a codex of the Pentateuch, and place it upon the child, and say, 'Let this child observe what is written in this book.' They [also] should put a quill in one hand and writing materials in the other so that he might merit becoming a

---

scribes the exegetical and teaching activities within the Bible. He divides them into scribal activities, legal exegesis, haggadic exegesis, and mantalogical exegesis. His division concords with the activities of the rabbis in their own exegetical activities. Fishbane examines the terminology in Neh. 8 on pp. 107-9.

4. Mishnah *Abot* 1.1. "Moses received the Torah at Sinai and handed it on to Joshua, Joshua to the elders, the elders to the prophets. The prophets handed it on to the men of the Great Assembly. They said three things: Be deliberate in Judgment. Raise up many disciples and make a fence around the Torah." *The Ethics of the Talmud: Sayings of the Fathers,* ed. R. Travers Herford (New York, 1962).

scribe expert in the Torah of God."[5] Ten men, a prayer quorum, gather in the home shortly after the child has been circumcised. The ten men constitute an *'edah*, a community in which worship with all appropriate rites can occur. In that sense they constitute a representation of the Jewish community, since all would most likely not be able to gather in the home of the child. Probably a larger group had witnessed the boy's circumcision in the synagogue. However, the connection with the circumcision is demonstrated by the garments the child wears in his crib, the same as those worn at the earlier ceremony. Now that the child has been physically introduced into the covenant of Abraham through the removal of his foreskin, this gathering acts out a symbolic ritual that dramatizes one of the liturgical formulae at the circumcision. At the rite of circumcision the community recites, "As this child has entered the covenant of Abraham, so may he enter the study of Torah, the marriage canopy, and a life of good deeds." In *Mahzor Vitry* the placement of the codex of the Pentateuch upon the child symbolizes both the commandments contained in the book and the life of Torah study he will be expected to pursue. The ritual of placing the codex onto the child is explicated by reciting the formula "May this child fulfill what is contained in this [book]." The placing of the quill and writing materials in the hand of the child might call attention to the phrase in Ezra 7:6 that he was a "scribe expert in the Teaching of Moses which the Lord God of Israel had given." The quill and writing equipment represent another ritual expressing the idealized life of the male child: that he should engage in a life of learning and fulfilling the commandments as symbolized by the book, and that he should also become one of the elite scholars capable of teaching and applying the law.

Following the cradle ceremony, *Mahzor Vitry* describes a ceremony for the first day a child begins the study of Torah outside the home. This ceremony is also recorded in the *Sefer HaRokeach* of the German pietist author Rabbi Eliezer ben Judah of Worms. It provides another opportunity to observe the appropriation of idealized study and learning from the biblical passages we have thus far examined:

> When a man introduces his son to the study of Torah, they write the letters on a slate or tablet. They wash the child and dress him in clean garments. They bake three loaves made of flour with honey. An unmarried woman kneads the dough. They also boil three eggs for him, and bring him apples and other types of fruit. They make an effort to find an important scholar to bring the child to the school. They put the child under the folds of his garment, and bring him to the synagogue. Then they feed him the loaves baked in honey,

---

5. *Mahzor Vitry*, ed. S. Hurwitz (Nürnberg, 1923), p. 628.

the eggs, and the fruit. After that they read him the letters which they have covered with honey, and they say to the child, "Lick [these letters]." The child is then returned to his mother while he is still covered with a veil. When they begin to teach him, they entice him, but ultimately they may put a strap to his back. They begin his instruction with the book of Leviticus. They accustom him to move his body when he studies. When the child reaches the verse "This shall be an eternal statute for you" (Lev. 16:34), he reads it as if he were in a community of worship *(ke"eyn tsibbur)*, and they make a festive meal for the occasion. . . . "And I will account it to them (the children of Israel) as if they had sacrificed the blood and innards on the altar." Therefore they make him a feast like the one on the day of his circumcision, when the child's blood was really diminished. A person who enjoys this festive meal is obliged to bless the child and say, "May God enlighten your eyes in His Torah." This blessing follows from the one said at the circumcision, "As this child has entered into the covenant of circumcision, so may he enter into the study of Torah."[6]

This charming ceremony of eating cakes and licking the tablet with letters traced in honey is far more than enticing pedagogy and motivation for future study, as Elliot Wolfson and Ivan Marcus have clearly demonstrated.[7] Their research points out links between various parts of the ceremony and German Pietism *(Hassidut Ashkenaz)* and its esoteric traditions. *Mahzor Vitry's* commentary on this ceremony connects it with biblical verses from Exodus 19, the moment of revelation at Sinai. This initiation ceremony also recapitulates the three biblical passages we have previously discussed. The sensory elements of the assembly at Sinai are joined to the reading/literary elements of the Ezra assembly. To these two collective affirmations of the educational ideal the initiation into learning joins an additional element — the ceremony of circumcision, now extended from the inscription of the covenant in the flesh to ingesting the letters of Torah, thus to become a reader of Torah. The close connection between the home and the synagogue community at the rite reinforces the two environments in which the child will receive his learning and apply it throughout his life. The missing element in these texts for many modern readers is the synagogue as a place for instruction. The synagogue in premodern Jewish history is a place for assembly and for prayer, but it is not by necessity the place for school or learning.

6. *Mahzor Vitry*, p. 628.

7. Elliot R. Wolfson, "Erasing the Erasure: Gender and the Writing of God's Body in Kabbalistic Symbolism," in *Circle in the Square: Studies in the Use of Gender in Kabbalistic Symbolism* (Albany, N.Y., 1995); Ivan G. Marcus, *Rituals of Childhood: Jewish Acculturation in Medieval Europe* (New Haven, 1996). Cf. also Lawrence Hoffman, *Covenant of Blood: Circumcision and Gender in Rabbinic Judaism* (Chicago, 1996), which focuses on the connection between the rite of circumcision and blood sacrifice in Judaism.

Our survey of selected biblical passages and the rites of initiating young boys into learning in medieval France has provided some insights into the educational framework of premodern Jewish communities. Who constituted the community? Both men and women are present in the biblical assembly, but with a clearly delineated patriarchal hierarchy. Women are present, but they are not teachers.[8] Premodern Jewish communities were marked by a hierarchy of teachers and students. Biblical prophets and elders yield to the rabbi and *Talmid* (student), as the rabbinic world of second-century Palestine compiled the texts of oral Torah that would serve, together with Scripture, as the common curriculum for the assembled Jewish communities.

Communal Unity and Diversity

The diptych of biblical and medieval religious assemblies is a juxtaposition, a pastiche of literary elements from vastly different societies and cultures. If we move to a more historical grounding for our survey of community and education, we would suggest that the synagogue provides the point of intersection between the individual family and the Jewish community assembled as a juridical body, empowered to conduct the affairs of common good. The synagogue is an institution that may reach back into biblical antiquity. However, most scholars today believe its functions comport more easily with the Hellenistic world. In either case, we have archaeological evidence that synagogues existed in the world of late antiquity and throughout the dispersion of the medieval world.[9]

One can certainly associate three major aspects of Jewish religious life with the synagogue. It is primarily a *Beit Tefillah*, a place where communal prayers take place three times daily, on the Sabbath and Jewish festivals. A second function, associated with the synagogue, may not always have taken place precisely within the synagogue: it was a *Beit Midrash*, a place where Torah (written and

8. On the erasure of women from biblical assemblies of covenant, see Judith Plaskow, *Standing Again at Sinai: Judaism from a Feminist Perspective* (San Francisco, 1990), who also provides a hermeneutics of retrieval for women. Her hermeneutical efforts make the biblical erasure all the more glaring.

9. Cf. Steven Fine, *This Holy Place: On the Sanctity of the Synagogue during the Greco-Roman Period* (Notre Dame, Ind., 1997). See Dan Urman and Paul Flesher, *Ancient Synagogues: Historical Analysis and Archaeological Discovery* (Leiden, 1995), for evidence about the nature of the synagogue in antiquity. For the medieval period, see *Rabbinischen Responsen zum Synagogenbau*, ed. and trans. B. Kern-Ulmer (Hildesheim, 1990); F. Cantera Burgos, *Sinagagos Espanolas* (Madrid, 1984); Rachel Wischnitzer, *The Architecture of the European Synagogue* (Philadelphia, 1964); G. Nahon, *Inscriptions hebraiques et juives de France medievale* (Paris, 1986).

oral) was studied and taught. Finally, the synagogue was a *Beit HaKnesset,* the locus of Jewish communal gathering both for celebration and juridical functions. The latter would include the management of communal assets such as charitable funds, a hostel for travelers, the cemetery, and the ritual bath. It is not always possible to establish that the synagogue served as the locus of these three functions simultaneously, but it is significant that all are attributed to this single space. It was not inherently sacred space, but it provided the locus for the preparation for and living out of the life of Torah.

From our modern perspective it is the literature of the house of study that provides much of the information about the history of education formation. The literary genres associated with the oral Torah, Mishnah and Talmud, contain a wide variety of descriptions of the interaction between rabbis and their disciples.[10] These documents, which reflect the world of the rabbis in the eastern Roman Empire and the Persian Empire, are rich in their attempts to prescribe courses of study, master/disciple relationships, and even pedagogy. From the literary genre of midrash, whose compilation we may associate with Jewry in the eastern Roman and later Byzantine Empire, we possess what many scholars believe to be the rich sermonic literature of the synagogue. Whether these midrashim are the real texts of the sermons or simply literary artifices created independent of an oral presentation, they reveal a rich texture of concern to synthesize written Scripture with rabbinic teaching. Many of these homiletical collections advocate in their explicit message, and more importantly by their rhetorical structure, a lifetime of continuous study. From the sixth century onward a tradition of liturgical poetry, *piyyut,* provided a significant aesthetic dimension to the festival prayers. However, many of these poems also had a pedagogic aim, providing yet another distillation and dissemination of rabbinic teaching. Here I would suggest that the genre of *Azharot* read on Pentecost provides a pedagogical literature that promoted the rabbinic orientation toward the oral Torah.[11]

How did these literary products of Jewry in late antiquity reach and form successive generations of Jews throughout the Mediterranean and European dispersion until the seventeenth century? Was there a uniform set of institutions that made the transmission of this literature their task? The Islamic conquest of the seventh century and the subsequent Abbasid empire seems to mark a water-

10. For bibliography and a summary of the scholarly questions about education during the rabbinic period and the genres of rabbinic literature, see H. L. Strack and G. Stemberger, *Introduction to the Talmud and Midrash* (London, 1991), and J. Neusner, *Introduction to Rabbinic Literature* (New York, 1994).

11. I. Elbogen, *Jewish Liturgy: A Comprehensive History* (Philadelphia, 1993), describes the function of religious poetry in the synagogue.

shed in the development of Jewish community life. The Jews of Baghdad and its immediately surrounding communities were entrusted with the leadership and collection of taxes for the newly centralized caliphate. The rabbinic houses of study in Palestine and in the successor states of the eastern Roman Empire continued their activities. However, Jewish communities throughout the Islamic empire were under the jurisdiction of the centralized bureaucracy of Baghdad a political reality until about the mid–eleventh century.

It must be recalled that the Jewish communities that lived under Islamic hegemony also participated in a broad culture of Arabic knowledge. The variety of their occupations often required learning beyond what was required to participate in the ritual life of Judaism. Their "secular" curriculum is beyond the scope of this paper, but it is important to remember that Jews who lived in the Islamic culture, particularly on the Iberian Peninsula, transformed many genres of Islamic literature into Jewish forms of poetry, moral tales, and philosophy. Many Jewish authors from the Islamic world utilized the grammatical and lexicographical genres for a more thorough understanding of Jewish sacred writ. At present it may suffice to say that, as Goitein indicates, much of this learning in Arabic studies was the possession of the "upper classes," and therefore the subjects were taught at home.[12] A number of ethical wills written either by Iberian Jews or émigrés from Iberia to Provence or Italy indicate that the broader Arabic curriculum was part of the home library.[13] Another indication that education in Arabic subjects may have taken place within the individual household in Iberia is the interaction of patrons and poets that Gerson D. Cohen has called "court culture."[14]

If we set aside the broader concerns of the symbiosis between Jewish and Islamic culture, we might observe that from the eighth through the eleventh century the Islamic imperial capital developed a remarkable series of institutions to disseminate the Babylonian Talmud as the central document of Jewish life.[15] The transformation came about through the activity of collegia of rabbis in Baghdad who became the agencies for licensing judges to serve in the Jewish

12. S. D. Goitein, *A Mediterranean Society: The Jewish Communities of the Arab World as Portrayed in the Documents of the Cairo Genizah*, vol. 1 (Berkeley and Los Angeles, 1967), introduction.

13. *Hebrew Ethical Wills*, ed. and trans. Israel Abrahams, facsimile edition of 1926 with introduction by Judah Goldin (Philadelphia, 1976).

14. Gerson D. Cohen, *The Book of Tradition of Abraham ibn Daud* (Philadelphia, 1969), introduction.

15. Most of our knowledge about these communities and their activities derives from documents in the Cairo Geniza, which was discovered at the end of the nineteenth century. Our discussion here is based on S. D. Goitein, *A Mediterranean Society*, vol. 2, *The Community* (Berkeley, 1971), pp. 171-209.

dispersion. These collegia, called *Yeshivoth,* do not resemble the educational institutions we associate with modern Jewish authors such as Chaim Potok. Rather than schools that prepared students for study, they were established as a collegium of rabbis who were organized in a hierarchical manner. At their head was a *Gaon* who was also known as *Resh Metivta,* the head of the Yeshiva. The Yeshiva was a place where scholars would gather and expound the Bible and sacred writings, interpret and apply the law, and decide questions of law that were raised by local communities. In the fall and spring, judges from the dispersion would gather in *Kallah* to hear the *Gaon* and his assistant, the *Meturgeman,* lecture about a talmudic tractate. In addition, the *Gaon* would respond to questions of local interest. Parallel to the lectures delivered by the *Gaon* were lectures given to a broader public, most likely merchants.

It was the questions put to the *Gaon* that were then sent back to the communities. If there were no questions immediately to hand, the teacher often suggested some. Often the questions would attempt to resolve conflicts between the practice of the local communities and the practices in Iraq. While promoting the hegemony of their interpretation of the Talmud, the *Gaonim* were careful to allow sufficient latitude for individual communal practices so that the bond between community and Yeshiva would remain firm.[16] The literature of *She'elot uTeshuvot,* Responsa, would become a most productive genre among the most learned Jews both in the Islamic and the European cultural environments. As we shall see, European rabbis lacked the centralized institutional governing structure of the *Gaonic* academies.

Within the Jewish communities living under Islamic hegemony there were continuing opportunities for what we might call "adult education." The synagogue seems to have been where classes in the study of Scripture met as often as three times per week, some of which were taught by leaders known as *Rosh Kevutzah,* the head of a group. This might suggest that groups of adults would gather either in the synagogue or at a nearby location known as *Midrash* for these lessons. Within these communities there were also what we might call "elementary schools." Some were located within the synagogue building, others met in either the house of a teacher or a space rented for purposes of instruction. According to Goitein, upper-class students received tutoring in the home of their parents. There is ample documentation about the communal charitable institutions providing for orphans. From personal letters, Goitein gives a rather bleak assessment of these schools for poor children. There seems to have been

16. Lawrence A. Hoffman, *The Canonization of the Synagogue Service* (Notre Dame, Ind., 1975), examines this delicate balance between local and central authority with respect to liturgical customs.

very low regard for the *melamed tinoqot*, the elementary teacher. His major task was to prepare the child to participate in the synagogue service. Therefore the curriculum emphasized learning to read and memorize portions of the Pentateuch and its Aramaic translation. There seems to be no explicit reference to regular prayers taught to children, but students were taught the *piyyutim*, or poetic elaborations that were part of the festival liturgies. Toward this end, children asked to participate in the service.

Our brief survey of premodern Jewry under Islam indicates some continuities with the paradigms of community described in the first section of this paper. It is clear that the political organization of the Abbasid empire and the competitive but symbiotic relationship between Judaism and Islam produced a hierarchy of institutions for educating younger people and sustaining a learned elite. However, the centrality of the liturgical recitation and scriptural lectionary cycle in the life of the community at prayer in the synagogue remained constant. What seems to have been unique in the ascendant period of Islamic cultural hegemony is the removal of the central teaching authority to the yeshivoth in Baghdad. This form of intercommunal organization declined after the twelfth century. With the rise of Ottoman rule in the Mediterranean and the *Reconquista* by Christians in Spain, the synagogue and local communal organization became the predominating institution within non-European Jewry.

Northern European Jewry and its community organization seems to have a greater continuity with the Jewry of late antiquity. F. Baer attempted to explain this continuity based on the development of Jewry in Europe's roots in the Byzantine Jewry.[17] Northern European Jewry did not participate in a culture of centralized institutions. The development of these communities came about through the urbanization which began in the Carolingian period (800-1050).

We know these earliest communities were founded by families from northern Italy who were merchants, and who also idealized piety and Torah learning.[18] In the cities of the Rhineland and then throughout Europe north of the Alps and Pyrenees, the community assembled provided the location for settling

---

17. Yitzhak F. Baer, "The Origins of Jewish Communal Organization in the Middle Ages," *Binah* I, 59-82 (an English translation and summary of Baer's original Hebrew article published in *Zion* [1950]: 1-41). H. H. Ben-Sasson, "The Northern Jewish Community and Its Ideals," in *Jewish Society through the Ages,* ed. H. H. Ben-Sasson and S. Ettinger (New York, 1971), pp. 208-19, provides a contextualization of Baer's thesis within the developments of Christian political organization and theory.

18. A. Grossman, *Reshit Hachme Ashkenaz* (The beginnings of northern European Jewry) (Jerusalem, 1978), provides biobibliographic surveys of the leaders of the Rhenish and Lotharingian Jewish communities. I. A. Agus, *The Heroic Age of Franco-German Jewry* (New York, 1969), provides valuable information but tends to idealize the early leaders.

disputes. Social control and litigation took place through two forms of coercion: expulsion from the community and the ability to interrupt the prayer service. Interruption of the prayer service by an individual who did not consider the local court to have dispensed justice validates the claim of the synagogue to act as the central locus of the community. Therefore educational institutions in Europe — harking back to late antiquity — had two primary trajectories: the preparation of individual males to participate in synagogue life and, for those who had the inclination and capacity, a curriculum that would lead to advanced ability to engage in the ongoing process of talmudic dialectics and the application of Jewish law.

With respect to the universal preparation of males for participation in synagogue services, it seems that most males during the earlier Middle Ages studied at home with members of their family. Ephraim Kanarfogel's survey of education in the high Middle Ages indicates that elementary education — reading and prayers — was held in very low regard. Despite the talmudic injunction that teachers must be hired in every city with twenty-five students, he has found little evidence that such institutions actually existed.[19] The customary solution was to engage tutors for orphans. Or when individuals did not have sufficient resources, they set up various forms of cooperation to pay the tutor. There were also a group of teachers who taught Scripture in the vernacular. These *poterim* have left evidence of their work in manuscript glossaries, which place Hebrew and Old French in parallel columns.[20] Vernacular translation of the Hebrew was also part of the synagogue service and of some home rituals in medieval France, Germany, Spain, and Italy.[21] Evidence of the work of these *poterim* suggests that Jews also engaged in vernacular consultations with Christian scholars at Cîteaux and the Abbey of St. Victor in Paris, concerning the meaning of Hebrew words in Scripture.[22] It is not certain whether biblical teaching in Old French belonged entirely to the elementary stages of education.

From the late eleventh through mid–twelfth century, Jewish scholars such as Rabbi Solomon b. Isaac of Troyes (Rashi), Rabbi Joseph Kara, Rabbi Samuel ben

19. Ephraim Kanarfogel, *Jewish Education and Society in the High Middle Ages* (Detroit, 1992).

20. Menahem Banitt, "The *La'azim* of Rashi and of the French Biblical Glossaries," in C. Roth, *World History of the Jewish People: The Dark Ages* (New Brunswick, N.J.: Rutgers University Press, 1966), pp. 291-96.

21. Cf. *Mahzor Vitry*, ed. S. Hurvitz (reprint, Jerusalem, 1962), p. 234; M. Güdemann, *Geschichte des Erziehungswesens* (reprint, Amsterdam, 1978).

22. Cf. Beryl Smalley, *The Study of the Bible in the Middle Ages*; Philippe Delhaye, "L'organisation scolaire aux XIIe siécle," *Traditio* 5 (1947): 211-68; and *Andreas de Sancto Victore: Expositio in Ezechielem*, ed. Michael Signer (Turnhout, 1991), pp. xxi-xxxvii.

Meir, and Rabbi Eliezer of Beaugency focused their literary work on biblical studies. To these names we might also add Rabbi Abraham ibn Ezra and the Kimhi family, who transmitted the legacy of Iberian Jewry's lexicographical approach to France, Italy, and Provence. The commentaries written during this period focused on a biblical exegesis emphasizing the *peshat,* or "plain meaning," which often meant minimal transmission of the classical rabbinic understanding of Scripture. I have argued elsewhere that one can discern evidence of how Scripture was taught on the basis of a careful reading of these commentaries.[23]

By the middle of the twelfth century a new form of talmudic study emerged in northern Europe, and this became the most prevalent mode of talmudic study for the next century. Known as *Tosafot,* or "additions," it began with the writings of Rabbi Solomon b. Isaac of Troye's grandson, Rabbi Jacob b. Meir. Dialectics and a rigorous comparison of all parallel passages of the talmudic text characterized this form of study. Again, it is impossible to determine how many students engaged in this highly sophisticated form of Talmud analysis. But by the mid–thirteenth century it had spread from England in the west to Vienna in the east.[24]

The education of rabbis in Europe for the next three hundred years would take place in an urban environment. Students would come to great masters of talmudic dialectics, absorb their method and their teachings, and go on to serve as preachers and teachers in other communities. In the later Middle Ages the rabbinate moved toward greater professionalization. However, it was the mental acuity of a rabbi either in dialectical argument or in his ability to apply the law that advanced his reputation and career.

Beyond these talmudic skills, which they seem to have reserved for their disciples, the later Middle Ages witnessed the rise of Jewish preaching, sermons often being delivered in the vernacular and then rewritten in Hebrew. They were spoken as part of the synagogue services for Sabbath and festivals, for weddings and funerals, and upon the occasion of great political events. From the texts of these sermons it is possible to discern the level of popular Jewish learning and the dissemination of mystical and philosophical ideas as they became applied to the classical texts of the rabbinic tradition.[25]

23. Michael A. Signer, "Rabbi Joseph Kara: Exégèse et Enseignment," *Archives Juives* 18, no. 4 (1982): 60-63; but also the criticism of Kanarfogel, pp. 184-85 n. 126.

24. There is no monograph on the Tosafists and their method in English. Cf. Kanarfogel, pp. 66-85. E. E. Urbach, *Ba'ale HaTosafoth,* 2 vols. (Jerusalem, 1980), is the most complete account of the Tosafists and their methods. On rabbinical education in late medieval Germany, see Israel Jacob Yuval, *Scholars in Their Time* (in Hebrew) (Jerusalem, 1988).

25. Marc Saperstein, *Jewish Preaching: 1200-1800: An Anthology* (New Haven, 1988), provides a survey of the literary genre as well as translations of sermons with excellent annotations.

Beyond the Synagogue

Our survey of the premodern Jewish community has focused on how participation in synagogue worship and communal deliberation was the aim of religious formation. This has focused our attention on the preparation of male members of the community for participation in the synagogue and a lifelong study of Torah. While we have noted the contrasting communal organization of Jews who lived under Islam and those who lived under Christian rulers, we have described only two paths of education: elementary studies in the reading of Scripture and Talmud, and more advanced study of Talmud and rabbinic literature, which might lead the individual to become a rabbi.

The erasure of women from the paper until this point has been intentional. In the great majority of cases — and there are exceptions — women were not expected to be part of the daily routine of public liturgy, which also included reading from the Torah scroll or the prophetic lection. They were excluded because they were exempt from what the rabbis called "time-bound commandments" (those rites and rituals to be performed within a limited temporal scheme). Maimonides' twelfth-century codification of Jewish law rationalizes the exclusion of the woman from the *Beit Midrash* in the following manner:

> Women, slaves, and minors are free from the obligation to study Torah, but a father is obliged to teach his son Torah as Scripture states, "You shall teach them to your son to speak about them." However, a woman is not obliged to teach her son Torah, because only the person who is obliged to study is obliged to teach.
>
> A woman who has learned Torah gains reward, but it is not the same reward as for a man, because she is not commanded to study. A person who does something which he is not commanded does not receive the same reward as one gains for a commandment he has done, but gains a lesser reward. Furthermore, even if she does gain reward, the Sages have commanded that a man not teach Torah to his daughter because the majority of women do not have the intellect which is directed toward real Torah study. Rather, they create frivolities of Torah according to their impoverished intellect. The sages said, "A man who teaches his daughter Torah has taught her lechery (Sotah 3,4)." In what cases does this ruling apply? It applies to teaching her the Oral Law. However, with regard to Scripture, *a priori* he should not teach her, but if he does teach her it is not considered lechery.[26]

26. Maimonides, *Mishneh Torah*, Laws of Torah Study, chaps. 1:1 and 13.

Despite the strictures set forth by Maimonides, we know that during the premodern period there were exceptional women who were learned in the oral law. Rabbis consulted them about Jewish laws having to do with the preparation of food.[27] The restrictions against teaching women Torah might have precluded their learning Hebrew, but it did not render them illiterate. A vernacular literature seems to have served women's religious life. They read paraphrases of the weekly scriptural portions, which included rabbinic homiletical material such as *Tsenah U'renah*.[28] We have prayer books containing women's religious poetry from the later Middle Ages.[29] Another genre of popular devotion, *Tekhinnes*, seems to have inspired compositions by women as well as men.[30]

Devotional literature in Hebrew and the vernacular for men and women seems to have grown in popularity during the later Middle Ages. The invention of the printing press enabled a wider dissemination of this literature. Books of stories, hymns, and ethical exhortation popularized many of the ideas that had been developed by pious fraternities of men bringing them from the synagogue or the yeshiva into the Jewish home.

In this shift of the balance from an "assembly" of Hebrew readers toward a multiplicity of extrasynagogal groups, the Jewish community made its first steps toward modernity. It was not so much urbanization or an increasingly rationalized economic status that constituted modernity for Jews. Rather, it was the growing positive estimation of their surrounding cultural climate that motivated western European Jews. While they continued their devotion to the written word, they shifted their loyalty from Hebrew to vernacular texts. This suggestion about the fragmentation that characterized Jewish communities from the sixteenth century onward may place too much emphasis on written texts. However, I believe it is one path toward understanding why the young Moses Mendelssohn made the journey from Dessau to Berlin.[31] He may have gone there to continue studying with his rabbi, but it was as a tutor for women

27. *Jewish Women in Historical Perspective*, ed. Judith Baskin (Detroit, 1991).

28. Yaakov ben Yitzchak Ashkenazi (1550-1628), *Tz'enah ur'enah: The Classic Anthology of Torah Lore and Midrashic Comment*, trans. M. Stark Zakon (Brooklyn, N.Y., 1983-84).

29. Many of these prayers have been translated in *Women Speak to God*, ed. and trans. Marcia Cohn Spiegel and Deborah Lipton Kremsdorf (San Diego, 1987).

30. The connection between women and modernity, especially Jewish women and vernacular languages, is made in Natalie Zemon Davis, *Women at the Margins: Three Seventeenth-Century Lives* (Cambridge, Mass., 1995).

31. Alexander Altmann, *Moses Mendelssohn: A Biographical Study* (Birmingham, Ala., 1973), and David Sorkin, *Moses Mendelssohn and the Religious Enlightenment* (Berkeley and Los Angeles, 1996), provide thorough analyses of the cultural forces that shaped Mendelssohn's career.

in a patrician Jewish household that he launched the project of translating Hebrew Scripture into German. With this movement from Hebrew to German the process of modernizing the education of the Jewish community began.

Practice beyond the Confines
of the Medieval Parish

John Van Engen

Belief and practice at the local level have proved hard to get at in medieval Europe. Texts abound from devout monks and nuns, thoughtful intellectuals, extraordinary mystics, and norm-setting prelates. But what about "ordinary" people in all the thousands of parishes across Europe? Do we know what they practiced, what Christian faith meant to them, how they learned what they believed or did? They, after all, made up the vast majority of the "faithful," each baptized as a baby, most not literate, many confined to limited social and cultural spaces in rural villages or small towns. More pointedly, could they, born into a society where Christian faith reigned as public law, exercise any meaningful choice? Or was choice by definition an act of dissent, even heresy (the original meaning of the Greek word *hairesis*)? Was not obedience the mark of belief? These questions, so seemingly straightforward, pose genuine problems for historians. We have too few sources that record or reveal, that truly open up for us, the worlds of local religious practice, and many scholarly arguments about how to interpret those we have. Just as crucially, historians have reached no consensus on how to think about personal practice in a society where religion functioned as public law. It is tempting, for us looking back, to move toward either extreme, to imagine the medieval church as a mythic iron age of superstition and coercion (the Protestant and enlightened visions that fostered its repudiation and also glorified dissenters) or as an equally mythic golden age of devotion and harmony (the romantic and restoration visions that fed into Roman Catholic revivals). To make matters more complicated, both views rest in part on texts: those of devout and educated believers who practiced their religion ardently, those too of ardent reformers who critiqued widespread abuse and negligence.

Incalculable distances must have yawned, then as now, between all the norms issued as prescriptive texts and ordinary practices lived out day to day in all their variety. Some historians have turned this perception of distance into a vision of duality: If lived religion was not the same as normative religion, and if texts throw up contrary images, why not simply recognize opposing poles? Why not project into the medieval past two distinct religious worlds, that of the churchmen and that of the people, of prelates and of peasants?[1] As evidence for the people's religion, scholars of European folklore, going back a century and more, focused on those practices that seemed most non-Christian, at least in origin (magic, charms), and those figures with shamanlike roles (witches, fortune-tellers, and so on, with women in prominent roles). This tendency grew more pronounced after the 1960s, when students of history turned empathetically to those who resisted established conventions or themselves stood outside the circles of power, peoples passed over earlier and deserving of study: heretics, dissenters, witches, mystics, pagans. Peasants, though making up fully 90 percent of the populace, could also count as "marginals." Not only were they exploited socially for their labor, crushed under medieval lordship; as rural people they lived distanced from a church built on privilege, often given, so it was said, to practices dismissed or critiqued by their superiors as "superstition."[2] Some scholars have taken this interpretive direction still further: all such suspect practices represent collectively the religion peasants perpetuated or fashioned for themselves, quite apart from churchmen, a religious world thus only distantly related to normative Christianity — one, further, that drew upon deeper religious traditions, the vestiges of an alternative Europe or pagan Middle Ages.[3]

This debate goes on, and always will, for it springs in part from charges lev-

---

1. Many historians took this approach a generation ago. Perhaps most influential and thoughtful among medieval historians was Jean-Claude Schmitt. See now, for instance, his "Religion, Folklore, and Society in the Medieval West," in *Debating the Middle Ages: Issues and Readings*, ed. Lester Little and Barbara Rosenwein (Malden, Mass., 1998), pp. 376-87, which is responding in part to my "The Christian Middle Ages as an Historiographical Problem," *American Historical Review* 91 (1986): 519-52, though his article (and the introduction to it, pp. 308-9) have mischaracterized my position. For the deeper background of notions pertinent to "popular religion," see François André Isambert, *Le sens du sacré: fête et religion populaire* (Paris, 1982).

2. For this turn in medieval historiography toward the "margins," see now Paul Freedman and Gabrielle Spiegel, "Medievalisms Old and New: The Rediscovery of Alterity in North American Medieval Studies," *American Historical Review* 103 (1998): 677-704. For an impressive study of the ways peasants were regarded, positively and negatively, also in religious terms, see now Paul Freedman, *Images of the Medieval Peasant* (Stanford, 1999).

3. See, for instance, Ludo Milis, ed., *The Pagan Middle Ages* (Rochester, 1998).

eled already by medieval and Protestant reformers, deeply dissatisfied with various practices they knew firsthand and observed all around them. Extreme dualist positions have given way in recent years, however, to the recognition of a wide spectrum, with attitudes ranging from devotion to indifference and a mix of beliefs and practices not easily fit under broad labels like "churchly" or "popular." Bipolar models — the clergy and the people, the devout and dissenters — fail to account for all the overlapping, even contradictory practices and attitudes that cut across simple social or religious lines. When people said charms over a sick family member or a newly plowed field, were they invoking an alternative religion or a supplemental one, demons or local saintly presences? Or were they simply trying with all means available to appease forces beyond their control, not worrying how some practice might exactly fit Christian belief? When a parish priest used a host as a charm, even held one in his mouth to seduce a woman, was he going over to the "people's" side or simply sharing in multiplying beliefs about the powers inherent in the consecrated Body? So too, when people joined dissident or heretical or mystically inclined groups, were they openly rebelling or taking religion seriously and into their own hands? Did they even perceive a nonnegotiable line, a clear boundary — the Cathars called themselves the "true" Christians, as did the Lollards — before objections were raised and boundary markers enforced? Do microstudies of particular heretics or dissenters or local "deviants" permit us to infer a larger alternative world dexterously hidden from sight? Is that approach different, on reflection, from those of historians who inferred from selected devout texts and ardent practitioners a larger silent world of devotion?

Over the last decade or two historians have begun to focus more on local centers of religious life, the thousands of parishes set up every few miles across medieval Europe — work well represented in this book by Goering's essay. Images of success, even of thriving religious practice, on this local front, especially in recent studies of the later Middle Ages, are now threatening to swing the interpretive balance rapidly and forcefully to the other end of the spectrum. Parish organization worked, these studies seem to say, thoroughly mapping Europe into grid of sacred spaces, forming people into local communities, whatever the varieties of practice and complexities of allegiance.[4] By the twelfth century, Susan Reynolds contends, parishes served as fundamental units of human organization and governance.[5] By 1400, according to Eamon Duffy's *Stripping of*

---

4. See, most recently, with a helpful introductory essay, Katherine L. French, *The People of the Parish: Community Life in a Late Medieval English Diocese* (Philadelphia, 2001).

5. Susan Reynolds, *Kingdoms and Communities in Western Europe, 900-1300* (Oxford, 1984), pp. 79-100.

the Altars, parish religious life in England, rich and satisfying, so animated people of faith that the subsequent interventions of Tudor reformers must be regarded as acts of raw hostility, greedy attacks upon living communities.[6] The fifteenth-century parish in Switzerland, according to Peter Blickle's equally influential *Communal Reformation,* had become effectively organized, with an unanticipated historical result. For years churchmen had manipulated parish obligations to extract material support and spiritual obedience, fomenting a simmering anticlerical furor. A well-organized parish, however, enabled people to take charge of their own religious lives, even to undertake a reforming rebellion.[7]

All this talk among historians of success in parish religion, by whatever measure, comes as something of a surprise, perhaps a reaction. A good generation ago historians in France found medieval parochial practice shockingly lax and indifferent — as measured against categories set up by historical sociologists. Their "finding" prepared the way for a generation of scholars who argued that effective "Christianization" took place only in the postmedieval era[8] — a viewpoint partly reinforced subsequently by the "confessionalization" school of early modern historians, who saw the disciplines of Christian life imposed effectively only by the new reforming regimes. Work this past generation on shrines and saints' cults as well as dissident groups has tended to foster the impression as well, or even set out from the assumption, that medieval parishes were at best functional frameworks for obligatory observance, and at worst, centers of exploitation and power in the name of religion. For their part medieval church historians have identified a revolutionary pastoral mission launched after the year 1215, thus silently conceding earlier failures. With this mission came powers, coercive and pastoral, usually summed up in the call for annual confession, construed at times as directed as much at achieving "control" as providing "care."[9]

To argue then, by contrast, for the effectiveness and importance of parishes in molding religious practice, even for initiatives that came "bottom-up" as well as "top-down," raises new and probing questions. This essay attempts to open

6. Eamon Duffy, *The Stripping of the Altars: Traditional Religion in England, 1400-1580* (New Haven: Yale University Press, 1992).

7. Peter Blickle, *Communal Reformation: The Quest for Salvation in Sixteenth-Century Germany* (Atlantic Highlands, N.J., 1992). See, for instance, the essays in *Kommunalisierung und Christianisierung,* Zeitschrift für Historische Forschung, Beiheft 9 (Berlin, 1989).

8. See especially Jacques Toussaert, *Le sentiment religieux en Flandre à la fin du moyen âge* (Paris, 1963).

9. See Jacques Le Goff and Jean-Claude Schmitt, "Au XIIIe siècle: une parole nouvelle," in *Histoire vécue du peuple chrétien,* ed. Jean Delumeau (Paris, 1979), pp. 257-79.

up that interpretive issue from just one angle, raising the question of local choices in religious practice. However fully and effectively people participated in the routines of parish life, however reluctantly or indifferently, however resistantly (as in the case, say, of Lollards), the parish ordinarily formed the center of Christian belief and worship, becoming for most, as well, the focal point of human life from christening through marrying to burying.[10] No historical generalization can recapture the distinctive histories and wide variation that came with each parish, or indeed the degree of allegiance or obligation felt by any individual parishioner. But two cautionary notes must be entered, to recapture the tension as well as the possibilities located in practices surrounding local religious life. The medieval parish functioned, first, as an authorized public authority. For medieval people a parish meant social life and ecclesiastical obligation as much as personal devotion. Its bell tower called people to prayer and to Mass; it also kept time for work and served as a military bulwark. Stone churches marked the prestige of religious life but also, as official church visitors complained, might double for grain or animal storage, with markets held outside the front doors, even on Sundays or feast days. On every visit to a village church people saw the altar in the choir and the crucifix hanging at the front of the nave, but also, on their way, the tithe barn and the vicar's house to remind them of their economic obligations. A parish represented, at once, obligation and allegiance. An individual, at any given time, might think of his or her parish with a sense of belonging, as his or her place in the world, but also as a center of duties and taxes. People might choose to go there to pray; they had no choice but to have their children christened there, and as well to pay tithes, make confession, and be buried in its churchyard — until the friars challenged that monopoly, in towns at least. All this produced a mix of obligation and participation exceedingly difficult to disentangle, for them and for historians. Take the "churching" of new mothers, their ban from church after childbirth as unclean, then their procession to church with newborns. What might be construed as a shaming of women and their sexuality often functioned, it seems, as a way of celebrating a new mother. The same ambiguity runs throughout: keeping up the nave, part of the people's responsibility, could prove a vexing financial burden or a source of local pride and ownership, even of demonstrative competition, or both.

Second, fascination with the parish and its growing effectiveness should not obscure other religious potentialities in the neighborhood, nor the real limits of a parish's reach. However central each "mother church" (as they were

10. David Cressy, *Birth, Marriage, and Death: Ritual, Religion, and the Life-Cycle in Tudor and Stuart England* (Oxford, 1997), sets this out wonderfully for a slightly later period.

called), however deeply it marked people's lives with christening, marrying, burying, and weekly observances, it never monopolized religious practice. Take the household, for instance. While its religious practices are mostly lost in the shadows, tantalizing hints suggest that children learned the fundamentals — especially how to say the Lord's Prayer or creed, how to conduct themselves in prayer, what to practice as virtue or avoid as vice — at the hearth of their own homes, not at church, and especially from their mothers, not from priests. Boys who went on to become prominent as monks, preachers, or bishops were often said in later *vitae* to have been opened to devotion, sensitized to religious life, by the teaching and example of their mothers, not their parish priest.[11] Add to this the whole world of shrines and cults and saints, these proliferating across every local landscape at their own rate and under their own energies. Take, too, all the practices and rites that historians have labeled or lifted out as "non-Christian." They did exist, to varying degrees and at varying times, just beyond the parish or alongside it or even virtually within it. Their reality was presumed, either passed over as nonthreatening for the priest and the essentials of the faith or as too deeply a matter of local custom to bear challenging without severe consequences, or sometimes indeed as rivals. For medieval parishioners, this essay presupposes, the supernatural was at work freely and powerfully in the world all about them, not confined to the parish, likewise not confined to rival or alternative religious practices.

Historians must take up a more complex story, multiple opportunities and shaping religious influences at work inside and outside parish structures and routines. One may accord full recognition to the parish, and full recognition to the reality of alternatives and of anticlericalism, and still not account for the complexity of local religious life. This essay attempts to frame the issue a little differently, without contesting the realities of either parishes or dissenters. It asks about choices at the local level, religious choices and dynamics available beyond parish routines and duties, and in particular those not perceived as moving people into the category of dissenters. "Choice" is a deceptive word for medieval historians, dealing with a society where so much was conceived and expressed in terms of power and hierarchies, duties and responsibilities. Further, beyond the force of lordly authorities, very real group constraints exercised their power as well. Especially in local settings community pressures and expectations, probably more than lordly demands, moved people to act as their

11. Very little work has been done on this as yet, but see the essays in *La religion de ma mère: Le rôle des femmes dans la transmission de la foi*, ed. Jean Delumeau (Paris, 1992). On the theoretical level, that of the "feminine divine," see the work of Barbara Newman, for instance, her "God and the Goddesses: Vision, Poetry, and Belief in the Middle Ages," in *Poetry and Philosophy in the Middle Ages: A Festschrift for Peter Dronke,* ed. John Marenbon (Leiden, 2001), pp. 173-96.

neighbors or fellow parishioners did. And yet there were choices, group and individual, not in every village, not always equally for men and women, not equally for all social classes. More, everyone knew it, had always known it, and presumed it. Group choices probably had an easier time of it than individual, though that is a distant historical reality hard to generalize about. Depending upon the place, there might be few choices, or in fact a whole range. This was not a systematized set of options — quite the contrary. And so to present as organized what lay by definition beyond prescribed routines would violate the inherent sense of variety, even whimsy and playfulness, that, in my view, most fundamentally characterized these practices. So they are presented here in series, not as a system.

The Cult of Saints

Saints and their shrines began to transfigure the European landscape long before parishes and their priests. Even after a grid of parishes was put in place, saints continued to operate as independent personalities, surprising presences all-around. Their cults might coalesce with parish observances, commonly in a side altar or a subordinate chapel. But as easily and as often, saints transformed an independent chapel, also a hilltop or wooded cove, into a holy place where people chose to gather — more fervently perhaps than for weekly worship in their parish — to pray, to plead their needs and desires, to encounter a heavenly being. All the recent scholarly work on saints and their cults points to an abiding sacral reality, which medieval prelates took entirely for granted. In an exhortatory work setting out the moral claims on each social estate, Bishop Rather of Liège/Verona, addressing ordinary peasants in the 930s, placed the saints immediately after God as deserving reverent attention, before churches, priests, and tithes. "If you wish to be a good Christian, be a worker *(laborator)* who is not only just but constant, content with your own, defrauding no one, doing injury to no one, reproaching no one, slandering no one. Fear God, pray to the saints, attend church, honor priests, offer tithes and first fruits to God, give alms as you are able. Love your wife, know no other woman."[12] Ordinary people living the Christian life, imagined here as peasant and male, were to show fear toward God and direct their requests to saints. These heavenly beings enjoyed a powerful appeal as independent and somewhat unpredictable supernatural presences, often personal. Their stories and deeds attracted loyalty and

---

12. Rather, *Praeloquia* 1.2, ed. Ried, Corpus Christianorum, Continuatio Mediaevalis 46A.5.

devotion. Their lives modeled "heroic" practice; their relics sacralized altars and sites for prayer and miracles; their intercession mediated divine power.

Saints and their cults might antedate or supersede church structures. Willehad in Bremen offers an early and instructive example of the former. Charlemagne had sent this Anglo-Saxon missionary to act as religious overseer and future bishop after conquering the Saxon lands. During Willehad's lifetime these northern peoples had mostly resisted his person and preaching. But after his death a cult sprang up around his grave, miracles were attested, and two generations later (ca. 860) so many people streamed in from nearby villages to pray at his tomb and honor his saintly powers and presence that his church needed expanding. With this cult Bremen's position as an episcopal see, it turns out, was secured — not by his missionary work.[13] The story may seem, in this retelling, much too simple, but it captures a sense of how perceived sacrality could transform place and power. Generally the German landscape was transfigured less by new and local saints such as Willehad than by imported ancient saints (Mary, Peter, Lawrence, and so on), appropriated locally through the transfer or "theft" of relics, bringing to their region the presence of already acclaimed holy people.[14] In the case of Bremen (one reason the record exists), the cult and the church came together, which is typical for stories of founders and patrons.

Villagers left their homes, later also their village churches, to pray at Willehad's tomb. Why? The saint whose body lay in a tomb or under an altar or in a reliquary, people believed, dwelled already in heaven, where he could intercede before Christ, the ultimate healer and judge. That was the divine beauty of it. People of all social classes left their usual settings and prostrated themselves mentally and physically before a chosen saint, sometimes practicing rites peculiar to a shrine in order to effect specific ends, thus lying overnight in touch with the tomb to gain healing or seeking from it a drop of oil or water or dust. They sought there what they could not find in their home church: the presence of a divine power made manifest in miracles of healing, as well in supernatural interventions to render justice or resolve troubles. People acknowledged the saint's intercessory powers with gifts at the shrine, also with votives that acted as emblems for their story (a cane to mark the healing of a crippled leg), and they took home blessed medals as tokens of the saint's continued presence.

13. Ansgar, *Vita Willehadi* 8: *Monumenta Germaniae Historica Scriptores* 2.382-83.

14. This at least is the argument, generally accepted, of Lionel Rothkrug, *Religious Practices and Collective Perceptions: Hidden Homologies in the Renaissance and Reformation*, Réflexions historiques 7.1 (1980), with an important list of shrines on pp. 203-41. The process of importation lies at the heart of Patrick Geary's *Furta Sacra: Thefts of Relics in the Central Middle Ages*, rev. ed. (Princeton, 1990).

They also learned the saint's story, hearing it read or told at the shrine, taking away elements that spoke to their needs or aspirations, remembering or invoking it when they confronted further troubles in their lives. Saints came in great numbers and variety, a range of personalities and powers to meet differing human needs, inclinations, or aspirations. A whole array might populate the mental and spiritual universe of a given person or community, but all in local landscapes: heavenly personalities at work in their own world, busy presences made manifest in holy deeds and powers in their very region, whether inside or outside the parish church.

It was one thing to leave home and walk an hour or a half-day to pray at a nearby shrine or church, but another to walk a whole day or many days to pray in the presence of a special saint or at a very special site. This was to go on pilgrimage.[15] Traveling to distant shrines, to Rome or Jerusalem or Compostela and its shrine of Saint James, transported an individual into a different spiritual world. This was an act of piety and devotion, also perhaps an arduous journey to atone for evils at home. Grave sinners (murderers, for instance) were enjoined to do penance by way of pilgrimage, and thereby took upon themselves, in effect, a temporary and redemptive banning. They were to break out of all ordinary social and religious practices, to launch themselves upon ascetic travel and thus discipline their bodies and concentrate their minds. Pilgrimage, to say it another way, removed believers from daily routines, including notably parish routines and obligations. It focused their minds on Christ or the saint commemorated, and impressed on their perception of the holy a new sense of tactile space and divine presence, a "place to pray," as they ordinarily put it. In 1102-3, just after the crusaders captured Jerusalem, an Anglo-Saxon named Saewulf traveled all the way to the sepulcher of the Lord, as he put it, to pray.[16] A German pilgrim named Theodericus traveled to Jerusalem in the 1150s or 1160s, and explained: the holy places of our Savior displayed his bodily presence, were filled still with the mysteries of his humanity and of human redemption. He narrated this pilgrimage for readers who could not make the journey themselves, so they could thereby learn always to keep Christ in mind, to love his memory, to suffer with Christ along the way, eventually to gain his heavenly kingdom. Beyond Jerusalem and Rome new sites emerged: Saint Thomas of Canterbury, and countless regional sites, also controversial ones such as, much later, the bloody host at Wilsnack in Germany. Regional sites allowed the less

---

15. There is an outstanding bibliography on pilgrimage in *Wallfahrt kennt keine Grenzen* (Zürich, 1984), pp. 543-68, and some recent interpretive essays in *Pilgrimage Explored*, ed. J. Stopford (York, 1999).

16. *Peregrinationes tres*, ed. R. B. C. Huygens, Corpus Christianorum, Continuatio Mediaevalis 139.59.

privileged, perhaps also the less devout, to undertake manageable pilgrimages at crisis points in their lives: to intercede for loved ones, to do public penance, to orient their inner life in prayer.

Parishes attempted, like bishops earlier, to co-opt for themselves the key elements in the cult of saints: dedicating their main altar to a particular patron whose relics were kept there, allowing additional shrines or cults at side altars, fostering devotions in smaller circles, sometimes claiming oversight over local shrines. But local cults remained independent and unpredictable, as Schmitt demonstrated in the cult of a holy greyhound, Saint Guinefort. Such shrines could expand and contract in waves of devotion entirely independent of the local parish and its cults or routines. After the Roman Church established formal canonization procedures in the thirteenth century, "new" saints had more difficulty gaining full or universal recognition, though local cults continued to flourish, perhaps with somewhat increased risk of intervention if they appeared somehow excessive or false. For the historian these "new" saints and new cults, likewise the miracles attested of them, give witness to religious practices and expectations apart from those associated with the great canonized figures (usually in orders). All the most gripping needs of families and individuals, including violence against children or the ills wrought by warfare, came to expression in their stories, and especially the miracles performed.[17]

One of the more remarkable of the local and new cults to attain universal recognition was that of Elizabeth (d. 1231), daughter of the Hungarian king, who gave her life to serving the poor in poverty. She became a model for those establishing an urban hospice/hospital to serve the sick, destitute, and homeless in the new cities. At least in the German-speaking lands of central Europe, her cult spread almost as rapidly as that of her male contemporary in Italy, Francis of Assisi, and she was one of the few contemporary saints taken up into the *Golden Legend* and preached across Europe. For all her attractiveness as the paradigmatic figure of a new urban Christian charity, she also embodied the full powers of a saint. At her death her body oozed sweet-smelling aromas and healing oils, and birds spontaneously sang. Within only four years of her death (1231-35) her tomb at Marburg had gained fame as a major pilgrimage site, one to which people turned, after they had given up on others, as their newest and last hope. More than seven hundred healing miracles were attested in writing in this short time alone, the pilgrims and the healed coming from widespread regions of the German Empire. She also gained recognition as patron of the Teutonic Order of knights, more strikingly, thus linking her back, ironically, to power and privi-

---

17. See Michael E. Goodich, *Violence and Miracle in the Fourteenth Century: Private Grief and Public Salvation* (Chicago, 1995), for some compelling accounts.

lege.[18] And yet the rapid spread of her cult had as much to do with the attractive story of her Christlike life as with the miracles worked at her shrines and the protection she afforded clients.

A spiritual landscape marked by devotion to local and universal saints intersected with — or may legitimately be put in tension with — the grid of parish observances, thereby returning us to our larger question. Veneration was a matter of choice, not obligation. People had little choice about where they would be christened, married, or buried, and where or when they paid tithes. But they could choose which saints to pray to, when to light a candle in their honor, to which they offered gifts, to which they turned personally for healing or intercession or intervention. These prayers or rites or medals were always to some degree personal, always in varying states of adaptation to local usages and new needs. Choices in turn grew out of experience. Saints could, for instance, also prove vengeful, jealously protecting with curses and plagues the peoples or properties entrusted to their keeping. They might also be found wanting, failing to deliver as promised or hoped — this not normally recorded in a shrine book dedicated to recalling the qualities of a saint. Yet it was a common experience, and a common anxiety. Witness those people who claimed to find healing at Elizabeth's tomb only after giving up in despair elsewhere (a motif in many stories). Pursuing choices, or making choices, about saints' cults without repudiating the religion of the parish or its patron saints: this is one area where religious practice at local levels found genuine freedom of expression and movement.

Through the high and later Middle Ages the full array of inherited cultic figures persisted, and indeed became ever more fully available in images, shrines, and stories. Recent scholars have noted particularly the attention paid to antique women (Catherine, Barbara, and so on) as well as figures addressing contemporary need (Roche as protector against plague). For the purposes of this essay three broader points deserve notice. There was, first, ever greater emphasis upon Christ's humanity, especially his passion and particularly his wounds, this perhaps fostered by Franciscans but soon generalized and reaching into local places by way of, for instance, the Veronica (the face of the suffering Christ imprinted on a veil), the instruments of the passion, and the stations of the cross. Second, Marian veneration, first fostered especially by Cistercians, expanded ever more broadly in universalizing patterns (Marian chapels or side altars) and at local sites ("Our Lady" of such and such a place or of such and such a need or devotion). Indeed, Marian shrines proved paradigmatic as

18. The best orientation is by way of *Elisabeth von Thüringen: Persönlichkeit, Werk und Wirkung,* ed. Kaspar Elm (Marburg, 1982).

wellsprings of divine mercy, and Marian devotions as formative of an ideal human piety (see Clark's paper in this volume) — the "feminine divine" plainly important, especially when contrasted, as it often was in word or image, with a "judging Lord." Importantly, third, the eucharistic host was itself enshrined for veneration, commonly now in monstrances, and each year processed through town during the new feast of Corpus Christi. In special cases such as the controversial shrine at Wilsnack in the mid–fifteenth century, bleeding hosts became the objects of special devotions and enthusiasms.

All these devotions share, with respect to the larger question in this paper, noteworthy structural analogies. They focus upon elements central to the religious practices of the parish establishment: the passion, the Eucharist, Mary the mother of God (often assimilated to mother church). But in each case the object of devotion and prayer has become separated out as a matter of cult, thus personalized and transformed into an item of choice. People might turn to any of these, for reasons of need or devotion or both, as an individual practice, not the required Easter duty or the Holy Week observances or simple obedience to mother church. Cultic practices, in other words, proved so powerful, as matters of devotion and of choice, that they effectively appropriated distinctive elements from parish religion and turned them into items of individual choice rather than communal observance.

In the later Middle Ages, lastly, the cult of saints — though never losing the crucial element of access to heavenly powers (pilgrims to Elizabeth's shrine also lay on her tomb or rubbed dust on sick limbs) — cultivated more richly the paradigmatic aspect, saints as exemplary of Christian virtues and lifestyles. While the intercessory element never ceased, the exemplary dimension grew. Images and especially stories played an ever larger role. Adopting saints' names, which only really took off in this later era, presumes it, claiming for one's self, or rather one's child, attributes known from the story (also of course, the saint's protection). Saints' lives had always been presented to people as heavenly and exemplary, worthy of reflection during their prayers. But churchmen self-consciously added an educational element, most famously and influentially in the *Golden Legend,* an attempt by Dominicans about 1260 to present summary accounts of all the saints useful for preachers in making sermons. From the later thirteenth century onward, moreover, this (and other collections of saints' lives) was translated repeatedly into the vernacular languages.[19] These stories circulated widely and achieved a remarkably strong place in popular culture,

19. See now Werner Williams-Krapp, *Die deutschen und niederländischen Legendare des Mittelalters* (Tübingen, 1986). For an accessible translation, see now Jacobus de Voragine, *The Golden Legend: Readings on the Saints,* trans. William Granger Ryan, 2 vols. (Princeton, 1993).

alongside the stories people told in taverns or at court. That is to say, the stories of saints came alive for people as importantly as the actual cult or shrine, and indeed were to come alive in their own languages through telling and retelling (also depiction in stained glass, wall paintings, altar paintings, tapestry, sculpture). Here again choice was paramount: people could choose which stories to hear or tell or appropriate, which names to adopt, which images to venerate or to obtain for their own household. The cult of saints allowed people, without rejecting parish obligations, to shape their religious lives according to personal needs and predilections.

Preaching

From the ninth century onward synodical statutes enjoined priests to instruct their parishioners in the meaning of the Gospel readings and the essential articles of the creed, together with the vices and virtues and the Ten Commandments. Exactly how much instruction actually went on, and in what form, is nearly impossible to tell, even in the later Middle Ages. People expected priests to perform the sacramental mysteries and to lead worship; they seem not to have expected much formal teaching or preaching. Repeated injunctions from prelates and complaints in visitation records about ignorant priests indicate that preaching was not ordinarily a memorable feature of parish life. It had been otherwise in late antiquity when great Roman bishops, Augustine, Ambrose, John Chrysostom, and numerous others, deployed the full power of the rhetorical art to instruct and persuade urban populations. But the transition from bishops preaching in Roman cities to priests instructing country parishioners took place over generations, and much was lost along the way. Preaching gained new importance in medieval Europe from the twelfth century onward, but in entirely different circumstances and with a different meaning — a point that must be registered firmly over against various post-Reformation expectations or patterns. Preaching came to people from time to time — but mostly as an unusual event, something beyond the parish, therefore a matter of choice.

Many twelfth-century reformers spent a phase of their lives as "wandering preachers" before settling into religious communities or as prelates. Such preachers operated in an extraordinary way: gathering audiences in open fields or town squares, choosing their own topic and text. Many were regarded with suspicion or jealousy, also accused of straying into false teaching or invading parishes. But they apparently met with an eager response. Late in the twelfth century demand appears to have increased, and some regular clergy — including, in southern Germany, a Cistercian and an Augustinian canon — undertook the preparation of sermon cycles in the vernacular. These more "orthodox" sermons in German were largely based upon those of the Latin Fathers (those Roman bishops) or Carolingian authors (who summarized and transmitted them: see Cavadini's essay in this volume). They circulated widely in manuscript,[20] but their exact usage as well as their audience outside the monastery is hard to fathom.

When freewheeling preachers entered medieval parishes, they were sometimes welcomed, sometimes resisted. Churchmen increasingly came to fear them as heretical, thus Waldensians who set up to preach in the vernacular or Cathars who taught a dualist worldview. So prelates moved to control preaching generally. They would seek to limit it, in principle, to those directly under a bishop's authority (including parish priests) — a point insisted upon again around 1400 over against Lollards, the New Devout, and others. Yet exceptions of all kinds persisted, including some women. And just after 1200 a striking exception emerged to this strict hierarchical view, represented most famously by the lay preacher Francis of Assisi. Some clerics concocted an entirely innovative notion. Whereas religious orders had been committed for centuries to withdrawal from the world and to prayer, they organized themselves instead to pursue public preaching in the world. Such was especially the Order of Preachers founded by Dominic Guzman between 1215 and 1221. At Cologne, then the largest city in German-speaking lands, an early Dominican brother named Henry reportedly set the whole town buzzing and sparked a revival that directed people toward a special devotion to the name of Jesus.[21] In Italy, in the "Alleluia" revival of 1233, preachers persuaded warring factions in cramped cities to seek peace, and the brother-preachers themselves acted on occasion as mediators and political arbiters.[22] Dominicans, later Franciscans and all the other mendicant friars as well, brought enormous learning to their preaching.[23] But they aimed at far more than eloquence. They considered their preaching truly effective if people lined up afterward to make their confessions.

20. There is an enormous literature on medieval preaching in German, some of it dated and much of it marred by confessional concerns. Basic orientation to the literature (with bibliographies) by Georg Steer, in Ingeborg Glier, ed., *Die deutsche Literatur im späten Mittelalter, 1250-1370*, Geschichte der Deutschen Literatur III/2 (Munich, 1987), pp. 318-38.

21. Jordan of Saxony, *Libellus de principio ordinis predicatorum 79*, ed. H. C. Scheeben (Rome, 1935), p. 63.

22. See now Augustine Thompson, *Revival Preachers and Politics in Thirteenth-Century Italy: The Great Devotion of 1233* (Oxford, 1992).

23. See now Michele Mulchahey, *"First the Bow Is Bent in Study": Dominican Education before 1350* (Toronto, 1998).

Just one example for the purposes of this essay. The preaching tours of a German Franciscan named Berthold of Regensburg (d. 1271), across southern and central Germany in the 1250s, made news everywhere. In distant England Roger Bacon took note, as did Salimbene in Italy, and claimed that Brother Berthold single-handedly converted more people than all other Dominicans and Franciscans combined. Stubborn sinners, one chronicler reported, would give up their former lives in the wake of his preaching, openly make confession, and seek to make amends.[24] Berthold attracted thousands, bursting the limits of any church, even the open space in front of most churches. So he set up in city squares or open fields. He had a pulpit constructed to raise him above the surging crowds, released a feather to test the wind, and then preached with the wind at his back so his voice would carry.[25] Berthold and his brothers kept sermon notes in Latin. Within a generation these were recast in German, leaving us an approximation of how he sounded.[26] Though friars followed the liturgy's Gospel lessons and saints' days, Berthold also preached topical sermons. These caught on and were chosen for distribution in the vernacular.

Berthold's method was to link topics central to Christian life (fasting, penance, duty) to common images or metaphors. He pointed, for instance, to the seven planets in the sky above, linked by name in German to the seven days of the week, and made them visible points of reference for the seven virtues. Thus Sunday, named after the brightest and most needed heavenly body, should call to mind what is most needed, namely, faith. Just as looking into the sun too much blinded the eyes, he noted, so people should not worry their faith excessively. When people looked up into the heavens, they should think of heaven and the celestial virtues, should remember too that planetary bodies influenced only nature, that is, the body and health, not the will. For memory purposes Berthold might link Gospel stories to common human features, thus the man with five talents to five fingers, toes, and senses. Each talent, people should remember, must be returned to God "doubled," meaning a renewed faithfulness in office, craft, or occupation as well as in the use of time, and above all in love of neighbors.

Berthold's message employed a new medium but was not generally a new message, and he could put matters very plainly. God commanded four things:

24. These testimonies to Berthold's preaching, and many others, were collected in the preface to a first edition: *Berthold von Regensburg, Predigten,* ed. Franz Pfeiffer (Vienna, 1862), pp. xx-xxxii.

25. *Berthold von Regensburg, Predigten,* p. xxiii (a later Swiss chronicler who claimed to report what he had heard from eyewitnesses years earlier).

26. For the enormous problems surrounding authorship and editions, see now the *Verfasserlexikon* (1978), 1:817-23.

right belief, obedience (to guard against mortal sin), right deeds (no heaven without good acts), and giving up enmity (patience enough to hold no one in envy or hatred).[27] Berthold rarely threatened. He crafted his sermons to shape souls. The greatest wisdom in the world, he began one sermon, is to guard the soul from mortal sin; that is the craft of saints. Master artisans know every possible craft, but without the craft of guarding souls humans are fools.[28] It is the stuff of a thousand books in Christendom, he added, but for people to learn this craft they must come to sermons![29] Berthold was inviting them, through this new medium, to acquire for themselves the bookish wisdom of protecting the soul into eternity. He rendered this craft as a kind of folk wisdom, offering three items learned better through hearing sermons, he declaimed, than through acquiring the learning of professors at Paris or Bologna. First, always take counsel before acting: with your own heart, with fellow humans, and with God. Second, never put off doing good useful to your soul and praiseworthy to God, whether saying your prayers or giving alms. Third, think at all times on your final end.[30] In one of his elaborate images, in fact a mixed metaphor, Berthold likened heaven to eternal profit or gain and placed it like a castle on a hilltop. A few, the saints and martyrs, walked straight up the steepest path to claim it, as did monks and nuns. Most people wound their way slowly and circuitously up the hill by the wagon road. The spoked wheels of their wagon represented four forms of mercy that carried them along: mercy on the soul by way of repentance and a change of will; mercy on present-day martyrs, namely, the poor and the sick and the homeless; mercy on those suffering for their sins in purgatory; and mercy on those still caught in deadly sin (the avaricious, for instance) who wander the path the wrong way.

Preaching worked if it effected a change of will: so the basic concepts of penance were never far from these sermons. In one on penance Berthold laid out its threefold steps. Since sin begins in the inner being, the heart must be turned to contrition; since it is advanced by words, the mouth must speak it aloud in confession; and since it is carried out in deeds, good works must render satisfaction. Berthold took up objections to each he had heard from people. About confession, for instance, they complained that it was too embarrassing and shameful to say aloud to a priest what they had done — there were no confession boxes as yet — especially when it was also commonly said that the priest's "wife" would later hear and tell all. Berthold rejected this, but then sug-

27. Berthold, *Predigten* II, "On Twelve Sinners," ed. Pfeiffer-Joseph Strobl, 2:211.
28. Berthold, *Predigten*, ed. Pfeiffer, 1:1.
29. Berthold, *Predigten*, 1:5.
30. Berthold, *Predigten*, 1:6-8.

gested they find a mendicant priest if necessary, one other than their own, who would lead them into repentance. The point of hope, he insisted, was that any who made their way through all three steps would never be put to shame by the devil, not in this life or the next. Fifty years after Lateran Council IV had made confessing annually to your "own" priest a matter of Christian obligation (and a defining feature of the parish), Berthold foresaw preaching and confessing as working outside the parish more effectively both personally and spiritually.

Preaching was associated in most people's minds, in short, with a space and an occasion other than the parish and its ministrations. It might be one of the mendicant churches in town, designed with great halls to accommodate large crowds and pulpits to project the preacher's voice. It might be an open field or a town square. In the later Middle Ages, especially in Germany and Italy, towns hired famous preachers (often mendicants) to preach a Lenten series in preparation for the Easter duty. In this case the space was public (usually the town square) and the funding civic; the aim, beyond parish duties, was to lift the moral and religious tone of the entire community. Friar-preachers or hired preachers, moreover, were not bound by the readings for a given Sunday or feast day. They could pursue topics of interest to the people (often moral and social issues), they could employ stories (called exempla) and various other devices to hold attention, they could move people with all the rhetorical arts available to them in the people's own language. And above all, this was not Sunday duty: people could choose to come, or not. Or they could visit a mendicant church on Sunday because they wished to hear a more thoughtful or persuasive exposition of the Gospel. Odd as it may seem, therefore, especially over against images of the church from the late antique and post-Reformation worlds, preaching must be understood in the high Middle Ages as largely an activity of choice: people removing themselves from their parish to be moved by instruction or exhortation in their own language in a space set up for that purpose, with a preacher aiming singularly at that end.

Private Religious Societies

Just as people could choose to look beyond their parishes to shrines and saints for divine intercession and heavenly models, and beyond their own priests to extraordinary preachers for exhortation and guidance, so throughout the Middle Ages they looked beyond the parish for paradigms of religious perfection. The triumph of the monastic ideal in late antiquity meant that Christian perfection came to be reckoned as a complete renunciation of the self to serve the kingdom of Christ, thus all property, all sexual and familial ties, all self-will.

Monastic houses predated parish churches in many cases, and in the religious hierarchy monks and nuns stood highest as exemplars of the perfect life. The professed, in orders, were simply "the religious." Others might become associated with them but in subservient roles, by giving over themselves and their properties, for instance, at the end of their lives in return for prayers, or following monastic practices at a distance and in limited ways as oblates or tertiaries. The prestige accorded the religious affected laypeople in varying ways. They might, at one extreme, be inclined toward a kind of passive resignation, simply leaving religious life as such to professionals, as a matter beyond their own duty or doing. They might also look to acquire benefits at a distance: by visiting these powerhouses of intercession on a particular holy day or establishing prayer links through gifts of land or children. Alternatively, some people might seek to emulate monastic life within the restrictions of lay and parish life. Whether and how monasteries influenced people beyond their walls remains under dispute for the early Middle Ages.[31] But after 1200 or so, many more people began seeking out ways to act in some measure as "religious," not by joining monasteries but by organizing private societies within or beyond the parish and pursuing a devotional life there. They might, most simply, especially at the end of the Middle Ages, form a "confraternity": a group, for instance, to facilitate common religious observances as members of an artisan group, which also helped bury members, maintain a side altar, or even hire a chantry priest to say Mass. People also formed confraternities dedicated to specific devotions, say, like-minded devotions to the Virgin in the form of the rosary prayers (a late medieval movement). Such confraternities, proliferating in the later Middle Ages, many of them loosely organized out of parishes, focused isolated devotional practices on a voluntary basis.

Other people, separating themselves out more dramatically but without taking vows, aimed to establish forms of life or spiritual practices modeled roughly on monastic life, thus common prayer or common meals or an informal commitment to chastity and simplicity. Historians, for lack of a better term, have called these people "semi-religious." They were especially influential in the Low Countries and in German-speaking lands, though also in Italy. They sought a religious life subject neither to the institutional arrangements of monastic profession nor to the obligations of the parish, and this could bring trouble from either side.[32] Securing the approval, or at least tolerance, of the parish

31. See, for one end of the debate, Ludovicus Milis, *Angelic Monks and Earthly Men: Monasticism and Its Meaning in Medieval Society* (Woodbridge, 1992).

32. For orientation to a large literature, see my "Friar Johannes Nyder on Laypeople Living as Religious in the World," in *Vita Religiosa im Mittelalter: Festschrift für Kaspar Elm zum 70. Geburtstag* (Berlin, 1999), pp. 583-615.

priest was essential to avoid suspicion, for theirs was a form of religious practice just beyond his jurisdiction and oversight.

The best known of these groups, here treated representatively, acquired the name Beguines, private religious women setting up in their own houses, often clustered at the far edge of a medieval town or near a supportive church. They voluntarily banded together to lead a religious life of simplicity, relative poverty, and chastity, with a daily round of prayer in the vernacular, charity toward orphans or the sick, and self-support through the work of their hands.[33] They never took vows, never joined a religious order as such, never wholly forswore property (several owned their houses or had inherited incomes). Yet they pursued religion at an intensity far beyond parish expectations, approaching that of life in a cloister. They sought to remove themselves, still as laywomen, from the routines of worldly life, and to sustain contemplative prayer in solitude. Central for them, ordinarily, was a pattern of prayer in their own tongue, often the so-called little hours of the Virgin or some other set of Psalms. Though these women belonged still in principle to their local parish, whenever their numbers and influence grew large enough they preferred to withdraw and seek pastoral guidance on their own terms, from a Franciscan or Dominican friar or by forming a church specially for their community. Theirs was a self-constructed religious life, designed for women in an urban setting, usually sanctioned by statutes agreed to jointly by the women themselves and the town's magistrates.

Their most famous exemplar, a kind of founding figure, was Marie d'Oignies. At an early age she persuaded her husband to turn theirs into a chaste marriage, and to give themselves over to care for lepers and the sick. She adopted for herself, apart from any monastic rule, an extraordinary ascetic regimen, with extreme fasting and night vigils, and was soon perceived as a person with supernatural powers of spiritual intuition. She knew the minds and hearts of sinners or troubled persons before they revealed themselves to her. Her father-confessor (and the author of her *Life*), the cardinal and preacher Jacques de Vitry, came to venerate her and to depend upon her more than she upon him. But churchmen worried about self-made communities with self-made religious exercises. Laywomen seeking a firsthand experience of God, with no formal training in theology, distancing themselves from parochial oversight and

33. For the large literature on Beguines, see now Andreas Wilts, *Beginen im Bodenseeraum* (Sigmaringen, Germany, 1994), an impressive local study that reviews the state of the question. In English, Edward McDonnell, *The Beguines and Beghards in Medieval Culture, with Special Emphasis on the Belgian Scene* (New Brunswick, N.J., 1984), and now especially Walter Simons, *Cities of Ladies: Beguine Communities in the Medieval Low Countries, 1200-1565* (Philadelphia, 2001).

with knowledge derived mostly from teachings and writings in their mother tongues: this could all too easily generate devotion or speculation, they feared, that would veer into the aberrant or the bizarre. And indeed, some of these women were perceived to cross the boundary of received orthodoxy — or at least were so charged. Marguerite Porete, the most horrific and famous case, paid with her life for writing in medieval French about souls "annihilating themselves" in total devotion, "emptying into God."[34]

Just as Beguines created their own religious communities beyond the parish, distantly modeled on monasteries, so they created a literature of devotion and religious experience in their own style and tongue, distantly modeled on religious writings in Latin for monks and canons. Mechthild of Magdeburg's *Flowing Light of Divinity* is a masterpiece of German literature and mystical exposition, as was Marguerite's in French despite its difficult prose and condemnation. The earliest of these writers was the Beguine Hadewijch, who composed the first substantial body of religious poetry and prose in Dutch, datable roughly to the mid–thirteenth century. All three women drew deeply on themes they knew from worldly literature, especially the poetry of love and lovemaking. These courtly themes and commonplaces, it must be inferred, were more familiar to them from their upbringing than was the distinctive monastic literature of formation that had flowered in twelfth-century monasteries in Latin. These women transformed those worldly themes into intense descriptions of the soul's pursuit of her divine lover, its longing to be united indissolubly with Christ, in Marguerite's case for the soul to empty itself entirely into quiet unity with the Godhead, in Hadewijch's for an experience of love as a "raging tempest."

Hadewijch's poems reveal a powerful form of teaching aimed at shaping both the outer and the inner life, while expressing a personal experience of the divine. Laying siege to Love, or seeking to "become Love," begins, she says, with ardent service, consisting in the works of mercy, serving strangers and the poor. It means suffering grief without knowing pain, performing service so constantly that it becomes effortless, keeping friendship with God's friends on earth. She who serves in this way, with all her heart and powers, will receive in time the consolations of Love.[35] Her writings went far beyond metaphors of chivalric service, however. In a prose letter on "living in the rhythm of the Trinity," she declares that the person who serves Love and unites with it/him thereby

---

34. See now Margaret Porete, *The Mirror of Simple Souls,* ed. and trans. E. Colledge and J. C. Marler (Notre Dame, Ind., 1999).

35. *Hadewijch, the Complete Works,* trans. Columba Hart (New York, 1980), poem 8, pp. 147-48.

also participates in the deeper mysteries of the Godhead. She imagines poetically grasping within her own person the procession of the Son from the Father, being herself thereby animated by the might, will, and work of the triune God.[36] That is to say, the basic teachings of parish life — acting in virtue, performing the works of mercy, loving God — have not been rejected. But they have become quite distinctly and personally appropriated; more, these women living in community beyond the parish have transmuted them into a personal language of love for, and experience of, the divine. Whether or not churchmen liked and trusted Hadewijch's command of language and sensitivity to religious experience, she wrote a personal theology in poetic form. For Beguines such teachings could well prove far more instructive, and indeed formative, than the ordinary accounts of Christian life proffered in the parish. Above all, this way of life offered a choice, one women could take on their own in their own town, apart from taking on the obligations of a professed religious life, yet distinct from the ordinary duties of parish life.

Drama in Church and in the Streets

In the later Middle Ages the Christian peoples of Europe devised ever more ways to enliven their religious beliefs, to appropriate them as practices outside the sacramental rites and worship led by clergy, even to experience them as entertainment. Dramatic representations of religious and moral themes came to abound, indeed became a fixed part of life in most towns. Nearly seven hundred examples still exist, with records of thousands of public performances.[37] Dramatic versions of the Christian story had begun inside churches (probably cathedrals, and probably in the tenth century), and in their earliest form re-enacted, in Latin, the women visiting the tomb on Easter morning. After 1200 drama moved out into the city square and reenacted, mostly or wholly in the vernacular, the entire passion and Easter story.[38] Controlled initially by churchmen who sang or chanted the text in Latin, these dramas were increasingly taken charge of by laymen, often by guilds or confraternities, who spoke their lines in the vernacular. Joined to major liturgical feast days, whether Holy Week or Corpus Christi (the feast of the Eucharist), the plays brought to life biblical stories or moral teachings and involved individuals or groups by way of mostly

36. Letter 17.

37. The essential edition, in five volumes, is Walther Lipphardt, *Lateinische Osterfeiern und Osterspiele* (Berlin, 1976).

38. There is an enormous literature on medieval religious drama. A good basic orientation for the German examples noted here by Hansjürgen Linke can be found in Glier, pp. 153-233.

voluntary participation. Once these religious dramas went into the streets and into the people's tongue, they acquired added characters and scenes: rowdy soldiers, greedy merchants, penitent women (especially Mary Magdalene converted from whoredom to holiness). In making this biblical drama their own, taking it out from under the auspices of clergymen, the people of medieval towns, especially in Germany, made the central biblical stories speak to their own experience of human life.

Dramatic productions offer a striking combination of "play" *(ludus)* and "exemplary teaching" *(exemplum).*[39] The biblical soldiers who guard Christ's tomb and lose their charge become objects of playful sport, including jabs at the incompetent and shrunken "manhood" of these "knights" — jokes meant to please a rowdy and sometimes irreverent audience. Artisans and shopkeepers also mocked their own: the women purchasing spices for Christ's tomb occasioned an ever expanding scene that turned on an apothecary (Krämer) and his wife who were made to embody — with much comic effect — all the vices of a greedy, bungling merchant household. No less surprising as a type of personal appropriation is the Mary who encounters Christ in the garden, represented as the Magdalene, the converted whore. This lowliest of urban sinners, a woman who sold her body, becomes the first to see the resurrected body and be assured of full forgiveness and everlasting life. This Mary tells a troublesome and disbelieving Thomas, in a subsequent story, simply to "shut up." Most of Christ's lines, taken over directly from the Gospel account, were sung in Latin, but in this story, treating belief and unbelief, he speaks here in the vernacular.[40] Still another scene, much beloved and an addition to the biblical narrative, was set in hell. It has Satan and Lucifer relishing all the souls they hold there, beginning with the pope. They enumerate in catchy rhymed verse a list of doomed souls, beginning with arrogant and vicious clergymen and ending with tradespeople, each corrupt in a distinct way. In the end Christ overwhelms hell by his sheer power and leads out by the hand those troubled souls on whom he has had mercy.

The designers of these dramatic presentations were clear about their didactic purposes, set out in an introductory speech. In one of the earliest extant plays (from Innsbruck), the "expounder of the play" instructed all, rich and poor, old and young, to sit on the ground and "take in" how their God came to

39. Strikingly, a Latin text from Benediktbeuron (also the provenance of an important early vernacular version) described the play with both words: *ludus, immo exemplum.* Lipphardt, no. 830 = 5:1711.

40. See, for instance, a newly discovered version: *Das Brandenburger Osterspiel,* ed. Renate Schipke-Franzjoseph Pensel, Beiträge aus der Deutschen Staatsbibliothek 4 (Berlin, 1986), pp. 57-61.

reign: how he rose from a bitter death to console humans, how he rescued from hell all who did his will. First the people must be quiet and sit down so they may hear Pilate and some Jews make a plan to place soldiers at the tomb (the first scene).[41] He goes on to set out all the scenes that were to follow. This play ended, as did many, with a final speech in which the apostle John called on all the seated people to rejoice over their rescue from hell, to pray God for eternal life, and to join in the Easter hymn "Christ arose."[42] In the Vienna version of this drama, the "expounder" says they are to join in singing so as to pay honor to the Lord, so all who wish to escape the pains of hell may have Christ's memory impressed upon their hearts.[43] In the passion plays the leader begins with even more personalized instruction: Hear, all you Christians, how the Creator of the world wandered through it with signs and teaching and then was murdered "by you" *(dorch dich)!* Mark this well in your understanding![44] For many the passion or creation lived more thoroughly in their minds and imaginations by way of these representations than by way of the priests' annual liturgical readings. People, often drawn in by membership in a guild, participated in these displays, as producers, actors, or audience, by choice, as a matter of entertainment as well as of devotion or instruction.

Literary Writing and Religious Practice

Storytelling, entertaining, and instructing by literary composition, sung aloud or privately read, constitute the oldest of human activities. Nearly from the beginning of a Christian presence in German-speaking lands, two authors self-consciously recast the Gospel in vernacular verse: the Old Saxon *Heliand* and Otfrid's rhymed Old German *Gospelbook.* Otfrid explicitly offered his verses to rival the obscene verses laypeople regularly sang, he said, so the sweetness of the Gospels in their own tongue might offset (literally "wipe out") secular wordplay. The memory of the Old German words, he hoped, would transform the hearers' acts and lift their thoughts toward heaven. Gospel tales in their own tongues might help discipline the waywardness of the five senses.[45] In the early

41. "Das Innsbrucker Osterspiel" (one of the earliest extant plays), in *Das Drama des Mittelalters,* ed. Eduard Hartl (1937; reprint, Darmstadt, 1964), pp. 136-37.

42. "Das Innsbrucker Osterspiel," pp. 188-89.

43. "Das Innsbrucker Osterspiel," p. 75.

44. *Das St. Galler Passionsspiel,* ed. E. Hartl, Altdeutsche Textbibliothek 41 (Halle, 1967), p. 56.

45. *Otfrids Evangelienbuch,* ed. Oskar Erdmann, 4th ed. by Ludwig Wolff (Tübingen, 1962), pp. 4-5. For the *Heliand,* see now G. Ronald Murphy, *The Heliand: The Saxon Gospel* (New York, 1992).

twelfth century a laywoman named Ava rendered in verse the lives of John the Baptist and of Christ. She concluded her life of Christ with verses teaching the seven gifts of the Holy Spirit: now, she said at the transition point, we should discover in the love of this holy God how the Spirit from on high might stir in our breast. Open, she ordered, your inner ears, so you may learn how to cultivate *(phlegen)* God.[46]

Just how far such poems spread outside the monastic houses where their manuscript copies are preserved is impossible to know. The difficulty with those writings we now classify more or less as "literary" is to know their audience. For while drama aimed to entertain and instruct, to draw in large public audiences, these literary writings mostly targeted far smaller circles of readers or listeners, private audiences in palaces or town houses or religious houses. In truth the great majority of the population remained illiterate, the cost of books out of reach. Importantly, too, in medieval Europe the virtues and individuals celebrated in vernacular literature often ran contrary to any notion of faithful practice: the prowess in battle of the epics, the tangled love of the romances, the wily deviousness of the fabliaux, the sensuous enticements of lyric. Singular emphasis on this aspect of medieval vernacular writing, however, reflects modern interests as much as the evidences of medieval writing. In the later Middle Ages religious literature flourished nearly everywhere in the vernacular, despite occasional attempts at suppression, or troubles such as those associated with the Lollards. Who can forget that the most profound theological reflections on medieval society came in the form of literary masterpieces, Dante's *Divine Comedy* or Langland's *Piers Plowman*?

Between the mid-eleventh and the early thirteenth centuries vernacular literature flourished at court. German writers applied the same verse, meter, and language to compositions with religious themes. These poems and lyrics took many forms: courtesy displayed to the Virgin and saints, battle scenes allegorizing spiritual struggles (adumbrated centuries earlier by Prudentius). *The Redemption,* a poem from the later thirteenth century and the region of Hesse, emulated the rhymes, easy flowing language, and verse forms of the epics, its prologue consciously imitative of Gottfried's *Tristan* — now celebrating divine redemption rather than human love. After a stunning opening on the beauties of the natural world as made by a triune God, the poet pretended he could not so invitingly ornament his language *(ich kan niht vil gesmieren/noch die wort bezieren)* like the poems of the Grail, of Iwein and Parcival, of Tristan and all the others. He would versify without rhetorical flowers, for his was seri-

---

46. *Die religiösen Dichtungen des 11. und 12. Jahrhunderts,* ed. Friedrich Maurer (Tübingen, 1965), 2:487.

ous speech *(dise rede ist [ein] ernstlich gesar)* delivered in plain words *(mit blozen worten unde bar)*. Yet his next verses, taking up the creation of time and the world, described the Redeemer's hand as "tender" *(so zart und so gehure)* in making his creatures, their making in turn modeled on "godly worthiness."[47] Throughout the author offers appealing stories (chiefly about Christ's life as redeemer) in the manner of great worldly epics, complete with dialogues to reveal inner states of being (for instance, Mary's at the annunciation). The poet carries his reader/hearer through the life of Christ, then seats the king and his queen (Mary) in heaven as rulers over all earthly kings. On introducing the last judgment, he reviews in verse the seven deadly sins and the Ten Commandments: so people might be found in the Redeemer's "band" *(schar)* at the crucial moment. After delivering threats and curses for a whole range of infidels, the poet ended with a prayer invoking the love *(minne)* the betrothed displayed to his "queen," and as well his "worthiness," manifest above all in the "worthy blood" that poured out of his wounds and forgave "our misdeeds" so people might enjoy "sweet" life.[48] Here was a poetic composition fit for the hearthside at court or at tavern, to rival any worldly notions of redemption and the good life, a literary interpretation in epic language of the Christian story — not the sort of thing heard in a parish from a priest.

For the purposes of a paper on formative practices, just one final example may be noted: literary writing that intriguingly united storytelling with moral teaching, worldly amusement with religious practice, literary form with preaching. Around 1300 a Dominican friar named Jacobus de Cessolis turned the game of chess and the pieces of the chessboard into an instrument for inculcating moral behavior. He preached a series of sermons at Genoa, at the same house that produced the *Golden Legend,* and then issued them as the treatise *A Little Book on the Conduct of Humans and the Duties of Nobles and People (Libellus de moribus hominum et officiis nobilium ac popularium).* Overnight this book on chess, like that on the saints, became one of the most oft-translated and reproduced books of later medieval Europe, yielding nearly three hundred extant Latin copies. Many noble households must have possessed it, for it was translated into the vernaculars in less than a generation. The book appeared twice in German verse before 1337, five times in all in German; twice in French before 1347; as well in Middle Dutch, Low German, Swedish, Czech, Italian, Catalan, Spanish. William Caxton turned it into English about 1474, and it became the second book printed in the English vernacular. He set it in a typeface that imitated the common *bastarda* in which noble folk read their

---

47. *Die Erlösung,* ed. Karl Bartsch (1858; reprint, 1966), pp. 5-6.
48. *Die Erlösung,* pp. 180-86.

romances and perhaps their devotional works. Nine years later he reissued it, this time with woodcuts representing each of the chess figures, apparently emulating what he saw in manuscript versions. Indeed, many of the manuscripts came in deluxe versions with wonderfully painted images of the social figures represented by each piece.

In a brief preface Friar Jacobus claimed that he first preached this material before the people (*ad populum declamatorie praedicassem*), presumably in the Genoese city square or the Dominican church. His "text" was not the Gospel, lives of the saints, or vices and virtues, but the game of chess, the pieces presumably held up one by one in the pulpit. When the local nobility asked that he turn it into a book, he agreed, and transformed this game into a cipher for the "governing of the moral life and battle of the human condition."[49] The greatest evil among human beings, thus the book began, lay in their failure entirely to fear displeasing God or offending others by living disordered lives. He described each of the chess pieces in the back row as figures (*repraesentare* = signifieth) of the nobility, that is, the king, the judges or assessors (alfili/elephants), the knights, the king's vicars or messengers (rooks/camels); and each in the row of pawns as figures of the people, thus peasants, smiths, notaries, money changers or merchants, physicians and apothecaries, innkeepers, gatekeepers or toll takers, and the footloose. He admonished his listeners/readers to imprint upon their minds the form of each piece, so that having it down "by heart," they might the more easily recall the battle and virtue taught in the game. He would achieve his purpose if this game, a symbol of noble leisure, were made into an "instrument for correction and instruction in the mores and virtues." This may sound a little dreary and disciplinary, but it was received with amazing interest, as a way to think about fundamental ethical issues in familiar and entertaining images. The church and churchmen, devotion and the mystical life, made virtually no appearance here (there were as yet no bishops in this game). Inner devotion was not the preferred reading of chess: the point was social and moral responsibility. The aim was to turn amusement — the game itself, this literary treatise full of exemplary stories and the stunning illuminations that often accompanied it — into moral practice. But the choice to hear or read or consider the book and its teachings was that of the person who acquired it, even if, as seems likely for some of the deluxe copies, it was acquired in part for display, a kind of medieval coffee-table book.

---

49. Printed copies of the original Latin text are now, ironically, hard to come by. I have used a manuscript version, Milan, Bibliotheca ambrosiana, D 32 inf.

Concluding Observations

In and around parishes after 1200, and increasingly so as the years went by, until reformation regimes moved to restrict various practices as a matter of reform, people could exercise religious choice beyond the structured routines of parochial duty. To set parish religion over against popular practice, to imagine parishes starkly as either working effectively or hardly working at all, is neither helpful nor accurate. Saints' cults were part of parish life and the saints' stories were taught there, but venerating shrines beyond the parish — traveling there to pray, do penance, or seek blessing, adopting a saint as protector or paradigm — represented an individual act of will, personalized and potentially highly formative. Some teaching, however halting, might be found in parishes on Sundays and feast days, but this powerful instrument of persuasion, taken in hand by professional preachers from outside the parish, gathered people in city squares or fields or "hall-churches." There, if they so chose, they could be instructed, moved to remorse, or simply entertained. To form a private religious community, to join up as a Beguine or member of a confraternity, was to appropriate for yourself, still as a layperson, aspects of "religion" in ways suited to your setting and gender. Easter liturgical drama began in the parish, but town plays made the biblical stories the people's own, allowed them to participate as audience, as actors, as producers, even, as the story lines expanded, as interpreters. In smaller circles people could choose to read or hear or sing in their own language, and sometimes in the finest literary expressions of the day, the stories, teachings, and dilemmas of Christian practice. In each of these domains, it deserves note, lay urban magistrates took increasing responsibility from the thirteenth century onward: they sought or protected local patron saints, hired preachers, issued statutes for Beguine houses, organized cycles of plays, and sometimes patronized literature.

If the parish represented duty, what everyone was minimally expected to do, practices beyond the confines of the parish represented choices, ways people could seek involvement, gain religious deepening or instruction or participation or amusement according to their needs and desires. These choices could undeniably run toward dissent: cults of "false" saints or demons or witches, preaching deemed rebellious or aberrant, private societies become independent religions or sectarian groups, literature that mocked the faith or fostered alternatives. Churchmen feared this, at times excessively, as when Beguines or Lollards or a new cult appeared. But most often various choices persisted, present as a "normal" part of medieval religion, domains of practice that could be personalized beyond routine obligations, opportunities outside the parish or within, willingly conjoined to parish obligations or pursued independently. Despite the wary or jealous eye of a priest, people took these practices for granted as accepted supernatural presences and possibilities, and acted on them in keeping with their own aspirations. The parish did not monopolize Christian practice, and practices outside the parish were not necessarily extra-Christian. The world of religious practice around local medieval parishes could be complex and variegated, even allowing for its authoritative structures. The post-Reformation churches, of whatever stripe, generally proved more anxious to limit possibilities and bring people into conformity with the pronounced ideals of a local community, in the name of a reform that would no longer brook quite so many choices inside or outside the local church.

Orality, Textuality, and Revelation as Modes of Education and Formation in Jewish Mystical Circles of the High Middle Ages

Elliot R. Wolfson

T his study will examine the mechanism by which the Provençal and Spanish kabbalists of the twelfth and thirteenth centuries were instructed in the traditions and practices considered unique to their groups. It focuses on the interplay between oral transmission of esoteric wisdom and the production of written texts either exegetical or revelatory in nature. Individuals in these circles required proper instruction in mystical matters pertaining to both true beliefs and right actions. To understand the social constitution of these groups, it is necessary to consider the means by which these traditions and practices were disseminated, the relative exclusiveness or inclusiveness of a given group as determined by pedagogical concerns. The more esoteric the means of transmission or the more recondite the doctrine, the more restrictive the group. A salient feature of the proliferation of Jewish mysticism in the high Middle Ages was indeed the apparent clash between novel and unprecedented forms of Jewish spirituality and the recurring claims that these forms represented the authentic and ancient traditions of Judaism. The complex issues that arise from these ostensibly opposing views require an exploration of the cultural forms for transmitting knowledge and practice in these mystical fraternities.

In the twelfth and thirteenth centuries Jewish mysticism was clearly an elitist enterprise far removed from what scholars today would call popular religious culture. There is little historical evidence that large numbers of people in any geographical area were influenced by mystical beliefs and practices. The extant historical documents provide relatively sparse biographical information about the Jewish mystics themselves. A significant number of textual compositions (especially from Castile in the later thirteenth century) come without attribution or with false attributions to ancient authors. For the most part, it seems that the kabbalists were practicing rabbinic leaders or men who had received training in the talmudic academies and were thus well versed in classical Jewish learning. It is doubtful that they were separated from society at large, as one might find in a Christian monastic order, for example, though there is good reason to assume that they belonged to small fraternities made up exclusively of fellow practitioners. These circles functioned autonomously, to some degree, laying claim to a secretive knowledge that explained the essence of Judaism and yet was not readily available to all Jews alike.

The issue of education, therefore, goes to the heart of the matter of identity formation on both the individual and the communal levels. The kabbalists were part of the larger world of rabbinic culture, which had a major role in shaping the identity of Jews in the Middle Ages as a unique community of belief vis-à-vis other religious traditions, principally Islam and Christianity. Even though the teachings and practices of the kabbalists were presumed to be esoteric, it was their overriding belief that their secret gnosis represented the truest and innermost dimension of Judaism — hence its relevance for the education and formation of Jewish society at large. How the educational process unfolded for the transmission of esoteric knowledge, however, remains unclear. Indeed, at the moment only the questions seem clear: Were there clandestine meetings in which the master orally communicated secrets to the disciples? Or were there study groups in which older esoteric documents *(megillot setarim)* were analyzed, interpreted, and expanded into more elaborate theosophical systems and/or mystical ideologies?[1] Or did the exposition of secrets emerge in the context of explicating traditional literary sources that were part and parcel of the medieval rabbinic library — talmudic legends, midrashic anthologies, and liturgical works, for example? If there were in fact study groups dedicated to the exegesis of mystical secrets, within what educational framework did they assemble?

---

1. The presumption that there were older esoteric documents circulating within elitist circles lies at the basis of Gershom Scholem's historical reconstruction of the origins of kabbalah, which privileges written texts over oral traditions as the primary conduit through which knowledge is transmitted. See D. Biale, *Gershom Scholem: Kabbalah and Counter-History* (Cambridge, Mass., 1979), pp. 133-34. Biale perceptively compares Scholem's view to Nachman Krochmal's description of "how the sefirot theosophy was first developed in Babylonia and was carried westward via Italy to Spain in various 'scrolls and small pamphlets'" (p. 134). Biale also suggests that Scholem's discussion of the influence of gnosticism on kabbalah reflects Krochmal's theory (pp. 28, 134, 138, 198).

Jewish Mysticism and the Hermeneutics of Esotericism

The most appropriate term to characterize the body of lore called Jewish mysticism is "esotericism," *hokhmat ha-nistar*, a set of doctrines deemed secretive and therefore transmitted only to a small circle of initiates.[2] In an essay published in 1936, Alexander Altmann noted that the "esoteric nature of mystical teachings in Judaism is expressed by the terms *sod* ('secret'), *sithrey Torah* ('mysteries of the Law'), and their equivalents. Obscure though the historical origins of Jewish mysticism are, and especially its connections with the various schools of prophecy, apocalyptic literature, and gnosis, a definite esoteric posture, setting down a precise form of transmission, had evolved as early as the tannaitic period."[3] Altmann went so far as to suggest that the exclusive transmission of mystical knowledge from master to disciple attested in rabbinic sources may be due to the influence of Hellenistic mystery religions. The notion of secret is essential.

Gershom Scholem, for his part, distinguished sharply between mysticism and esotericism. The former, he maintained, "means a kind of knowledge which is by its very nature incommunicable," insofar as the object of mystical experience is inexpressible in human language, whereas the latter involves "a kind of knowledge that may be communicable and might be communicated, but whose communication is forbidden."[4] The issue of esotericism, as delineated by Scholem, is much more critical in assessing the nature of what we call Jewish mystical speculation in its different varieties or trends. The experiential aspects of Jewish mysticism are to be contextualized within a hermeneutical framework predicated on some form of esotericism. To borrow the formulation of Antoine Faivre, "active esotericism is the privileged form of hermeneu-

2. The extreme form of secrecy affirmed by Jewish mystics when compared to other religious traditions has been noted by W. Stace, *Mysticism and Philosophy* (London, 1960), p. 57. Two helpful surveys on the nature of esotericism may be found in A. Faivre, "Ancient and Medieval Sources of Modern Esoteric Movements," in *Modern Esoteric Spirituality*, ed. A. Faivre and J. Needleman (New York, 1992), pp. 1-70, and Faivre, *Access to Western Esotericism* (Albany, N.Y., 1994), pp. 3-110.

3. A. Altmann, "Maimonides' Attitude toward Jewish Mysticism," in *Studies in Jewish Thought*, ed. A. Jospe (Detroit, 1981), pp. 201-2.

4. G. Scholem, "Jewish Mysticism in the Middle Ages," *The 1964 Allan Bronfman Lecture* (New York, 1964), pp. 3-4. Cf. the characterization of A. Faivre, "Esotericism," in *The Encyclopedia of Religion*, ed. M. Eliade (New York, 1987), s.v., 5:158: "Strictly speaking, gnosis should be distinguished from mysticism, even though they are usually found together. Mysticism, which is more 'feminine,' more nocturnal, voluntarily cultivates renunciation, although this does not exclude a taste for symbolism. Gnosis, more 'masculine,' more solar, cultivates detachment and is more attentive to structures."

tics."[5] The word "esotericism" is thus meant to convey the notion that there is an inner tradition that can only be conveyed to select individuals who ascertain or gain access to the secret through hermeneutics. This point has also been expressed by Moshe Idel: "Kabbalah is by definition an esoteric body of speculation; whether in its theosophical-theurgical explanation of the rationales for the commandments, or in the ecstatic trend dealing with techniques of using divine names, esotericism is deeply built into this lore."[6] Nothing is more important for understanding the mentality of the kabbalist than the emphasis on esotericism. The possession of a secret gnosis empowers the kabbalist, for he alone has the keys to unlock the hidden mysteries of the tradition.

Orality and Esotericism

In the writings of medieval Jewish mystics, esotericism is strongly linked to orality as the vehicle of transmission. In mystical texts the oral nature of the transmission of esoteric doctrines is underscored in an unprecedented way. The most common term used by Jewish mystics of this period to refer to their teaching is *qabbalah*, derived etymologically from the word *qibbel* (to receive), while the masters of the esoteric knowledge are called *ba'ale qabbalah* or *mequbbalim*. In this context the term *qabbalah* connotes reception of an occult lore or practice transmitted orally. The connection between esotericism and orality is affirmed in one of the most important documents for the study of early theosophic kabbalah, a letter written in the mid-1230s by Isaac the Blind, the Provençal master considered the source of the theosophic ideas and contemplative practices that influenced the major circle of Catalonian kabbalah.[7] In the letter Isaac reports that he has learned a lesson from the behavior of his "ancestors," i.e., his maternal grandfather, Abraham ben Isaac of Narbonne, and

5. Faivre, *Access to Western Esotericism*, p. 5. He writes: "The etymology of 'esotericism' clarifies the idea of secret by suggesting that we can access understanding of a symbol, myth, or reality only by a personal effort of progressive elucidation through several successive levels, i.e., by a form of hermeneutics."

6. M. Idel, *Kabbalah: New Perspectives* (New Haven, 1988), p. 253. More recently Idel has studied aspects of Jewish esotericism related particularly to preoccupation with exegetical devices; see his "Secrecy, Binah and Derishah," in *Secrecy and Concealment: Studies in the History of Mediterranean and Near Eastern Religions*, ed. H. G. Kippenberg and G. G. Stroumsa (Leiden, 1995), pp. 310-43.

7. G. Scholem, "A New Document on the Beginnings of Kabbalah" (in Hebrew), in *Sefer Bialik* (Tel Aviv, 1934), p. 144. In *Origins of the Kabbalah*, ed. R. J. Zwi Werblowsky, trans. A. Arkush (Princeton, 1987), p. 254, Scholem dates the letter to 1235.

his father, Abraham ben David of Posquiéres. They never allowed a word dealing with esoteric matters "to escape their lips and they conducted themselves with them [those not initiated into the secret doctrine] like men who were not versed in the [mystical] wisdom."[8] The intent of the letter was to express Isaac's anger at the dissemination of kabbalistic doctrines in northern Spain by his own students, presumably Ezra and Azriel of Gerona. Isaac criticized the composition of such treatises for, as he put it, "that which is written has no box" (ha-davar ha-nikhtav 'ein lo 'aron),[9] meaning the author cannot control the fate of a document's distribution after it has been composed. Isaac thus presents himself in this epistle as very reluctant to disclose matters publicly, especially through the medium of a written text.

Many textual examples demonstrate the reluctance of kabbalists in this early period to write any explanation considered to have been passed through a continuous chain of oral tradition. Indeed, mystics representing the three dominant trends of Spanish kabbalah in the thirteenth century — linguistic mysticism (those kabbalists whose principal interest consisted of speculating on the nature of the Hebrew alphabet), theosophic kabbalah (the system based on the doctrine of ten dynamic powers that constitute the *pleroma* of divine energies, most frequently referred to as the *sefirot*), and prophetic kabbalah (the system whose main focus is the attainment of a state of mystical ecstasy, characterized as *unio mystica,* through various meditative techniques including letter combinations and permutations of the divine names) — all profess that their respective teaching is a *qabbalah,* an orally received doctrine. Oral teaching was upheld as the main medium for transmission of esoteric ideas and practices. Thirteenth-century esotericism was characterized by a transition from an oral to a written culture, a process culminating in the composition and dissemination of the *Zohar* in the 1280s and 1290s. Yet there is ample evidence that kabbalists adhered to a code of esotericism that prohibited the complete exposure in writing of sensitive theological issues of a theoretical or practical nature.[10] Even Moses de León, who expounded freely on esoteric matters in his Hebrew writings and in the *Zohar,* occasionally adopted a more conservative approach and insisted on the need to conceal a matter or to withhold its full disclosure.[11]

---

8. Scholem, "New Document," p. 143. For a different rendering see Scholem, *Origins of the Kabbalah,* p. 200.

9. Scholem, "New Document," p. 143.

10. See Idel, *Kabbalah,* pp. 20-22.

11. See Y. Liebes, *Studies in the Zohar,* trans. A. Schwartz, S. Nakache, and P. Peli (Albany, N.Y., 1993), pp. 26-34; E. R. Wolfson, *Circle in the Square: Studies in the Use of Gender in Kabbalistic Symbolism* (Albany, N.Y., 1995), p. 150 n. 61. A reputed typological distinction between con-

Kabbalists probably were influenced in part by Maimonides, who likewise emphasized that the "secrets of Torah," which he located in accounts of the chariot and of creation, representing for him metaphysics and physics respectively, had to be explained orally. Maimonides goes so far as to say that "this knowledge was only transmitted from one leader to another and has never been set down in writing."[12] Maimonides also argued that this knowledge, hidden in parables in both scriptural and rabbinic texts, has never been set down in any systematic way.[13] In spite of the many differences in approach between Maimonides and the kabbalists, there is a basic similarity in the formal acceptance of esotericism that is linked with orality.[14] Maimonides assumed that the oral tradition consisted of philosophic doctrines cultivated by Jews but never

---

servatism and innovation is problematic if pushed too far. See M. Idel, "We Have No Kabalistic Tradition on This," in *Rabbi Moses Nahmanides (Ramban): Explorations in His Literary and Religious Virtuosity,* ed. I. Twersky (Cambridge, Mass., 1983), pp. 51-73 (on 71 n. 73, Idel acknowledges that in the zoharic text there are allusions to secrets that must be hidden, but he concludes that much more is revealed than is concealed); Idel, *Kabbalah,* pp. 210-18. A subtle approach is necessary, one that takes into account the possibility that within one thinker there may be a clash between the two approaches.

12. Maimonides, *Guide of the Perplexed,* trans. S. Pines (Chicago, 1963), 3, introduction, p. 415.

13. Maimonides, *Guide of the Perplexed* 1, introduction, p. 7; 1.33, p. 71; 3, introduction, p. 416.

14. See Altmann, "Maimonides' Attitude," pp. 200-219. The problem of secrecy and esotericism in Maimonides has been treated by a number of scholars from various methodological perspectives. The following list of representative studies is very selective: L. Strauss, "The Literary Character of the *Guide of the Perplexed,*" in *Essays on Maimonides,* ed. S. W. Baron (New York, 1941), pp. 37-91, reprinted in *Persecution and the Art of Writing* (Glencoe, Ill., 1952), pp. 38-94; Strauss, "How to Begin to Study the *Guide of the Perplexed,*" in Maimonides, *The Guide of the Perplexed,* trans. S. Pines (Chicago and London, 1963), pp. xi-lvi; Strauss, *Philosophy and Law: Contributions to the Understanding of Maimonides and His Predecessors,* trans. E. Adler (Albany, N.Y., 1995), pp. 95-96, 102-3 (regarding the approach of Strauss to Maimonides' esotericism, see K. H. Green, *Jew and Philosopher: The Return to Maimonides in the Jewish Thought of Leo Strauss* [Albany, N.Y., 1993], pp. 111-34); H. A. Davidson, "Maimonides' Secret Position on Creation," in *Studies in Medieval Jewish History and Literature,* vol. 1, ed. I. Twersky (Cambridge, Mass., 1979), pp. 16-40; A. Ravitsky, "Samuel ibn Tibbon and the Esoteric Character of the *Guide of the Perplexed,*" *Association for Jewish Studies Review* 6 (1981): 87-123; Ravitsky, "The Secrets of the *Guide of the Perplexed:* Between the Thirteenth and the Twentieth Centuries" (in Hebrew), *Jerusalem Studies in Jewish Thought* 5 (1986): 23-69, English version in *Studies in Maimonides,* ed. I. Twersky (Cambridge, Mass., 1990), pp. 159-207; Z. Levy, "Hermeneutik und Esoterik bei Maimonides und Spinoza," *Internationaler Schleiermacher Kongress, Berlin 1984,* ed. K.-V. Selge (Berlin, 1985), pp. 541-60; M. Idel, "*Sitre 'Arayot* in Maimonides' Thought," in *Maimonides and Philosophy: Papers Presented at the Sixth Jerusalem Philosophical Encounter, May 1985,* ed. S. Pines and Y. Yovel (Dordrecht, 1986), pp. 79-91; M. Fox, *Interpreting Maimonides: Studies in Methodology, Metaphysics, and Moral Philosophy* (Chicago, 1990), pp. 47-90.

committed to writing in a comprehensive or systematic manner. Jewish mystics, by contrast, made a claim for specific ideas that are, to a great degree, unique to the respective mystical systems and are thus not traceable to any one source.

The impact of Maimonides is particularly evident in one of the earliest systematic characterizations of kabbalah, found in Ezra of Gerona's commentary on Song of Songs. The treatise cannot be dated with any precision, though it was probably composed sometime in the late 1220s or early 1230s.[15] In his introduction Ezra traces the transmission of the knowledge of God's name as a chain from biblical antiquity (beginning with Abraham) to his own time: "From that time [the Sinaitic revelation] until now there has not been in Israel any generation that has not received the tradition of wisdom, which is knowledge of the name *(yedi'at ha-shem)*, through the order of the tradition *(qabbalah)*, the Oral Torah."[16] Yet in another passage he asserts that, since the destruction of the temple, "this wisdom had ceased in Israel." The efforts of sages who scattered references to the kabbalistic truths in the midrashim and the talmudic Haggadoth, he concludes, preserved remnants of the tradition for posterity.[17] As he puts it in another passage: "The words of the sages, blessed be their memories, are absolutely complete and perfect . . . all their words were said through the holy spirit by allusion in order to arouse the hearts of the enlightened ones, the kabbalists *(ha-maskilim ha-mequbbalim)*."[18] Ezra attempted hermeneutically to recast biblical texts in the light of kabbalistic theosophy, by reading the former through the lens of rabbis whose words had been theosophically transformed.

Ezra perceived his own time as propitious for the reconstruction of kabbalistic truths that ultimately went back through an oral chain to the beginnings of Judaism as recorded in biblical history. This may relate to his own advancing age and to the approaching of the sixth millennium in the year 1240, linked to much messianic speculation in eschatological works written in the twelfth and thirteenth centuries.[19] An implicit messianic rationale for disclos-

---

15. See Scholem, "New Document," p. 145; *Origins of the Kabbalah*, p. 374.

16. *Kitve Ramban* 2.478.

17. *Kitve Ramban* 2.479.

18. *Kitve Ramban* 2.498.

19. The significance of 1240 must be related to a conflation of the passage in Babylonian Talmud *Sanhedrin* 97a to the effect that the world endures for 6,000 years divided into three cycles of 2,000 years, the last one being the days of Messiah, and a conception that Jewish authors, beginning with Abraham bar Hiyya, apparently borrowed from Christian sources, particularly evident in Joachim of Fiore but going back to the Augustinian theme of seven *aetates mundi* from creation to consummation. The Christian apocalyptic idea involved the typological parallelism between the *hexämeron*, the six days of the week, and six ages of human history followed by the Sabbath corresponding to the seventh age of eternity. Appropriating this worldview, me-

ing esoteric wisdom, in my opinion, would explain Ezra's choice of an exegetical work on Song of Songs as the vehicle to communicate his ideas, for this scriptural book was understood from the rabbinic period as a messianic allegory. In Ezra's own words:

> For many years I have seen this and that [secret tradition] and I have kept quiet, and my hand has clapped my mouth,[20] until I entered the fifth grade[21] as it says, one [year] from the years of life.[22] I see that the day has declined before me and old age is quickly approaching; therefore I have undertaken to explain one of the twenty-four books that comprises delights, and speaks of glorious mysteries and secrets — and this is book Song of Songs. I will explain it according to my strength as I have received from my teachers, and I will attend to the rationales for the commandments, and illustrate the secrets of the account of creation.[23]

---

dieval Jewish authors identified each cosmic day with a period of 1,000 years, given the additional rabbinic teaching (based on the metaphor in Ps. 90:4) that each day of the Lord extends to a period of 1,000 years. Hence the six days of creation are the six millennia of history to be followed by a period of rest, which was construed either as total annihilation, the relative cessation of life, or the time of cosmic judgment. The acceptance of this parallel between cosmos and history resulted in the following symmetrical relation: just as Adam was created on the sixth day, so the sixth millennium was the appointed time of the messianic redemption when the original perfection of cosmos and humanity would be restored. Such a scheme of human history was adopted and transformed by a number of kabbalists in northern Spain in the thirteenth century. See the comments of J. Guttmann in his introduction to *Sefer Megillat ha-Megalleh*, ed. A. Poznanski (Berlin, 1924), pp. xiii-xiv; S. Heller-Wilensky, "Isaac ibn Latif: Philosopher or Kabbalist?" in *Jewish Medieval and Renaissance Studies*, ed. A. Altmann (Cambridge, Mass., 1967), p. 218; Heller-Wilensky, "Messianism, Eschatology and Utopianism in the Philosophical-Mystical Trend of Kabbalah in the Thirteenth Century" (in Hebrew), in *Messianism and Eschatology: A Collection of Essays*, ed. Z. Baras (Jerusalem, 1983), pp. 221-37; A. Funkenstein, "Nahmanides' Symbolic Reading of History," in *Studies in Jewish Mysticism*, ed. J. Dan and F. Talmage (Cambridge, Mass., 1982), pp. 139-41.

20. Cf. Job 40:4.

21. In the first edition of this work published in Altona, 1764, a scribal note suggests that the reference is to the time of death based on Babylonian Talmud *Berakhot* 10a, where the fifth world of David is connected with the day of death. See also Chavel's edition, p. 479. According to another reading, mentioned parenthetically in the first edition, the text here states that the author was fifty-one years old. See G. Vajda, *Le commentaire d'Ezra de Gérone sur le cantique des cantiques* (Paris, 1969), p. 44; I. Tishby, *Studies in Kabbalah and Its Branches* (in Hebrew), vol. 1 (Jerusalem, 1982), p. 12 n. 11.

22. A note in the first edition (cited by Chavel) suggests that this may mean one year beyond the life expectancy of seventy years. If that interpretation is correct, then Ezra apparently was seventy-one when he composed this treatise. See A. Jellinek, *Beiträge zur Geschichte der Kabbala*, vol. 1 (Leipzig, 1852), p. 33 n. 4.

23. *Kitve Ramban* 2.479-80.

Approaching the end of his life, Ezra felt compelled to commit to writing the kabbalistic secrets he received from his teachers. As his genre he chose an exegetical work on the Song of Songs, in which he offered mystical reasons for the commandments and the secrets of cosmology, two topics he considered essential to kabbalah.

Ezra's choice of this biblical text can be properly appreciated only in conjunction with an underlying emphasis on the imminent redemption set to occur in the sixth millennium according to the doctrine of cosmic cycles *(shemittot)* that he accepted:[24] "'For now the winter is past' (Song of Songs 2:11). This symbolizes the completion of the end and the departure of the exile. 'The blossoms have appeared in the land' (2:12). This refers to the approaching days of repose and the coming of the inheritance and rest."[25] In contrast to other kabbalists, including his younger colleague Nahmanides,[26] Ezra does not advocate the calculation of a specific date for the redemption. He cautions the reader: "Know that there are figures of speech *(meshalim)* in this book whose details cannot be explained in any manner, like 'the blossoms have appeared in the land, the time of singing has come, the song of the turtledove is heard in the land.' Concerning these [images] and others like them, we cannot examine them in detail but only explain that this is a symbol for the greatness of the coming days of rest, and the winter for the passing days of exile."[27] Sensitivity to the impending end of exile and the beginning of the redemption presumably lay behind Ezra's decision to write a commentary on the Song of Songs and to contextualize kabbalistic secrets in such a setting. A long-standing exegetical tradition, attested in the Targum to this book as well as in isolated midrashic comments,[28] read the song as recounting Israel's sacred history from the exodus from Egypt to future redemption.[29] What book could have served better than the Song of Songs to express the message of redemption as the sacred union of the masculine and feminine aspects of the divine? The kabbalistic reading of Song of Songs is concomitantly a messianic reading. It is not possible to separate the mystical and the messianic, for the story of Israel's exile and return,

24. See, e.g., *Kitve Ramban* 2.480, 499, 500-502.

25. *Kitve Ramban* 2.491. See H. Pedaya, "The Spiritual versus the Concrete Land of Israel in the Geronese School of Kabbalah" (in Hebrew), in *The Land of Israel in Medieval Jewish Thought,* ed. M. Hallamish and A. Ravitzky (Jerusalem, 1991), pp. 250-51.

26. On Nahmanides' messianic posture in light of the aggressive Christian missionizing in thirteenth-century Spain, see R. Chazan, *Barcelona and Beyond: The Disputation of 1263 and Its Aftermath* (Berkeley, 1992), pp. 172-94.

27. *Kitve Ramban* 2.480-81.

28. Collected in various works, such as *Shir ha-Shirim Rabbah.*

29. *Kitve Ramban* 2.480.

dramatized in the dialogue of the lover and beloved, reflects the rupture and re-unification of the masculine and the feminine in the divine.[30]

The essence of the kabbalistic tradition has to do with knowledge of the divine name, a notion found as well in fragments attributed to the kabbalists of Provence, Abraham ben David, Jacob ha-Nazir, and Isaac the Blind.[31] Such a characterization of kabbalah is also found in one of Ezra's epistles[32] and recurs in the writings of Azriel.[33] It is the basis of Asher ben David's treatise *Perush Shem ha-Meforash,* which begins with the statement, "we have received a tradition in our hands from our ancestors," concerning the theosophic meaning of the Tetragrammaton.[34] Identifying the name as one of the secrets of Torah or as part of the mystical praxis of "ascending to the chariot" is found in other writings from the medieval period, for example, in the northern French exegetes, Solomon ben Isaac of Troyes and his grandson Samuel ben Meir.[35] That kabbalah was construed in this way is critical, for it indicates a common heritage of Jewish esotericism.[36]

Secrets, Not Reasons

There is an important corollary to the claim that *qabbalah* refers to esoteric truths that have been transmitted orally. These truths cannot be deduced by the power

---

30. See Pedaya, "Spiritual versus the Concrete," p. 249.

31. See G. Scholem, *Reshit ha-Qabbalah* (Tel Aviv, 1948), pp. 73-74 n. 2. The centrality of the name in the kabbalistic thought of Isaac has been explored in detail by H. Pedaya, "'Flaw' and 'Correction' in the Concept of the Godhead in the Teachings of Rabbi Isaac the Blind" (in Hebrew), *Jerusalem Studies in Jewish Thought* 6 (1987): 157-285.

32. Scholem, "New Document," p. 155. In MS New York, Jewish Theological Seminary of America Mic. 1878, ff. 12a-b, a passage dealing with the containment of the ten *sefirot* in the Tetragrammaton is transmitted in the name of Ezra. This idea is briefly alluded to by Isaac the Blind. Inasmuch as the study of the *sefirot* is the distinguishing feature of theosophic kabbalah, and the *sefirot* are comprised within the name, it follows that kabbalah can be viewed as an esoteric tradition regarding the divine name.

33. See, e.g., the text published by Scholem, *Madda'e ha-Yahadut* 2 (1927), pp. 231-32.

34. Text printed in J. Dan, *The Kabbalah of R. Asher ben David* (in Hebrew) (Jerusalem, 1980), p. 13.

35. See Pedaya, "'Flaw and 'Correction,'" p. 157 n. 2. Traditions concerning the name are preserved as well by the German Pietists of the twelfth and thirteenth centuries (see J. Dan, *The Esoteric Theology of the Ashkenazi Hasidism* [in Hebrew] [Jerusalem, 1968], pp. 74-75) and by Abraham Abulafia and his followers in the thirteenth and fourteenth centuries (see M. Idel, *The Mystical Experience in Abraham Abulafia* [Albany, N.Y., 1988], pp. 14-24; Idel, *Kabbalah*, pp. 97-103).

36. See M. Idel, "Defining Kabbalah: The Kabbalah of the Divine Names," in *Mystics of the Book: Topics, Themes, and Typologies,* ed. R. A. Herrera (New York, 1993), pp. 97-122.

of reason or supposition *(sevara')*. This position is, prima facie, at odds with Maimonides, who stated explicitly that he had deduced knowledge of the secrets of Torah by conjecture and supposition rather than by their reception through divine revelation or oral transmission from a teacher.[37] Nahmanides wrote explicitly, in the introduction to his commentary on the Torah, that no one will understand the allusions he has made to the secrets of Torah by means of the intellect or understanding, but only through an oral reception, "from the mouth of a kabbalistic sage to an ear that receives" *(mipi mequbbal hakham le-'ozen meqabbel)*.[38] A host of kabbalists through the generations reject reason as a means of comprehending or ascertaining esoteric wisdom, in many instances relying on or paraphrasing the formulation of Nahmanides — for example, Abraham ben Eliezer ha-Levi of the fifteenth century and Hayyim Vital of the sixteenth century.[39] An anonymous text enumerated several introductory principles for the study of kabbalah: "The one who enters this wisdom must know that it is called *qabbalah* for one must receive it orally and it cannot be comprehended by the intellect for it is above the intellect, even above the first intelligible."[40]

An extraordinary collection of kabbalistic secrets (written in all probability in the first decades of the fourteenth century), transmitted in the name of an anonymous elder *(zaqen)*,[41] affirms the primacy of orality in the transmission of kabbalistic teaching: "Had you received this secret mouth to mouth, then you would have known who are the ones that enter the chambers of the king."[42]

37. Maimonides, *Guide of the Perplexed* 3, introduction, p. 416. A striking affirmation of the power of reason in the pursuit of mystical gnosis is found in *Zohar Hadash,* ed. R. Margaliot (Jerusalem, 1978), p. 25c *(Midrash ha-Ne'elam)*. R. Haggai is told that he can join R. Dostai in his excursion to visit R. Eleazar ben Arakh if he is capable of comprehending what he hears. To this challenge R. Haggai responds, "I have heard the matter of the supernal secret, I have contemplated it, and I have proposed an interpretation." The word I translated as "interpretation" is *sevara',* which has the connotation of logical supposition. The point of the passage, then, is that one must be able to discern the meaning of an esoteric matter through the exercise of one's own reason.

38. *Perush ha-Ramban 'al ha-Torah,* ed. C. Chavel, 2 vols. (Jerusalem, 1984), 1.7.

39. See E. R. Wolfson, "'By Way of Truth': Aspects of Nahmanides' Kabbalistic Hermeneutic," *AJS Review* 14 (1989): 105 n. 6.

40. MS New York, Jewish Theological Seminary of America Mic. 1990, f. 102a.

41. A brief description of this text is given by Scholem, *Origins of the Kabbalah,* p. 61. The text is referred to by Moses Cordovero, *'Or Ne'erav* (Tel Aviv, 1965), p. 23: *we-hakhi mukhah be-sodot ha-zaqen u-she'arav,* "Thus it has been proven in the secrets of the elder and his gates." In the manuscript I examined, however, I did not find a source for the custom that Cordovero attributes to this text, which involves sitting on the floor when kabbalah is studied.

42. MS Oxford, Bodleian Library 2396, f. 2b. The following oral tradition is reported on ff. 13a-b: "The eyes of the one who tastes the wine from that blessed cup will be illuminated, and he will see the supernal and lower beings. The pious of Israel *(haside yisra'el)* have the custom of

In another passage, after explicating the "secret of Abraham and Sarah," which involves more generally the mystical significance of masculinity and femininity, the author writes that "the elder did not want to elaborate this matter, and he warned us not to write that which we had received."[43] A strict code of esotericism is upheld in yet another passage, an elaborate exposition of the rabbinic idea that the building of the tabernacle reflects the creation of the world.[44] The initial transmission of the secret is oral, by means of a whisper.[45] This knowledge is imparted in a secondary sense to someone who has the power to deduce it on his own, to understand one thing from another.[46] This anonymous kabbalist assumes that the mysteries of Torah are communicated orally or discovered exegetically by someone with the requisite intellectual capabilities.[47] The most dramatic example occurs in a passage wherein the elder scolds his disciple for asking him why Elijah did not experience physical death: "He took hold of the hand of one of his students and brought him into the

---

placing on their eyes a drop of wine from the cup for the sanctification of Sabbath *(kos qiddush shel shabbat)* so that they will merit that blessed cup prepared for the righteous in the Garden of Eden. All this we received from the great rabbi, the pious one, master of secrets." Cf. f. 14b, where the custom to declare a holiday when the study of a book or a tractate was completed is cited in the name of the "midrash of our teacher, the elderly master."

43. MS Oxford, Bodleian Library 2396, f. 4a. The admonition not to write esoteric matters is repeated on f. 50b.

44. MS Oxford, Bodleian Library 2396, f. 36b: "I have received in this matter that he whispered in the ear of one of his students what you see alluded to here, and if you comprehend one thing from another, 'they will be yours alone, others having no part with you' (Prov. 5:17)."

45. The transmission of secrets by whisper reflects the rabbinic idea of the manner in which an esoteric matter is handed over by a master to a disciple. Cf. Babylonian Talmud *Ḥagigah* 14a; *Bere'shit Rabbah* 1:3, ed. J. Theodor and C. Albeck (Jerusalem, 1965), pp. 19-20, and the many parallel sources mentioned on 19 n. 10. The latter passage has been discussed by a number of scholars. See, in particular, A. Altmann, *Studies in Religious Philosophy and Mysticism* (Ithaca, N.Y., 1969), pp. 128-39, and G. Scholem, *Jewish Gnosticism, Merkabah Mysticism, and Talmudic Tradition* (New York, 1965), p. 58.

46. On the criterion of understanding one thing from another, cf. Babylonian Talmud *Ḥagigah* 11b, 13a. The complex relationship of oral reception, innovative exegesis, and revelatory experience is affirmed in a brief comment of Hai Gaon explaining the talmudic dictum that esoteric knowledge must be transmitted in a whisper, in *Otzar ha-Geonim: Thesaurus of the Gaonic Responsa and Commentaries* (in Hebrew), ed. B. M. Lewin (Jerusalem, 1931), 4.12, cited by Scholem, *Jewish Gnosticism*, p. 58 n. 10: "They whisper to him in whispers, give him the principles, he understands them, and from heaven they show him the mysteries of his heart." According to this text, esoteric knowledge is imparted by an oral transmission from the master to the disciple, but that knowledge must be interpreted by the receiver of the tradition by applying the general principles that have been disclosed, and this results in a heavenly revelation of the secrets that are lodged in the heart of the initiate.

47. Maimonides, *Guide of the Perplexed* 1.33, pp. 71-72.

room within a room. He said to him, 'Have I not rebuked you several times not to ask me this question before your comrades?'[48] The student trembled, and the master said to him, 'Place your head between your knees,[49] and I will whisper in your ears what I have received in the matter of Elijah.' The student covered his face in his cloak, placed his head between his knees, and the master whispered in his ear."[50]

The claim to orality professed by this anonymous kabbalist is linked to the view (also expressed by Maimonides)[51] that the writing down of doctrine could prove potentially dangerous insofar as it might lead to the misunderstanding of a sensitive theological issue by an individual not sufficiently trained in esoteric lore. Yet the threat of forgetfulness is so strong that transgressing the oral nature of transmission becomes inevitable, although the manner in which the secret is disclosed preserves the esoteric quality by being deliberately allusive (again the model seems to have been Maimonides, who advocated a form of esoteric writing to convey secrets).[52] One author comments: "I considered writing the matter in a greatly concealed allusion out of fear of forgetfulness."[53] Elsewhere he states that the small amount that is written of the mystical doctrines is for the sake of memory.[54] And he instructs the reader: "You must know that these chapters require an expansion of language and a complete tradition, but the little that has been mentioned is out of fear of forgetting the intention of the verses to which there have been allusions."[55] In a fourth passage the point is elaborated as a general hermeneutical principle:

What the disciple receives from his master he writes down on account of forgetfulness. We have received this wondrous and great secret, in which are

48. The precise language of rebuke is used in another context; cf. MS Oxford, Bodleian Library 2396, ff. 54a-b.

49. This posture is associated with inducing mystical trances or ecstatic states of consciousness. See P. Fenton, "La 'Tête Entre Les Genoux': contribution à l'étude d'une posture méditative dans la mystique juive et islamique," *Revue d'Histoire et de Philosophie Religieuses* 72 (1992): 413-26.

50. MS Oxford, Bodleian Library 2396, f. 30b.

51. Maimonides, *Guide of the Perplexed* 1, introduction, p. 6; 1.33, p. 71.

52. Maimonides, *Guide of the Perplexed* 1, introduction, pp. 7-8; 1.33, p. 80; 3, introduction, p. 416.

53. MS Oxford, Bodleian Library 2396, f. 7a. In the continuation of this passage the author proclaims that he can commit to writing angelic names because they will not be comprehensible to anyone except through an oral tradition.

54. MS Oxford, Bodleian Library 2396, f. 51b. On the transmission of chapter headings, cf. f. 24b.

55. MS Oxford, Bodleian Library 2396, f. 62b.

contained all wisdoms, from the great and known sage. Every enlightened person will understand from his words to the point where his intellect and expansive wisdom reaches. The sage said, "Come and I will show you great principles in these few words, and these words to which I allude are like grains of wheat in relation to all the results, labors, and benefits that derive from them."[56]

Ideally, esoteric matters are transmitted orally because their ultimate grounding lies in oral tradition. But we find a similar justification for writing down esoteric matters offered by Abraham Abulafia in his *'Or ha-Sekhel*, as a preface to his exposition of the secret concerning the motif of the image of Jacob engraved on the throne of glory:[57] "Verily, at this time that which was hidden has been revealed because forgetfulness has reached its limit, and the end of forgetfulness is the beginning of remembrance."[58] Abulafia believed cultural amnesia was a rationale for disclosing hidden secrets in an esoteric manner.

Abulafia, despite his prolific literary activity, maintained that the kabbalistic tradition in its essence — which involved knowledge of the divine name[59] — should not be conveyed in writing. Thus, in the context of explicating traditions regarding Enoch Metatron in *Sitre Torah*, one of his commentaries on Maimonides' *Guide of the Perplexed*, Abulafia reminds the reader, "All these matters, and others that are similar to them, are from the words of the sages of kabbalah; they possess wondrous secrets that are inappropriate to be written."[60] The esoteric reasons for the commandments, in contrast to their literal explanation, must also be transmitted orally.[61] Abulafia further claimed that the ecstatic techniques that he reported, principally various permutations of the divine names, had been transmitted orally through the generations. In

56. MS Oxford, Bodleian Library 2396, ff. 51b-52a.

57. Regarding this motif in Abulafia's writings, see E. R. Wolfson, *Along the Path: Studies in Kabbalistic Hermeneutics, Myth, and Symbolism* (Albany, N.Y., 1995), pp. 20-22 and 135-36 nn. 150-58. In that context I neglected to mention the pertinent discussion in *Hayye ha-Nefesh*, MS Munich, Bayerisch Staatsbibliothek 408, ff. 69b-70a.

58. MS Vatican, Biblioteca Apostolica ebr. 233, f. 97b.

59. See Scholem, *Major Trends in Jewish Mysticism* (New York, 1995), pp. 119-55, and the work of Idel cited in n. 35.

60. MS Paris, Bibliothèque Nationale héb. 774, f. 130a.

61. Cf. *'Imre Shefer*, MS Munich, Bayerisch Staatsbibliothek 40, f. 224b; *Sitre Torah*, MS Paris, Bibliothèque Nationale héb. 774, ff. 169a-b; *Hayye ha-Nefesh*, MS Munich, Bayerisch Staatsbibliothek 408, f. 10b. I have discussed these and other relevant passages in "Mystical Rationalization of the Commandments in the Prophetic Kabbalah of Abraham Abulafia," to appear in the proceedings of the conference in honor of Alexander Altmann held at University College, London, June 1994. See also M. Idel, *Language, Torah, and Hermeneutics in Abraham Abulafia* (Albany, N.Y., 1989), p. 64.

one of his many treatises still buried in manuscript, *Sefer Mafteah ha-Hokhmot,* Abulafia distinguished three levels of meaning in the text, corresponding to three levels of religious perfection: the simple or contextual meaning *(peshat)* for the class of the righteous *(saddiq);* the secrets of Torah known through philosophy or science *(sitre torah 'al derekh hakhme ha-mehqar),* i.e., the allegorical meaning, for the pious *(hasidim);* and the comprehension of the text as an amalgam of divine names for the prophets *(nevi'im).*[62] The way of reading associated with attaining prophecy represents the "true tradition" transmitted orally. In Abulafia's own words: "If you want to reach the level of Torah where you will be prophets, you must follow the way of prophets, for their way was to combine all of the [letters of] Torah, and to grasp it from beginning to end as the way of the holy names, as the true tradition *(ha-qabbalah ha-'amitit)* has come to us that the entire Torah is the names of the Holy One, blessed be He, from the *bet* of *bere'shit* (Gen. 1:1) to the *lamed* in *le'eine kol yisra'el* (Deut. 33:12)."[63] In his commentery *Sitre Torah* he distinguished three types of sages: prophets *(nevi'im),* forced by the divine influx to speak or to write; the wise of heart *(hakhme lev),* who speak through the Holy Spirit and also write books on the divine wisdom according to what they have received orally from the prophets or indirectly from their compositions; and philosophers *(hoqre mada'),* who attempt to understand the hidden matters through their own understanding and reason.[64] The mystical truth is based on an oral, prophetic tradition unique to the Jewish people that transcends the bounds of human reason.[65] The latter can contradict the former. Abulafia declared, "It is known by the kabbalists from amongst our colleagues, who received from the prophets who spoke with God and God spoke with them, that the philosophers erred in their minds with respect to many matters of faith."[66]

The most important source for Abulafia's formulation was Nahmanides, who likewise conceived the Torah in its entirety as composed of the names of God — the true tradition *(qabbalah shel 'emet).*[67] The exegetical decoding of the scrip-

62. See Idel, *Language, Torah, and Hermeneutics,* pp. 109-11.

63. MS New York, Jewish Theological Seminary of America Mic. 1686, f. 96a.

64. MS Paris, Bibliothèque Nationale héb. 774, f. 143a.

65. Cf. the description of kabbalah as knowledge of the name in *Sheva' Netivot ha-Torah,* in A. Jellinek, *Philosophie und Kabbala* (Leipzig, 1854), p. 9. The influence of Abulafia is discernible in Joseph Gikatilla, *Ginnat 'Egoz* (Jerusalem, 1989), pp. 343-44. Gikatilla identifies the "wisdom of Torah" as the "inner wisdom," which is compared to the nucleus of the circle apprehended only by Israel. The Torah is identified further as the twenty-two letters, which are comprised in AHW'Y, the letters of the divine name that add up to twenty-two.

66. MS Paris, Bibliothèque Nationale héb. 774, f. 140b.

67. G. Scholem, *On the Kabbalah and Its Symbolism,* trans. R. Manheim (New York, 1965), p. 38; M. Idel, "The Concept of Torah in the Hekhalot and Its Evolution in the Kabbalah" (in

tural text as an aggregation of divine names is, according to Abulafia, the true oral Torah that cannot be committed to writing.[68] Thus, in an epistle where he delineated seven hermeneutical paths, *Sheva' Netivot ha-Torah,* Abulafia described the seventh path as: "The truth and essence of prophecy, which consists of the matter of the knowledge of the comprehension of the essence of the unique name. . . . It is not appropriate to write in a book the substance of this path, which is called holy and sanctified, and it is impossible to transmit any traditions, even the chapter headings, except if the one who desires it has at first orally received knowledge of the forty-two-letter name and the seventy-two-letter name."[69]

Written texts at best contain allusions, or in the traditional idiom "chapter headings," that the enlightened will understand through the exercise of their own understanding. In a second passage Abulafia describes the requisite combination of oral reception and hermeneutical creativity: "The kabbalah brings forth the hidden from these matters, from potentiality to actuality, and it reveals the mysteries in them to each recipient *(mequbbal).* And the recipient, in accordance with his capacity, his receptivity, and his effort, brings forth what is in potentiality into actuality, for even though the kabbalah is transmitted to every enlightened person in general, not every one who hears it and receives it can bring it into actuality."[70] The only esoteric writing that is justified alludes to the secrets in such a way that he who has received the oral tradition will be able to interpret and expand the written allusions. In *Sitre Torah* Abulafia elaborated on this point, closely following the Maimonidean hermeneutic:

> There is no doubt that the enlightened can comprehend one thing from another. Therefore, the one who composes a book on a matter as deep as this

---

Hebrew), *Jerusalem Studies in Jewish Thought* 1 (1981): 52-55. The true tradition of which Abulafia speaks — that the Torah in its entirety is composed of the names of God — is known from other contemporary sources, including: the German Pietists (Dan, *Esoteric Theology,* p. 124 n. 45; Idel, "Concept of Torah," pp. 147-48; Idel, "No Kabbalistic Tradition," p. 54 n. 10; E. R. Wolfson, "The Mystical Significance of Torah-Study in German Pietism," in *Jewish Quarterly Review* 84 [1993]: 43-78); theosophic kabbalists (Scholem, *On the Kabbalah,* pp. 37-39; Scholem, "The Name of God and the Linguistic Theory of the Kabbala," *Diogenes* 79 [1972]: 76-77; Idel, "Concept of Torah," 23-49); and other rabbinic figures such as Sedeqiah ben Abraham, author of the halakic compendium *Shibbole ha-Leqet* (Idel, "Concept of Torah," p. 54 n. 10). Concerning his indebtedness to Nahmanides, see Idel, *Language, Torah, and Hermeneutics,* pp. 46-47, 66, 171 n. 88; Wolfson, "By Way of Truth," p. 117, n. 44.

68. See Idel, *Language, Torah, and Hermeneutics,* pp. 48-49.

69. Jellinek, *Philosophie und Kabbala,* pp. 4-5.

70. Jellinek, *Philosophie und Kabbala,* p. 12. Idel remarks that despite the innovative hermeneutical approach adopted by Abulafia, which resulted in his prolific literary activity, he still remained faithful to the view that what is truly esoteric cannot be written (*Kabbalah,* p. 254).

can rely on the knowledge of those who understand, for the book cannot adequately reveal the mysteries. . . . The rational faculty is obligated to speak of it and to assist him in comprehending what he has heard. . . . The intention is to reveal the hidden matter according to its need, to arouse the intellect to draw forth until it comprehends it with an enduring comprehension that will not be forgotten or obliterated.[71]

In another of his commentaries on the *Guide,* Abulafia noted that Maimonides revealed what he had to reveal so that the enlightened reader would understand, but he concealed matters so that the unworthy would not understand.[72] The Maimonidean resolution to the tension between the mandate to conceal secrets on the one hand and the need to reveal them on the other was widely adopted by kabbalists of the various schools in the thirteenth century.

The appeal to an oral transmission *(qabbalah)* appears in many anonymous tracts that deal principally with the mysticism of divine names or letters of the Hebrew alphabet, a mysticism that is virtually indistinguishable from magical praxis and is rooted in much older trends of Jewish esotericism. The first example, attributed to the circle of *Sefer ha-Temunah,*[73] originated in a group of Spanish mystics whose central concern was speculation on the letters of the Hebrew alphabet. This text represents a stage of Castilian kabbalah preceding the generation of the kabbalists referred to by Scholem as the "gnostic circle," which included Jacob and Isaac ha-Kohen, and their disciples, Moses ben Simeon of Burgos and Todros ben Joseph Abulafia. Some of these writings, including, most importantly, *Sefer ha-'Orah* of Jacob, reflect this concern with the mystical nature of the alphabet and the names of God.[74] In this circle are compositions dedicated to the mystical nature of letters, vowel points, and cantillation signs.[75] The relevant text (cited in accordance with the superior reading found in manuscript) reads: "The one who has received the [visual] form *(siyyur)* of the alphabet will then understand this great and awesome secret [concerning the name of God], for the ancient Geonim put a ban on the disclosure of this secret, which is the essential name, as it is written, 'A fountain

71. MS Paris, Bibliothèque Nationale héb. 774, f. 121a.

72. For Abulafia's extended discussion of this part of the *Guide,* cf. *Hayye ha-Nefesh,* MS Munich, Bayerisch Staatsbibliothek 408, ff. 69a-73a.

73. G. Scholem, "The Secret of the Tree of Emanation by R. Isaac: A Treatise from the Kabbalistic Tradition of *Sefer ha-Temunah*" (in Hebrew), *Qoves 'al Yad* 5 (1951): 67 n. 2.

74. D. Abrams, "'The Book of Illumination' of R. Jacob ben Jacob haKohen: A Synoptic Edition from Various Manuscripts" (Ph.D. diss., New York University, 1993).

75. See A. Farber, "On the Sources of Rabbi Moses de Leon's Early Kabbalistic System" (in Hebrew), in *Studies in Jewish Mysticism Philosophy and Ethical Literature Presented to Isaiah Tishby on His Seventy-Fifth Birthday* (Jerusalem, 1986), pp. 67-96.

locked, a sealed-up spring' (Song of Songs 4:12)."[76] The text ends with a chain of tradition, obviously based on the beginning of the Mishnah *Avot*:

> This is the tradition *(qabbalah)* received by Moses from the mouth of God at Sinai and he transmitted it to Joshua, and Joshua to the elders, and the elders to the prophets, and the prophets transmitted it to the members of the Great Assembly, for they were masters of wisdom *(ba'ale hokhmah)*, masters of tradition *(ba'ale qabbalah)*, masters of fear *(ba'ale yir'ah)*, masters of honor *(ba'ale kavod)*, concerning whom it is written, "the secret of the Lord is with those who fear Him" (Ps. 25:14). And they hid it within the secrets of the Talmud *(sodot ha-talmud)*, for it is all a tradition [given] to Moses at Sinai *(qabbalah le-mosheh mi-sinai)*.[77]

Prophetic Revelation and the Oral Chain of Tradition

The intricate relations of oral tradition and written transmission in Jewish mysticism can be clarified only by a comprehensive study of orality in classical Jewish sources. As a working hypothesis the following may be suggested: the role of orality in rabbinic culture is not to exhibit a conservative mind-set but the very opposite, i.e., to mask novelty and innovation, which in effect serves as an impetus or catalyst for more creativity. The few scholars who have more recently paid attention to the question of orality in the kabbalistic sources have tended to adopt the correlation of oral culture and conservatism.[78] Within the highly literate atmosphere of the rabbinic academies of late antiquity and the Middle Ages, and in geographical regions as distinct as Palestine, Babylonia, North Africa, and central Europe, the role of orality was never to inhibit intellectual experimentation. Oral tradition functioned as a means of fostering new ideas, new interpretations of traditional texts, or new rituals. Even if we accept at face value the assertion of Jewish mystics that esoteric traditions were transmitted orally, we need not posit that the exponents of these traditions were conservative in their orientation. The presumption that creative innovation is operative in the oral stage is supported both by an understanding of the specific role of orality in rabbinic culture as well as from a more general consideration of medieval European society, especially in the twelfth and thirteenth centuries

76. MS Oxford, Bodleian Library 1953, f. 24b.

77. MS Oxford, Bodleian Library 1953, f. 28a.

78. W. J. Ong, *Orality and Literacy: The Technologizing of the Word* (London and New York, 1982), p. 41. See B. Stock, *The Implications of Literacy: Written Language and Models of Interpretation in the Eleventh and Twelfth Centuries* (Princeton, 1983), pp. 15-16.

when new ideas were typically presented as the "old traditions." Medieval Jewish mystics should not be isolated from their Jewish heritage or from their immediate intellectual and social environment.

It is important to recall the chain of tradition *(shalshelet ha-qabbalah)* that appears in late thirteenth- and early fourteenth-century kabbalistic material. The obvious purpose of this chain is to explain the historical evolution of the kabbalah. According to one version of the *shalshelet ha-qabbalah,* the originator of the chain is the prophet Elijah, who revealed the secrets to Abraham ben Isaac, who then revealed them to his son-in-law, Abraham ben David, who in turn revealed them to his son, Isaac the Blind.[79] According to another version, Elijah revealed the secret gnosis to Jacob the Nazirite, who transmitted it to Abraham ben David, who in turn passed it on to his son, Isaac the Blind.[80] In yet another version Elijah revealed the secrets to David, the father of Abraham ben David, who revealed them to his son, who passed them on to his son, Isaac the Blind, who disseminated them to Ezra and Azriel of Gerona, and to Nahmanides.[81] Finally, another version of the chain reports the following sequence: Elijah, Isaac ben Abraham of Narbonne, Jacob the Nazirite, Abraham ben David, and Isaac the Blind.[82] That the chain begins in every case with Elijah attests to a remarkable self-awareness by later kabbalists that something new has appeared on the scene in twelfth-century Provence. The point was made by Scholem that the tradition of a revelation of Elijah may be regarded "as testimony that in this circle something really new had burst forth from the depths."[83] Through the notion of the revelation of Elijah, the kabbalists "wished to communicate something which obviously had not come to them through the traditional and generally accepted channels."[84] On the other hand, the choice of Elijah helped guarantee the tradi-

79. Shem Tov ibn Gaon, *Badde ha-Aron u-Migdal Hananel,* facsimile edition based on MS 840 in the National Library, Paris, ed. D. S. Loewinger (Jerusalem, 1977), 29; cf. Shem Tov ibn Gaon, *Keter Shem Tov,* in *Ma'or wa-Shemesh,* ed. J. Koriat (Livorno, 1839), 35b; Shem Tov ibn Shem Tov, *Sefer ha-'Emunot* (Ferrara, 1560), p. 35b.

80. Isaac ben Samuel of Acre, *Sefer Me'irat Einayim by R. Isaac of Acre: A Critical Edition* (in Hebrew), ed. A. Goldreich (Jerusalem, 1981), p. 84.

81. Menahem Recanati, *Perush ha-Torah* (Jerusalem, 1961), p. 73d. A similar chain of tradition is cited in the name of the "sages of truth" *(hakhme ha-'emet)* by Meir ibn Gabbai, *'Avodat ha-Qodesh* (Jerusalem, 1992), II.13, p. 102, and from there it is cited by Elijah Delmedigo, *Masref la-Hokhmah* (Basel, 1629), p. 15a.

82. According to the manuscript evidence cited by Scholem, *Origins of the Kabbalah,* p. 37 n. 61.

83. Scholem, *Origins of the Kabbalah,* p. 245. On the role of Elijah in Jewish mysticism, see also A. Wiener, *The Prophet Elijah in the Development of Judaism: A Depth-Psychological Study* (London, 1978), pp. 78-111.

84. Scholem, *On the Kabbalah,* p. 19.

tional and authoritative status of the content of that revelation, given Elijah's standing in the normative rabbinic tradition.

These chains of tradition are relatively late, and there is no clear indication in the earlier sources themselves that the Provençal or, for that matter, the Geronese kabbalists attributed kabbalistic teachings to Elijah.[85] We cannot be certain that the first kabbalists were aware of the problem this notion seeks to address, that of a seemingly innovative doctrine presented as tradition. The stated position of Ezra of Gerona or Nahmanides directly challenges the claim made by later kabbalists. Both Ezra and Nahmanides emphasized that the kabbalah represented an ancient Jewish lore, indeed part of the oral tradition par excellence (*torah shebe'al peh,* meaning literally), going back either to Abraham or to Moses.

While it is true that the early masters were depicted as preservers of a received tradition, the source was Elijah. Efforts to link the notions of orality and conservatism on the one hand, and written composition and innovation on the other, should be reassessed in light of the kabbalists' own admission that the chain of tradition began with a revelation of Elijah. The conserving tendency is predicated, in effect, on a prior innovative stage. The claim for linear reception, and thus the forging of an authoritative chain, is meant to legitimate what was revealed spontaneously by the prophet to the first link in the chain. The conservative trend, therefore, must be seen in dialectic relation to the innovative.

Orality as Exposition of Texts

It would be wise to consider the cultural context in which kabbalah flourished as being simultaneously oral and written. To state at the outset my hypothesis: there is no orality that does not presuppose textuality.[86] One should avoid the spectrum of an oral versus written dichotomy with a pure oral tradition on one

85. Scholem (*Origins of the Kabbalah,* p. 36) was of the opinion that even though the traditions relating to the appearance of the prophet Elijah to the earliest kabbalists first appear around 1300, everything indicates that they are drawn from traditional material going back to the first Spanish kabbalists. By contrast, I. Twersky (*Rabad of Posquières: A Twelfth-Century Talmudist* [Cambridge, Mass., 1962], p. 287) concluded that the claim for Abraham ben David's acquisition of knowledge through the medium of revelation "seems to be a later accretion."

86. A similar position regarding the interaction of orality and literary traditions in classical rabbinic culture has been affirmed by a number of scholars. See M. Jaffee, "How Much 'Orality' in Oral Torah? New Perspectives on the Composition and Transmission of Early Rabbinic Tradition," *Shofar* 10 (1992): 53-72; Jaffee, "Writing and Rabbinic Oral Tradition: On Mishnaic Narrative, Lists and Mnemonics," *Journal of Jewish Thought and Philosophy* 4 (1994): 123-46, and references to other relevant scholarly discussions given on 124 n. 2.

end and the written page of text on the other.[87] We must focus our attention rather on the interface of oral and written.[88] After all, we are speaking of groups within medieval Jewish society that demonstrated a high degree of literacy.[89] The circle of kabbalists in Catalonia and Castile were, in Brian Stock's terminology, "textual communities," for they demonstrate a "parallel use of texts, both to structure the internal behaviour of the groups' members and to provide solidarity against the outside world."[90] The role of orality, as shown by existing kabbalistic materials, was, to borrow the formulation of Stock, "to function in a reference system based on texts."[91] The center of gravity for the medieval kabbalists shifted from the oral to the written despite their claims to the contrary. I accept the probability that kabbalists imparted esoteric doctrines and practices through oral performance. My point is that for these medieval Jewish mystics, orality consisted primarily in the exposition of written texts. The oral tradition, *qabbalah,* is thus mainly textual, or text-related, and in that respect we do well to speak of orality intersecting with textuality.

87. A number of scholars of late have challenged a rigid dichotomization of orality and textuality in the Middle Ages and have opted for a symbiotic model whereby the two epistemic modes interact and interpenetrate. See F. H. Bäuml, "Medieval Texts and the Two Theories of Oral-Formulaic Composition: A Proposal for a Third Theory," *New Literary History* 16 (1984-85): 41-54; J. M. Gellrich, *The Idea of the Book in the Middle Ages: Language Theory, Mythology, and Fiction* (Ithaca, N.Y., and London, 1985); J. M. Foley, *The Theory of Oral Composition: History and Methodology* (Bloomington, Ind., 1988); Foley, "Orality, Textuality, and Interpretation," in *Vox Intexta: Orality and Textuality in the Middle Ages,* ed. A. N. Donne and C. B. Pasternack (Madison, Wis., 1991), pp. 34-45; Foley, "Word-Power, Performance and Tradition," *Journal of American Folklore* 105 (1992): 275-301; M. Calinescu, "Orality and Literacy: Some Historical Paradoxes of Reading," *Yale Journal of Criticism* 6 (1993): 175-90. See also the works of Stock cited in nn. 90 and 91 below.

88. I have borrowed this expression from J. Goody, *The Interface between the Written and the Oral* (Cambridge, 1987).

89. The history of Jewish literacy in the Middle Ages has not been written. For a preliminary study see S. C. Reif, "Aspects of Medieval Jewish Literacy," in *The Uses of Literacy in Early Mediaeval Europe,* ed. R. McKitterick (Cambridge, 1990), pp. 134-55. Although Reif's study is limited to Oriental Jewish communities living under the rule of Islam from the sixth to the eleventh centuries, many of his insights regarding Jewish literacy would equally apply to Jews in Christian Europe.

90. Stock, *The Implications of Literacy,* p. 90. According to Stock, from the beginning of the eleventh century, a new kind of interdependence arose between the oral and the written: "oral discourse effectively began to function within a universe of communications governed by texts" (p. 3). To my mind, this is a satisfactory model for the rabbinic conception of oral tradition in the medieval European centers, although it would apply equally to a much earlier historical period and different geographical locality.

91. B. Stock, *Listening for the Text: On the Uses of the Past* (Baltimore and London, 1990), p. 20.

Allow me a philological observation not sufficiently noted in the scholarly literature. The very terms *qabbalah*, "tradition," or *qibbalti*, "I have received," do not require an oral transmission that precludes any written evidence. The mode of presentation in the first document of the medieval kabbalistic tradition, the *Sefer ha-Bahir*, is midrashic: views are presented as the exegesis of select verses and placed into the mouths of rabbinic personalities.[92] There are no overt claims to the antiquity of the doctrines expounded, although this is implied by the literary presumption of the text, nor are any of the ideas legitimized through a continuous chain of oral transmission. This text is classified as a kabbalistic work, for we impute to it what we know from other documents that employ this term or related terms to name the transmission of an esoteric doctrine regarding the dynamic gradations *(sefirot)* of the divine.[93] In the *Bahir*, however, there are competing theosophies, reflecting the composite and highly redacted nature of the text, and in only one stratum is there a sustained reflection on the ten powers of the divine realm.[94] In one instance the word *qibbalti*, "I received," is used in connection with a theosophic reading of Exodus 20:11 according to which the six days of creation are transformed into symbols for six divine emanations.[95] In this case the *qabbalah* is an esoteric recasting of a biblical text in light of certain theosophical assumptions. In a second passage we read: "Rabbi Rehumai said, 'Thus I received *(qibbalti)* that when Moses wanted to know the knowledge of the awesome and glorious name, he said, "Show me Your glory" (Ex. 33:18). He wanted to know why one righteous person experiences goodness and another evil, and why one wicked person experiences goodness and another evil.'"[96] The problem of theodicy is here treated as knowledge of the name of God, and this is further associated with a reception of a tradition on the part of R. Rehumai. The passage is based on the interpretation of Exodus 33:18 in Babylonian Talmud *Berakot* 7a. The force of the locution

92. Scholem, *Origins of the Kabbalah*, pp. 39-44, 49-53; J. Dan, "Midrash and the Dawn of Kabbalah," in *Midrash and Literature*, ed. G. Hartman and S. Budick (New Haven, 1986), pp. 127-39.

93. See Scholem, *Origins of the Kabbalah*, pp. 49-198; M. Idel, "The Problem of the Sources of the *Bahir*" (in Hebrew), *Jerusalem Studies in Jewish Thought* 6, nos. 3-4 (1987): 55-72; H. Pedaya, "The Provençal Stratum in the Redaction of *Sefer ha-Bahir*" (in Hebrew), *Jerusalem Studies in Jewish Thought* 9 (1990): 139-64; E. R. Wolfson, "The Tree That Is All: Jewish-Christian Roots of a Kabbalistic Symbol in *Sefer ha-Bahir*," *Journal of Jewish Thought and Philosophy* 3 (1993): 31-76, revised version in *Along the Path*, pp. 63-88 and notes on 187-223.

94. For the purposes of this study, I am focusing on the use of the root *qbl* in the bahiric text, and thus I will not enter into the complicated question of protokabbalistic sources, oral or written, that may prove to be the foundation of the *Bahir*.

95. *Sefer ha-Bahir*, ed. R. Margaliot (Jerusalem, 1978), par. 57.

96. *Sefer ha-Bahir*, par. 194.

"I received," therefore, must be "I received an interpretation of the traditional source." On philological grounds the word *qibbel* in the *Bahir* denotes reception of an exegetical tradition.

Let me here note two other striking examples of this phenomenon. The first is from Moses ben Simeon of Burgos, a Castilian kabbalist active in the second half of the thirteenth century. He begins with a commentary on the forty-two-letter name of God: "We have a complete tradition from R. Hai, blessed be his memory, who received from the Geonim who preceded him, and from the sages who preceded the Geonim going back to R. Akiva and R. Ishmael the High Priest, may peace be upon them."[97] Whether or not Moses of Burgos himself is responsible for these traditions, he reports them as something he has received. In this context the force of the terms *qabbalah* and *masoret*, which I have rendered with the one English word "tradition," cannot be a direct oral transmission since Hai Gaon lived two centuries before Moses of Burgos. Here these terms signify that Moses of Burgos received through a textual channel an authoritative teaching attributed to Hai Gaon. The textual connotation of the word *qabbalah* is implied in a second passage from the same work: "After we have informed you that we have mentioned the sayings of those who speak by means of the Holy Spirit and the sages, blessed be their memory, regarding the status of the greatness of the aforementioned name [of forty-two letters], we will write the essence of the names in their vocalization as we have received and the variant readings that we have found in the writings of the Geonim, blessed be their memory."[98] One may be tempted to argue that in this case the expression "we have received" *(qibbalnu)* contrasts with "we have found" *(masa'nu)*. But the term *qibbalnu* signifies the act of orally receiving a tradition as authoritative, and the source of that tradition is a literary document. Thus, immediately after presenting the vocalizations of the forty-two-letter name, the author writes: "Now we shall begin to explain the meaning of the words and letters by way of proper tradition *('al derekh qabbalah nekhonah)* from the learned of the world, the kabbalists *(ge'one 'olam mequbbalim)*, from the secrets of their exalted and inner intentions that edify wondrous matters." The complex explanations offered by Moses of Burgos on the forty-two-letter name of God are drawn from existing texts that he may well have received from his teachers.

Along similar lines, the expression *shama'ti*, "I have heard," does not always

---

97. MS Oxford, Bodleian Library 1565, f. 93b. Scholem accurately described this composition as an anthology arranged from different sources (*Le-Heqer Qabbalat R. Yishaq ben Ya'aqov ha-Kohen* [Jerusalem, 1934], pp. 122-27).

98. MS Oxford, Bodleian Library 1565, f. 95b.

connote an aural reception. In medieval mystical texts, as in rabbinic sources,[99] the expression *shama'ti* can refer to a "hearing from books,"[100] i.e., comprehension of a written artifact or acceptance of the latter as authoritative. In a fragment of a letter addressed to Nahmanides on matters pertaining to prayer, an anonymous inquirer explained his reason for turning to the rabbi for guidance: "Even though I have found other sages of the kabbalah saying similar things, I have not heard [anything] from the holy mouth *(lo shama'ti ken mi-pi qadosh)* concerning the matter of prayer."[101] The writer of the letter is seeking to receive a response from Nahmanides concerning the mystical intention of prayer. The locution "to hear from the mouth" does not denote oral reception in a literal sense, but rather to receive a teaching from a certain authority, even if in written form.[102]

I do not mean to challenge entirely the reliability of a mystic's assertion that he has received such and such a tradition from a particular sage. Indeed, we find in many instances that the formulations *qibbalti mipi,* "I received from the mouth," and *shama'ti mipi,* "I have heard from the mouth," indicate the reception of that which has been transmitted orally. In many of these cases, however, what has been transmitted is a tradition recorded in written form, which the master passes on to his disciples in an oral way, i.e., in a context of teaching them by reading the recorded traditions and expounding upon them. These oral expositions of written traditions often themselves become texts at the hands of disciples, which in turn facilitate later oral and written exposition. A codex of kabbalistic sources from the thirteenth century — the manuscript written in a beautiful Spanish script and dated to the fourteenth or fifteenth

99. See B. Gerhardsson, *Memory and Manuscript: Oral Tradition and Written Transmission in Rabbinic Judaism and Early Christianity* (Copenhagen, 1964), p. 133 n. 4. To be sure, the general connotation of the word *shama'ti* in rabbinic texts is a literal repetition or memorization of a teaching that is considered to be an authoritative tradition, but there are passages wherein the connotation of this term is "I have deduced," "I have understood," or "I have learned."

100. I have borrowed this expression from U. Schafer, "Hearing from Books: The Rise of Fictionality in Old English Poetry," in *Vox Intexta,* pp. 117-36. The intersection of orality and textuality may also relate to the fact that the dominant mode of reading within the social setting of religious institutions in the Middle Ages was acoustical, i.e., one read with one's ears rather than with one's eyes. On the aural nature of reading in the medieval monastic setting, see Stock, *The Implications of Literacy,* pp. 408-9; I. Illich, *In the Vineyard of the Text: A Commentary to Hugh's "Didascalicon"* (Chicago, 1993), pp. 51-65.

101. MS Parma, Biblioteca Palatina 68, f. 76a.

102. To take one other illustration from a comparatively later text, the seventeenth-century compendium of halakic and kabbalistic sources, *Shene Luhot ha-Berit* of Isaiah Horowitz (Amsterdam, 1698), p. 355b: "I have heard with regard to this a wonderful matter in a manuscript." Here we have clear evidence that the locution "I have heard" functions in a literary context. That is, the author "hears" or comprehends a tradition that he has found in manuscript.

century, used by Johann Reuchlin in his *De Arte Cabalistica*[103] — assembled a variety of such materials: "I have written this book in which there are kabbalistic explanations so that I will remember what I have received from the great and elderly sages, men of understanding, blessed be their memory. And I adjure all my descendants to guard this book[104] so as not to show it to empty people who would destroy their souls by thinking thoughts they did not understand."[105] Oral traditions were not by definition nontextual. The function of oral transmission for the kabbalists was not to conserve ancient doctrines or practices in a rigid way, but to provide a context for innovative interpretation, expansion, and application. We can well imagine that disciples sat and learned from masters who taught orally the esoteric gnosis and techniques for mystical experience. These masters were, first and foremost, expositors of texts that preserved older traditions in some recorded form. The kabbalah, whether theosophic or ecstatic, is unequivocally related to textual explication.

The earliest reports about an oral tradition received from a teacher almost invariably involve the exposition of some text, either biblical, liturgical, or haggadic in nature. Thus, for example, the oft-cited remark of Ezra of Gerona reporting the tradition of Isaac the Blind: "Our teacher, the pious one, blessed be his memory, said: The essence of worship of the enlightened and those who meditate on His name is 'cleave to Him' (Deut. 13:5), and this is the great principle in the Torah concerning prayer and blessings, to harmonize his thought and his faith as if he were cleaving above, to unite the name in its letters and to comprise within it the ten *sefirot* like a flame that is bound to the coal."[106] The kabbalah, in short, is presented as an exegetical reflection on the verse from Scripture. It is likewise with the nature of the kabbalah for Isaac the Blind, as reported by another Geronese kabbalist, Jacob ben Sheshet. Reflecting on the Aramaic translation of Onkelos on Leviticus 13:18, Jacob wrote: "This is comparable to the explanation, 'He looked into the Torah,' He saw the essences *(hawwayot)* within Himself, for they were the essences from Wisdom, and from those essences, which were the essences of Wisdom, He discerned that they would be manifest in the future. Thus I heard this discourse in the name of the pious one, R. Isaac the son of R. Abraham, blessed be his memory."[107] The oral tradition in this case is an explanation of the haggadic motif found at the very beginning of the midrashic collection, *Bere'shit Rabbah,* regarding

103. See Scholem, *Origins of the Kabbalah*, p. 424.

104. The manuscript here reads *shem*, i.e., "name," but I have taken the liberty to assume that the correct reading is *sefer*, which has been rendered as "book."

105. MS New York, Jewish Theological Seminary of America Mic. 1887, f. 76a.

106. *Kitve Ramban* 2.522.

107. *Kitve Ramban* 2.409.

God's looking into the Torah as the vehicle of creation. Given the theosophic identification of God and the Torah, Isaac the Blind interpreted the rabbinic comment as an articulation of the idea that God gazes into his own image and contemplates the inner essences of Wisdom. The kabbalistic tradition, therefore, is essentially an exposition of the midrashic text. Interestingly enough, in the continuation of the passage Jacob ben Sheshet states that the kabbalistic interpretation of Isaac the Blind accords with the philosophical view expressed by Maimonides concerning God's knowledge of particular existents through self-contemplation. Even though the substance of the philosophic and kabbalistic sources may be identical, in an epistemological sense the two are distinguishable, for the former is a matter of knowledge *(yedi'ah)* and the latter of faith *('emunah)*.

In most instances the kabbalah is an explanation of some authoritative text, whether liturgical,[108] biblical,[109] or rabbinic.[110] Hence the claims *qibbalti,* "I received," and *shama'ti,* "I heard," signify the reception of an exegetical teaching as authoritative.[111] Interestingly enough, in his supercommentary on the esoteric allusions in Nahmanides' Torah commentary, Shem Tov ibn Gaon mentions secrets that he received orally from his teachers, Solomon ibn Adret and Isaac ben Todros.[112] The nature of these secrets, however, is very much related to textual exegesis, for example, in the mysteries associated with impregnation *(sod ha-'ibbur),*[113] levirate marriage *(sod ha-yibbum),*[114] sacrifices,[115] and Ezekiel's chariot.[116] In a similar vein Isaac of Acre stated that the disciples of Nahmanides reported that they received from his mouth that each occur-

---

108. MS New York, Jewish Theological Seminary of America Mic. 1878, f. 4b.

109. MS New York, Jewish Theological Seminary of America Mic. 1878, ff. 6b, 7a, 17a.

110. MS New York, Jewish Theological Seminary of America Mic. 1878, f. 7b.

111. There are, of course, reports of oral traditions regarding the sefirotic potencies and/or the divine names that are not necessarily linked to specific texts. Cf. Shem Tov ibn Gaon, *Keter Shem Tov,* pp. 36b, 47b. To take another example, the anonymous author of *Ma'arekhet ha-'Elohut* (Mantua, 1558), p. 66b, remarks that Solomon ibn Adret reported that he received from Nahmanides that the word *siyyon* is one of the technical names for the ninth emanation. The textual nature of the oral tradition is underscored in a second passage from this work where the author relates having heard that the repetition of the word *mayim* in the legend about Akiva's warning to the other rabbis (according to the version in Babylonian Talmud *Ḥagigah* 14b) has symbolic significance.

112. In one place, *Keter Shem Tov,* p. 34a, Shem Tov records a numerological explanation of the word *hit'azzar* in Ps. 93:1, which he heard from his teacher, who had heard it from R. Shlomo ha-Qatan. The oral tradition is linked specifically to an exposition of a biblical text.

113. Shem Tov ibn Gaon, *Keter Shem Tov,* p. 29a.

114. Shem Tov ibn Gaon, *Keter Shem Tov,* p. 31b.

115. Shem Tov ibn Gaon, *Keter Shem Tov,* pp. 32b, 41a-42a.

116. Shem Tov ibn Gaon, *Keter Shem Tov,* p. 39a.

rence of the Tetragrammaton in Scripture refers to the supreme divine being, the Cause of Causes *('illat ha-'illot)*.[117] The oral tradition was an interpretative strategy for reading the biblical text.

I do not envision the recasting of talmudic Haggadoth, or the commentaries on the prayers, as a secondary process in the formulation of kabbalistic doctrine, functioning therefore as a kind of *'asmakhta'* in traditional rabbinic literature, i.e., textual support for an autonomous doctrine. On the contrary, I suggest that we look at the process of formation of these ideas as a result of an inner hermeneutic whereby there is a gnostification of haggadic and liturgical texts. Here I am deliberately using Scholem's terminology. However, I do not suggest that the gnostification occurs from the outside, i.e., through the imposition of an extrinsic system on Jewish material, but rather from the inside.[118] It is possible that the kabbalah contains the elaboration of ancient Jewish mythologoumena reflected in the doctrines of gnosticism, Mandaeanism, or Judeo-Christianity.[119] But it is also possible that the parallels between these forms of gnosis and kabbalah can be explained by similar hermeneutical developments occurring independently at two periods of history.[120]

The thesis I have presented, that there is no orality that does not presuppose textuality, lends support to the claim that at the oral stage itself there is innovation, specifically as exposition of texts. From the perspective of hermeneutical method there is no discernible difference between the oral and the written stages of transmission. Let us consider once more Nahmanides, who explicitly described kabbalah in the most conservative terms as a corpus of limited secrets passed through the generations in a continuous chain of oral tradition.[121] I have

117. *Sefer Me'irat Einayim*, p. 219. Cf. Shem Tov ibn Gaon, *Keter Shem Tov*, p. 40b.

118. See Scholem, *Origins of the Kabbalah*, pp. 66-67. Scholem's views regarding gnosticism and its relationship to Judaism are complex. See discussion in Idel, *Kabbalah*, pp. 30-31, and the critique by I. Tishby, "Upheaval in the Research of Kabbalah (On: M. Idel, *Kabbalah: New Perspectives)*" (in Hebrew), *Zion* 54 (1989): 210-13. For more recent reviews of the question, see N. Deutsch, *The Gnostic Imagination: Gnosticism, Mandaeism, and Merkabah Mysticism* (Leiden, 1995), pp. 1-17, and J. Dan, "Jewish Gnosticism?" *Jewish Studies Quarterly* 2 (1995): 309-28.

119. See Idel, *Kabbalah*, pp. 31-32.

120. Tishby articulates a similar position to the one I am advocating, although he does not place the same emphasis on the hermeneutical dimension ("Gnostic Doctrines in Sixteenth-Century Jewish Mysticism," *Journal of Jewish Studies* 6 [1955]: 146).

121. This aspect of Nahmanides' kabbalah has been championed by Idel, "We Have No Kabbalistic Tradition on This," and *Kabbalah*, pp. 20, 212, 253-54. In a more recent publication Idel asserts that, according to Nahmanides, understanding is a tool for the reception of secrets, but not for the extracting of secrets from the text ("Secrecy, Binah and Derishah," p. 331). See also Idel, "R. Moshe ben Nahman — Kabbalah, Halakhah, and Spiritual Leadership" (in Hebrew), *Tarbiz* 64 (1995): 535-80, esp. 550-56.

argued that, in spite of Nahmanides' declarations, he expanded the range of kabbalistic secrets through a consistent and innovative hermeneutical posture vis-à-vis Scripture, often read through the lens of rabbinic Haggadah. I have further suggested that a major source for Nahmanides' kabbalistic explanations was the *Sefer ha-Bahir,* received by him as a literary document and read as part of the traditional Haggadah.[122] I find little evidence that Nahmanides ever relied on a purely oral tradition. Kabbalistic secrets emerged from an exegetical effort to fathom the text. In many cases in Nahmanides' commentary, the literal sense, in his view, converges with the esoteric or kabbalistic.[123] If there were in fact received traditions, then they did not inhibit or restrict the exegetical process. The deep secret, the esoteric truth, thus arose from and within the hermeneutical relation of the reader to the text.

The key exegetical term Nahmanides employs to bridge the gap between text and interpretation is *remez,* which signifies an allusion or hint encoded in Scripture.[124] The belief affirmed by Nahmanides, that all wisdom, including esoteric wisdom (*ma'aseh merkavah,* the account of the chariot, and *ma'aseh bere'shit,* the account of creation) and exoteric science about the natural world, is contained in the Torah, necessitates the further belief that the biblical text either explicitly or implicitly discloses the different types of wisdom.[125] Particu-

---

122. Wolfson, "By Way of Truth," pp. 153-78. M. Idel, in his introduction to *The Book Bahir: An Edition Based on the Earliest Manuscripts* (in Hebrew), ed. D. Abrams (Los Angeles, 1994), p. 4 n. 24, expresses doubt regarding my claim that the *Bahir* was the main kabbalistic source for Nahmanides with respect to at least two topics, the doctrine of the *sefirot* and the secret of impregnation *(sod ha-'ibbur).* See, however, "By Way of Truth" (pp. 177-78 n. 237), where I mentioned that Nahmanides' essentialist interpretation of the *sefirot* did not parallel the view expressed in the *Bahir.* More importantly, the main thrust of my argument concerned support for kabbalistic ideas. When the issue is framed in that way, I still think it is correct to conclude that, for Nahmanides, the *Bahir* is the critical text, for he often relies on that source to validate his kabbalistic exegesis.

123. D. Berger, "Miracles and the Natural Order in Nahmanides," in *Rabbi Moses Nahmanides,* p. 112 n. 19; B. Septimus, "'Open Rebuke and Concealed Love': Nahmanides and the Andalusian Tradition," in *Rabbi Moses Nahmanides,* p. 21 n. 37; Wolfson, "By Way of Truth," pp. 129-53.

124. Wolfson, "By Way of Truth," pp. 164-65.

125. *Perush ha-Ramban 'al ha-Torah* 1.3. Nahmanides' position bears a striking resemblance to the orientation of the German Pietists, who likewise emphasize that all wisdom, including the secrets, are contained in the Torah. See H. Soloveitchik, "Three Themes in the *Sefer Hasidim,*" *ASJ Review* 1 (1976): 314 n. 7. One text not mentioned by Soloveitchik, but which is very close to the position of Nahmanides, is Eleazar of Worms, *Perush ha-Rav 'Ele'azar Mi-Germaiza' 'al Sefer Yesirah* (Przemyśl, 1883), p. 1b: "The Torah begins with the *bet of bere'shit* and ends with the *lamed* of *le-'eine kol yisra'el* [the numerical value of *bet* and *lamed* is thirty-two, the number of the paths of wisdom] to teach you that everything is alluded to in the Torah

larly significant is Nahmanides' reflection on this issue in his sermon *Torat ha-Shem Temimah*:

> I am perplexed for I see that the Torah speaks of the account of creation *(ma'aseh bere'shit)* and cosmology *(hokhmat ha-yesirah)*, but I do not know where it alludes to the account of the chariot *(ma'aseh merkavah)*. The supernal chariot *(merkavah ha-'elyonah)*, which is the knowledge of the Creator, is written in the Torah, but I do not see where there is an allusion *(remez)* in the Torah to the chariot of the palaces *(merkavah shel hekhalot)*. Perhaps it was an oral tradition until Ezekiel and Isaiah came and gave it textual support.[126]

Nahmanides entertains the possibility that there was an oral tradition regarding the lower chariot, not written in the Torah. Even in this case he maintains that the upper chariot, which is the gnosis about God, is written in the Torah.

With respect to secretive matters, then, one might say that, according to Nahmanides, the Torah, much like Apollo as described by Heraclitus, "neither declares nor conceals, but gives a sign."[127] The master of esoteric knowledge is one who can read or decode those signs. I submit that such reading is a form of extracting the secret from the text. To be sure, from one perspective the tradition *(qabbalah)* is independent of the scriptural text, and precisely on account of that tradition the text is interpreted in a particular way. The point is made clear in Nahmanides' statement that "the account of creation is a deep mystery that cannot be understood from scriptural verses, and it is not clearly understood except through the kabbalah going back to Moses, our master, [who received it] from God. Those who know it are obligated to conceal it."[128] On the surface it appears that Nahmanides blatantly denies the possibility of extracting

---

(ramuz ba-torah) . . . but it is hidden from people, and the secrets of Torah were only given to those who fear him, 'the secret of the Lord is with those who fear Him' (Ps. 25:14)." Cf. Eleazar of Worms, *Sefer ha-Shem*, MS London, British Museum 737, ff. 205b-206a. Eleazar acknowledges that through the interpretative method, which he refers to by the technical term *talmud*, one can greatly multiply the production of books that make explicit that which is inherent in the scriptural text — a point all the more remarkable in light of the explicit claim in *Sefer Hasidim* (ed. J. Wistinetzki and J. Freimann [Frankfurt am Main, 1924], par. 986) that the production of novel interpretations *(ledabber hidushim)* is one of the major temptations that the pietist must overcome. See, in particular, the text of Eleazar published by J. Dan, *Studies in Ashkenazi-Hasidic Literature* (in Hebrew) (Ramat Gan, 1975), pp. 46-47, and the analysis in I. G. Marcus, *Piety and Society: The Jewish Pietists of Medieval Germany* (Leiden, 1981), pp. 69-70.

126. *Kitve Ramban* 1.161.

127. C. H. Kahn, *The Art and Thought of Heraclitus: An Edition of the Fragments with Translation and Commentary* (Cambridge, 1979), pp. 42-43.

128. *Perush ha-Ramban 'al ha-Torah* 1.9 (ad Gen. 1:1).

the esoteric gnosis (related specifically to the account of creation) by exegetical means from the text of Scripture.[129] Nahmanides' insistence that Scripture cannot yield secrets except to one who has received the tradition is equivalent to his claim that reason is of no avail on these matters. In truth, Nahmanides utilized both reason and exegetical principles to elicit the mysteries encoded in Scripture. My interpretation is confirmed by Nahmanides' celebrated remark concerning the prohibition of illicit sexual relations: "We do not possess in our hands any tradition *(davar mequbbal)* about this, but according to supposition *(sevara')* there is in this matter a secret of the secrets of creation *(sodot ha-yesirah)*, which is conjoined to the soul, and it is in the category of the secret of impregnation *(sod ha-'ibbur)* to which we have already alluded."[130] Nahmanides acknowledges that he is not the recipient of an authoritative tradition to explain these biblical verses, but he surmises on the basis of reason that the matter is related to the secrets of creation. The hint that he does offer indicates that he knew perfectly well the secret of illicit sexual relations and precisely for that reason concealed more than he revealed.

Conclusion

When we get beyond the spoken word implanted in our ears by the kabbalists' own language, we realize that oral tradition and written transmission were two stages in a dialectical and hermeneutical process rather than conflicting moments in the evolution of Jewish mysticism. The education and formation of the medieval kabbalists was such that esoteric traditions, transmitted either orally or in written documents, were conservatively received and innovatively expanded. In the final analysis the kabbalist of this period was first and foremost a biblical exegete. When we bear this simple fact in mind, it becomes clear that the Catalonian and Castilian mystical fraternities in the most exact sense were textual communities.

---

129. See Idel, "R. Moshe ben Nahman," pp. 550-51.
130. *Perush ha-Ramban 'al ha-Torah* 2.101 (ad Lev. 18:6).

The Thirteenth-Century English Parish

Joseph Goering

Religious life in the Middle Ages evokes images of grand Gothic cathedrals. These magnificent monuments to art, culture, and devotion dominate our mental notions of the medieval church and of the religious life of its people. We imagine these churches as towering over the landscape and dwarfing the inhabitants of the town and of the surrounding countryside, and we may conclude that medieval people were similarly dominated by a rich and powerful church that overwhelmed their ordinary and everyday lives. In truth, the cathedral church played a very small part in the lives of most medieval people. They would visit it on special occasions, and it attracted pilgrims and other visitors from distant places, but the cathedral was not the parish or proper church of more than a handful of people. Medieval people received most of their education and formation in faith in their local communities and parish churches, and so it is to the parish that we now turn.

The medieval parish church, unlike the bishop's cathedral, was divided conceptually, and often financially, into two portions: one, including the sanctuary and high altar, was the preserve and responsibility of the parish priest, and the other, including the nave and church porch, was primarily in the care of the parishioners. This distinction between priest and people is an important one in the medieval community; it was jealously guarded by both parties and extended into many areas of the religious life of local communities. In particular, it helped shape two different sets of expectations and two different regimes of education and formation, one for priests and another for parishioners. The creative tension between the two is one of the hallmarks of the medieval period.

Priests in the Parish

The modern idea of the parish priest as someone who should be a skilled preacher, teacher, counselor, and pastor of souls was created during the twelfth and thirteenth centuries; hitherto those tasks had been expected only of the bishop or of learned members of monastic communities. The notion that the local priest should be the bishop's true and full vicar as preacher, teacher, and judge in the parish marks the beginnings of the modern pastorate, and the new expectations of the parish priest brought new demands upon the clerics carrying out these tasks. Thus the education of the parish priest underwent a radical transformation in the thirteenth century.

At the beginning of the thirteenth century the parish priest was primarily a member of the local community. His strongest loyalties were to the local landlord who had appointed him, and his duties were shaped by the traditional expectations of the local community. He was the guardian of the local cultus, charged with making God present in the community at the Mass and in the sacraments and sacramentals, such as the blessings of homes, families, crops, and livestock. He might be married or keep a concubine (or "hearthmate"); he might have paid for his office or inherited it from his father; and he almost certainly would have had little formal education beyond learning song and chant, and perhaps the rudiments of Latin letters, at a local school.

By the end of the century a new understanding of the parish priest and his role was taking root. His behavior was henceforth to be judged less by the standards and customs of the local community than by universal standards set forth in the church's canon law. His education, too, was expected to reflect the latest teachings of the schools and universities springing up in towns and cities throughout Europe. Like the ideal parson in Chaucer's *Canterbury Tales,* he was expected to be a student as well as a priest, able to read the liturgical books in the parish, but also to own and read some of the treatises, reference books, and pastoral summae produced in ever increasing numbers during the thirteenth and subsequent centuries. In addition to his traditional activities in the parish, he was expected to exercise new forms of pastoral care: to teach his flock, by word and by example, the doctrines of the schools and the disciplinary decrees of the councils; to preach to them regularly; and to transmit to them, especially through the sacrament of penance, the intricate details of the law and moral theology as understood in the schools. Even if such an ideal was not always (perhaps not often) attained in the parishes, it reflects the new standards according to which parish priests would henceforth be formed and educated.

If this picture of the parish priest seems to us familiar, it is because of the eventual success of this thirteenth-century project. Our modern views of what priests and ministers should be and how they should act have been shaped by these early developments. But there is a gap between theory and practice in every society, and often an even larger gap between the historical realities of a past culture and our modern and anachronistic expectations of it. With this in mind, let us describe as carefully as possible the education and forming of a typical village priest in England in the middle of the thirteenth century.

The medieval parish priest began his life as a simple parishioner in a local community. He shared the same experiences as the other laypeople we describe below. At an early age he might have attended the song or grammar school in his parish, where he would have learned to recite the basic prayers, to chant and sing the liturgy, and to read Latin letters with proper accentuation and pronunciation (although perhaps without much comprehension). To judge from entries in the bishops' registers of this period, many clerics had not availed themselves even of these limited educational opportunities before ordination, and bishops frequently required ordinands to make good their educational deficiencies by attending a local song or grammar school before being permitted to exercise the care of souls.

Boys destined to become priests in a parish would receive the clerical tonsure, or haircut, that set them apart from others in the community, and they would begin a period of apprenticeship where they learned the skills necessary for fulfilling the pastoral office. They might continue to live at home, or be taken into the household *(familia)* of the local priest. During this apprenticeship they became familiar with the multifarious details of the Christian liturgy. They would serve the priest at Mass, singing the responses and some of the readings, and accompany him in reciting the canonical hours, insofar as these were kept in the parish churches. They would assist the priest in performing the rites and rituals that constitute the church's sacraments, learning firsthand, for example, the prayers and gestures of the baptismal ceremony, accompanying the priest to the graveyard for burials and to the church porch for marriages.

By the age of twenty they could be ordained to the first of the three major orders (subdeacon, deacon, and priest). This step, which involved the forsaking of marriage and the commitment to a life in the church, would usually be taken only when an appointment to an ecclesiastical benefice, which would provide a living, had been secured. Once installed in a parish but before being ordained to the priesthood, a few clerics went off to the schools and universities, using the fruits of their benefice to support higher studies, and appointing a vicar to fulfill most of the pastoral duties in their stead. But of those who took advantage of the opportunity for higher education, few returned to serve as simple parish priests; most would find employment in the higher reaches of the ecclesiastical hierarchy. Nor was there much incentive for the local clergy to spend time in the schools before returning to their parochial duties. Most remained in the parish, serving as full-time assistant clergy until, at the age of thirty, they were qualified for ordination as priest in a parish.

By this time the priest was considered fully formed and capable of directing the liturgical and sacramental life of the local church. In particular, he should know his way around the standard booklets that were to be kept in all parishes: a *computus* or calendar, necessary for determining the feast and fast days throughout the year; a sacramentary, containing the liturgies of baptism, the eucharistic consecration, marriage, and extreme unction; liturgical books such as a lectionary, an antiphonary, and a missal; a homiliary, with readings from the Fathers for each of the feast days; a penitential, giving direction about what kinds of penances to assign to various sins; and a ritual, giving the various forms of the blessings, for holy water and salt, for swords and plowshares, for eggs and candles, as well as instructions for celebrating the church's sacramentals, from the purification of new mothers to the last rites and burial ceremonies.

The cleric's practical education continued after his installation as parish priest, as he encountered all the pastoral, administrative, and political problems associated with his profession. But so did his formal education, and it is in this that his experience differed significantly from that of local priests in previous centuries. He was expected to attend regularly a gathering of the clergy in his vicinity, convoked each month by one of the senior priests. During the thirteenth century these meetings of the rural (or "arch-") deanery were often used for the dissemination and study of disciplinary decrees and pastoral handbooks published by the bishop of the diocese. For example, in the diocese of Worcester during the 1240s, every priest was expected to obtain a copy of the diocesan statutes and of a little summa explaining the Ten Commandments, the seven deadly sins, the latest teachings on penance, and the articles of faith. He was to bring these copies with him to the monthly meeting, and there to practice reading them out and explaining them. A substantial fine was levied on priests who failed to obtain, and to understand, the texts.[1]

Such provisions marked the first concerted attempt to make written materials readily available to the parish priest for education through reading, and to ensure that priests would actually read and understand them. When Bishop Robert Grosseteste preached to the parochial clergy of his diocese of Lincoln in the 1240s, he encouraged them to spend the time between the early morning mass and their midday meal in reading, and he probably had in mind the study

---

1. See J. Goering and D. S. Taylor, "The *Summulae* of Bishops Walter de Cantilupe (1240) and Peter Quinel (1287)," *Speculum* 67 (1992): 575-93.

of one of these small pamphlets or handbooks. If none were available, they were to read their liturgical books and especially to study the Gospel readings for the following Sunday, so they could explain them, in simple words, to the parishioners at Mass. Ever a realist, Grosseteste goes on to say that this is how priests who can read Latin with understanding should spend their mornings; if they are unable to read the texts for meaning, they should seek out a neighboring priest, who would kindly explain the Gospel reading to them.[2]

By the end of the thirteenth century it could be taken for granted that every parish priest should understand the essential elements of the Christian faith in such a manner that he would be able to teach and preach them publicly to his parishioners. Lists of essential matters had been tacitly agreed upon during the course of the century, and set out in a manner that could be easily learned and taught; these would become the basic elements of Christian "catechesis" from that time on. The syllabus circulated in 1281 by John Pecham, the archbishop of Canterbury, is a representative example.[3] It includes: (1) fourteen articles of faith, derived from the Apostles' Creed, seven pertaining to the Trinity and to each of the divine persons, and seven concerning the humanity of Christ; (2) the Ten Commandments, understood as three obligations toward God and seven governing relations with neighbors; (3) the two Gospel precepts added to the commandments: "Thou shalt love the Lord thy God . . . and thy neighbor as thyself"; (4) seven works of mercy, as described in Matthew 25: feed the hungry, give drink to the thirsty, clothe the naked, harbor the stranger, care for the sick, visit those in prison, bury the dead; (5) seven deadly sins (and their offspring): pride, envy, wrath (or hatred), sloth, avarice, gluttony, and lust; (6) seven principal virtues: the four "cardinal" or "political" virtues (prudence, justice, temperance, and fortitude) and the other three, called "theological" (faith, hope, and charity); (7) the seven sacraments of grace: baptism, confirmation, penance, eucharist, extreme unction, holy orders, and matrimony. These elements of Christian teaching were preached from pulpits, woven into stories and stage plays, painted on walls, and generally spread about in every possible medium. Even the simplest priests in the most isolated communities could scarcely have remained entirely ignorant of them. Indeed, the priest was expected to be able to explain the meaning of each of these to his people at appropriate times.

2. From Grosseteste's sermon beginning "Scriptum est de Levitis"; the text is printed in J. Goering and F. A. C. Mantello, "The *Meditaciones* of Robert Grosseteste," *Journal of Theological Studies*, n.s., 36 (1985): 122 n. 16.

3. *Councils and Synods, with Other Documents Relating to the English Church, II,* A.D. 1205-1313, ed. F. M. Powicke and C. R. Cheney (Oxford, 1964), 2.900-905. For the development of such lists in the twelfth and thirteenth centuries, see J. Goering, *William de Montibus (c. 1140-1213): The Schools and the Literature of Pastoral Care* (Toronto, 1992), pp. 75-99.

Increasingly during the thirteenth century the behavior and belief of the parish priest was shaped not just by his own fallible understanding of the difficult texts of the ancient Scriptures, or by personal and local standards of acceptable conduct, but by the living law of the church, which sought to give tangible form, in its norms and institutions, to the precepts of law and gospel. His inclusion within the effective scope of the international, juridical culture of "Christendom" had far-reaching consequences. The canon law was less a set of rules and regulations than a sophisticated means of shaping behavior and deciding difficult questions concerning faith and morals. Its "rules" were distilled from the Holy Scriptures, from the authoritative judgments of popes and church councils, and from the interpretations of these texts by ancient and holy writers. It was a living law because application of these "rules" to particular cases and circumstances was continually being discussed and debated by scholars, both ecclesiastical and lay, and adjudicated by experienced members of the church's hierarchy.

For instance, the Scriptures make abundantly clear the importance of repentance for sins. King David's penances (recalled regularly in the reciting of the "penitential Psalms") were renowned, and both John the Baptist and Jesus began their public ministries, as recorded in the Gospels, with a call to repentance (Matt. 3:2 and 4:17). This penitential precept was given liturgical and pastoral form in various ways throughout the Middle Ages, most notably by the Fourth Lateran Council of 1215, which required that every Christian confess his or her sins personally to the parish priest at least once a year. In providing thus, the council made it incumbent on every parish priest to make arrangements for every man and woman in his parish to come to confession, and to learn how to hear their confessions and assign proper penances for the sins confessed. It also required all bishops to arrange for hearing the confessions of all priests and clerics in their dioceses, and to confess their own sins regularly to qualified confessors. What had been a widespread custom now became a juridical requirement whose proper fulfillment could be insisted upon, whether by parishioner, priest, or prelate. This uniform minimum requirement quickly became the focal point of much jurisprudence. Could a parishioner confess to a neighboring priest rather than to his or her own? What should one do if one's proper priest was incompetent or indiscreet? What should a priest do about parishioners who refuse to come to confession? These and many other questions were answered not according to the whims of individual priests and parishioners, but according to the best theological and juridical minds of the era, and the answers were continually being refined in scholastic discussions and judicial appeals. Simple parish priests quickly became accomplished jurists (relatively speaking) and more or less sophisticated confessors, who saw themselves as accountable to, and supported by, a larger body of learning and expertise than any one of them could be expected to master through his own efforts.

This juridical culture not only touched questions of penance and confession but extended to nearly every aspect of moral behavior and religious practice. Parish priests became the local authorities for advice on all sorts of knotty questions, from the validity of vows and oaths to questions of criminal responsibility and ethical malfeasance. So, too, could priests be held accountable for their own behavior, in the church and outside of it, by parishioners who had learned or surmised the disciplinary norms of the church and could turn to neighboring priests, rural deans, archdeacons, or the bishop and his representatives for support and redress. The surviving records of the thirteenth-century parish often reflect a litigious and seemingly acrimonious side of life in local communities, but the other side of the story is the importance of law, and the ecclesiastical institutions that embodied it, in forming and educating a people of faith.

The expectation that the local priest should be the church's primary provider of pastoral care and formal Christian education, especially through preaching and teaching, gradually gained acceptance during the thirteenth century. This view emerged from the top, especially from the teachings and reforms of school-trained clergymen. But the eventual success of this project was not inevitable, nor would it be an unmixed blessing. Resistance to this new ideal of the parish priest as scholar and preacher was encountered at many levels, and for a variety of reasons. Few parish priests had the interest or the wherewithal to master the book learning necessary for keeping up with the teachings of the schools, and few parishioners thought their parish priest would be better if only he had spent some time in the schools. It would be a mistake to assume that the new ideal was embraced wholeheartedly by very many.

Medieval parishioners rarely considered these new experiments in educating the parish priest of crucial interest or importance. The parish priest was, in the Middle Ages, as in most other periods, a person set apart. As someone who handled the sacred mysteries, he was seen as different. If not necessarily holy, he was at least accountable to God and to the community in a different way than were others. By virtue of his office he received certain kinds of wealth, authority, and prestige that marked him as a "noble" or notable person. In England he came to be addressed as "Dominus" (Lord) rather than "Father," and to exercise some of the same judicial, political, and ceremonial prerogatives as others of the petty nobility. The social distance thus created was important for the functioning of the medieval parish. Laypeople by and large had little desire to be like their parish priest, or to do the kinds of things he did. Their religion was "vicarious" in the sense that the priest was their vicar, or representative, in dealing with the formal mysteries of the faith. He was the one who needed to understand the mysteries, to perform the rites and rituals correctly and in a timely fashion. He was expected to live in a way that was worthy, before God and the community, of such a ministry. Those among the laity who did wish to emulate the priest would normally pursue a clerical vocation themselves, or associate themselves with one of the many forms of religious communities, for men and women, that were flourishing in thirteenth-century England. But such people were never a large proportion of the population.

Among those things they expected of, or desired from, their parish priest, the laity seems rarely to have included the duty of teaching and informing them concerning the faith. Rather, they expected their priest to provide the services for which they accorded him his wealth, authority, and prestige. First and foremost, these were the services of the cult. He was expected to make God present in the local community every day in the sacrifice of the Mass; to bring God's blessings to their children, houses, fields, and flocks in the form of the Latin blessings provided in the authoritative books; to intercede for them and for their dead in the prayers of the liturgical hours; and to be prompt in visiting the sick and dying. He was looked to not for friendship and personal support, but for the professional services of ritual intercession and reconciliation. As president of the official cult, the priest also played an indispensable but limited role in the community, especially as the keeper of the calendar and as the guardian of the sacred vessels and objects — the consecrated host, the holy oils, and the statues, images, and crosses around which many popular devotions and religious activities were organized.

The parish priest's opportunities for exercising such formal educational activities as teaching, preaching, and hearing confessions, although real and important, were strictly circumscribed in the practice and traditions of the thirteenth-century parish. The priest could teach a few young boys (and sometimes girls) in his song or grammar school, but no one seemed to think such an education might be desirable for all laypeople. He was also expected to preach regularly, teaching parishioners about virtues and vices, the Ten Commandments, the sacraments, and so forth. Such sermons were to be preached "at least four times a year,"[4] but we have no evidence that even this minimum requirement was strictly observed. In many cases both priest and parishioners seem to have preferred that such teaching be done by visiting preachers, often Dominican or Franciscan friars, who were skilled at attracting a willing audience and

---

4. *Councils and Synods* 2.900-901; cf. Siegfried Wenzel, "Vices, Virtues, and Popular Preaching," *Medieval and Renaissance Studies* 6 (1976): 28-54.

preaching compelling sermons. Likewise, although every parishioner was required to confess his or her sins to the parish priest at least once a year, we have every reason to believe that these annual confessions were often more in the nature of ritual gestures (and important as such) than a detailed baring of soul and conscience. Those parishioners who wished to make a detailed examination of conscience and a searching confession would have been more likely to seek as special confessor, or "soul friend," one of the Dominican or Franciscan friars specially trained in the hearing of confessions, or even a neighboring priest, who would be suitably distanced from the entanglements and allegiances of local politics and society.

These limitations on the educational activities of the parish priest were not meant to belittle his importance in the medieval community, but rather to suggest that his value lay elsewhere, at least in the minds of the parishioners. For them the priest's primary responsibility remained the administration of the parish and the maintenance of its cult. He was the community's vicar before God, and the guardian of the sacred mysteries. His clerical dignity and his distance from the day-to-day life of the parish were more highly valued by them than was his possible contribution to their community through teaching and personal counseling. Moreover, by circumscribing the important areas in which the priest's knowledge and expertise could be exercised, parishioners maintained their own vital role in shaping the Christian life of their communities.

"Popular Religion"

Most thirteenth-century parishioners saw formation in faith not as a clerical monopoly, or even much of a clerical responsibility, but rather as a family and community activity. Nor was it narrowly centered on the parish church, at least not on the sanctuary and around the altar, which was the priest's domain, but on the nave, the church porch, the churchyard, and the streets and houses of the town or village. For lack of a better term, we can refer to this complex of customs and traditions as "popular religion," to distinguish it from the official cult, centered on the person of the priest and the formal Latin liturgy. Popular religious practices, some originating in pre-Christian observances, developed and flourished in constant dialogue (and occasional tension) with the normative practices of the ordained clergy. Many of these practices formed a kind of para-liturgy, reproducing an aspect of the official cult in a form that fostered lay initiative and a degree of lay control. One example is the multiplication of small chapels, associated with the parish church but staffed by a priest who was hired by a group of laypeople to say "private" masses for their own intentions. Another is the growth of popular prayers, such as the rosary, which allowed laypeople to imitate with their own prayers, and at their own times and places, the more sophisticated prayers said in church and cloister by priests and religious. Countless other examples of popular practices based on the liturgy and images of the official cult could be mentioned, from the adoration of the cross on Good Friday to the eucharistic processions of the feast of Corpus Christi and the prayers for the dead in cemeteries on the feasts of All Souls and All Saints.[5]

Rituals of healing, fortune-telling, weather prognostication, blessing and cursing, and of course fertility have a long history in human society. These continued to flourish throughout the Middle Ages, and have caused some modern authorities to question whether medieval Europe was "Christian" in any meaningful sense of the term. But to label these practices "superstitious" and dismiss them as "magical" is to read backward into the Middle Ages a modern and materialistic religious sensibility, one that is problematic in its own way and unhelpful in understanding the life and thought of medieval (and modern) people. For medieval Christians, from the most learned clerics and sophisticated nobles to the humblest parishioners, religion was not simply an intellectual or even a moral doctrine, but a way of life that brought one into intimate contact with the powers that rule the universe. Religion consisted especially in finding appropriate ways of relating to this divine reality, of receiving God's protection, and of appropriating the benefits accruing to the faithful servants of the true God.

In such a world, opportunities for prayer, worship, and invocation of God and the saints were in no way restricted to the official activities of the cult. Historians, who have tended to approach questions of religious education from an intellectual and clerical point of view, have naturally emphasized the importance (or lack of importance) of the sacraments and preaching. For medieval villagers, however, these were only a small element in the vast array of religious activities that encompassed their lives. Some idea of the scope of these popular rites, rituals, and devotions can be gained by attending first to the ecclesiastical sacraments and the activities that surrounded them, and then working outward, into the community, to describe other sacramental and religious acts.

The first of the church's sacraments is baptism. Medieval baptisms were complex affairs, both ritually and socially. Centered on family groups rather

---

5. For a recent evocation of these popular religious devotions in a slightly later period, see Eamon Duffy, *The Stripping of the Altars: Traditional Religion in England, 1400-1580* (New Haven and London, 1992). See also André Vauchez, *The Laity in the Middle Ages: Religious Beliefs and Devotional Practices,* ed. D. Bornstein, trans. M. J. Schneider (Notre Dame, Ind., 1993).

than the entire community, they marked the point at which an infant was received into the church, and into an extended family. The essential element of the rite was the invocation of the Father, Son, and Holy Spirit, accompanied by a threefold immersion in or infusion of water. The trinitarian formula, "in nomine Patris et Filii et Spiritus sancti" (in the name of the Father and the Son and the Holy Spirit), was known to all, either in Latin or in the vernacular, and provided one of the best, and most effective, introductions to the mysterious Christian doctrine of the Trinity. It also became a popular charm for warding off evil, and for blessing oneself and others. The rite of baptism also included a series of exorcisms (with salt) and anointings (with oil) that brought home the power of the Christian God, as well as the seriousness of the enemy who was overthrown by the sacred actions. Also included was a form of catechesis — a profession of faith, mirroring the articles of the Apostles' Creed, that was made by the parents and sponsors. The presence of sponsors, or godparents, for the child was one of the most important popular elements in the rite; insisted upon by the laity, it offered an opportunity for extending the family beyond its normal bloodlines and created "spiritual" ties that often proved to have political and economic importance as well.[6]

The Eucharist, wherein bread and wine brought to the church's altar were transformed into the body and blood of Christ, was appropriated by the people in a number of ways. Attendance at the Mass, although often encouraged, seems not always to have been of primary importance. It was enough to know that the priest was making God present regularly in the community in this way. Reception of the Eucharist by the laity, although infrequent, was an important event at Easter and on one or two important feasts such as Pentecost or Assumption Sunday. The right to receive Communion at these times was jealously guarded, and the order of precedence for receiving it was one of the ways social status was established and upheld in many communities. Although only the priest would communicate regularly, the body and blood of Christ in the eucharistic elements were the focus of a great deal of popular piety and devotion. People began attending Mass to be present when the priest elevated the bread and the wine and spoke the words of consecration that effected the eucharistic miracle. They were quick to provide expensive candles to burn before the cupboard in which consecrated hosts were reserved, in honor of the sacrificial body thus present in their sanctuary. The feast of Corpus Christi, established in the early thirteenth century at Liège, largely at the insistent behest of some pious women there, was quickly taken up throughout Europe. It was celebrated with popular processions and all manner of civic and social festivi-

6. See J. H. Lynch, *Godparents and Kinship in Early Medieval Europe* (Princeton, 1986).

ties, serving to draw attention to the power of the body of Christ present in the local community in the Eucharist.

The sacrament of penance also provided opportunities for religious participation and formation. After the requirement of the Fourth Lateran Council, the practice of private confession to a priest was confirmed as a common religious responsibility shared by everyone in the community. As such, the language and methods of the confessional provided a common language for talking about the ethical dimensions of everyday life. The materials for confession — the seven deadly sins; the Ten Commandments; sins against God, self, and neighbor; and sins of omission as well as commission — became part of the common language of all European cultures. We do well not to overestimate the power of the confessional itself in reforming and shaping behavior; ethical formation continued to be then, as it is now, something imparted most effectively by the family and close personal acquaintances. But the confessional and penitential culture that developed in medieval Europe, and was shared by people of both sexes and of every class and station in life, certainly helped to establish a set of standards and norms that was common to all, and that could be drawn upon, and appealed to, in all political, social, and personal activities. These examples, drawn from the sacraments of baptism, Eucharist, and penance, illustrate some of the ways major sacraments performed by the priest were adapted and "popularized" by the laity.

This penitential culture also gave birth to new forms of lay spirituality. Penances were performed, increasingly, not just for one's own sins but also for the sins of others. An intricate spiritual economy developed, in which one could draw on the merits of others to help pay one's own spiritual debts, and vice versa, either in this life or in the afterlife of purgatory. In this way care for souls became a popular, and not just a clerical, activity. The extraordinary richness of penitential activities undertaken for the sake of souls, both living and dead, is one of the most striking aspects of later-medieval popular religion.[7]

While church teaching from that time on focused primarily on the major sacraments, church practice valued a wide variety of sacred actions and encouraged (or sometimes only tolerated) a great deal of popular initiative in the use of sacred signs and symbols. The theological distinction between the seven major sacraments and a myriad of minor sacraments, or "sacramentals," was first introduced in the schools during the second half of the twelfth century. The large corpus of "blessings" *(benedictiones)* that survive, in haphazard fashion, in

---

7. See J. Le Goff, *The Birth of Purgatory,* trans. A. Goldhammer (Chicago, 1981); R. M. Haines, "The Indulgence as a Form of Social Insurance," in *Ecclesia Anglicana: Studies in the English Church of the Later Middle Ages* (Toronto, Buffalo, and London, 1989), pp. 184-91.

diocesan liturgical books and in other medieval manuscripts suggests the scope and practical importance of sacramentals in the life of a medieval village community. These blessings were all in Latin and written for use by the priest. Most were carefully composed, some with poetic grandeur. The precise content of the prayers might have been lost on most parishioners (even on many priests), but the picture which emerges from a consideration of the surviving evidence is one of a flourishing culture of sacred actions in which the priest and people interacted to bring blessings upon the daily life of the community and protect it from harm.[8]

The blessings selected for inclusion in medieval liturgical books for use in parishes varied widely from place to place, but as an ensemble they provide a valuable index to the important events in the lives of parishioners. In the Sarum (Salisbury) manual the blessings of salt, water, and bread are followed by songs to be sung on Christmas Eve, by the ritual for blessings on Candlemas (the feast of the purification of the Virgin, February 2), and by the ceremonies associated with the Lenten penitential season and Easter in the parish. Details concerning these celebrations must be sought in other sources, and we have no diaries or descriptions to give us firsthand accounts of the parishioners' or the priests' activities. Occasional notices, however, allow us a glimpse of their special interests and concerns. Thus, for example, when England was under papal interdict for six years, from 1208 to 1214, all the parish churches were locked and all public services were banned. Special permission was sought, and granted by the pope, for setting up the crucifix outside the church on Good Friday so that the parishioners could exercise their customary devotions in that place, albeit without accompanying liturgical ceremony.[9] The Sarum manual continues with the ceremonies surrounding baptism, a ceremony for the churching of women after childbirth, a marriage ceremony, and another service for those setting out on pilgrimage. Each of these liturgical services was provided by the parish priest, but always at the request of the parishioners, who were also involved in organizing the wide range of social affairs that accompanied such important events in people's lives.

Next the manual provides a long series of blessings to be used on a variety of occasions in the parish. The blessing of the sword of a new knight was part of a larger social drama involving the local gentry. The blessings for meat, cheese, butter, eggs, and fancy breads (pastillarum) on Easter Sunday marked the end of the community's Lenten fast. Blessings for new fruits, seed, apples (on the

---

8. The following discussion is based on the *Manuale ad usum . . . Sarisburiensis*.

9. See *Selected Letters of Pope Innocent III concerning England (1198-1216)*, ed. C. R. Cheney and W. H. Semple (London, 1953), pp. 107-9.

feast of Saint James, July 25), and "for what-you-will" *(ad omnia quaecunque volueris)* indicate some of the range of agricultural and economic activities for which the services of a clergyman might be employed. These are followed by a blessing for the shields and clubs used in the judicial duels of English common law, even though the Fourth Lateran Council of 1215 had declared that the ordeal and duel were no part of canonical procedure, and that the clergy ought not be implicated in them,[10] and also blessings for weak eyes (perhaps of special importance for craftspeople who do close work, such as seamstresses, cobblers, and the like) and for ships. The blessings of salt and water, beginning with an exorcism of the salt ("I exorcise you, creature salt . . ."; *Exorciso te creatura salis)* and concluding with a mixing of the salt into the exorcised and blessed water, produced the holy water that was used in countless ways, in the church, and in the homes, shops, and fields of the parishioners. Holy water was also sprinkled over the bread that was blessed at the conclusion of the Sunday mass, and then distributed to the people as they left the church.[11]

Other devotions proliferated, with and without encouragement by the priest and clergy. Statues and images of patron saints were erected in every parish, and these saints were treated as valuable members of the local community. They were honored with flowers, clothing, drapery, and candles, and given a place of honor in community celebrations. These saints, as represented in their images, were the special protectors and intercessors for individuals and for the whole community, and were expected to repay their devotees in this life and the next. The list of these popular practices, the details of which varied from village to village and from county to county, could be extended indefinitely.

Conclusion

In summary, two educational regimes can be identified in the thirteenth-century parishes. One was designed especially for clerics; it emphasized the intellectual and ethical content of the Christian faith and drew its inspiration and direction from the teachings of the schools of law and theology. The other, cultivating close personal and community allegiances to Christ and his saints, was based on traditional religious practices. In the thirteenth century it flowered in countless new devotions, such as the adoration of the Eucharist host, purgatorial piety and prayers for the dead, and impetration of the images of the saints.

10. See *Councils and Synods* 1.49.

11. See E. L. Cutts, *Parish Priests and their People in the Middle Ages and England* (London, 1898), pp. 298-305.

Although these represented two different educational regimes, they did not constitute two solitudes. Scholastic theologians were as devoted to popular pieties as were the laity, and uneducated people were busy incorporating parts of the scholastic teachings into their own thought and behavior. The two regimes were thus held in tension; neither was thought to represent the totality of the Christian faith. The end of the Middle Ages may be marked by the triumph of the learned regime in parts of Europe, where it gradually became the norm for all Christians, and the relegation of popular practices to the realm of magic and superstition. In some places, especially in northern Europe, the transition was well under way by the sixteenth century; in others it is a transformation that is not complete even in the twenty-first.

The Cult of the Virgin Mary and Technologies of Christian Formation in the Later Middle Ages

Anne L. Clark

An anecdote from the early decades of the Dominican Order relates the following incident. An elderly Carthusian monk, extremely devoted to the Virgin Mary, prayed to her that she might teach him how to please her with his service. "What is appropriate for a lover, do for me," he was told by the Virgin, who appeared to him one day as he prayed. But what is that? he questioned. "Love, praise, and honor," the Virgin replied. He fell to the ground, pleading to be taught how to love, praise, and honor her. Her response: "Go to the Dominicans, because they are my brothers, and they will teach you." The Dominicans' personal devotions as well as their sermons, Mary affirmed, exalted her with love, praise, and honor.[1]

---

1. This anecdote is an expanded version of a story in *Vitae Fratrum Ordinis Praedicatorum,* written ca. 1256-59. For the original and expanded versions, see Gerard of Frachet, *Vitae Fratrum Ordinis Praedicatorum,* ed. Benedict Maria Reichert, Monumenta Ordinis Fratrum Praedicatorum Historica 1 (Louvain: Charpentier & J. Schoonjas, 1896), pp. 41-42. Gerard's work includes many assertions of Mary's particular favor for the Dominican Order as well as their particular veneration for her. The Dominicans were not alone in seeing their order as especially dedicated to Mary. For examples of comparable Cistercian claims, see Hélinand of Froidmont's view of the Cistercians as the liege men of the celestial queen (*Patrologia Latina,*

Much of the research for this paper was done while I was on sabbatical in 1994-95. I would like to thank the University of Vermont and the School of Historical Studies of the Institute for Advanced Study and especially Giles Constable for their support of this research. I would also like to thank Robert Somerville and Barbara Newman, who read earlier versions of a related paper that became the basis for this essay; Philip Soergel and Kevin Trainor, who gave me very insightful critiques of this essay; and Laurel Broughton, who has generously shared with me her database of miracles of the Virgin in English manuscripts.

In this story the monastic piety of the Carthusians, the preaching and pastoral care of the Dominicans and the lay piety nourished by the preachers' sermons are all grounded in the veneration of Mary. The public articulation of faith, the personal experience of religious emotion, and membership in a community were created and experienced as devotion to Mary. The purpose of this paper is to explore ways in which images of Mary and practices of devotion to her were integral to the formation of communal and personal Christian identity. I will focus on the twelfth through fourteenth centuries, examining the cult of the Virgin Mary in the technologies of Christian formation. By technologies of formation I refer to the processes by which individuals came to think and act as Christians. These processes train cognition and behavior so that the basic teachings of the Christian religion can be activated and reinforced in the routines of daily life as well as in moments of heightened significance. This is not to suggest that the disciplining of perception and behavior is totally determinative. Rather, particular beliefs and ways of being in the world, taught to be experienced as natural and proper, will always vary in practice in their persuasiveness and the style in which they are appropriated by different people.

At first glance this focus on Marian devotion may seem tangential to appropriating the story and teachings of Jesus, the presumed fundamental aim of Christian formation. This issue — the relationship between devotion to Mary and devotion to God — elicited varied responses from medieval Christians. To some the affective outpouring of devotion to Mary was not understood as detracting from God but was itself praise of God. The Franciscan friar Conrad of Saxony (d. 1279) asserted this view in his commentary on the Ave Maria: "Since, as blessed Jerome says, 'No one doubts that whatever is worthily assigned to his Mother belongs completely to the praise of God,' I have hoped to express the praise and glory of our Lord Jesus Christ by means of the praise and glory of his most glorious mother, and thus have taken as my subject the very sweet salutation to his mother."[2] Conrad's rationale for Marian veneration became well known in the later Middle Ages: there are 247 extant manuscripts of his work with provenances from across western Eu-

---

212, col. 495), or Caesarius of Heisterbach's story about Mary's affirmation of the Cistercians as "the best friends I have in the whole world." See *Dialogus Miraculorum*, ed. Joseph Strange (Cologne: H. Lempertz & Co., 1851), p. 60.

2. Conrad of Saxony, *Speculum seu salutatio beatae Mariae virginis ac sermones mariani*, ed. Pedro de Alcantara Martinez (Rome: Collegium S. Bonaventurae ad Claras Aquas, 1975), p. 141. The view attributed to Jerome was in fact that of Paschasius Radbertus (died ca. 860). For Paschasius, see *De assumptione sanctae Mariae virginis*, ed. Albert Ripberger, Corpus Christianorum, Continuatio Mediaevalis 61C (Turnhout: Brepols, 1985), p. 119.

rope.[3] Did the same sentiment underlie a rewriting of the Te Deum, the ancient hymn of praise to God, into "Te Matrem laudamus, Te Virginem confitemur . . ." [We praise you, Mother, we confess you, Virgin]? The author of this text, which is found in a twelfth-century prayer book from the Benedictine nuns' monastery at Saint Emmeram, praised Mary in these glorious creedal cadences without bothering to justify the relationship between praise of God and praise of Mary.[4] If we hold in tension the explicit theologizing of Conrad and the unstated motives behind the "Te Matrem laudamus," we may refrain from squeezing Marian devotion into a tidy theological picture that relates all elements to each other. The description of Dominican preaching as focused on teaching how Mary "is to be loved, praised, and honored" indicates the subject of this study: the cultivating of relationships with Mary and the contours of those relationships.

The anecdote about Dominican devotion and preaching suggests the diffusion of monastic and mendicant spirituality into the lives of ordinary parish Christians. Marian devotion during the later Middle Ages is often traced back to new expressions of intimate prayer and meditation that developed in Benedictine and then Cistercian monasteries, and were taken up with great fervor by Franciscan and Dominican preachers who introduced this piety into lay practice.[5] The nature of surviving materials — texts composed within learned milieux — makes a picture of diffusion from monastic/mendicant circles into popular consumption readily understandable. And yet the diffusion model can easily be oversimplified if made to imply a dichotomy of power and passivity,

3. For the manuscript transmission of this text, see *Speculum seu salutatio*, pp. 113-32. The equivalence between praising Christ and Mary is also asserted in Bernard of Clairvaux, *De laudibus virginis matris*, Homily 4, chap. 1, in *Sancti Bernardi Opera*, ed. J. Leclercq and H. Rochais (Rome: Editiones Cistercienses, 1966), 4.46. Not everyone accepted this equivalence; see Anne L. Clark, "An Ambiguous Triangle: Jesus, Mary, and Gertrude of Helfta," *Maria: A Journal of Marian Studies* 1 (2000): 37-56.

4. The Saint Emmeram prayer book (Munich, Bayerische Staatsbibliothek MS Clm 14848) is discussed in Franz Xaver Haimerl, *Mittelalterliche Frömmigkeit im Spiegel der Gebetbuchliteratur Süddeutschlands*, Münchener Theologische Studien 4 (Munich: Karl Zink Verlag, 1952), pp. 21-22, and a brief excerpt of the hymn is given in Stephen Beissel, *Geschichte der Verehrung Marias in Deutschland während des Mittelalters* (Freiburg: Herderliche, 1909), p. 314. An English translation of this hymn can be found in [Pseudo] Bonaventure, *The Mirror of the Blessed Virgin Mary (Speculum Beatae Mariae Virginis) and the Psalter of Our Lady (Psalterium Beatae Mariae Virginis)*, trans. Mary Emmanuel (St. Louis: Herder, 1932), pp. 294-97.

5. See, e.g., the following two very useful essays, which are excellent introductions to medieval Marian piety: Elisabeth A. Johnson, "Marian Devotion in the Western Church," in *Christian Spirituality: High Middle Ages and Reformation*, ed. Jill Raitt, World Spirituality 17 (New York: Crossroad, 1989), pp. 392-414, esp. 392-93; Carol M. Schuler, "The Seven Sorrows of the Virgin: Popular Culture and Cultic Imagery in Pre-Reformation Europe," *Simiolus* 21 (1992): 5-28, esp. 7-11.

with preachers as the active agents and lay folk as the passive recipients of their teaching.[6] Even professional preachers recognized that teaching the faith was a complex process with many agents. Rare testimonies catch some of the complex ways in which "nonprofessionals" actively engaged in shaping religious behavior: stories about a Beguine who came to Paris to buy the *Summa of Vices and Virtues*, which she then lent in quires to various priests to aid them in their preaching;[7] holy women living in the world such as Umiliana dei Cherchi and Margaret of Cortona, who were described as living sermons;[8] or a woman in the diocese of Lincoln who warned her two adulterous neighbors to desist from their illicit activity on the feast of All Saints and to turn instead to their faith.[9] We may not often be able to hear the voices and see the gestures of laypeople as they engaged in active processes of shaping each other and even, occasionally, influencing their teachers. But I will try to highlight the evidence that suggests where these voices and gestures were most likely found.

Only a small fraction of these processes can be examined here, and I have chosen to present materials that best illuminate the various mechanisms by which Christian values were disseminated and appropriated. The following composite picture is not meant to serve as an ideal or universal type, but rather is intended to suggest the proliferation of various, sometimes divergent, activities in which a person's or community's relationship to the Virgin Mary was cultivated.[10] To this end I will focus on four related subjects: prayer, preaching

6. The relationships of spiritual guidance between male clerics and female visionaries or holy women, which might also suggest a diffusion of piety from learned male authority to subordinate female audience, in fact challenges the diffusion model. Often the male clerics functioned as much as students or protégés of the women rather than their teachers. See, e.g., John Coakley, "Friars as Confidants of Holy Women in Medieval Dominican Hagiography," in *Images of Sainthood in Medieval Europe*, ed. Renate Blumenfeld Kosinski and Timea Szell (Ithaca, N.Y.: Cornell University Press, 1991), pp. 222-46; Anne L. Clark, "Repression or Collaboration: The Case of Elisabeth and Ekbert of Schönau," in *Christendom and Its Discontents: Exclusion, Persecution, and Rebellion, 1000-1500*, ed. Scott L. Waugh and Peter Diehl (Cambridge: Cambridge University Press, 1996), pp. 151-67.

7. Cited in D. L. d'Avray, *The Preaching of the Friars: Sermons Diffused from Paris before 1300* (Oxford: Clarendon, 1985), p. 2.

8. See John Coakley, "Friars, Sanctity, and Gender: Mendicant Encounters with Saints, 1250-1325," in *Medieval Masculinities: Regarding Men in the Middle Ages*, ed. Clare A. Lees, Medieval Cultures 7 (Minneapolis: University of Minnesota Press, 1994), pp. 91-110.

9. Text edited in Stephen L. Forte, "A Cambridge Dominican Collector of Exempla in the Thirteenth Century," *Archivum Fratrum Praedicatorum* 28 (1958): 127.

10. For example, although most of the evidence I examine below is from the twelfth to fourteenth centuries, in Bavaria it is only in the late fifteenth century that there is evidence for widespread Marian devotion. See Philip M. Soergel, *Wondrous in His Saints: Counter-Reformation Propaganda in Bavaria* (Berkeley: University of California Press, 1993), pp. 25-26.

and teaching, the localization of Mary's presence in painting and sculpture, and the ways in which images of Mary articulated the boundaries of the Christian community.

"Blessed Is the Fruit of Your Womb"

Crucial to Christian formation is prayer, and prayer to Mary, whether in public liturgy or private meditation, shows how Christians learned about their faith and became Christian through acts of petition and praise. By the later Middle Ages four major feasts commemorated events in Mary's life: her nativity, the annunciation, the purification, and the assumption. This liturgical schedule, at its most basic, represented a cycle of obligatory observances that drew people to church to celebrate past events. But these feasts sometimes became intimately tied as well to the present welfare of local communities. In parts of Germany the feast of the assumption (August 15) was celebrated with a ritual for blessing herbs. The plants, loose or in bundles, were carried by the people into the church and placed on the altar. There they were blessed, with specific reference made in the blessing either to the celebration of Mary's assumption or to Mary's intercession in the blessing. Then blessed herbs were taken home as protection against all manner of harm.[11] As one prayer from a fourteenth-century manuscript beseeches the Lord:

> Through the assumption of the most holy virgin Mary, pour out the blessing of your strength upon these herbs, so that all who carry these herbs with them may not be condemned by judgment or fire or water, nor feel the wound of iron, nor ever suffer infamy, envy, mockery, opprobrium, magic, accusations, wrath, subjugation, the diverse machinations of anyone, jealousies, illusions, trickeries, or sadness. And if a pregnant woman has the herbs with her at the time of birth, may she be freed and not die, and in whatever home they are found, may it endure neither scandal nor danger.[12]

In this prayer the annual commemoration of Mary's triumph over death and bodily corruption became the setting in which products of the earth and human labor, blessed in Mary's name and worn on the bodies of the devout, served as a reminder and source of God's protection.

Beyond the major liturgical feasts, the Virgin was praised and petitioned in

---

11. See Adolph Franz, *Die Kirchlichen Benediktionen im Mittelalter*, 2 vols. (Freiburg: Herdersche Verlagshandlung, 1909), 1:398-413.

12. Franz, 1:409-10.

a wide range of prayers and hymns. Outstanding among them is the Ave, a combination of the salutations of Gabriel and Elizabeth from the Gospel of Luke (1:28, 42).[13] This popular prayer, highlighting Mary as a pregnant woman, underlies Mary's continued association with fertility, pregnancy, and childbirth. The power associated with Mary's birthing process was believed to be physically present in one of the most important relics of Mary, the tunic at the cathedral of Chartres said to be the chemise she wore when she gave birth to Jesus.[14] The mysteries attributed to this birth process inspired many devotional reflections. In a psalter of the Virgin composed in a French Cistercian abbey and popular especially among the Beguines of Liège in the thirteenth century, the absence of male seed in Mary's conception of Jesus is compared to the seemingly spontaneous generation of worms in rotting flesh.[15] Thus French Cistercian monks and Flemish Beguines — both somewhat learned communities dedicated to lives of virginity — sang Mary's praises with repeated Aves and this hymn rejoicing in Mary's mysterious fertility.

Outside the communities of chaste men and women, Mary became a patron of the reproductive processes of women. The association between Mary and reproductive aims dated back at least to the early Middle Ages. The Virgin was sometimes invoked in prayers for infertile women, as can be seen in a tradition preserved in the Gelasian Sacramentary: "Omnipotent and everlasting God, who did not deny maternal affection to that sacred ever virgin Mary, who gave birth to our Redeemer, graciously concede that through the prayers of that same Mother of God your servant may be worthy to be a mother."[16] Here Mary

13. For a history of the development of this prayer, see H. Leclercq, "Marie (Je vous salue)," in *Dictionnaire d'archéologie chrétienne et de liturgie,* ed. Fernand Cabrol and Henri Leclercq (Paris: Librarie Letouzey et Ané, 1907-53), 10:2043-62.

14. According to the thirteenth-century collection of miracles associated with the cathedral, the chemise was given to the cathedral in the ninth century by Charles the Bald. In the fourteenth century copies of the chemise were given to men to wear in battle. See Laura Spitzer, "The Cult of the Virgin and Gothic Sculpture: Evaluating Opposition in the Chartres West Facade Capital Frieze," *Gesta* 33 (1994): 143.

15. The psalter "Ave porta paradys" is found in Giles G. Meersseman, *Der Hymnos Akathistos im Abendland,* vol. 2, *Gruß-psalter, Gruß-orationen, Gaude-andachten und Litaneien,* 2 vols. (Freiburg: Universitätsverlag, 1960), pp. 79-96. For the popularity of this text, see Judith H. Oliver, *Gothic Manuscript Illumination in the Diocese of Liège (c. 1250–c. 1330),* Corpus of Illuminated Manuscripts from the Low Countries 2 (Leuven: Uitgeverij Peeters, 1988), pp. 38-40. The use of this image, while perhaps not decorous, suggests a thoughtful theological perspective: the worm that is conceived without male seed (i.e., Jesus) is the worm by which the serpent is destroyed. And a picture of decay (consumption by worms) is reshaped into a picture of life.

16. *The Gelasian Sacramentary: Liber Sacramentorum Romanae Ecclesiae,* ed. H. A. Wilson (Oxford: Clarendon, 1894), p. 270.

is cast as both a woman blessed with fertility (albeit virginal fertility) and as the intercessor for the sterile woman.

Other rituals less public than Mass prayers also linked Mary with reproduction. The blessing performed at the bed of a woman endangered in childbirth, found in a twelfth-century German ritual, instructs the officiant, presumably a cleric,[17] to thrice touch the woman's belly at her navel, then her right side, then her left side, reciting a prayer in which Mary's birth of Jesus was invoked to beseech the infant to be born.[18] Another twelfth-century manuscript includes a similar prayer: "Anne brought forth blessed Mary; Mary brought forth Christ without any pain or tribulation; Elizabeth brought forth John and did not grieve. Christ called to Lazarus who was dead for four days and said, 'Lazarus, come forth.' And I adjure you, infant, by the Father, Son, and Holy Spirit, to come forth and withdraw from this woman, whether you be living or dead."[19] Mary is here placed among a company of childbearing women and, as in several other such blessings,[20] is recognized for a peculiarly successful birth, that is, one without pain.

Even as other saints became associated with safe childbirth,[21] the connection between Mary and giving birth remained. Frequent miracle stories tell of Mary's benevolent intercession in childbearing, even in "unexpected" cases, like the Jewish woman who successfully petitioned Mary's help in giving birth[22] and the pregnant abbess who was discreetly delivered of her child by the intervention of Mary.[23] A series of three songs on the life of Mary, written in Middle High German by a priest named Wernher (ca. 1172), was envisioned, at least by

17. According to the editor of this text, the Latin formula with its biblical references, transmitted in a liturgical manuscript, is strong evidence that the blessing was composed and used by clerics. Often such formulae are found in books which make no distinction betwen these bedside rites and ecclesiastical services. This practice of bedside ritual, at least as it was officiated by the clergy, became less common after the thirteenth century. See Franz, 2:197-98.

18. From Munich, Bayerische Staatsbibliothek MS CLM 100. Found in Franz, 2:198.

19. From Munich, Bayerische Staatsbibliothek MS CLM 19411. Found in Franz, 2:199-200. Franz notes that the phrase "come forth and withdraw" is from an exorcism formula.

20. Franz, 2:200 n. 6; p. 201 n. 8; p. 202 n. 2.

21. For example, Saint Margaret. See Franz, 2:199.

22. This story was included in the collections of Vincent of Beauvais (*Speculum historiale,* bk. 7, chap. 99) and of Johannes Herolt.

23. Vincent of Beauvais, *Speculum historiale,* bk. 7, chap. 86. H. L. D. Ward, *Catalogue of Romances in the Department of MSS in the British Museum* (London, 1893), vol. 2, cites seventeen manuscripts in which it circulated. Other manuscripts are listed in Beverly Boyd, *The Middle English Miracles of the Virgin* (San Marino, Calif.: Huntington Library, 1964). For other vernacular transmissions, see Paule V. Bétérous, *Les Collections de miracles de la vierge en gallo et ibéro-roman au XIIIe siècle,* Marian Library Studies 15-16 (Dayton: University of Dayton, 1983-84), p. 685.

its author, as a talisman for safe childbirth. He declared that in all houses where this poem is found, no woman in childbirth should fear death and all children will come into the world in good health.[24] In the vita of Margaret of Ypres, written in 1240, the Virgin Mary appears to the holy woman prostrate in prayer for her sister who was dying in childbirth. Mary assures the health of both the dying sister and the infant, and the story concludes with this miracle of successful birth.[25]

Yet this patron of safe childbirth was usually portrayed as giving birth in an entirely unnatural way. This unnaturalness was strikingly expressed in the work of a fourteenth-century woman who herself had experienced the pains of childbirth, Birgitta of Sweden. Her famous visions of witnessing Mary's childbearing fuse concern for realistic detail (e.g., reference to the afterbirth) with an affirmation of the unusualness of this birth (e.g., the afterbirth suddenly appearing neatly wrapped in a clean cloth).[26] The tradition of sanitizing Mary's birth continued in vernacular dramas, such as the fifteenth-century N-Town cycle play in which a smiling Mary proclaims, to the midwives' disbelief, that her birth was painless and clean.[27]

This evidence about devotion to Mary as childbearer and as patron of childbirth raises two important questions. First, how much weight should be attached to prayers to or about Mary, especially those recited in Latin, within the process of religious formation? Hélinand of Froidmont (d. after 1229), in a sermon for the feast of the assumption of Mary, offers a glimpse of how the name of Mary could function in a ritual context. "When the sweetest name of Mary is heard in church," he declared, "immediately the stony hearts of the laity are shaken as if struck by a certain hammer of piety. They lift their hands and eyes to heaven and they beseech help from Mary; and like ships in danger, they frequently look to the star that they know."[28] Hélinand's comment describes a mode of listening and being stimulated to devotion — triggered by the sound

24. Volker Honemann, "Wernher," in *Dictionnaire de spiritualité, ascétique, et mystique, doctrine et histoire,* ed. M. Viller et al. (Paris: Beauchesne, 1932-), s.v.

25. Thomas of Cantimpré, *Vita Margarete de Ypris,* ed. in G. Meersseman, "Les Fréres Precheurs et le mouvement dévot en Flandre au XIIIe siècle," *Archivum Fratrum Praedicatorum* 18 (1948): 68-130, at 119-20.

26. Birgitta of Sweden, *Revelations,* trans. Albert Ryle Kezel (New York: Paulist, 1990), pp. 202-4. For an examination of Birgitta's visions, see Kari Elisabeth Borreson, "Birgitta's Godlanguage: Exemplary Intention, Inapplicable Content," in *Birgitta: hendes vaerk og hendes klostre i Norden,* ed. Tore Nyberg (Odense, 1991), pp. 21-72.

27. *The N-Town Play,* ed. Stephen Spector, Early English Text Society, SS 11 (Oxford: Oxford University Press, 1991), pp. 158-60.

28. Hélinand of Froidmont, Sermon 21: "In Assumptione B. Mariae, II," in *Patrologia Latina,* 212, col. 649.

of Mary's name rather than all the particular theological details being expressed — that could be the means of participating in a formal liturgy as well as in the more urgent prayers intoned at bedside during childbirth.

Second, how were the theological messages encoded in the images of Mary as patron of childbirth appropriated, particularly by women concerned with fertility and reproduction? Even the popular medium of the vernacular drama participates in the theological activity of asserting Mary's difference from women in this ostensibly most "natural," most "biological" of activities. For women facing their own much messier and more dangerous experiences of birth, did Mary's unnatural birthing render her distant and irrelevant to their own experience? Or did the images of her unnatural birthing, confirming Mary's difference from all other women, render her all the more powerful and thus a more appealing intercessor?[29] Theresa Coletti has argued that in social practice, "medieval people seem not to have been terribly troubled by Mary's impossible difference."[30] Although we cannot know how every woman responded to the complex symbol of Mary, we can see what they were exposed to — vernacular poetry and plays, the blessings and prayers that were said to them and over them. And with these sources we begin to sense what women themselves participated in, how ritual shapes those who enact its forms and speak its words. What we do know for certain is that women in this period participated in a world in which one of the crucial moments of their life offered the potential for a direct and physical relationship to Mary.

The invocation of a pregnant Mary in the Ave was also part of a much wider range of practices than those associated strictly with reproduction. In a new form of monastic devotion in place at least since the mid–eleventh century, the Office of the Blessed Virgin Mary, the prayer was recited at each of the canonical hours.[31] There is also evidence that from the mid–twelfth century the

29. For some reflections on these questions, see Penny Schine Gold, *The Lady and the Virgin: Image, Attitude, and Experience in Twelfth-Century France* (Chicago: University of Chicago Press, 1985), pp. 68-75. Marina Warner, *Alone of All Her Sex: The Myth and the Cult of the Virgin Mary* (New York: Random House, 1976), emphasizes that the distinctiveness of Mary was something that primarily made Mary an alienating symbol for women. Warner's analysis, however, makes little use of what evidence there is for understanding medieval women's relationships with Mary. Her focus is much more on suggesting what the representations of Mary reveal about men's attitudes toward Mary and toward women.

30. Theresa Coletti, "Purity and Danger: The Paradox of Mary's Body and the Engendering of the Infancy Narratives in the English Mystery Cycles," in *Feminist Approaches to the Body in Medieval Literature,* ed. Linda Lomperis and Sarah Stanbury (Philadelphia: University of Pennsylvania Press, 1993), pp. 65-95.

31. The earliest extant manuscripts of these offices, one from a Benedictine monks' community (British Library Cotton MS Tiberius Aiii) and one from a Benedictine nuns' commu-

Ave was part of regular lay devotion. Heriman of Tournai (d. 1147) described the devotional practice of Ada, the wife of Theoderic of Avesnes, who recited the Ave Maria sixty times a day: twenty times lying prostrate, twenty times kneeling, and twenty times standing. Theoderic's nephew Gosceguin is also said to have replicated this practice of the sixty daily Aves, and to have tried to persuade his soldiers to do so as well.[32]

By the late twelfth century regional church synods began to mandate that the Ave be recited as a standard prayer, along with the Pater Noster and the creed. A council in Paris (1198) dedicated to pastoral improvement simply said priests were always to exhort the people to pray the Lord's Prayer, the creed, and the salutation of the blessed Virgin.[33] In 1237 it was decreed at the council in Coventry: "We ordain that every Christian man and woman recite each day seven times the Our Father, because one must praise the Lord seven times a day, according to the Prophet who said, 'I have praised you seven times a day.' Likewise seven times the Ave Maria, and twice the creed. They should be frequently warned to do this and should be forced to know it" (23.432). Some synods gave explicit directions that children be taught these prayers. Richard Poole's Constitutions for Salisbury (1217) declared that priests should gather one or two children and teach them, who should then instruct others (22.1107-8 [c. 4]). When the prescriptions appear in the context of campaigns against heresy, there is much more emphasis on the need for effective teaching. The Council of Béziers in 1246 ordered simple and distinct teaching "lest anyone later be able to allege the veil of ignorance." To this end, "children from the age of seven are to be brought to church by their parents on Sundays and feast days to be instructed in the catholic faith and to learn the salutation of blessed Mary, the Pater Noster, and the creed" (23.693 [c. 7]).[34] According to the Synod of Le Mans (1247), priests were to warn their parishioners to send their children as well as their husbands and wives to be instructed in the three basic prayers at church. This synod emphasized the necessity of believing such articles of faith as the

---

nity (British Library Royal MS 2BV), make similar use of the Ave despite their otherwise differing arrangements of prayers and readings. See *Facsimiles of "Horae de Beata Maria Virgine" from English MSS. of the Eleventh Century*, ed. E. S. Dewick, Henry Bradshaw Society 21 (London: Harrison and Sons, 1902).

32. Heriman of Tournai, *Liber de restauratione S. Martini Tornacensis*, in *Monumenta Germaniae Historica, SS*, 14.298-99.

33. *Sacrorum conciliorum nova et amplissima collectio*, ed. J. D. Mansi (1757-98, 1901-27; reprint, 1960-61), 22.681 (c. 10). Parenthetical references in the remainder of this paragraph are to this work.

34. A similar canon was promulgated by the Council of Albi in 1254, which was also convened for the extirpation of heresy. See 23.837 (c. 18).

virginity of Mary, without seeking a reason as to how or why it was true (23.756, 735). After decreeing that children are to be diligently taught the three basic prayers as well as the sign of the cross, the Council of Norwich (1257) acknowledged that sometimes adults are ignorant of these prayers. Therefore priests were ordered to test their knowledge when they came to confession (23.966-67). The Council of Liège (1287) declared that parents and godparents had the duty of teaching children these prayers (24.889). Synods in Bergen in Norway (1320), Drontheim (1351), and Skalholt (1354) also required that all believers must learn and often pray the Ave.[35]

The minimal rudiments of Christian knowledge that priests were exhorted to teach the laity extended in this period to include this prayer to the Virgin.[36] To this end some councils even stipulated that exposition of the Ave should take place in the appropriate vernacular language,[37] and vernacular versions began to appear in the thirteenth century.[38] Early in this period of conciliar legislation Thomas of Chobham could still distinguish between the absolute necessity for laypeople to know the Pater Noster and creed (they must be able to recite them to receive penance) and the less stringent requirement of knowing the Ave (they should learn it if they could).[39] This distinction would have ceased to have much significance if parish priests of the thirteenth and fourteenth centuries had taken seriously the mandates that so many regional synods were promulgating. That a fourteenth-century manual for domestic management could instruct women to glaze sugar or cook eggs by putting them on the fire "for the span of an Ave Maria" suggests how well known the Ave was as-

35. Beissel, p. 230.

36. On the cognitive element of faith, see John Van Engen, "Faith as a Concept of Order in Medieval Christendom," in *Belief in History: Innovative Approaches to European and American Religion*, ed. Thomas Kselman (Notre Dame, Ind.: University of Notre Dame Press, 1991), pp. 19-67, esp. 36-38.

37. Beissel (p. 230) refers to councils of the fourteenth and fifteenth centuries that required instruction in German or Prussian. The councils cited above did not stipulate vernacular instruction of the Ave even though some of them did require vernacular instruction for a different — emergency — circumstance: the instruction of laypeople, especially expectant mothers, on how to baptize a newborn infant whose life was endangered. See, e.g., Synod of Exeter (1287), Mansi, 24.786; Council of Liège (1287), Mansi, 24.888 (c. 2).

38. On Aves in the vernacular, see Nicole Bériou, Jacques Berlioz, and Jean Longère, *Prier au Moyen Age: Pratiques et Expériences (Ve-XVe siècles)* (Turnhout: Brepols, 1991), p. 287 n. 18 (the earliest example is from the thirteenth century); John Edwin Wells, *A Manual of the Writings in Middle English, 1050-1400* (New Haven: Yale University Press, 1916), pp. 350-51, 530 (earliest examples from ca. 1250); Haimerl, pp. 150-51 (examples in two prayer books, one written in 1402, one in 1475).

39. Thomas of Chobham, *Summa confessorum*, ed. F. Broomfield (Louvain and Paris, 1968), art. VI, dist. III, qu. IIII, quoted in Bériou, Berlioz, and Longère, p. 199 n. 76.

sumed to be, at least for laywomen.[40] Thus the kitchen and what we may consider "secular" activity could be a site where prayer to Mary became the very measure of time and a site of religious formation of children who were within earshot as the eggs were cooked or sugar glazed.[41]

The Ave Maria was a prayer, a channel of devotion or religious sentiment directed to Mary, and there was another form of encouragement — more appealing perhaps than the decrees of synods — to recite it. Many stories of Mary's favor bestowed upon those who recited her prayer or even just the two words "Ave Maria" circulated in Latin and the vernaculars.[42] Collections of these stories — when not linked to the promotion of a particular shrine — seem to have originated and circulated within monastic circles and then were compiled as preaching aids in the mendicant orders.[43]

These miracle stories, while always encouraging devotion to Mary and frequently promoting a specific devotion such as the Ave, cannot be reduced to a simple message of devotion for the sake of reward. They often suggest a more subtle message in which devotion to Mary is part of a complex religiosity. One popular story tells of one woman who beseeched Mary to intervene on her behalf by punishing another woman who was having an affair with her husband.[44] Mary appears to the wronged wife and tells her she is unable to execute

40. *Le Ménagier de Paris, traité de morale et d'économie domestique*, ed. Baron Pichon, quoted in Danièle Alexandre-Bidon, "Des Femmes de bonne foi: La religion des mères au Moyen Age," in *La Religion de ma mère: Les femmes et la transmission de la foi*, ed. Jean Delumeau (Paris: Les Éditions du Cerf, 1992), p. 122. This collection of essays has much material relevant to the themes of religious formation.

41. See Alexandre-Bidon, "Des Femmes de bonne foi," for other ways in which the religious education of children was primarily women's work.

42. There is no adequate systematic catalogue of all extant stories. For a view of the range of stories, one can consult the description of Cambridge, Sidney Sussex College MS 95, a late-fifteenth-century compilation of 500 miracle stories. See M. R. James, *A Descriptive Catalogue of the Manuscripts in the Library of Sidney Sussex College, Cambridge* (Cambridge: Cambridge University Press, 1895), pp. 76-109.

43. R. W. Southern, "The English Origins of the Miracles of the Virgin," *Medieval and Renaissance Studies* 4 (1958): 176-216; Evelyn Faye Wilson, *The "Stella Maris" of John of Garland Edited Together with a Study of Certain Collections of Mary-Legends Made in Northern France* (Cambridge: Wellesley College and the Medieval Academy of America, 1946); and Marie-Anne Polo de Beaulieu, "Des Histoires et des images au service de la prédication: La *Scala Coeli* de Jean Gobi Junior (+1350)," in *De l'homélie au sermon: Histoire de la prédication médiévale*, ed. Jacqueline Hamesse and Xavier Hermand, Publications de l'Institut d'Études médiévale: Textes, Études, Congrès 14 (Louvain: Université Catholique de Louvain, 1993), pp. 279-309.

44. I am using three sources for this story: Guibert of Nogent, *Liber de laude s. Mariae*, in *Patrologia Latina*, 156, cols. 573-74; *Miracula de beata virgine*, London, British Library Addit. MS 18929, f. 83v (an example of a monastic collection; the thirteenth/fourteenth-century manu-

such vengeance because the adulteress has regularly served her by praying the Ave with great reverence. "Extremely indignant, the lawful matron said to Mary, 'Never again will I honor you since you do not disdain to listen to the prayers of such a vile woman.'"[45] Later the two women met, and the wife expressed her despair that even Mary would not help her due to the other woman's devotion. The adulteress was immediately overcome with compunction and repented of her sin.

Modern readers of this story may at first be struck by the way the recitation of the Ave is represented as a prophylaxis against legitimate punishment for sin.[46] Mary is portrayed as literally unable to do anything against the adulteress who praises her with the Ave. And yet it is not her protection from harm that is the most significant benefit the adulteress receives from her relationship with Mary. Ultimately the miracle of the story is her conversion. And this miracle is also the benefit Mary bestows upon her other propitiant, the wronged wife. Mary does not grant the wife her wish, which was punishment of the adulteress, but she does not abandon the wife to despair. Instead she ends the crisis with a resolution beyond what the wife was able to imagine. The story thus creates a world in which the lives of those who venerate the Virgin experience unexpected beneficence. This is not to suggest that devotion to the Virgin necessarily undermined conventional morality.[47] What may initially seem subversive of traditional morality — the power gained by a ritual act protecting the adulteress from justice — is indeed a significant part of the dynamic of devotion. The story graphically portrays how the individual is empowered by her recitation of a prayer that renders Mary incapable of punishing her.[48] Yet the story also dem-

---

script comes from the Benedictine Abbey of Saint Peter's in Erfurt); Jean Gobi, *Scala Coeli*, ed. Marie-Anne Polo de Beaulieu (Paris: Édition du Centre National de la Recherche Scientifique, 1991), pp. 438-39 (an example of a mendicant preaching tool). As is usually the case with Marian miracles, each text tells the story in a somewhat different way. For other Latin versions, see T. F. Crane, "Miracles of the Virgin," *Romanic Review* 2 (1911): 247-48. For vernacular versions, see Bétérous, p. 686.

45. London, British Library Addit. MS 18929, f. 83v. All versions consulted relate a comparable expression of the wife's threat to withdraw her veneration.

46. Heriman of Tournai's description of the prayer of Ada and Gosceguin, referred to above, also suggests that repetition of the Ave could serve as a shield against just punishment.

47. Cf. Jutta Held, "Marienbild und Volksfrömmigkeit: Zur Funktion der Marienverehrung im Hoch- und Spätmittelalter," in *Frauen, Bilder, Männer, Mythen: Kunsthistorische Beiträge*, ed. Ilsebill Barta et al. (Berlin: Dietrich Reimer Verlag, 1987), pp. 43-44, who argues that such legends subverted ecclesiastical order.

48. In one version of this story, there is a hint of magic associated with the praying of the Ave: the wife accuses the mistress of "seducing the Mother of God with her incantations." This version also has the most dramatic climax: the repentant adulteress vows perpetual chastity and becomes a nun. See Crane, "Miracles of the Virgin," p. 247. The provenance of this version is not known.

onstrates that the power of the individual's prayer was not something she could wield according to her own wishes or was even aware of. A scenario that seems to diverge from a conventional system of morality becomes the means for reinforcing the most traditional goal: conversion from sin. The story envisions a world in which this process of conversion is enabled by the relationship that individuals have cultivated with the mother of God.

Like so many other miracles of the Virgin, this story portrays a concrete means of cultivating that relationship. "Every day, on her bare knees, she said the angelic salutation," relates Jean Gobi, author of a version of this story closely linked to public preaching.[49] That same version describes the wife going to the altar of the blessed Virgin and speaking to Mary there. Lives are to be structured by such practices as daily kneeling in prayer or visiting the church to present oneself physically before an image of Mary. While they speak of the miraculous and the extraordinary, these stories are more concerned with inculcating the mundane, the routine of devotion understood as the context in which a virtuous Christian life can be led.

Taking refuge in Mary through frequent, emotive recitation of the Ave was not a devotion reserved for uneducated laity. We have already seen the inclusion of the Ave in a regular *cursus* of monastic daily prayer in the Office of the Blessed Virgin. A thirteenth-century manual for the instruction of Dominican novices declared that Mary will not abandon those who "with devotion in their hearts repeat the angelic salutation five hundred or a thousand times a day."[50] Gerard of Frachet tells stories of Dominican friars engaged in regular recitation of the Ave as part of their own devotion.[51] The very popular *Vita Christi* of Ludolph of Saxony (d. 1377)[52] cites Bernard of Clairvaux as authority for this type of devotion: "For you, Virgin Mary, to hear this angelic verse, the Ave, was like a kiss. Indeed most blessed one, you are kissed as often as you are devoutly greeted by the Ave. Therefore beloved brothers, go to her image, bend your knees, and press kisses upon it, and say the Ave."[53]

---

49. Jean Gobi, *Scala Coeli*, p. 438.

50. *Libellus de instructione et consolatione novitiorum* 4.3, cited in Raymond Creytens, "L'instruction des novices dominicains au XIIIe siècle après le ms. Toulouse 418," *Archivum Fratrum Praedicatorum* 20 (1950): 145.

51. Gerard of Frachet, *Vitae fratrum* 46, 57, 119, 161.

52. For the sources and the influence of Ludolph's work, see James H. Marrow, *Passion Iconography in Northern European Art of the Late Middle Ages and Early Renaissance: A Study of the Transformation of Sacred Metaphor into Descriptive Narrative*, Ars Neerlandica 1 (Kortrijk: Van Ghemmert, 1979), pp. 12-14.

53. Ludolph of Saxony, *Vita Jesu Christi*, ed. A.-C. Bolard, L.-M. Rigolot, and J. Carnandet (Paris and Rome: Victor Palmé, 1865), p. 26.

It was through the regular recitation of prayers to the Virgin that laypeople could join congregations that paralleled the organized prayer life of professed communities of monks, nuns, and friars.[54] The first congregation of the Virgin founded in Milan in 1232 by the Dominican Peter of Verona initiated a development that would also spread to the Franciscan Order (with the founding of congregations in Bagnorea, Osimo, Recanati, and Reggio in 1257). This seems to have become a popular means outside Italy as well for mendicants to attract crowds to their sermons.[55] The expressed goal of these groups, usually comprised of both lay and professed members and led by a friar, was to promote devotion to Mary. In general, the major obligations incumbent upon members of the congregations included participation at monthly assemblies, attendance at weekly preaching services usually held on Wednesdays at the conventual church of the friars, the recitation of daily prayers, some financial contribution, and charitable works that recall the compassion of the Mother of Mercy. The monthly assemblies as well as the four major feasts of the Virgin were usually celebrated with processions in which members of the congregation marched through the church and adjoining cloister, sometimes through the city streets, bearing lit candles and singing vernacular hymns of praise to Mary.

Membership was usually open to women as well as men in the Marian confraternities, although with significant differences in their roles.[56] The statutes of the Congregation of the Virgin in Arezzo, dating from 1262, include the following stipulation:

> Because to God there is no distinction or difference between a man and woman in performing the works of salvation, we wish that women as well as men be received into the saving company of this congregation. Like the men, women are obligated to recite the daily prayers for the living and the dead, either in church or at home, and they are obligated to offer the suffrages for the

---

54. On belonging to an identifiable group as a significant aspect of late medieval culture, see Caroline Walker Bynum, "Did the Twelfth Century Discover the Individual?" in *Jesus as Mother: Studies in the Spirituality of the High Middle Ages* (Berkeley: University of California Press, 1982), pp. 82-109.

55. Gilles Meersseman, "Études sur les anciennes confréries dominicaines: Les congregations de la Vierge," *Archivum Fratrum Praedicatorum* 22 (1952): 5-176. My sketch of the general life of the confraternities is based on Meersseman's article and collection of documents.

56. Apparently not all Marian congregations originally accepted women. For example, at Utrecht women were not admitted until three years after the congregation was founded in 1403, and then their admission was limited to forty. See Meersseman, "Études," documents 69-70, pp. 163-64. On women's participation in fifteenth-century rosary confraternities, see Anne Winston, "Tracing the Origins of the Rosary: German Vernacular Texts," *Speculum* 68 (1993): 634.

dead members of the congregation . . . and they are obligated to gather on the appropriate Sunday of the month, and on the four feasts of the glorious Virgin Mary, mother of God, and on the feast of All Saints . . . unless there is a personal impediment or a family duty.

Other obligations of membership, most notably almsgiving, were also waived for female members, and women could not be chosen rectors or counselors, the lay officers of that confraternity.[57] Even though women and men were distinguished in the roles they could undertake in the Marian congregations, the praise of the Virgin was here understood to be a devotional act of universal appeal and access.[58] Consequently, it was a practice that brought both laymen and laywomen more fully into the public ambit of Christian expression.

The significance of belonging to a special group, sometimes given material reality in the inscription of members' names in the congregation's record book,[59] does not lie in any peculiarity of the congregations' devotional and charitable practices. Rather, its power resides in the ways standard beliefs and practices were encouraged and took on a special aura. Even when there is not a distinctive Marian theology in the sermons preached to the congregations or in the devotions practiced, there is a compelling sense of specialness generated by the voluntary commitment of the individuals to a congregation. Thus the rule of the congregation of the Virgin at Perugia that required confession four times a year and Communion twice transformed the obligations of annual Communion and confession of the Fourth Lateran Council (1215) by simply intensifying it in the name of Marian piety.[60] Furthermore, membership in these congregations was a means of drenching the week in devotional practice: the

57. Meersseman, "Études," document 18, pp. 102-5. Unlike the statutes of the congregation of Arezzo, which said that men *(vires)* were to be chosen for officers, the statutes of the congregation of Perugia (1312) did not indicate that its offices were to be held by men (document 47, p. 140).

58. This is in contrast to another type of congregation, that of the flagellants, in which women were not members. See John Henderson, "The Flagellant Movement and Flagellant Confraternities in Central Italy, 1260-1400," in *Religious Motivation: Biographical and Sociological Problems for the Church Historian,* ed. Derek Baker, Studies in Church History 15 (Oxford: Basil Blackwell, 1978), pp. 154-55; Ronald Weisman, "Cults and Contexts: In Search of the Renaissance Confraternity," in *Crossing the Boundaries: Christian Piety and the Arts in Italian Medieval and Renaissance Confraternities,* ed. Konrad Eisenbichler, Early Drama, Art, and Music Monograph Series 15 (Kalamazoo: Medieval Institute Publications, 1991), p. 212.

59. See, e.g., the statutes of the congregation in Perugia, Meersseman, "Études," document 47, p. 140.

60. Meersseman, "Études," document 47, p. 140. For the Latin text and English translation of this canon of Lateran IV, see *Decrees of the Ecumenical Councils,* ed. Norman P. Tanner, 2 vols. (London: Sheed and Ward; Washington, D.C.: Georgetown University Press, 1990), 1:245.

statutes of Arezzo required daily visits to church for prayer;[61] members of the congregation at Imola were granted an indulgence of forty days for joining in the evening rite of singing Mary's praise and bringing lamps in her honor every day for a whole year;[62] and as many as 240 to 250 sermons were preached each year in Dominican churches with confraternities, and the theological sophistication of some of these sermons suggests that lay hearers were eager for serious religious engagement.[63] Laypeople in congregations also created public religious media, commissioning paintings and rebuilding churches.[64] Thus congregations dedicated to the Virgin may be seen as one of the most concrete institutional structures through which Marian devotion, integrated into the regular temporal and spatial/civic framework of lay life, was part of the process of Christian formation.

Preaching Mary and Mary as Preacher

Intimately related to prayer was the strong cultivation of Marian devotion in preaching and teaching. Teaching about Mary took place in many settings. The most obvious we have already encountered: the instruction and explication of the Ave Maria by parish clergy. Treatises dedicated to this task, such as that of Conrad of Saxony, began to appear in the thirteenth century.[65] Sermons about Mary were preached on the four great Marian feasts,[66] but teaching about Mary was not limited to these occasions. The degree to which Mary could pervade preaching can be seen in "Mariales," sermon collections in which each piece is

61. Meersseman, "Études," document 18, p. 106.

62. Meersseman, "Études," document 50, pp. 143-44.

63. G. Meersseman, "La Prédication dominicaine dans les congrégations mariales en Italie au XIIIe siècle," *Archivum Fratrum Praedicatorum* 18 (1948): 149, and Meersseman, "Études," 31.

64. See, e.g., Ellen Schiferl, "Italian Confraternity Art Contracts: Group Consciousness and Corporate Patronage, 1400-1525," in *Crossing the Boundaries*, pp. 121-40. See also Meersseman, "Études," document 30, p. 118, for a contract between the congregation of S. Maria Novella in Florence and the Siennese painter Duccio Buoninsegni, for the execution of a painting of the Virgin and her Son.

65. For other examples of Latin texts commenting on the Ave, see Conrad of Saxony, *Speculum seu salutatio*, p. 71 n. 42. Vernacular examples include Gautier de Coincy's *Salus Nostre Dame* and the commentary found in Munich, Bayerische Staatsbibliothek MS Gall. 34 (discussion and abridged translation in Bériou, Berlioz, and Longère, pp. 280-82).

66. Examples of sermon collections for these feasts are Innsbruck, UB 364, described in Johannes Baptist Schneyer, *Repertorium der Lateinischen Sermones des Mittelalters für die Zeit von 1150-1350* (Münster: Aschendorff Verlagsbuchhandlung, 1969), 7.651-52, and Bartolomeo da Breganze, *I "Sermones de beata virgine" (1266)*, ed. Laura Gaffuri, Fonti per la Storia della Terraferma Veneta 7 (Padua: Editrice Antenore, 1993).

focused on Mary. For example, Jacobus de Voragine, author of the extremely popular *Legenda aurea*, compiled an alphabetically arranged collection of 160 Marian sermons.[67]

The praise of Mary's virtues and encouragement to seek her patronage are ubiquitous, but preachers could also shape the images of Mary they articulated when addressing specific audiences. In a sermon directed to Benedictine nuns that denounced, among other things, nuns who wandered outside the cloister and were being corrupted by their interactions with secular people, Jacques de Vitry (d. 1240) ended with a cautionary exemplum about devotion to Mary. A nun was tempted by the love of a young man to leave the cloister one night. To leave, she had to pass the altar of Mary "at which she was in the habit of bowing and saluting the Virgin in the presence of her image." As she passed by the altar, she began from habit to bow and say the Ave before the image. Her fear paralyzed her and she returned to the dormitory. Since her plan was similarly frustrated on many subsequent nights, she finally decided to refrain from her usual devotional practice. She passed by the image without bowing or greeting it, and the devil immediately received power over her and inspired her with such audacity that she abandoned the convent and followed her concupiscence.[68] This story repeats many of the same themes we have seen before: the encouragement of a habit of saying the Ave that coordinates physical and mental attention by focusing it on an image, and the efficacy of a habit that ensures Mary's protection. Yet in this sermon Mary's saving intervention is not the climax of the story. Instead, a picture of failed devotion is preached.

Jacques did not tell a popular story here — it did not circulate widely outside the context of his original model sermons.[69] In contrast a similar story enjoyed wide currency. Caesarius of Heisterbach, a Cistercian contemporary of Jacques, tells of Beatrice, a nun who was sacristan of her convent and fervent in her devotion to Mary. Driven by lust to leave the convent, she first went to the altar of the Virgin and laid the keys upon it, acknowledging her inability to

---

67. The collection was written ca. 1292-98. For a description of its contents, see Schneyer, 3.273-83. For a more complete list of its manuscript transmission, see Thomas Kaeppeli, *Scriptores Ordinis Praedicatorum Medii Aevi*, 4 vols. (Rome: Istituto storico Dominicano, 1970-93), 2:367-68.

68. Text found in Jean Longère, "Quatre sermons *ad religiosas* de Jacques de Vitry," in *Les religieuses en France au XIIIe siècle*, ed. Michel Parisse (Nancy: Presses Universitaires de Nancy, 1985), pp. 249-59.

69. I know of only one other example of its transmission: a Middle English version in British Library MS Addit. 25,719. Cf. Thomas Frederick Crane, *The Exempla or Illustrative Stories from the Sermones Vulgares of Jacques de Vitry* (1890; reprint, New York: Burt Franklin, 1971), p. 160.

withstand her temptation. She leaves, is corrupted, and becomes a prostitute. Fifteen years later she returns to the convent in secular dress, only to discover that the Virgin Mary has taken her place and that no one even knows she was gone.[70] The contrast between these two stories is instructive. Caesarius's story was included in many other collections of Marian miracles, which were often compiled as preaching aids.[71] In these collections the story could be adapted to whatever religious goal or audience a preacher might wish to address. But Jacques's story was actually integrated into a model sermon addressed to a particular group of people: women who professed virginity but were often suspected of lasciviousness. The divergent (though not contradictory) images of Mary presented in these two stories remind us that the symbol of Mary could be used in different ways for the formation of different constituencies and that gender conventions (e.g., suspicions about nuns' lasciviousness) shaped the ways in which the symbol of Mary was deployed in preaching.

While preaching remained the primary medium for formal teaching throughout the later Middle Ages, teaching about Mary took place in other settings as well. In the twelfth century the liturgical dramas of Good Friday began to feature a vernacular passage expressing the lament of Mary at the foot of the cross. These portrayals of Mary in grief, sometimes accompanied by directions for imitative gestures such as weeping, were written to "excite emotions of piercing agitation and produce a more intense participation of the people in the representation of the Passion of Christ."[72] New vernacular devotional literatures also focused on the compassionate suffering of Mary. Short compositions such as the Middle English "Dispute between Mary and the Cross" of the fourteenth century (with other versions in Middle Dutch, Provençal, and Latin) became increasingly popular. This text tells the whole of the Christian faith, with Mary posed as both poignant questioner of faith and as intercessor saving people from hell.[73] There is pathos in her interrogation of the cross, but her suffering, in this case, is never completely divorced from her power. It is because she gave up her Son that she is now in a position to save the faithful. "The Dispute between Mary and the Cross" demonstrates how Mary could become a symbol that enabled both the effective exposition of the faith as well the channeling of

70. Caesarius of Heisterbach, *Dialogus Miraculorum* 7.34, pp. 42-43.

71. Ward, *Catalogue of Romances in the Department of MSS in the British Museum*, vol. 2, cites eight examples; Boyd, *The Middle English Miracles of the Virgin*, cites one. Other manuscripts include Paris, Bibl. Nat. MS Lat. 18134.

72. Sandro Sticca, *The "Planctus Mariae" in the Dramatic Tradition of the Middle Ages*, trans. Joseph R. Berrigan (Athens: University of Georgia Press, 1988), p. 120 and passim.

73. See Wells, p. 417. For a sketch of the Latin foundations of the new vernacular devotional texts, see Schuler, "The Seven Sorrows of the Virgin."

emotion. Thus like prayer, teaching about Mary worked on the emotional as well as the cognitive level of Christian formation.

Not only was Mary a major subject of preaching and teaching; she was also envisioned as a teacher herself: "Mary, having been divinely instructed in all mysteries from the beginning, could then better reveal the truth to the writers and preachers of the Gospel."[74] So Bernard of Clairvaux saw Mary as the one who taught the Evangelists and the first generation of Christian preachers. But for Ludolph of Saxony the issue of Mary as teacher was fraught with tension: "Mary was the mother of the Teacher of all, and she herself was a teacher, although she could not publicly teach by words because of her sex, but she wished to teach by example."[75] He too could affirm the tradition that Mary taught the apostles and even say that "they had frequent recourse to her as if to a master." Yet three chapters later he asserted that Mary's teaching could not be an oral proclamation of truth; such an image of Mary might undermine the gender convention that women should be silent.[76] Ludolph's remark gives us a rare glimpse into some of the tension generated by the femaleness of Mary when she was used within the most overt processes of religious formation, that is, preaching and teaching.

Localization and Presence

Ludolph of Saxony's exhortation to kiss an image of the Virgin and pray the Ave in front of it, Jean Gobi's story of an image of Mary speaking to a wronged wife seeking vengeance, Jacques de Vitry's story of a nun greeting Mary by bowing before her image — all encourage a practice of seeing Mary and of interacting with her as localized and present in the material images that represent her. Since the tenth century particular churches and monasteries had become important pilgrimage sites based on their possession of miracle-working Marian relics or images. Some of these sites developed reputations for particular kinds of miracles (e.g., Chartres with the chemise worn by Mary during the birth of Jesus was associated with the cure or resuscitation of injured or dead children),[77] and many important Marian pilgrimage sites north of the Loire were

74. Bernard of Clairvaux, *De laudibus virginis matris*, in *Sancti Bernardi Opera*, ed. Leclercq, Homily 4, chap. 6, p. 52.

75. Ludolph of Saxony, *Vita Jesu Christi*, p. 56.

76. For debates about women preaching, see Nicole Bériou, "Femmes et prédicateurs: la transmission de la foi aux XIIe et XIII siècles," in *La Religion de ma mère*, pp. 66-68.

77. Spitzer (p. 142) notes that although Chartres also had a reputation for the cure of ergotism, it is the Virgin's intervention for dead or threatened children that predominates in the miracle records.

associated with the outbreaks of *mal des ardents* or ergotism that occurred in 1089, 1094, and 1128.[78] As Gabriela Signori has argued, the development of these Marian pilgrimage sites was usually directly linked with other pastoral efforts of bishops and cathedral clergy to consolidate their dioceses. Just as pilgrimage to a wonder-working image or relic created the experience of a personal relationship with a powerful and compassionate Mary, it simultaneously strengthened the connection of the individual to the hierarchical diocesan structure.[79] Thus the cathedral dedicated to Mary embodied the church as institution and as society of believers, it proclaimed and enacted the leadership of the cathedral within the diocese, and as a physical building, it localized recourse to Mary.[80]

The localization of the presence of the Virgin took on new dimensions with the vast proliferation of Marian sculpture and paintings in what Michael Camille calls the newly visual culture that emerged in the thirteenth century: "There were literally thousands of representations of this subject [i.e., the Virgin] in wood, stone, alabaster, metal, and ivory, and of every conceivable size and shape. They were placed in multifarious contexts and produced with varying degrees of artistic skill."[81] From the twelfth to the fifteenth centuries many new motifs appeared: the pietà; Mary in her childbed; Mary nursing Jesus; the standing Madonna with child; the *vierge ouvrant* (a statue of a seated Madonna whose body opened up to reveal an image of the Trinity); Mary as a child with her mother, Saint Anne; Mary receiving Communion; the Schützmantelmadonna (Mary with her protective cloak held over her devotees, also known as the "Mother of Mercy"); and the seven sorrows of Mary.

This proliferation of Marian images is not simply a fact of art-historical interest; the images emerged in new patterns of devotional practice. For example, a fourteenth-century breviary included in its office of the blessed Virgin "a salutation of all the limbs of the Virgin by which she humbly served the Lord Jesus Christ." This devotion, which was said to be more pleasing to Mary than any other service, should be said "before an image of the Blessed Virgin."[82] Images

---

78. Gabriela Signori, "Marienbilder im Vergleich: Marianische Wunderbücher zwischen Weltklerus, städtischer Ständevielfalt und ländlichen Subsistenzproblemen (10.-13. Jahrhundert)," in *Maria, Abbild oder Vorbild? Zur Sozialgeschichte mittelalterlicher Marienverehrung*, ed. Hedwig Röckelein, Claudia Opitz, and Dieter R. Bauer (Tübingen: Edition Diskord, 1990), pp. 72-74.

79. Cf. Spitzer, "The Cult of the Virgin and Gothic Sculpture."

80. Signori, pp. 62-66.

81. Michael Camille, *The Gothic Idol: Ideology and Image-Making in Medieval Art* (Cambridge: Cambridge University Press, 1989), pp. 224-25.

82. From the Soyons Breviary, Paris Bibl. Nat. MS lat. nouv. acq. 718, quoted in Sixten Ringbom, "Devotional Images and Imaginative Devotions: Notes on the Place of Art in Late Medieval Private Piety," *Gazette des Beaux-Arts* 73 (1969): 170.

of "the piety of Mary," that is, any image of Mary worshiping Christ such as at his birth or in the temple, could become models for pious imitation.[83] Images that represented Mary's compassionate suffering — at the crucifixion or holding the dead body of her Son — and images that represented Mary's sovereign power to protect those who take refuge in her, as in the Schützmantelmadonna, embodied for their beholders the two contrasting sides of their celestial mother.

The role of images within Christian formation sometimes met with criticism. Because theological justification for images within Christian practice rested in part on their didactic value, images were occasionally condemned for their misrepresentation of Christian teaching.[84] And there is some evidence that the new proliferation of images may have bred contempt, or at least indifference. Writing around 1220, Gautier de Coinci vernacularized a Latin story about a Muslim who owned a painting of the Virgin and fastidiously cared for it. In response to his doubts about the incarnation, the Virgin's breasts lifted up from the painting and emitted streams of oil. The inevitable conversion of the Muslim ensued. But for Gautier the moral of this story is not simply the truth of the incarnation nor even the reality of Mary's compassionate presence in the image. The incident is explicitly interpreted as a reproach to those who do not honorably revere their Madonnas.[85]

Medieval explanations about the role of images in religious formation were usually given in gender-neutral terms: that images teach the faith and arouse devotion. However, Dominique Rigaux suggests that such views particularly addressed women, because women usually had the responsibility of spiritual education for young children and were usually considered less educated than men. Thus images were more likely to figure prominently in women's religious life, whether because of their use of them in training their children or their own less formally educated piety.[86] Furthermore, because women were more readily

---

83. F. O. Büttner, *Imitatio Pietatis: Motive der christliche Ikonographie als Modelle zur Verähnlichung* (Berlin: Gebr. Mann Verlag, 1983), p. 65.

84. For example, in 1402 Jean Gerson condemned the *vierge ouvrant* as suggesting that the whole Trinity was incarnate (cited in Camille, pp. 231-32); François LePicart (1504-56) condemned the representations of Mary in childbed as suggesting that Mary experienced pain in childbirth. See Larissa Taylor, *Soldiers of Christ: Preaching in Late Medieval and Reformation France* (New York: Oxford University Press, 1977), pp. 111-12.

85. Gautier de Coinci, *Les Miracles de Nostre Dame*, ed. V. Frederic Koenig, 4 vols. (Geneva: Librairie Droz, 1966-70), 3:23-34. Ringbom interprets this story as evidence for the private ownership of images, but the emphasis seems to be on the veneration of images on altars in churches. See Ringbom, p. 160.

86. Dominique Rigaux, "Dire le foi avec des images: une affaire de femmes?" in *La Religion de ma mère*, pp. 72-73.

identified with physicality and embodiment, there may have been greater cultural support for women to incorporate images — that is, physical objects — in their religious lives.[87] This is not to suggest an absolute dichotomy between men's and women's religious formation. Rather, it suggests that a significant dynamic within late medieval Christian formation was often more visible in women's lives than in men's.

One example of a woman's Marian piety focused by images can be seen in the vita of Umiliana dei Cherchi, a Florentine woman who became a Franciscan tertiary after the death of her husband. The vita was written shortly after her own death in 1246 by Vito of Cortona, a Franciscan friar. It is the picture of the life of a woman whose holiness was understood to be simultaneously extraordinary and exemplary. In this portrayal of her life of prayer and visitations by divine grace, Umiliana is said to have owned a painted panel of the blessed Virgin, which she kept in her cell and revered by adorning it with crystal and amber seals.[88] When her young daughter died in her presence, Umiliana prostrated herself in front of the image and tearfully begged Mary to restore her daughter. After Umiliana made this prayer and blessed her daughter with the sign of the cross, "a wonderful and beautiful child stepped out from that panel, went to where the girl lay, and blessed her. At this, her daughter arose restored and the child disappeared" (396). For the author of this text the painting of the Virgin is not only the focus of prayer, but the site where the Virgin and her Son enter into the world of their needy devout. In another episode Umiliana tries to extinguish a fire that is burning the cloth which covers the image. But the blaze turns out not to be an earthly fire, and the author uses this story to announce a lesson about devotion to Mary: "It must be believed that this fire represented the fire of the Holy Spirit by which Christ inflamed Umiliana, due to the merits of his glorious Mother, whom Umiliana greatly served" (398).

Umiliana's devotion to Mary and the rewards of this service are most fully asserted in the description of her death. Out of reverence for Mary, Umiliana wishes to die on a Saturday, the day on which the Virgin was especially commemorated (398-99). The death scene that follows hardly fits hagiographical conventions. Clerics and their sacraments are notably absent, surprising especially since the vita attests to the frequent presence of a Brother Michael who was Umiliana's confessor (389, 391-93, 395, 398). Instead, Umiliana's female companion, probably Gisla, who is named in the prologue of the text as her guardian

---

87. See Caroline Walker Bynum, "The Female Body and Religious Practice in the Later Middle Ages," in *Fragmentation and Redemption: Essays on Gender and the Human Body in Medieval Religion* (New York: Zone Books, 1991), pp. 195-222.

88. Vito of Cortona, *Vita b. Aemiliana seu Humilianae*, in *Acta Sanctorum*, May IV.395. Parenthetical references in the following text are to this document.

during her illness (385), turns to what appears to be a veritable shrine in the cell. The painting of Mary is also the repository of Marian relics; candles, incense, and holy water are kept there as well as another painting, that of Mary and the dead or dying Christ. The companion uses these objects to fortify Umiliana in her struggle with the devil. The image of Mary with her dying loved one is placed on the chest of her other dying loved one, and the ritual succeeds in preparing Umiliana. The devil flees from her bedside and Umiliana dies in peace. The life that was led in the physical presence of Mary ends with physical contact between painting and body, and the reassurance of Mary's escort of the soul to her Son. Instead of receiving the body of Christ from the hands of a priest, Umiliana receives the image of Mary and Christ on her body at the hands of a woman, and awaits the reception of her soul into the hands of Mary.

The images in this story do not simply serve the purposes usually envisioned by theologians: as didactic reminders or even stimulants of devotion.[89] The images structure the contours of the relationship between Umiliana and Mary, and literally are the media of their interaction.[90] The physical object — the painting of Mary — served as a focus of prayer, a site of divine contact with this world, and as portable talisman to be put on the body. The image of Mary enables Umiliana and Gisla to enact a ritual of communion and last anointing, a tableau that suggests a style of women's piety in which devotion to Mary embodied in her images existed as an alternative to sacerdotally mediated ritual. At the same time, the vita of Umiliana reinforces the picture drawn from our other testimonies — that all Christians were encouraged to understand the presence of Mary localized and embodied in images that were increasingly available in churches, on street corners, and even in their own homes.

The Formation of Boundaries

As we have seen, Christians both learned about their faith and "activated" it in their daily lives through prayer, preaching about Mary, and relating to Mary in material images. These processes of becoming Christian were closely tied to an articulation of what was not Christian. The enthusiasm for praising Mary's pure body as enclosed garden, closed gate, holy tabernacle, along with other

89. For the inadequacy of using medieval theological views for understanding actual devotional practice, see Jeffrey Hamburger, "The Visual and the Visionary: The Image in Late Medieval Monastic Devotion," *Viator* 20 (1989): 161-82.

90. Cf. the suggestive discussions in Camille, pp. 220-41; and Hans Belting, *Likeness and Presence: A History of the Image before the Era of Art,* trans. Edmund Jephcott (Chicago: University of Chicago Press, 1994), p. 300.

such images of sealed entity,[91] coupled with the assertion of Mary as exemplary Christian, rendered her a powerful image in the construction of the perceived enemies of such purity and faith. Just as the "Dialogue between Mary and the Cross" or sermons preached to Marian congregations could use Mary as a means of explicating the entire Christian faith, so the image of Mary could function as the touchstone of membership in that faith.

As early as the mid–ninth century the response "Gaude Maria virgo" began to be incorporated in the monastic antiphonaries for the feast of the purification. In this chant Mary is said to have destroyed all heresies. It continues: "Let the unfortunate Jew blush / who says that Christ was born from the seed of Joseph."[92] It is the defilement of Mary's body — her natural impregnation by Joseph — that encapsulated for a Christian audience the whole of Jewish faith by making it the diametrical opposite of their own. The composition of this chant was set in a miraculous framework: the mid-ninth-century *Musica disciplina* of Aurelian describes the chant as the divinely inspired utterance of a blind Roman man. By the thirteenth century this story had been elaborated to provide a polemical context. Jews taunt the Roman with the impotence of Christ to cure his blindness and with their denial of Mary's virginity. The Jews then agree to convert if his eyesight is restored, which occurs as the blind man sings this responsory and verse before the altar of Mary on the feast of her purification.[93]

The thirteenth-century version of this story resembles many stories that circulated widely in miracle collections. A significant element of many of these stories is the pathos generated by the portrayal of Jewish violence against innocent Christian purity. For example, Jean Gobi records a story of a Jewish woman in labor who beseeches the aid of Mary and then painlessly gives birth to a healthy boy. She takes him to a church and they are both baptized. Her husband then comes and kills the child. When the wailing of the wife arouses the neighbors, he flees and the only refuge he can find is in a chapel dedicated to Mary. He falls before her image and condemns himself as a wolf who slew a lamb. He pleads for her help, saying he now believes that the true God was incarnated and born from her with her virginity intact. When the neighbors arrive, they are stunned at his request for baptism. At his baptism the dead child begins to stir in his mother's arms. All praise the Virgin, the former Jew is freed, and he dedicates himself to writing against Jewish falsehood about Mary.[94] What is most striking about this story is how the basic Christian narrative of

91. See Coletti, p. 89 n. 15.

92. Louis Brou, "Marie, 'Destructrice de toutes les hérésies' et la belle légende du répons *Gaude Maria Virgo*," *Ephemerides Liturgicae* 62 (1948): 321-22.

93. Brou, pp. 322-26. Cf. Crane, "Miracles of the Virgin," p. 257.

94. Jean Gobi, *Scala Coeli*, in *De l'homélie au sermon*, pp. 445-47.

the life of Christ is retold here: A Jewish woman gives birth painlessly to a boy. This innocent lamb is slain by a wicked Jew. The grieving mother holds her dead son in her arms, but he is restored to life, and the community is united in its faith. This story narrates not only how devotion to Mary saves one in distress, but also how the paradigmatic events of history continue to be replayed in the Christian present.

This story is one of the less violent miracle tales, some of which end with the disappearance or death of incorrigible Jews. A well-known story recounts the theft of an image of Mary by a Jew, who then hid it in a privy. Having done this, "he ceased to exist, suddenly struck by a sudden death."[95] For the audience of these stories Mary literally was the embodiment of their faith — hers was the body that had to be preserved against the defilement of heresy or denial. This fear of pollution projected on the outsiders to the faith is graphically expressed in this story of the defiled image. The formation of Christian belief and practice was inextricably entwined with an articulation of those who were enemies of that order. As Christian identity was formed, it was formed in relationship to what was seen as its absolute negation. Stories of the Virgin's miraculous power gave Christians the power to imagine the negation of those threats.

The negation of those threats did not remain on the imaginative level of stories about Marian miracles. The later Middle Ages was a period of substantial violence by Christians against Jews. Stories circulated in sermons about the conversion of Jews to Christianity because of Mary's benevolent intercession and about the death of Jews owing to their profanation of Mary. Such preaching activities, particularly associated with mendicant friars, focused lay attention on the "problem" of Jews in their midst.[96] As Jeremy Cohen has argued, the banishment of Jews from most of western Europe by the end of the Middle Ages suggests that the aggressive anti-Jewish ideology that emerged in the thirteenth century must have been successfully articulated for and understood by laypeople.[97]

---

95. Jean Gobi, *Scala Coeli*, in *De l'homélie au sermon*, p. 451. This story circulated widely and is cited in modern scholarly literature as "Mary Image Insulted." See Gavin I. Langmuir, *Toward a Definition of Antisemitism* (Berkeley: University of California Press, 1990), p. 242, for a discussion of this story within the larger framework of his thesis about Christian irrationality and projection of doubt on Jews. Also, see now Miri Rubin, *Gentile Tales: The Narrative Assault on Late Medieval Jews* (New Haven: Yale University Press, 1999), pp. 7-39.

96. See, e.g., William Chester Jordan, "Marian Devotion and the Talmud Trial of 1240," in *Religionsgespräche im Mittelalter*, ed. Bernard Lewis and Friedrich Niewöhner, Wolfenbütteler Mittelalter-Studien 4 (Wiesbaden: Otto Harrassowitz, 1992), pp. 61-76.

97. Jeremy Cohen, *The Friars and the Jews: The Evolution of Medieval Anti-Judaism* (Ithaca, N.Y.: Cornell University Press, 1982), pp. 226-27. Cf. Robert Chazan, *Daggers of Faith: Thirteenth-Century Christian Missionizing and Jewish Response* (Berkeley: University of California Press, 1989), pp. 170-81.

The razing of synagogues, such as that in Nürnberg in 1349, to be replaced by shrines dedicated to the Virgin,[98] suggests that Marian stories envisioning the disappearance of Jews — either by conversion or death — became part of a larger process of forming western Europe as an exclusively Christian society.

Conclusion

The symbol of Mary was ambiguous. That ambiguity was often related to her femaleness: she is a mother, but one in whom the pollutions of birth are sanitized; her compassionate patronage of those devoted to her is held in tension with a system of justice that is often associated with a penitential system represented by the clergy; she is the best of all teachers but also the model of female silence; she has extraordinary power, yet she is vulnerable to defilement by the pollution of unbelief. Any articulation and deployment of the symbol of Mary was marked by the anxieties about femaleness that were also a part of medieval Christian culture. Because the differentiation of gender was so central to medieval Christian religious life, it makes sense that the contours of devotion to Mary would reflect tensions about gender roles as well as contribute to the work of differentiating gender. Accordingly, in the cult of the Virgin we can see how a symbol understood to be universal (Mary as the mother of all Christians) is taught to be experienced differently by different groups (e.g., pregnant women or professed nuns). And we can see how that universality functioned as a means by which the boundaries of the "universal" community were constructed.

The ambiguity of the symbol of Mary also allows us to rethink the processes of religious formation. We may be tempted to imagine that the teaching and absorption of a religious identity takes place with the communication of the most basic beliefs of the tradition, that is, the transmission across generations of a stable and comprehensible creed. Evidence from the cult of the Virgin suggests that the ambiguity of personal relationships may prove a better model for understanding how people in western Europe in the later Middle Ages came to experience themselves as living a Christian life. Children, women, and men were taught to perceive the complexly gendered figure of Mary acting in their lives as a response to their own words and gestures of devotion.

---

98. See Hedwig Röckelein, "Marienverehrung und Judenfeindlichkeit in Mittelalter und früher Neuzeit," in *Maria in der Welt: Marienverehrung im Kontext der Sozialgeschichte 10.-18. Jahrhundert,* ed. Claudia Opitz, Hedwig Röckelein, Gabriela Signori, and Guy P. Marchal, Clio Lucernensis 2 (Zürich: Chronos Verlag, 1993), pp. 279-307.

Just as none of us claims to fathom completely the total being of a beloved, so devotion to Mary was a relationship that could not be neatly mapped. The Marian cult provided Christians with the possibilities for a life in which physical space could be organized by the localization of Mary's presence; bodily experience could be formed by the wearing/bearing of Marian images or objects blessed in Mary's name, by gestures of obeisance, or by health that was understood to be protected by Mary; and time could be structured by the length of the Ave Maria, by the weekly schedule of a confraternity's assemblies, by the annual cycle of Marian feasts. These factors did not determine the experience of any one Christian in completely predictable ways; rather, they provided a set of behavioral possibilities for the faithful to achieve a diversity of potential goods, ranging from a successful childbirth to eternal salvation. This organizing of time, space, perception, emotion, and the body enabled men and women to experience their lives as participating in a world they understood as Christian, as a world in which a maternal compassion was a potent expression of divine love.

THE REFORMATION ERA

Luther and Formation in Faith

David C. Steinmetz

The first generation of Protestant leaders faced a task that was in large measure unprecedented. It was their task not merely to form a younger generation in the Christian faith, but to re-form an older generation that had in their estimation been formed in the Christian faith incorrectly. The proponents of the new measures agreed that children had to be taught the creed and the Lord's Prayer as their parents and grandparents had been taught before them. But parents and grandparents also had new lessons to learn. They had to be taught to take Communion in both kinds (like the heretical Hussites in Bohemia) and to do it at least four times annually (the de facto medieval norm was once a year). Furthermore, they were encouraged to abandon the recitation of the Ave Maria (a prayer particularly comforting to women in childbirth) and to leave their private devotions to the privacy of their own home. Church was no longer regarded as the appropriate place for the audible recitation of private prayers, especially prayers for the dead. Audible private prayer should not be offered during the celebration of the new ritual and certainly not while the pastor was consecrating the bread and wine. The list of holidays was shortened, and the colorful processions of the consecrated host on Corpus Christi and the relics of the saints on feast days were canceled. Masses for the dead were abruptly stopped, and the endowments that supported them were put to other uses. The celebration of the Eucharist, much less frequent under the new regulations than in the old church, was no longer a rite to be observed by the laity, who had remained prayerful spectators, but a communal meal in which all the laity were expected to participate. In short, the early years of the Protestant Reformation marked a very disorienting time for a great number of people who had always thought of themselves as good Christians and who had difficulty understanding the new order that put their old status in doubt.

Ignatius Loyola, Luther's contemporary and one of the principal founders of the Society of Jesus, conceived of his task as the conversion of Christendom to Christianity. What Ignatius hoped to assist was the process by which ordinary parishioners, many only half-committed to the church and the Christian faith, could become better followers of Jesus Christ. Although Luther did not think of his task as the conversion of Christendom to Christianity, he could have affirmed it as an appropriate goal. What set him off from Ignatius was his radical rethinking of the principles according to which such a conversion could and should occur. Before Christendom could become truly Christian, it had to abandon old habits of thinking and acting and embrace a new vision of what being an authentic Christian implied. In Luther's view the late medieval church suffered not so much from a failure to implement its own traditional principles — as Ignatius thought — but from a misguided and uncritical commitment to the wrong principles.

Return to Sources

The Lutheran program for the re-formation of Christendom began with an appeal to Christian antiquity.[1] There was, of course, nothing in the sixteenth century less revolutionary and more traditional than an appeal to the past. Sixteenth-century Christians, both Protestant and Catholic, shared a strong cultural assumption that what is older is better than what is new. That assumption applied not only to religion but to civic and cultural relations, art and architecture, law and custom, economic and agricultural practices — in short, to the whole range of activities and beliefs that gives human society its character. The modern notion that new things are generally better and ought in a well-ordered society to supplant what is older was, on the whole, an idea that had not yet found a home in sixteenth-century Europe. The cultural bias was in favor of what was sound, tested, ancient, and rooted in the collective experience of generations.[2]

---

1. The first article of the Augsburg Confession begins with a reaffirmation of the decisions of the Council of Nicea. Article XXII, dealing with Communion in both kinds, appeals to Cyprian and ancient custom against the modern practice of denying the cup to the laity. For the appropriate texts, see *The Book of Concord*, ed. and trans. Theodore Tappert (Philadelphia: Fortress, 1959).

2. See in this connection the valuable anthology *Manifestations of Discontent in Germany on the Eve of the Reformation*, ed. Gerald Strauss (Bloomington: Indiana University Press, 1972).

An appeal to Christian antiquity had been a strong motif in reform movements throughout the Middle Ages. When the mendicant orders (the Franciscans, Dominicans, Carmelites, and Augustinians) were founded, their apologists could point to what they regarded as a more ancient form of the religious life than the cloister: namely, the circle of disciples around Jesus, who had abandoned their small properties in order to follow a leader who had nowhere to lay his head. The mendicants called such a life of poverty and itinerant preaching the *vita apostolica* (apostolic life). Who can forget the picture of Francis of Assisi stripping himself of his possessions in order to marry the widow, Lady Poverty, and to take for his cloister the highways of the world? *Nudus nudum Christum sequens.*

When Christian humanists suggested that scholars ought to return *ad fontes* (to the sources), to the oldest and best manuscripts of ancient Christian and pagan writings rather than rely, as earlier scholars had, on later translations or adaptations, they were stating as a philological principle a theme deeply embedded in Christian consciousness. The water of a stream is purest near its source; like a mountain spring, Christian antiquity represents a purer form of Christianity than its contemporary manifestations. If this is true, then the cry of Christian reformers must always be "back to the past," to the purer form of ancient Christianity that can serve as norm and inspiration for the reform of church and society in the present.

The Lutheran form of the appeal to the past rested on the conviction that many so-called ancient traditions of the Catholic Church were not ancient at all, but represented innovations introduced into Catholic life and thought at a later, often a much later, stage of the church's history. Like old English customs that cannot, on closer inspection, be traced back beyond the reign of Queen Victoria, the church promulgated customs and ideas as ancient that could not be traced in unbroken succession to a period earlier than, say, the pontificate of Gregory VII (r. 1073-85) or the codification of canon law by Gratian (d. ca. 1159) or the introduction of scholastic theology by Peter Lombard (d. 1160) — to mention three possible turning points suggested by different Protestant authors.

When the bishop of Carpentras, Jacopo Cardinal Sadoleto, accused Calvin and the reformers of Geneva of introducing innovations and novelties into the communities they reformed, Calvin turned Sadoleto's argument on its head.[3]

---

3. John Calvin, *Ioannis Calvini Opera Selecta,* ed. Peter Barth (Munich: Chr. Kaiser, 1926-59), 1:437-89. Sadoleto's text is printed in his *Opera quae extant omnia,* vol. 4 (Verona, 1737-38). For further discussion of this question, see David C. Steinmetz, "Luther and Calvin on Church and Tradition," in Steinmetz, *Luther in Context* (Bloomington: Indiana University Press, 1986), pp. 85-97. See also *John Calvin and Jacopo Sadoleto: A Reformation Debate,* ed. John C. Olin (New York: Harper and Row, 1966).

The Catholic claim to antiquity, argued Calvin, was a formal claim without material justification. The Catholic Church was riddled with innovations introduced over centuries of inattention and theological laxity. By submitting themselves to Scripture and the writings of the ancient fathers, the Protestant communities were purging themselves of such unwanted innovations and returning to a more ancient and therefore purer form of ecclesiastical life and thought. Luther, who seems to have read and admired Calvin's letter, was in fundamental agreement with its argument.[4]

It may be important to point out that Luther and Calvin did not think the church had died. There were undoubtedly some scattered sectarians who hinted darkly at the demise of true Christianity in the Middle Ages, but such a notion was repudiated by the larger bodies of Lutheran and Reformed Christians. God had remained faithful to his promise not to forsake the church. The gospel had been preached and heard by faithful souls from the time of the apostles until the present day, even in a church that in recent centuries had proven to be unreformed and resistant to change. If it was no longer obvious to the naked eye that the Church of Rome was still the body of Christ, one could nevertheless be assured that even this church contained *vestigia ecclesiae,* traces of the true church.[5]

The goal of the Reformers was not to supplant a dead or dying church with a new Christianity, as though God had written "Ichabod" over a moribund Christendom and repudiated his covenant. Their goal was a reformed Catholic Church, built upon the foundation of the prophets and apostles, purged of the medieval innovations that had distorted the gospel, subordinated to the authority of Scripture and the ancient Christian writers, and returned to what was best in the old church. As they saw it, it was this evangelical church, this reformed and chastened church, that was the church catholic. It was the innovators in Rome who could no longer pretend to be genuinely catholic and whose claim to be the custodians of a greater and unbroken tradition was patently false. What the Protestants thought they offered was a genuine antiquity, one that stretched back to Peter and Paul and not merely to Lombard and Gratian.

The slogan later generations of Protestants used to describe this reform was the battle cry *sola Scriptura,* "Scripture alone!"[6] While it is true that the re-

4. Though there are small differences between Luther and Calvin on this question, the similarities are far more important. See again Steinmetz, *Luther in Context,* pp. 85-97.

5. The standard translation of the *Institutes* is by Ford Lewis Battles, ed. John T. McNeill, in Library of Christian Classics, vols. 20-21 (Philadelphia: Westminster, 1960). On this question see John Calvin, *Institutes* 4.2.11.

6. See Anthony N. S. Lane, "*Sola Scriptura?* Making Sense of a Post-Reformation Slogan," in *A Pathway into the Holy Scripture,* ed. P. E. Satterwhite and David F. Wright (Grand Rapids: Eerdmans, 1994), pp. 297-327.

formers were at first optimistic that it would be possible to teach and preach a theology that was wholly biblical, they rarely intended to exclude theological sources that were nonbiblical. *Sola Scriptura* generally meant *prima Scriptura* (Scripture first), Scripture as the final source and norm by which all theological sources and arguments were to be judged, not Scripture as the sole source of theological wisdom.

For Melanchthon and Calvin, though less so for Luther, the Reformation was an argument almost as much over the writings of the early Christian Fathers as over the meaning of Scripture. Typical of the level of interest in early Christian authors, even among reformers who did not edit or translate ancient Christian writings, are Luther's marginal annotations on Augustine and Jerome and Calvin's marginal annotations on a Latin edition of Chrysostom.[7] Even internal Protestant controversies, like the bitter dispute over the Eucharist between John Calvin and the Lutheran theologian Tileman Hesshusen, often had a large patristic component in them.[8] In short, the Protestant appeal to antiquity included the early Christian writers as well as the Bible, even if the Protestant reformers felt that patristic teaching could not have the last word. What the Fathers taught should always be judged in the light of the clear and unchangeable teaching of Scripture. Still, when all was said and done, Luther and Calvin were optimistic that the greater weight of patristic teaching supported their reform or, at the very least, the greater weight of the teaching of the better Fathers. For his part Luther was content to leave Origen and Jerome, whose exegesis he mistrusted, to Erasmus, if he could have Augustine.

Reform

The Reformation was not a wholesale attack on Christian tradition, and Luther was not inclined to quarrel with every traditional doctrine taught by the late medieval Catholic Church. In the Smalcald Articles (1537) Luther confessed that his reform movement accepted the teaching of Nicea on the Trin-

---

7. Calvin's annotations have been particularly well studied. See Alexandre Ganoczy and Klaus Müller, *Calvins handschriftliche Annotationen zu Chrysostomus: Ein Beitrag zur Hermeneutik Calvins* (Wiesbaden, 1981). Cf. David C. Steinmetz, "Calvin and the Patristic Exegesis of Paul," in *The Bible in the Sixteenth Century,* Duke Monographs in Medieval and Renaissance Studies 11, ed. D. C. Steinmetz (Durham, N.C., and London: Duke University Press, 1990), pp. 100-118.

8. David C. Steinmetz, "Calvin and His Lutheran Critics," *Lutheran Quarterly* 4, no. 2 (summer 1990): 179-94.

ity and of Chalcedon on the two natures of Christ. He thought such teachings were true not because they were promulgated by general councils of the church and so were inspired by the Holy Spirit (as some Catholic theologians might have argued), but because the ancient councils had clarified the true meaning of Holy Scripture. Since Luther was convinced that the weight of sound exegesis supported the Fathers, he was as energetic in his rejection of the radical antitrinitarianism of the Protestant left as any conservative Catholic apologist. Luther differed with Rome over a long series of important theological issues, among them: penance, preaching, justification by faith, the meaning of baptism, and the mode of Christ's presence in the Eucharist. But he acknowledged that there were important issues on which they did not disagree at all. The medieval Catholic Church did not need to be recalled, corrected, and reformed on every point of doctrine. In the merciful providence of God, the Catholic Church had provided on some issues a constant witness to the truth. On such issues the Lutheran laity needed to be formed in the Christian faith as it had traditionally been taught, but not reformed from earlier errors.

There were, of course, some issues on which no agreement was possible. For example, while Luther honored Mary as the mother of the Lord (the *theotokos* or *Dei parens*) and as an outstanding example of faith, he was unwilling to accord her any honor as an intercessor for the church. She was not for him the sympathetic Queen of Heaven whose compassion softened the harsh judgments of her unsympathetic Son. Accordingly, he dropped the Ave Maria from the prayers that the Lutheran laity were taught. Mary did not, of course, disappear from the Lutheran Bible, and Conrad Porta, pastor of Eisleben, exalted the biblical image of Mary as a model for young girls in his *Jungfrawenspiegel* (1580).[9] But any hint that Mary should be regarded as intercessor or, even worse, *coredemptrix* was ruthlessly excised from Lutheran theology. No more prayers to Mary were authorized for women in childbirth, and no more catechetical instruction was offered in Marian devotion. A true Christian prays the Pater Noster but not the Ave Maria.

Luther also broke with medieval asceticism and the ethic that exalted virginity over chaste sexual practice in marriage. Lutheran laity were no longer instructed that a faithful monogamous marriage was an inferior state for a Christian (more of a compromise to accommodate human weakness than an ideal to which Christians should aspire) or that monastic life and rigorous ascetic practices were pleasing to God. One can take as an example of the new anti-ascetic

---

9. Conrad Porta, *Jungfrawenspiegel*, ed. facsimile of 1580, ed. Cornelia Niekus Moore (Bern: Peter Lang, 1990).

spirit the Lutheran reconsideration of the question of clerical marriage.[10] Although the ban on clerical marriage was total by the sixteenth century,[11] many clerics (how many is unclear) found themselves unable or unwilling to live up to the lofty rhetoric of clerical celibacy. The archbishop of York, Thomas Cardinal Wolsey, had an illegitimate son, Thomas Wynter, whose existence he did not deny. In central Europe clerics who found the celibate life too demanding were permitted to live in a sexual relationship with a housekeeper, contingent on the payment of an annual tax to the bishop.[12] Heinrich Bullinger, the Protestant reformer of Zürich, was the child of such an informal clerical family. Nevertheless, despite these arrangements being given a quasi-official sanction, the housekeeper was still regarded by the townspeople as the priest's whore. Canonically the priest and his unofficial wife were living in a state of mortal sin. In a particularly poignant exchange of documents, Huldrych Zwingli, who had slept with a young woman in a former parish, petitioned his ordinary, Bishop Hugo von Hohenlandenberg of Constance, for permission to marry, which was denied.[13] Zwingli was also secretly married to a widow, Anna Reinhart — as many people knew.[14]

Protestants attempted to correct the problem of clerical celibacy by denying the theoretical foundation on which it stood. Luther and his followers attacked the celibate ethic with its distinction between commands and counsels and its preference for virginity over matrimony. They insisted that celibacy was a charism, a gift given to some but denied to others, and therefore could not be made a general law. They authorized clerical marriage and encouraged the integration of the pastor into normal family life. In place of saints who were models

10. For a defense of celibacy against Protestant criticisms of the institution, see Johannes Eck, *Enchiridion locorum communium adversus Lutherum et alios hostes ecclesiae,* ed. Pierre Franekel, in *Corpus Catholicorum* 34 (Münster in Westfalen: Aschendorffsche Verlagsbuchhandlung, 1979), pp. 222-30. English translation by Ford Lewis Battles, *Enchiridion of Commonplaces against Luther and Other Enemies of the Church* (Grand Rapids: Baker, 1979).

11. The Second Lateran Council of 1139 pronounced the marriage of clerics in major orders invalid.

12. Steven E. Ozment, *The Reformation in the Cities* (New Haven: Yale University Press, 1975), pp. 58-61. Following Oskar Vasella, Ozment notes: "Clerical marriage would have been a great financial loss to the bishop of Constance."

13. Zwingli explains his brief affair with the daughter of a barber in Einsiedeln in a letter to Heinrich Utinger in Zürich dated December 5, 1518. See *Huldreich Zwinglis Sämtliche Werke,* vol. 7, ed. E. Egli, G. Finsler, and W. Köhler, Corpus Reformation 94 (Leipzig: M. Heinsius Nachfolger, 1911), pp. 110-13. The bishop himself was known to be intimate with the widow of the former burgomaster of Constance. See Cameron, *European Reformation* (Oxford: Clarendon, 1991), p. 44.

14. G. R. Potter, *Zwingli* (Cambridge: Cambridge University Press, 1976), pp. 78-81. Frau Reinhart had been Zwingli's concubine before their marriage. Their secret marriage was publicly announced before the birth of their first child.

of sexual self-denial and asceticism, the Protestants substituted the minister's family as a model of the Christian home.

There were, of course, difficulties with immediately implementing the new ideal of pastoral marriage. Upstanding middle-class families were not always willing to marry their daughters to former priests and permit them to inherit the beds so lately occupied by the priest's whore.[15] It was not uncommon for former priests and nuns to marry each other and for the children of such clerical families to intermarry as well. But the trend was, in any case, clear. The attack on the theoretical foundations of clerical celibacy allowed the Protestants to replace an off-again, on-again institution of clerical celibacy with a married order of ministers, whose marriage and family life were integral to their ministry. The Protestants ended what they regarded as the embarrassment of the erratic enforcement of clerical celibacy by abolishing the institution. The institution could no longer be maintained when the theological foundation that supported it was repudiated.

Continuities

However, the relation of the Lutheran movement to the medieval Catholic Church was not merely one of affirmation and denial. In many instances the Lutherans retained traditional practices and institutions but radically revised the underlying ideology. The pastoral office of preaching provides a sterling example of a traditional activity with a nontraditional intellectual foundation. What gave new force to the reconceived office of preaching for the Lutherans was Luther's new theology of the Word of God.

Luther's Reformation was not just a movement dedicated to the study of the Bible; it was dedicated to the spoken Word of God. It was not the Word of God written but the Word of God preached that formed the center of a renewed Christianity as early Protestants conceived it. When Heinrich Bullinger of Zürich wrote in the Second Helvetic Confession of 1566, "The preaching of the Word of God is the Word of God," he was speaking for a broad ecumenical front of early Protestantism, Lutheran as well as Reformed.[16] The words were

15. Even when the former priest's character was beyond reproach, many laity still regarded a married clergyman as something illegitimate and forbidden. The attitude lingered on even among people whose formal theological allegiance had shifted. Notorious in this respect was the attitude of Elizabeth I of England toward the spouses of married clergy, including the wife of Matthew Parker, her carefully selected archbishop of Canterbury.

16. *Bekenntnisschriften und Kirchenordnungen der nach Gottes Wort reformierten Kirche*, ed. Wilhelm Niesel (Zollikon-Zurich: Evangelischer Verlag, 1938), p. 223: "Praedicatio verbi Dei est verbum Dei."

Bullinger's, but the underlying theology was in substantial harmony with Luther's. Christianity is not, as both Thomas Müntzer and Luther asserted (though on different occasions and in different senses), a scribal religion, and the self-revelation of God is speech before it is text.

Luther's emphasis on the spoken word had, of course, some parallels in late medieval thought. Recent scholarship has shown how important was the spoken word in the rhetorical traditions of Italian civic humanism. The humanists understood that human beings are more than calculating reason, as scholastic theology seemed to them to assume. To be human is to have a will and emotions as well as an intellect. Many humanists, therefore, looked upon the spoken word as an instrument to move human beings, to inspire them to action, and thereby to shape public policy.[17] The mendicant orders, likewise, had always laid heavy emphasis on the spoken word in preaching and teaching. "Preach the Word" was as much a Dominican or Augustinian slogan as it was Lutheran or Reformed. While one ought not make too much of the relationship of early Protestantism to the mendicant orders, still a good number of early converts to Protestantism came from mendicant orders, including Robert Barnes, O.E.S.A.; Martin Bucer, O.P.; Bernardino Ochino, O.F.M.Cap.; John Bale, O.Carm.; and Conrad Pellikan, O.F.M.

Equally important as a late medieval parallel was the renewed emphasis on preaching in the free imperial cities. The laity in several late medieval cities in the Holy Roman Empire had laid aside funds to pay for a *Leutpriester,* a priest whose principal function was to preach on Sundays and feast days, leaving the ordinary liturgical services to the parochial clergy. The most famous *Leutpriester* in the sixteenth century was the preacher in Strasbourg, John Geiler of Kaysersberg, who died before the Reformation began.[18] Another famous *Leutpriester,* who subsequently identified himself with the Reformation, was the Swiss preacher Huldrych Zwingli. Like the humanists, these publicly funded preachers laid emphasis on the spoken word; like the mendicants, they laid emphasis on the spoken Word of God.

And yet there were differences. However important the preached Word was to the mendicants and the late medieval princes of the pulpit, it was still ancillary to the sacraments. The sermon was understood theologically as an invitation to baptism, penance, and Eucharist, where alone saving grace was dispensed. It was not the preacher in the pulpit, however eloquent, but the priest at

17. On the education of the orator, see Jean-Claude Margolin, *Humanism in Europe at the Time of the Renaissance,* trans. John Farthing (Durham, N.C.: Labyrinth Press, 1989), pp. 61-63.

18. For the career and thought of Geiler, see E. Jane Dempsey Douglass, *Justification in Late Medieval Preaching: A Study of John Geiler of Keisersberg,* Studies in Medieval Reformation and Thought 1 (Leiden: Brill, 1966).

the altar, however inarticulate, who stood at the center of medieval worship.[19] It was the Word joined to the elements of bread and wine and water through which God saved the faithful of every generation, not the words of preachers. The sermon moves sinners to the sacraments but is not itself a sacrament.

For Luther there was one means of grace, the voice of the living God; this voice once spoke by the prophets and apostles and now speaks again in the proclamation of the church. Preaching became for him a third sacrament, coordinate with baptism and the Eucharist and largely replacing the sacrament of penance. The power of the keys, the power to bind and loose from sin, was exercised through the preaching of the gospel. No sacramental power as such was thought by him to reside in ordination or in ecclesiastical offices. Office bearers were authorized by the Word they carried. They had no authority that was not the authority of the gospel they preached. It was through the preached Word that God justified sinners and pardoned sin. Even the sacraments of baptism and Eucharist were redefined as the visible Word of God.

In the face of this radical theology of the Word of God, the old hierarchical distinctions of *potestas ordinis* (power of order) and *potestas iurisdictionis* (power of jurisdiction) simply collapsed for Luther. There is no order higher than the order of the preacher of the Word of God; there is no jurisdiction greater than the jurisdiction exercised by the pastor of a local congregation. Apostolic succession is succession in apostolic teaching. Christians in the present are linked to the first generation of apostles, not by an unbroken succession of bishops, but by an unbroken succession of preachers of apostolic doctrine. Lutheran ministers are not priests forever after the order of Melchizedek. That is a priesthood that belongs to Christ alone. Lutheran ministers belong to an *ordo praedicatorum,* an order of preachers that stretches from the patriarchs to the present. For them it is the pulpit, not the altar, which is the throne of God, and the sermon, not the Eucharist, which is the ladder that links heaven and earth.

The Lutheran sermon was the principal instrument for the swift and effective reeducation of the laity; it augmented, supported, and reinforced the catechisms, pamphlets, and broadsides that poured from the evangelical presses. But the reconceived sermon was not regarded as mere instruction in faith and morals, however edifying. The sermon was never reducible to the sum of its teaching. What Luther had in mind was not a homily in the old sense but preaching as the *viva vox Dei* (living voice of God). Preachers have nothing to offer but human speech. However, through their voices, all too quickly stilled, God speaks an eternal Word that will never pass away. The sermon, as Luther

---

19. Geiler attempted to argue for the primacy of preaching, but without great success. See Douglass, pp. 82-91.

understood it, was a *Thettelwort,* or "deed word," rather than a *Heißelwort,* or "naming word." It does not merely call existing things by their correct names, like Adam naming all the beasts in Paradise; it calls new things into existence like God on the first day of creation. Preaching of the Word of God is never mere speech, any more than baptism is mere water or the Eucharist mere bread and wine. In preaching, as in the Eucharist, the operative word is *est* (is) and not *significat* (means); God is truly, not symbolically, present and active. The preacher does not merely point to a God who is distant; God is not distant but present in, with, and under the material elements of human language.

The pastor who absolves sinners from their sins in private confession is only exercising the preaching office in an individual rather than a corporate setting.[20] In both settings it is the promise of God, whether proclaimed from the pulpit or whispered in conversation, that binds and looses from sin. Of course, the pastor and only the pastor may exercise the power of the keys in public, through preaching, just as the pastor and only the pastor may preside at the Eucharist. However, any baptized Christian may exercise the power of the keys in private conversation, since all Christians have the right and obligation to bear God's Word of judgment and grace to each other. Luther is unwilling to make private confession a clerical monopoly, though he regards the confession of one's sins to a pastor a good and wholesome practice so long as it is not turned into a binding law (a position with which Calvin agrees).

Luther's Catechism

All three strategies — the reaffirmation, the denial, and the reinterpretation of earlier Christian tradition — are evident in Luther's catechetical writings. In 1529, after a visitation to parish churches that convinced Luther of the depth of the educational crisis facing him, he wrote a short catechism for use in both the home and local churches. Although catechetical instruction was nothing new in the history of the church, the development of printing technology in the late fifteenth century made it possible for catechetical manuals to be widely distributed to clergy and laity at a comparatively small cost. Over the forty years following the first printing of Luther's catechism, more than 100,000 copies were printed and sold. The catechism was eventually included in the *Book of Concord* as one of the fundamental confessional documents of the Lutheran churches.[21]

20. Luther's discussion of confession in the *Large Catechism* makes many of these points clear. *The Book of Concord,* pp. 457-61.

21. The *Small Catechism* can be found in *The Book of Concord,* pp. 337-56; the *Large Catechism,* pp. 357-461.

Luther's catechism was not the first to be written and published in German. The first German catechism, called *A Fruitful Mirror or Small Handbook for Christians*, was written in 1470 and revised in 1480 by the Observant Franciscan friar, Dietrich Kolde of Münster.[22] Kolde had written the book less as a manual of instruction for the young than as a handbook for mature Christians who were preparing themselves for the annual confession of their sins that must precede their obligatory participation in Easter Communion. It was a mirror, as the title suggests, into which Catholics could look for aid in an honest and informed self-examination. Kolde's catechism, like Luther's, was a popular manual. It went through nineteen editions in the fifteenth century and at least twenty-eight thereafter. It was also translated into several early modern vernacular languages. It may very well have been the single most popular catechism in late medieval Europe; it was certainly the most popular in German-speaking lands.

There are, of course, a number of formal similarities between the two catechisms. Both offer text and explanations of the creed, the Our Father, and the Ten Commandments. But Kolde offers a great deal more: the Ave Maria together with other Marian prayers and devotions (though without ascribing to her the title of *theotokos* and omitting the request for her intercession in the hour of death), five ecclesiastical rules, seven deadly sins, nine alien sins, six sins against the Holy Spirit, several open and mute sins, the great sins of the tongue, six conditions for forgiveness, seven signs of the state of grace, lessons on how to confess and hear Mass, seven works of corporal mercy, seven works of spiritual mercy, seven gifts of the Holy Spirit, seven points for daily reflection, nine conditions that lead to sin, three things that astonish the devil, five signs of a good Christian, reflections on how women should carry infants during pregnancy and how parents should rear their children as Christians, with some concluding considerations of the art of dying well.

Luther's difference from Kolde can easily be illustrated by considering what he says about confession. At first glance it may appear that Luther has kept, in unaltered form, the medieval sacrament of penance, commending the private confession of sins to one's pastor. On closer inspection, however, it becomes apparent that the old sacrament has not escaped significant alteration by Luther, since it rests for him on a new ideological foundation. Luther distinguishes two kinds of confession in the *Small Catechism* and three kinds in the *Large Catechism*. The two kinds, repeated in both catechisms, are secret confession to God

22. The English translation of *A Fruitful Mirror* is easily accessible in Denis Janz, *Three Reformation Catechisms: Catholic, Anabaptist, Lutheran* (New York and Toronto: Edwin Mellen Press, 1982), pp. 31-130.

264

and private confession to a pastor. The third kind, mentioned only in the *Large Catechism,* is confession to another Christian brother or sister. The absolutely fundamental and indispensable confession each Christian must make is to God alone. In such a confession Christians lament their particular sins and ask for a renewal of grace, as they do in general when they pray the Lord's Prayer. Confession in private to another Christian or to a pastor is not required, since Christians cannot be governed by any law in this matter and must use such confession voluntarily. At the same time, Luther deplores what he regards as the abuse of Christian freedom by some slovenly Christians (his actual term for them is "pigs") who never take advantage of the opportunity to confess their sins in private to their pastor.

Luther's formula for confession to a pastor or fellow Christian is fairly simple. It is not necessary to list all the sins one has committed since one's last confession or to indicate the number of times one has committed an offense and describe the circumstances of each. It is enough to confess generally that one is a sinner in constant need of God's grace and to provide a few specific examples of the kinds of sins one has in fact committed, especially the sins that trouble one's conscience. The obligation to recount one's sins in detail and to omit nothing turns what ought to be a joyous moment of absolution and reconciliation into a legal obligation that terrifies sinners. The best preparation Christians can make for confession is to reflect on the Ten Commandments and to reexamine the conduct of their lives in the light of each precept. If, after such a careful review, one is still unaware of any particular sin that should be confessed (a state of affairs Luther regarded as highly unlikely), it will still be sufficient for penitent Christians to offer only a general confession of their sins. Better that sinners make only a general confession than that they concoct sins they did not commit in order to satisfy their confessor. The confessor, after asking whether the penitent believes the promise of forgiveness in the gospel, should declare the penitent forgiven in the name of the Holy Trinity. The absolution will be effective not because the pastor shares a common priesthood with Christ, but because the Word of God binds and looses from sin.

Unlike Kolde, Luther did not regard his catechism primarily as a manual for penitents to prepare them for participation in the modified rite of confession he still retained. The catechism was rather a handbook of basic Christianity. It retained and continued the medieval tradition of the instruction of the laity in the creed, the Lord's Prayer, and the Ten Commandments, adding a section not found in Kolde on baptism and the Lord's Supper and omitting the Ave Maria. The *Small Catechism* represented what Luther regarded as the proper and essential knowledge for every Christian, stripped down to its bare fundamentals and elucidated clearly and concisely. In his *A Simple Way to Pray:*

For Master Peter the Barber (1535), Luther demonstrated how such a basic catechetical knowledge could provide the foundation for a rich life of prayer, not only for Peter Beskendorf the barber but also for Martin Luther himself.[23] In matters catechetical, all Christians remain beginners. As one cannot grow beyond Christ, so one cannot grow beyond the catechism. In the Christian life progress is made by clinging ever more tightly to the fundamentals.

Kolde, who died in 1515 in Cologne, never read Luther's catechism or had any reason to anticipate the religious and theological upheaval that would divide Catholic Europe in the decade after his death. But the teaching of his catechism on confession moves in a fundamentally different direction from Luther's. For example, Kolde was not satisfied to restrict the preparation of sinners prior to confession to a review of their lives in the light of the Ten Commandments, important as the Ten Commandments undoubtedly were. Kolde wanted penitents to consider as well the seven deadly sins, the six sins against the Holy Spirit, the sins of the tongue, the five ecclesiastical rules, and the nine alien sins. The need for detail derives from the nature of the sacrament itself. Penitents must list in detail the mortal sins they have committed since their last confession, because what is not confessed cannot be forgiven. Christians who want their sins pardoned must make a good, i.e., thorough and probing, confession of their faults. While God will not hold sinners accountable to confess sins they have genuinely forgotten, he will not forgive sins they have concealed. Detailed confession is not optional, as Luther later suggested, but obligatory for all Christians at least once a year. A good, i.e., effective, confession is priestly, detailed, and obligatory.

Kolde also warns his readers how important it is to find a competent confessor. It was unthinkable to him and his contemporaries that confession to a layperson could result in the pardon of one's mortal sins. Only persons who share in the priesthood of Christ through the sacrament of ordination have the authority to absolve people from sin. The power to absolve is conferred by ordination and not by baptism. Even the authorizing force of the gospel is not enough to sanction lay confession, if ordination by a bishop in apostolic succession is missing. Not every priest was authorized by his bishop to hear confession of every sin. There were what the late medieval church called "reserved sins," whose absolution lay beyond the competence of the ordinary parish priest. Adultery, for example, was reserved to the bishop to absolve by himself or by such deputies as he chose to authorize. Certain crimes against church

---

23. See in this connection *D. Martin Luther, Werke,* Kritische Gesamtausgabe 38 (Weimar: Hermann Bhlaus Nachfolger, 1912), "Eine einfultige weise zu beten fur enen guten Freund," pp. 351-73.

property, such as arson, could only be forgiven by the pope or his deputies. Kolde was therefore desperately concerned that penitents understand these limitations on the authority of the parochial clergy and make a good confession to a competent priest. Mortal sins absolved by a priest who had no authority over them remain unforgiven on the heads of the sinners who committed them.

While there is a good deal in Kolde's catechism with which Luther could agree and still other matters about which he would have been indifferent, it is nevertheless clear that the change of theological vision necessitated a change of penitential practice. Lutheran laity were still encouraged as they had always been while members of the old church to confess their sins to their pastor, three or four times a year, if possible. They were no longer required to detail their sins in confession or to worry whether their confessor was competent to absolve them. Moreover, they were permitted to confess their sins to each other and to offer to each other the Word of the gospel that binds and looses from sins. The new theology required the institution of new practices appropriate to it and the writing of new catechisms to explain both theology and practice to a laity formed in the old habits of thought and action. The Lutheran clergy affirmed the creed, denied the Ave Maria, and reinterpreted the keys. They taught the laity to do the same.

At the same time, it is important to remember that Luther was reluctant to specify the ideal shape of the Christian life in too great detail. He could even oppose the *imitatio Christi* of the later Middle Ages, noting sarcastically that a successful imitation would require Christians to be born of a virgin, have brown eyes, and walk on water. Such an imitation piety is the antithesis of what Luther regards as a proper theology of vocation, namely, his conviction that Christians are called to serve God in their own space and time and not in the space and time of the apostles. He was also passionately opposed to any attempt to turn the Bible into a hagiography, a Hebraic *Lives of the Saints* that offers perfect models to the aspiring. An afternoon spent reading and contemplating the dysfunctional families in Genesis and Judges should put an end forever to the elevation of the all-too-human characters of the Bible into the company of the morally unflawed. Luther confessed that he drew far more comfort from the failings of the biblical characters than from their virtues. If God could save heroic sinners like Jacob and Samson and David, he could certainly save less energetic sinners like Martin Luther.[24]

Perhaps even more important for understanding Luther's reluctance to spec-

---

24. For an example of Luther's preference for the failings of the biblical characters over their virtues, see my "Luther and Tamar," in *Luther, Faith, and Human Sexuality, Lutheran Theological Seminary Bulletin* 73, no. 1 (winter 1993): 3-15.

ify the form of the Christian life too narrowly is his conviction that the essential form of the Christian life is freedom. The old church had prescribed so many things narrowly by canons, rules, regulations, and anathemas that it had succeeded in turning the freedom of the gospel into a law. Christ is not Moses and the gospel is not a book of rules. There is no single pattern of true Christianity any more than there is a single pattern of human existence. Christians have been liberated through faith in Christ to live in love. Such freedom is not created by books of rules, and books of rules cannot nurture and sustain it. True Christians trust Christ for salvation rather than their fidelity in keeping fasts, going on pilgrimage, offering the corporal acts of mercy, or observing the days of holy obligation. Their good works are the spontaneous overflow of their lively confidence in God. Luther celebrated the diversity of the life of faith and resisted the efforts of canonists, old and new, to narrow and restrict what, in his view, God had created free and unbounded. Keeping a fast or breaking it may equally well be acts of Christian devotion. What matters is the faith from which the deed is done.

Results

Things do not always work out exactly as planned. The reeducation of Latin Christendom in a Christian faith and practice shaped by the theology of Luther was more difficult to achieve than early Lutherans anticipated. To begin with, other voices were raised in the Protestant camp that dissented from Luther, sometimes over minor matters like the celebration of a feast, sometimes over serious issues like the celebration of the Eucharist. Even dedicated Lutherans found themselves caught in fierce internal struggles between Philippists and Gnesio-Lutherans over the meaning of Luther's theological heritage. Moreover, Catholic theologians did not yield Scripture or the early Christian Fathers to the Protestants without a fight. Thomas de Vio Cardinal Cajetan, who had made a name for himself as a philosopher and interpreter of Thomas Aquinas, dropped his philosophical studies in order to write a series of biblical commentaries that would demonstrate to Protestants and Catholics alike that the literal sense of the Bible supports Catholic theology. Domingo de Soto at Salamanca and Ambrosius Catherinus Politus at Rome similarly attempted to show that Protestants had misread Paul.[25]

25. Domingo de Soto, O.P., *In Epistolam divi Pauli ad Romanos commentarii* (Antwerp, 1550), p. 5: "Quocirca non sola fide (ut falso ipsi praedicant) sed fide per charitatem operante iustificamur. . . ." Ambrosius Catherinus Politus, O.P., *Commentarius in Omnes divi Pauli et alias septem Canonicas Epistolas* (Venice, 1551), p. a2: "Nam si nostrae aetatis tractores spectemus (qui numerus hodie multus est) eorum longe maior pars haeretici sunt. . . ."

In spite of all obstacles to the re-formation of Catholic laity, Protestants, both Lutheran and Reformed, made measurable progress toward their goals. By midcentury a permanent self-perpetuating Protestant culture had developed. The older ex-Catholic leadership of former priests, nuns, friars, and monks was slowly replaced by a new leadership that had never attended Mass, much less said one, and by a laity that had never confessed its sins to a priest, gone on pilgrimage, invoked patron saints, made a binding vow, or purchased an indulgence. Monastic foundations like the cloisters at Riddagshausen, Wienhausen, and Gandersheim were no longer cloisters to them but schools for men or evangelical communities for women. By the end of the century the Protestants had not only transformed formerly Catholic universities like Rostock and Leipzig into centers of Protestant intellectual life, but had founded new universities like Helmstedt and Giessen that had no memory of a Catholic past.

While Protestants continued to write anti-Catholic polemics, their treatises lacked the passion and sense of betrayal of the polemics written by the first generation. Protestants were permanent outsiders with their own fixed institutions, parishes, confessions, catechisms, and settled sense of identity. They harbored no illusions about reunion and felt no twinges of nostalgia for a church that had never been their home. Unlike their grandparents, they cherished no hope for an evangelical reformation of the Catholic Church and settled into a mode of permanent opposition.[26] In all these respects the third generation of Protestants differed from the first. The Reformation began as an argument among Catholic insiders; it continued as an argument between Catholics and former Catholics until well past the middle of the century. The transformation of a movement led by former Catholics into a movement led by traditional Protestants took two generations to effect. Luther, Zwingli, Calvin, Hubmaier, Hooper, and Melanchthon were not Protestants in the way Voetius, Ames, Turrettini, Perkins, Wollebius, and Spener were. Indeed, the extent of the difference between them may prove in the end to be the best measurement of the success of their reform program.[27]

---

26. Richard A. Muller, in *Post-Reformation Reformed Dogmatics* (Grand Rapids: Baker, 1987), 1:15-52, argues that the discursive, polemical theology of the early Reformers, aimed at the reform of abuses in the life and thought of the medieval Catholic Church, was replaced by a more sophisticated, dialectical theology, aimed at protecting and establishing the Protestant churches.

27. Readers who would like to pursue these questions further are encouraged to read Euan Cameron, *The European Reformation* (Oxford: Oxford University Press, 1991); Eamon Duffy, *The Stripping of the Altars: Traditional Religion in England, 1400-1580* (New Haven: Yale University Press, 1992); Gerald Strauss, *Luther's House of Learning: Indoctrination of the Young in the German Reformation* (Baltimore and London: Johns Hopkins University Press, 1978); and *A Faithful Church: Issues in the History of Catechesis*, ed. John Westerhoff and O. C. Edwards (Wilton, Conn.: Morehouse-Barlow, 1981).

Zwingli and Reformed Practice

Lee Palmer Wandel

T he Reformation was forged in specific communities, first in German-speaking Europe, then in French- and Dutch-speaking Europe. Theologians and laity in small towns, in principalities, eventually in states such as England, Scotland, and the Netherlands worked, sometimes harmoniously but more often with friction, or even outright acrimony, to articulate and institute visions of true Christian belief and practice. The Protestant traditions that come down to us today are not the pure expression of a single theologian's vision but the product of negotiations with local communities and their practices, of adaptations to the specificities of Christianity as it was lived in particular places. They are the product of dialogues held throughout the century, traceable only in shadows in our sources, between those formally trained in theology and biblical scholarship — the pastors and preachers — and the laity, who brought to "Reformation" their own understandings of the nature of God, of Christ, and of the sort of life one lived in accord with God's will.

One community in particular became exemplary for others in the early years of the Reformation. In the 1520s, throughout southern Germany and Switzerland, those who held to the primacy of Scripture in determining the shape and practice of Christianity, that is, "evangelicals" as they called themselves, looked to Zürich for their ideal of Christian life and practice.[1] With less

1. In the early years of the Reformation, debates on where "authority" resided divided along lines that would eventually become "Protestants" and "Catholics." "Evangelicals," as they called themselves, called "Protestants" after 1529, accorded the text of the Bible, "Scripture," not exclusive but supreme authority in determining Christian doctrine and practice. Where human "custom" or "practice" differed from that which they understood Scripture to be describing, those customs and practices were rejected. Scripture was "God's Word," God's express com-

friction than others had encountered in Strasbourg, Augsburg, even Nuremberg, the reforming party worked with the town council to institute a Christian liturgy and ethic that held to the Word of God as understood in Zürich.[2] There all the rituals, the patterns of behavior, as well as the material culture of Christianity had been tested against the text of Scripture, each form, gesture, or implement compared with those described, often but fleetingly, in the narrative of Christ's life. And there, in the early 1520s, in public debates and before the town council, lived and spoken and taught Christianity was reformed to accord with God's will as the people of Zürich found it articulated in Scripture.

The Swiss reformer Huldrych Zwingli (1484-1531) lived his entire reforming career in Zürich. There in dialogue with magistrates, peasants, shoemakers, carpenters, as well as the other clergy in the town, Zwingli articulated "Reformed" Christianity: liturgy that returned to the early church for its form and shape; doctrine that was derived immediately from Scripture; a practice of Christianity self-consciously mimetic of the early church. It is difficult to recapture the dynamic of the Reformation in any town. Some voices are much harder to recover than others: theologians typically left behind a body of printed texts, while the laity of the communities in which they lived and worked remain largely silent in the sources, their effects on the theologians' formulations often discernible only in the direction of the theologians' polemics. In the following description of reformed practices in Zürich, we rely heavily upon Zwingli's words, his formulations. Although others are largely silent, we must remember that his views were not worked out in isolation. Zwingli's theology was dialogic: he came to formulate doctrine in Zürich sometimes in conversations, sometimes in conflict with others whose visions did not match his own. His understanding of baptism was developed in opposition to the Anabaptists, against whom he would assert infant baptism, though there was clear scriptural basis

---

mand for the human church. "Catholics" did not dispute the authority of Scripture, just its singularity, its isolation in evangelicals' treatment of it; Scripture was to be read in the context of "tradition," some fifteen hundred years of readers whose own interpretations informed Catholic understandings of the text, and with whose interpretations contemporary Catholic theologians held themselves to be in dialogue. Many evangelicals also looked to Swiss cantons for an ideal of political autonomy. See Thomas A. Brady, *Turning Swiss: Cities and Empire, 1450-1550* (Cambridge, 1985).

2. On the history of the Reformation in Zürich, see Ulrich Gäbler, *Huldrych Zwingli: His Life and Work,* trans. Ruth C. L. Gritsch (Philadelphia, 1983); Gottfried Locher, *Die Zwinglische Reformation im Rahmen der europäischen Kirchengeschichte* (Göttingen and Zürich, 1979); Robert Walton, *Zwingli's Theocracy* (Toronto, 1967); and most recently, chap. 2 in my *Voracious Idols and Violent Hands: Iconoclasm in Reformation Zurich, Strasbourg, and Basel* (Cambridge, 1994).

for adult baptism after "conversion."[3] Iconoclasts challenged Zwingli and the town council to recognize the specific effect of images in people's understanding of the nature of Christ.[4] His understanding of Communion was developed over time, within the social and religious dynamics of Zürich, in dialogue with friends such as Leo Jud, Johannes Oecolampad, and Martin Bucer, and in opposition to Luther. The Reformation in Zürich was forged in the specific social and political dynamics of the town, defined self-consciously over against other models of reformation forged elsewhere. In it were echoed many differing conceptions of Christian belief and practice, even as certain voices, Zwingli's especially, come through most clearly to us today. The vision of Reformed Christianity Zwingli delineated seems largely to have accorded with the spiritual needs of the people of Zürich: there are few traces of the sort of resistance the pastors in Strasbourg or Calvin in Geneva faced.

The reformation achieved in Zürich quickly became a model, a point of reference, for villages and towns, theologians and lay men and women, in part because the Reformed liturgy in Zürich broke more dramatically with medieval practice than the liturgy Luther and his affiliates instituted in Wittenberg.[5] The liturgy in Zürich was not altered in detail, but essentially re-formed: the movements of the minister, the vessels of the Eucharist, the location of baptism and Communion — gestures, patterns of behavior, objects, location — were self-consciously delineated anew to accord more precisely with the written text of Scripture, and in equally self-conscious repudiation of medieval practices. Perhaps even more important in contemporaries' eyes than the drama of the Reformation in Zürich, however, was the central place accorded the practice of Christianity — liturgy and ethics — in the formation of the Reformed community of Christians in Zürich and, by extension, in the formation of all Christian communities.

For Zwingli faith was *practiced* — that practice is what he called "worship"

3. On Zwingli's relations with the Anabaptists, see Locher, *Die Zwinglische Reformation,* chap. 13, for a summary of the scholarship to 1979; most recently, Mira Baumgartner, *Die Täufer und Zwingli: Eine Dokumentation* (Zürich, 1993). The Anabaptists came to form one boundary for Zwingli, and Luther another, for the scope of the difference he could accommodate in visions of reform. For Zwingli the Anabaptists — many of whom had been his close friends and associates in the early years of reformation in Zürich — threatened the community of Christians with fragmentation: their demand for purity and their enactment of exclusion meant the diminution of the Christian community to a community of the select. This dimension of their vision of reform led Zwingli, after some four years of negotiations, to repudiate his early friendships and to accept the use of force in the suppression of their group.

4. Wandel, *Voracious Idols,* chap. 2.

5. For a comparison of liturgical reforms, see Fritz Schmidt-Clausing, *Zwingli als Liturgiker: Eine liturgiegeschichtliche Untersuchung* (Göttingen, 1952).

(Gottesdienst). One's actions and one's belief could not be separated: the one did not exist autonomously of the other. Zwingli had been deeply influenced by the fourth-century Church Father Augustine, and his Neoplatonist conception of the nature of human beings. Following Augustine, Zwingli saw human nature in terms of a struggle between the spiritual and the physical, in which human nature was inevitably "drawn" to the physical world and struggled against its "seductions."[6] Those seductions were not narrowly sensual or sexual, but mental as well; one's human nature, one's existence as creature, as embodied, physical, led one to take up those images, metaphors, gestures — what one saw, touched, heard, and felt — in an effort to understand the nature of God, of Christ, of the Holy Spirit, and of the relationship between God and humankind. For Zwingli, as for Augustine, human thinking could struggle to be autonomous of its physical environment and of its own embodiment, yet the fact that the soul was embodied meant for both that human thinking, even about the nature of God, could never be free of its material conditions or its dependency upon material referents for any discussion or conception of the very nature of the invisible, infinite, intangible, and uncircumscribable God. Thus for Zwingli the "externals" — ceremonies, rituals, gestures, even architecture — could not be dismissed as unimportant. Unlike Luther, who held ceremonies and images to be *adiaphora,* extraneous to faith, Zwingli attended closely to what we might call the "culture of Christianity": the rituals, the media of expression, the patterns of behavior, and all the rich variety of physical forms — painted and sculpted images, ornately detailed liturgical objects, choir screens, crucifixes, albs, stoles, even the churches themselves.[7] Where those practices were wrongly formulated, wrongly conceived, they involved the weak in faith in a wrong theology, a wrong understanding of the nature of God. In instituting the Reformed liturgy in Zürich, he would attend closely to the location, the gestures, the implements, even how the minister was dressed, as well as stipulate precisely the words the minister and the congregation would speak.

There is considerable debate among historians how much "the common people," the laity, "understood" of the theology so vehemently debated in the sixteenth century. For Zwingli the very question itself is badly posed, its conceptual divisions misplaced: the knowledge of God and the formal study of theology were not to him the subject of study and its discipline of study, but two

6. For the following discussion of Zwingli's anthropology and ethics, see my *Always among Us: Images of the Poor in Zwingli's Zurich* (Cambridge, 1990), chap. 2; Gottfried Locher, *Zwingli's Thought: New Perspectives* (Leiden, 1981); Peter Stephens, *The Theology of Huldrych Zwingli* (Oxford, 1986), chap. 6.

7. Wandel, "The Reform of the Images: New Visualizations of the Christian Community at Zurich," *Archiv für Reformationsgeschichte* 80 (1989): 115-24.

distinct entities. Knowledge of God could come through the formal study of theology — as distinct from the formal study of Scripture — but for Zwingli, that study was not the best medium for increasing one's knowledge of God. Quite the contrary, the formal study of theology as it had been pursued in the schools — ungrounded, according to Zwingli, in close biblical study and isolated from the praxis of Christianity, ethics and liturgy — could not lead to the true knowledge of God. For Zwingli the knowledge of God derived from Scripture and was forged — tested and strengthened — in the praxis of faith. Worship — honoring God and his commandments — was not "mere ritual" but theology enacted, Christology lived.

With reformation in Zürich the practices of the medieval church were one by one brought under scrutiny, evaluated against the text of Scripture, and rejected or reformed, their purpose and place carefully articulated in sermon and law. Forbidden were all processions, including those held on Palm Sunday, with the "Palm ass" (Palmesel), and on Corpus Christi, both long popular; the sale of or belief in indulgences and their particular system of penance; monstrances which enshrined the host, itself having become more reliclike in people's devotions. The number of holy days was reduced from some two hundred to less than one hundred.[8] Following the teaching of evangelical theology, the Zürich town council reduced the number of sacraments from the medieval seven to two: baptism, performed within days of the birth of each child, and Communion, celebrated four times a year at Christmas, Easter, Pentecost, and "Autumn."[9] So, too, education was re-formed: formal education in the languages and text of Scripture began in youth and could continue throughout life for those men who wished to pursue an ever deeper understanding of God's Word. The reformed practice of Christianity was to encompass as well the conduct of the members of the community, which the town council regulated. The conduct of the poorer members of the Christian community — whose outward physical condition most accurately represented humanity's spiritual poverty before God — was to provide a model of Christian ethics. The conduct of married couples, also regulated by the town council, provided another model: of Christian fidelity and companionship.

8. Reformed holy days included all Sundays; Christmas; Saint Stephen's Day (the first martyr of the Christian church, December 26); Easter and Easter Monday; Pentecost and Pentecost Monday; All Saints' Day (November 1), which became Twelve Commandments' Day; Circumcision Day; Ascension Day; Candlemas (February 2); Annunciation Day; Mary's Ascension Day (August 15); John the Baptist's Day (June 24); Mary Magdalene Day (July 22); and for a time, Saints Felix and Regula Day (September 11). See Heinrich Bullingers Reformationsgeschichte, ed. J. J. Hottinger and H. H. Vögeli, vol. 1 (Frauenfeld, 1838) (hereafter B), p. 328.

9. Gäbler, p. 106.

While Luther looked to his catechism for the formation of the faithful, Zwingli's understanding of human nature led him to encompass more in his conception of "formation." If we look at what the "practice" of Christianity encompassed in sixteenth-century Zürich, we see that it drew upon a broad range of media — the preached word, the written word, gestures, and printed images — and comprised rituals as well as institutions, ethics as well as liturgy. The "education" in theology and the "formation" of faith encompassed much of public life in Zürich and a good deal of private life as well. Christians were educated in *environments:* of words written and spoken, of rituals, and of patterns of behavior. Throughout Zürich in the 1520s and 1530s Scripture permeated conversations. In legislation behaviors were regulated for their adherence to Christian ethics. In Zürich "worship" encompassed not merely the liturgy, but ethics: both were the praxis of faith, at once affirming and strengthening it, and forming it, educating it. As we shall see more fully, the Christians of Zürich grew to maturity and practiced their faith surrounded by the sound of Scripture, its mimesis in the gestures of their minister and the forms of their liturgy, and the enactment of its ethical mandates in the conduct of their neighbors.

Any discussion of that education must break apart an integrated environment of words, acts, and images. The following, therefore, is organized to recapture something of the *process* of that education. We begin with baptism, which marked the entry of each human being into the Christian community. With baptism an individual was initiated into what are here called *environments*, in order to capture how the Word of God permeated life in sixteenth-century Zürich, and to recall that every Christian, in entering a church to worship, found himself or herself within a specific visual environment of architecture, whitewashed walls, and carefully chosen liturgical objects. Christians, in other words, were educated verbally and visually throughout their lives and throughout the town of Zürich. Those environments are divided into the place of worship, where the infant would be brought for his or her introduction to Christianity; the Word of God, which was printed, preached, read aloud, and studied; and patterns of behavior, or ethics, in which Scripture was enacted, made visible in manner, gesture, conduct within the community. We conclude with Communion, the proper reception of which, for Zwingli, was the culmination of the formation of Christian faith. This still constitutes a division, though one, I hope, that does less violence to the complexity of "formation" in sixteenth-century Zürich. Lost nonetheless are the visual dimensions of preaching and reading, the complex of visual, aural, and tactile experience in the places of worship, and the visual and aural dimensions of ethical behavior — its mimesis and its invitation to mimesis. We cannot but disrupt the rhythms of that education, so familiar to the people of Zürich, which, over time, would have become integrated into the rhythms of daily life. We begin with baptism, the initiation into that education.

Baptism: Initiation into the Community of Christians

Zwingli preserved two sacraments[10] of the medieval seven: baptism and Communion. The first ritual marked each person's individual entrance into the community of Christians. As Zwingli would stipulate so forcefully in his debates with the Anabaptists, baptism was a rite of initiation. For Zwingli baptism did not itself save a person — salvation could come to anyone in the freedom of God's will. Baptism placed the individual within the boundaries of a community defined by its ethics and its practices, as well as its theology. In the medieval tradition baptism made one a Christian; in Zwingli's Zürich God made one a Christian, but baptism made one a member of a community of Christians, in which one could become stronger in faith and clearer in spiritual understanding. Each member of the congregation participated in baptism individually once, at center as recipient, and then throughout his or her life collectively with all those who had been baptized, as witness and as guarantor for the community. It was a rite of initiation, which reaffirmed the boundaries and the obligations of the community's membership.

The sacrament of baptism was reformed in 1525. On August 10 Ulrich Aberli was baptized in the Grossmünster, in German, with simple water, and "without oaths, salt, blessed liquids, crosses, or chrism."[11] He was baptized as a recently born infant, in church, not at home, as Anabaptists had begun to practice.[12] Zwingli's radically simplified service represented to the congregation key aspects

---

10. "It was only with reluctance that Zwingli used the term [sacrament], because it is foreign to the Bible, and because it is saddled with the Roman concept of grace. . . . But for ecumenical and apologetic reasons he accepts the traditional concept, and takes up a widely-recognized summary of Augustine's sacramental doctrine: 'A Sacrament is a sign of a sacred thing.' Zwingli explains immediately: 'I believe the sacrament to be a sign of a sacred thing, that is, of effected grace.'" Locher, "The Characteristic Features of Zwingli's Theology in Comparison with Luther and Calvin," in *Zwingli's Thought*, pp. 214-15.

11. B, p. 112.

12. Anabaptists were distinguished by their claim that baptism was an adult ritual, for those who chose voluntarily to live the "true Christian life," a life that did not accord with Zwingli's understanding of a "true Christian life." For examples of the Zürich magistracy's efforts to ensure infant baptism, see, for example, *Aktensammlung zur Geschichte der Zürcher Reformation*, ed. Emil Egli (Zürich, 1879; reprint, Nieuwkoop, 1973) (hereafter EAk), documents 566, 618, 621, 622, and 982 (all references in EAk are to document numbers). For baptism in church, not in the home, see EAk 632.

of his conception of the Christian community: its obligations, its agency in the formation of faith, its inclusiveness and diversity.[13] The pastor opened by invoking God's help. His first words to the congregation were a request for someone to take responsibility: "Do you wish to have this child baptized in the baptism of our Lord Jesus Christ?" The parents then held the child while the pastor spoke of Christ's singular role as Savior. Then followed a prayer intimating something of the dynamic Zwingli envisioned between the congregation and individual faith: "Therefore let us pray to God on behalf of this child for faith and that the outward baptism becomes internal through the Holy Spirit and this grace-rich water *(gnadrychen wasser)."* A second prayer narrating God's interventions in the story of human damnation followed on this one. And then the pastor read Mark 10:13-16: "Let the children come to me, do not hinder them; for to such belongs the kingdom of God." Children belonged to that Christian community, even as it took on the responsibilities of their proper care: "so we will, as much as we are able [*mögend*], bring him this child, that is: with baptism, take up this child in his community and give him [the child] the sign of the bond and of the people of God." The pastor then reminded the congregation that in baptism they had promised to help the child live a godly life. Only after the pastor's representation of divine agency in human life, of the importance of people of faith to that agency, and these promises, was the child baptized "in the name of the Father, the Son, and the Holy Ghost." The final image presented to the congregation was the child before them at the last judgment.

The Place of Worship

Baptism marked each person's first entry into the church. It was, in other words, also the introduction into a complex environment of images, words, and modes of behavior. Education took *place.* It occurred within specific material contexts — the differing interiors of the three churches in Zürich the laity used. Zwingli preached in the Grossmünster, the main church of the town, founded by Charlemagne on the relics of the town's earliest martyrs, Felix and Regula. Second in size and age was the Fraumünster, in which a number of guilds and artisanal confraternities had endowed altars and masses — in which they had invested and felt themselves to have a place to worship. The oldest and smallest parish church in Zürich was Saint Peter's.

---

13. *Huldreich Zwinglis Sämtliche Werke* (hereafter Z), vol. 4, ed. Emil Egli, Georg Finsler, Walther Köhler, and Oskar Farner (Leipzig, 1927), Corpus Reformatorum (hereafter CR), 91:680-83.

That material context was important enough to some of the people of Zürich that they risked their lives to alter it to accord with God's Word. By the time the Zürich town council instituted the reformed sacraments of baptism and Communion, the churches of Zürich had been "cleansed" of their "images": the altars, the stone sacrament houses and sculptures had been smashed into paving stones; the elaborately carved multiple-winged retables, the sculpted images, the carved figures mounted on columns, the wooden crucifixes had been broken into wood for the poor; the gold and silver liturgical implements and candlesticks had been melted down for their precious metals, and their gemstones were sold; the murals had been painted over; the interiors whitewashed.[14] The sacraments were set in interiors free of color, free of graphic, painted, or sculpted form; Communion took place at a simple table, using crude serving vessels;[15] children were baptized in a simple font; and by the end of the 1520s hymns were no longer accompanied by the rich tones of the organ. The sermon, the liturgies of baptism and Communion, communal prayer and worship took place within a space whose visual content had been radically altered: no colors distracted, no sculptures gave specific form to the narratives of the Gospel, no altars brought resonances of sacrifice and death to the Communion — the walls were white, silent of their older presences, and returning the eyes of the congregation to their pastor and their neighbors, the "true images of God."

The "Word"

The education of each Christian took place in an environment of words. In the Reformation the Word of God came alive. The text of Scripture was translated and published, in Zürich from the German New Testament in 1524 to the full Bible of 1531.[16] It was published in editions of varying quality. Froschauer's magnificent edition of 1531, with its woodcuts by Hans Holbein, or the Luther Bibles with their hand-colored woodcuts by Lucas Cranach were at one end of spectrum. At the other were the editions crudely illustrated, printed on coarse paper, unbound, yet offering to those much poorer the same texts, the same German translations. The published text was read, most often aloud, in homes

---

14. For a fuller description both of the interiors of the churches of Zürich and of the specific acts of iconoclasm, see *Voracious Idols*, chap. 2.

15. B, p. 367.

16. There is considerable dispute about how much of Luther's translation the Zürich Bible "used." See Locher, *Die Zwinglische Reformation*, pp. 162-63.

and workplaces. Jesus' words were quoted, his acts cited. The passages of the four Gospels and the Pauline Epistles permeated the conversations of those who called themselves "evangelicals." Pamphlets by artisans such as Utz Eckstein in Zürich drew comfortably upon a broad range of scriptural references.[17] Christians in towns throughout the empire could hear Scripture quoted in daily conversation, in the home, in the workplace.

The most dramatic and important medium for the formation of faith of literate and illiterate, rich and poor, man and woman, parent and child was, however, preaching.[18] Children probably received their earliest education from the sermons they heard accompanying their parents to church from infancy on. In Zürich the Word of God was preached in all the churches, to the full congregation on Fridays as well as Sundays and all holy days,[19] and to any who were interested on other days of the week as well. Zwingli, Jud, Engelhard, and later, Bullinger, as well as dozens of preachers throughout the countryside, preached week after week, each in his church.[20] In Zürich the pastors looked to the Old Testament prophets for their inspiration, their austere black scholars' robes contrasting with the colorful priests' albs, stoles, and robes, their manner of delivery "biblical" rather than "classical." Each week parents as well as children would stand or, if they brought their own stools, sit in the church and listen to sermons of varying length.

The "Word of God" became aural as it had not been for a millennium. No longer merely the point of departure for sermons, it became the centerpiece and substance of sermons.[21] Here was no "Bible," no text, but "the

17. Miriam Usher Chrisman, *Conflicting Visions of Reform: German Lay Propaganda Pamphlets, 1519-1530* (Atlantic Highlands, N.J., 1995).

18. By all accounts, preaching was *the* mode of the Reformation — more than images, more than songs, more than any other cultural medium or mode of expression, sermons carried people, moved them, educated them in the visions of reformation so many different preachers, whether clerical or lay, aristocratic or artisan, were articulating. Preaching was the first demand of those peasants and artisans who rebelled against their spiritual and secular lords in 1525, setting off the largest revolt in European history. In Zürich, on January 1, 1519, Zwingli began his first sermon as an explication of the text of the Gospel of Matthew. In Zürich the laity did not need to demand an evangelical preacher who would give them "the true Word of God"; they had him from the start.

19. For a list of holy days, see n. 8.

20. For a list of the clergy in Zürich in 1525, see EAk 889. For lists of clergy, both Catholic and Reformed, in the canton as well as the town, who attended the First Synod on April 21, 1528, see EAk 1391. For a list of preachers in the canton of Zürich, 1532-80, see Bruce Gordon, *Clerical Discipline and the Rural Reformation: The Synod in Zurich, 1532-1580*, Zürcher Beiträge zur Reformationsgeschichte 16 (New York: Peter Lang, 1992), chap. 6.

21. Cf. John O'Malley, *Religious Culture in the Sixteenth Century: Preaching, Rhetoric, Spirituality, and Reform* (Brookfield, Vt., 1993), chaps. 3-5.

Word": God speaking in his Son's embodied voice and actions and through his Son's disciples to humanity. As that "Word" was preached, it acquired sound: it was heard through human voices by living communities of those who gathered as "the faithful," who identified themselves as those who believed the content of the speaking. Indeed, for Zwingli only the faithful *could* hear the true content of this "external Word," the read or preached Word of God — that "Word" was subject to "that word the heavenly Father preaches within our hearts."[22] In keeping with the radical freedom he accorded the working of the Holy Spirit, Zwingli held that preaching could not bring about faith nor could the "external Word," the aural experience of the text of Scripture, effect faith. It could and did help to form faith, however, to educate people in God's will.

The "Word of God" was preached: in each sermon the preacher read from the text of Scripture, then explicated it. Indeed, "Reformation" meant that only the "Word of God" might be preached. In Zürich the first formal step toward the reform of all Christian practices, taken at the end of the First Disputation in January 1523, was the town council's institution of the principle of scriptural authority.[23] Scripture was to be the authority for determining true and authentic Christian doctrine and practice. The second major step occurred in the wake of the Second Disputation in October 1523, when the town council held the Mass and images to the test of Scripture, and began what would be continuing efforts to assure the true representation of Scripture. All pastors were to preach "the holy Gospel clearly and truly according to the spirit of God":[24] "Take care that God's Word is faithfully preached among you . . . and when you see how this alone brings glory to God and the salvation of souls, then further it, regardless of what this one or that one may say. For the Word of God makes you pious, God-fearing people."[25]

It is harder to recapture the experience of those sermons than of any other aspect of Christian practice in the sixteenth century or earlier. We have the texts

22. "Quod eo verbo, quod celestis pater in cordibus nostris predicat." Z, vol. 3, ed. Emil Egli, Georg Finsler, and Walther Köhler (Leipzig, 1914) (CR 90), p. 263.

23. "All people's priests, pastors, and preachers should preach in their town, land, and domains nothing other than what they may prove with the holy Gospel or otherwise with right Holy Writ" (EAk 327).

24. EAk 436. For later efforts to call preachers back to the true Word of God, see, for example, EAk 1536. In October 1532 the Zürich town council issued yet another mandate for the "restitution and improvement of certain deformations and abuses now committed by the servants of the Word of God" (EAk 1899).

25. Zwingli, "A Faithful and Solemn Exhortation to the Swiss Confederates," quoted in Locher, "In Spirit and in Truth: How Worship in Changed at the Reformation," in *Zwingli's Thought*, p. 4.

of some of Zwingli's sermons,[26] but those texts were probably not verbatim records of what was preached — they may be based upon notes that others took during the sermon or they may be later versions of a text that had been preached, revised, lengthened, expanded, altered in any number of ways. Those texts, as any who has seen more than one performance of any play or oration knows, only give clues to the performance itself: where were the inflections, the pauses, the thundering emphases, where the exultant facial expressions, where the head bowed, where the hands outstretched in supplication or raised in invocation? Very little is known about the preaching of others than Zwingli. Heinrich Bullinger, Zwingli's friend and successor in Zürich, offers us a glimpse of Zwingli's own style of preaching, a fleeting insight into one of the most charismatic and effective preachers of the age of preachers: "In his sermons he was most eloquent (*flyssig*), simple, and understandable, so that many heard him willingly, and there was a great rush of people to his sermons. . . . His speech was graceful and sweet. For he spoke idiomatically and was unwilling to use the usual pious chatter, the confusion thrown down from the pulpit, or unnecessary words."[27] And its effect: "There was soon a rush of all sorts of people, in particular the common man, to these evangelical sermons of Zwingli's, in which he praised God the Father, and taught all people to place their trust in God's Son, Jesus Christ, as the single Savior."[28]

When Zwingli took up his post as lay priest in Zürich in January 1519, he captured the attention of a new congregation by breaking the traditional order of sermons, which had followed specific texts of Scripture set to specific days in the liturgical year. He began with the first words of the first Gospel, Matthew, which he then explicated, continuing through the Gospel to its end. In the weeks that followed he moved in this same way through Acts, then the epistles to Timothy.[29] He taught his congregation to hear the words of Scripture, to hear the "words of God," as he would call them again and again, not excerpted to fit a particular time of year or in snippets, but as texts, narratives, whose meaning one worked to discern and whose meaning pertained to the conduct of daily life. "Scripture," the written Word, became the "gospel," the spoken

26. "We do not possess a single manuscript of Zwingli's sermons. He always spoke extempory, and did so daily throughout the years. The writings that have come down to us are mostly in Latin (used as a form of shorthand) and only partially fashioned. A series of special sermons, which he developed and published by request, grew into doctrinal writings" (Locher, "In Spirit," p. 9).

27. B, p. 306. When Carlstadt visited Zürich, by contrast, many found his speech unintelligible (EAk 2002).

28. B, p. 12.

29. Bullinger describes what Zwingli preached his first four years in Zürich (B, p. 51).

Word.[30] It acquired a new kind of effect, a theatrical presence, as its very words were spoken, *performed*. As people could hear Christ speaking, they were confronted much more forcefully with the content of his ethical imperatives and his descriptions of Christian behavior.

Zwingli, himself a gifted preacher, understood well the efficacy of preaching. He sought first to achieve the freedom to preach the text of Scripture, then to control how that preaching was done and toward what ends. In his sermon "The Shepherd," delivered at the Second Disputation and published in March 1524, Zwingli outlined what he believed to be the responsibilities of the preacher to his congregation: the care of his "flock," for acting as a "true shepherd" meant preaching the true Word of God, seeking in deed and in word to teach his flock how to live by the two commandments of Christ (to love God above all others and to love others as oneself), and then leading them to maintain that life.[31] In 1528 the town council instituted the synod, which would oversee not only the content of the sermons of all preachers in the canton, but the orthodoxy of their liturgical practices and the propriety of their conduct of their public and private lives.[32]

All children would hear preaching. In the Reformation in Zürich, all formal and public education, primarily of boys but also of girls, was turned to the purpose of teaching children to read Scripture.[33] This formal education was reformed more slowly than other practices. When the Latin master at the Grossmünster died in 1525, the town council gave his authority over the organization of schooling to Zwingli, who began to reconfigure the process of education along the lines of humanist biblical scholarship: the boys were to be in-

30. Cf. Marjorie O'Rourke Boyle, *Erasmus on Language and Method in Theology* (Toronto, 1977).

31. "Der Hirt," in Z, 3:1-68. On June 30, 1530, Zwingli published a second treatise, "Concerning the Preaching Office," in response to the preaching of Anabaptists. In it he was more concerned with the abuse of the preacher's authority within his congregation than with detailing further the nature of the office and its responsibilities. Like Luther, he was confronted with two "abuses" he had helped to engender: the great autonomy and authority of preachers in the early years of the Reformation and the singular authority of Scripture, which Zwingli had called for, led to (1) individual preachers inviting their communities to rebel against all authority, including the magistracy of Zürich, which supported Zwingli's vision of reformation, and (2) these preachers finding their authority in their differing readings of Scripture. See "Von dem Predigtamt," in Z, 4:369-433.

32. EAk 1391, 1714, 1757, 1899, 1941. For accounts of sermons the town council found heterodox, see, for example, EAk 938. On the synods in Zürich, see Gordon, *Clerical Discipline and the Rural Reformation*.

33. The magistracy sought to ensure the schoolmaster's financial autonomy in order to protect this primary responsibility; EAk 576b.

structed in Christian ethics and in those languages that would enable them to read Scripture, Latin first, then Greek, and when they had mastered these two languages, Hebrew, the most difficult of all.[34] One of his first acts was to hire the humanist scholar of Greek and Hebrew, Jakob Ceporinus, to teach those languages in Zürich. According to Zwingli, the school had two goals: "doctrine and discipline."[35] The German schoolmaster was to instruct the youngest children in prayer and the faith every Saturday and to take to church those whose parents did not do it themselves. The Latin schoolmaster was to take those youths old enough to study Latin to the Friday sermons, where the chancel was to be made free for them, that they might not be distracted from closely hearing the Word of God.[36]

It was not until 1532, however, that the magistracy formally reorganized education in Zürich.[37] The students were to use their time efficiently; when the bell struck, they were to begin immediately to read and to listen, until the bell struck again an hour later. The day began with the Lord's Prayer and ended with a psalm; on Tuesday, Thursday, and Saturday the Carmina was to be sung at the end of the day. There were to be two hours of instruction before midday, from six to seven and from eight to nine, and a total of three after midday, from noon to one, from one to two, and from three to four. On Fridays the second, third, and fourth "orders" were to listen to the sermon in the church. Those students who had already studied Latin (that is, those who had already received some instruction) were to read solely in Latin; those who would not, who spoke incorrectly or ungrammatically, were to be punished. The curriculum was designed to move students from the most rudimentary reading and writing skills in Latin, the first order, to fluency and mastery, the fourth order. These levels were not so much connected to a particular age as to proficiency in a particular level of linguistic mastery.

For a small percentage of boys in Zürich,[38] the end point of their formal

34. "By reorganizing the curriculum of the Latin school, Zwingli was able to institutionalize Bible exegesis, which had been carried on only incidentally and cursorily heretofore in Zurich" (Gäbler, p. 100). Zwingli outlined his ideal curriculum in 1523 in "Quo pacto ingenui adolescentes formandi sunt," Z, vol. 2, ed. Emil Egli and Georg Finsler (Leipzig, 1908), pp. 526-51, which he translated and published in 1526 as "Wie man die Jugend in guten Sitten und christlicher Zurcht erziehen und lehren soll," in Z, vol. 5, ed. Emil Egli, Georg Finsler, Walther Köhler, Oskar Farner, Fritz Blanke, and Leonhard von Muralt (Leipzig, 1934), pp. 427-47.

35. EAk 757 (June 1525). For one of his budget proposals, see EAk 1585 (June 1529), in which he speaks explicitly of support for poor students.

36. EAk 1780.

37. For the following description, see EAk 1896.

38. Only a minority of children received formal education in Zürich, as elsewhere, and the education of boys received the attention of reformers. Gender and choice of career affected

education was the *Prophezei,* or Prophecy, a group of advanced students, clergy, and interested adult laymen, which Zwingli organized in 1525. The Prophecy's sole purpose was the study of the Bible, through readings of a single text in all three biblical languages, Latin, Greek, and Hebrew.[39] According to chronicler Johannes Kessler, it met at 8:00 A.M. every day but Fridays (market days) and Sundays in the chancel of the Grossmünster.[40] The scholars stood, each with his own Bible before him, at a lectern *(Gestuhl)* ordered for that purpose. They opened always with a prayer for guidance in their reading and interpretation. Usually Caspar Megander opened the study of the day with a text from the Latin Vulgate.[41] Then the Hebrew scholar — first Ceporinus, then, after his death, Conrad Pellikan — would read the text from the Hebrew Bible, clarifying in Latin the meaning of particular words.[42] Then Zwingli would read the Greek text from the Septuagint and translate it into Latin, comparing the two as he read and calling attention to nuances in the Greek, dimensions of meaning that were not explicit. After these readings, usually Jud, but sometimes Zwingli, would clarify in "good German" the opacities of language and the ambiguities of meaning in the text.[43] Thus these scholars and students applied their ever deepening knowledge of the languages to their understanding of the text of Scripture. At the end of each day's study, Zwingli would preach in German to those who had assembled in the church while the scholars worked.[44]

Scripture permeated life in Zürich. Not only did it serve as the sole authority in determination of questions of doctrine, liturgy, and ethics. It was the substance of each week's sermons: at once the central text and the focus for consid-

---

both access to certain forms of education and the content of that education. Women seem to have had less access to the open and formal biblical education of the *Prophezei* than did men. We have but a brief passing reference to women's education in Zürich, and no evidence from which to determine how much or how many women participated in biblical study. Artisans were far less likely to pursue the sort of humanist or university education in languages and scriptural interpretation than were the children of clergy, merchants, urban patriciates, or other prosperous town dwellers. Those intended for the clergy would pursue a much deeper knowledge of biblical languages than those who might study Latin as a part of their training for urban and court professions.

39. For a more detailed description of the activity of the *Prophezei,* see Locher, *Die Zwinglische Reformation,* pp. 161-63, and "In Spirit," pp. 27-30.

40. For this and the following description of the study of biblical languages, see *Johannes Kesslers Sabbata,* ed. Emil Egli and Rudolf Schoch, Historische Verein des Kantons St. Gallen (Saint Gall, 1902), pp. 203-4.

41. *Johannes Kesslers Sabbata,* p. 203.

42. Ceporinus died in March 1525. Pellikan was appointed on April 21, 1526, to teach Hebrew (EAk 955).

43. The term is Kessler's; see *Johannes Kesslers Sabbata,* p. 204.

44. Locher, "In Spirit," p. 29.

eration in pursuit of its true meaning. Copies of the Bible were to be found in homes and workplaces; passages from Scripture might be read aloud before a family or among artisans. Conversations referred to specific texts of Scripture, by way of authority or exemplar. Legislation invoked Scripture as its guide in the formulation of policy. Scripture was the centerpiece of intellectual life in Zürich: the acquisition of the languages necessary for the most informed and nuanced reading of the texts was merely the beginning of a lifelong education, the purpose of which was the pursuit of true understanding of Scripture. The Word of God was the clearest revelation of God's will; the better one understood that text, the more closely one might discern God's will.

Patterning the Christian Life

At the same time they were first acquiring the knowledge of biblical languages, then applying that knowledge to a close reading of the texts of Scripture, those students, from first order to fourth, were learning moderation, temperance, obedience, and humility — the virtues of the pious Christian. Schoolmasters taught, in other words, not only Latin, Greek, then Hebrew, but also what it was to be modest, humble, and to love one's neighbor. Those students who would not or could not learn such conduct — the disobedient and truculent — were to be expelled.

Scripture was to be enacted: it was to be made visible in the conduct of the faithful, in the very patterns of their daily conduct, in their relations with one another, in their manner, demeanor, dress. In the 1520s the Zürich town council, citing Scripture, defined the proper conduct toward those less fortunate, the proper conduct of the poor, and the proper conduct of spouses.[45] All Christians were to conduct themselves modestly, to dress modestly — no jewelry, no elaborate collars, no expensive cloths — to live peaceably together. No Christian gambled, played cards, had commerce with prostitutes, behaved arrogantly or belligerently. Christian conduct, in other words, encompassed not only the nature of relations between human beings — the ideal of Christian brotherly love — but also how one appeared, the outward manifestations of humility, modesty, devotion: manner, gesture, demeanor, dress, livelihood, and the use of one's time.

For Zwingli "worship" encompassed not only liturgy, those formal rituals

45. The marriage court was established May 10, 1525 (EAk 711). On the marriage court and its extensive jurisdiction in questions of morals, see B, pp. 369-72, 377-80; and the important work of Walther Köhler, *Zürcher Ehegericht und Genfer Konsistorium* (Leipzig, 1932), pt. I.

instituted historically as "the works of the people," that is, the formal practice of religion, but the very ways one lived one's daily life as a Christian: one's daily conduct, one's manner, one's dress. "Honoring God" was also an ethical imperative. One acted in ways Scripture specified. The ideal of human conduct derived from how Christ had lived; relations with others were modeled on those the Gospels depicted among Christ, his disciples, and the many different kinds of strangers. In all one's acts one had the potential to honor — or dishonor — God. We have seen part of Zwingli's reasoning already: unlike Luther, he did not hold outward action as severable from inward belief. For Zwingli, and for Calvin, living one's life in accord with God's commands was the clearest evidence of one's efforts to fight one's own sinning nature.

For Zwingli, as for Augustine, sin was no more than self-love: sin consisted in valuing oneself over others and conceiving of others and of God in terms of one's own self. It was to conceive of God in terms of one's own experience as embodied, physical. It was to measure others in reference to oneself, to enter into social relations out of self-interest. Worship was the counteraction of self-love. The worship of God was the movement of the soul, from self-love, self-orientation, to God and outward to others: honoring them, according humanity equal value to oneself, and according God greater value than oneself. "Worship," for him, was purely and simply "to honor God." For Zwingli, one honored God not merely in those momentary rituals of formal religion, but day in and day out, in the conduct of one's life, in the mundane details: in one's gestures, in one's dress, in every act of a Christian — for acts indicated the orientation of a life as much as words did.

All these efforts at education were understood in Zürich as an aid to the work of the Holy Spirit.[46] If education was intended to provide the skills to gain access to Christ's teaching on the true Christian life, it was the Holy Spirit, for Zwingli, that made possible both the understanding of the content of those words and the enactment of their dictates. Only the truly faithful in spirit could live the sort of ethical life Christ had delineated. Like all Protestants, Zwingli held that faith could not be acquired, but came, as a gift freely given, from God: no act or desire of any human being could bring faith to him or her. And that faith led one into community: God's presence and the activity of the Holy Spirit moved the faithful to enter the community of Christians specifically in order to practice their faith. A community was the context, for Zwingli, within which each Christian expressed his or her faith. Faith led one to love one's "neighbor": to enter into the sort of relations of obligation from which the true Christian

---

46. In this, the language of the legislation itself echoes Zwingli's own position on the efficacy of the Holy Spirit in the reformation of each individual life.

community was forged. Faith could only be practiced, for Zwingli, and thereby strengthened, within the community of Christians.

The presence of the Holy Spirit led each Christian to love God above all others and to love his or her neighbor as himself or herself. During his years in Zürich Zwingli came to define more precisely what those two commands meant. Love of God meant first the rejection of the cult of saints, the medieval penitential system, and the use of images in acts of worship. Love of God led the pious to spend their lives in service to God, as "God's instrument," following his will as it revealed itself to them. It meant a life devoted to listening carefully and closely to the Word of God — a life of reading Scripture or listening to the Bible being read, or for the more pious a life of study of those languages that would enable them to come that much closer to the true meaning of God's words. It also meant conforming the conduct of one's life to what Christ had taught, by the example of his own conduct and of the parables. The life that honored God was humble: modest in speech, manner, and dress. There were no extravagances in it: no expensive clothing, no rich food; no dramatic gestures of asceticism or self-abuse. It was a life emptied of luxury: no pearls or other jewelry; no clothing of fine detail or expensive cut or cloth, no slashed sleeves, no wasted materials. And it was a life free of artifice. The Christian life would have none of the many techniques and devices Renaissance men and women had used in the pursuit of their ideal of beauty: no makeup, no plucked foreheads or brows, no bodices, no dyed hair.

Zwingli invoked the love of neighbor in many different contexts, from his efforts to speak to the grievances of those "common men" — peasants, artisans, laborers, small shopkeepers — who rebelled in 1524-25,[47] to those he called back to his fold from the Anabaptists in the later 1520s. What love of neighbor meant in the conduct of one's life, however, received its fullest explication in the legislation on poor relief.[48] There the town council called upon the people of Zürich to watch their "neighbors," to discern both signs of poverty and of righteous living, and to contribute to the communal fund for the relief of those who were both authentically poor and morally righteous. A "neighbor" might be indigent, without home or shelter, with many children and no employment. What made another person a "neighbor" was not physical proximity in the sense of neighborhood, nor did it derive from social place or political affiliation. It did not derive from what Zwingli called "false brotherhoods," those guilds and fraternities organized by craft or interrelated industries. What made

47. The largest rebellion in the history of Germany has been given many names: the German Peasants' Revolt, the German Peasants' War, the Revolution of 1525, the Revolution of the Common Man. For a fuller discussion, see Peter Blickle, *The Revolution of 1525*, trans. Thomas A. Brady and H. C. Erik Midelfort (Baltimore, 1981).

48. For a fuller explication of this argument, see my *Always among Us*.

a person a "neighbor" was shared faith and right conduct — the inner experience and outward expression of the love of God.

For Zwingli differences of gender, social place, and political power were of less consequence than differences of strength of faith, rectitude of life, and depth of understanding of God's will and design. Strength of faith and rectitude of life were God's gift — autonomous of any human construct, any human relation. Education in Zürich was intended to enable right faith to discern more accurately and fully God's will for the conduct of one's life and the content of one's belief. Different Christians had differing access to the complex education Zwingli helped form in Zürich: women had less access to the study of Scripture and its languages than men; artisans had less access than the sons of merchants; those intended for the clergy had fullest access. Each Christian, however, was to have access to some of that education, and all were to have access of one kind or another to its core: God's Word.

Communion

Communion or, as it was called in Zürich, the Supper was at once the affirmation of that Christian community into which each individual was initiated at baptism and the culmination of an education that began with baptism. If we imagine that moment as Zwingli described it, we glimpse something of the nature of the Christian community he envisioned. Zwingli never suggested that all would share the same depth of understanding of the central theological issue — the nature of Christ's presence — but argued consistently over time that the faith of each individual member of the congregation would link that person to others. Indeed, Zwingli did not hold that all present at Communion were necessarily believers, in opposition to the sorts of exclusions Anabaptists practiced, even that all had received the gift of faith. His vision of the community at the moment of Communion differentiated among the presence or absence of faith, degrees of faith, degrees of theological understanding and subtlety, at the same time that he insisted Communion reinforced community. The community enforced at Communion did have boundaries, however, defined according to the ideal of Christian behavior legislated in Zürich: excluded from Communion, according to Zwingli, were adulterers; pimps; prostitutes; drunks; those who lent at excessive interest or collected unjust tithes; blasphemers, including those who continued to hold Mass; and idolaters.[49]

49. "Ratschlag betreffend Ausschließung vom Abendmahl für Ehebrecher, Wücherer, usw," in Z, 4:25-34.

In Reformed Zürich Communion was held four times a year: Easter, Pentecost, "Autumn," and Christmas. While medieval practice had been to offer Communion at least once a week, at Sunday Mass, since the Fourth Lateran Council of 1215 Christians had been required to take Communion only once a year, at Easter.[50] Christians took Communion in Reformed Zürich to commemorate not only Christ's death and resurrection but also his birth and Pentecost; Christians also took it near the former All Saints' Day, when human sanctity had been celebrated, which was renamed, to commemorate God's agency, Twelve Commandments Day or Reformation Day. Communion, in other words, served to mark those moments of God's greater presence in the world, both at the time of Christ and in Christian history.

Zwingli had hoped that Communion would be celebrated every Sunday throughout the year.[51] Perhaps it was to become a part of that complex of education he had instituted: the earliest formulations of the full service he published, "The Action or Practice of the Supper," included men and women speaking alternate lines of a "song of praise," of the creed, and of Psalm 113, verses 1-9.[52] This earliest form also posited the fullest participation of the entire congregation; his later version, which was formally instituted in Zürich after Easter, April 16, 1525, kept much of the same text, but the clergy were to do all the readings.[53]

We have no description of the Communion service as practiced in Zürich. We have only Zwingli's guidelines for what was to be said and done, by minister and by congregation, though those seem to have been largely normative. Perhaps most important, Zwingli's Communion service explicitly rejected the solitary performance of the priest and brought the congregation to encircle the Communion table. The congregation thereby became more than witnesses; they belonged physically to the reenactment of the Last Supper.

Two themes run through Zwingli's Communion service: thanksgiving and

---

50. Thus, while the Zürich practice reduced the availability of Communion to the faithful, it increased the required number of times each Christian must take Communion, from one to four.

51. Apparently this hope was never realized. The town council would not agree to such frequency, a conflict paralleling almost exactly Calvin's conflict with Geneva.

52. "Aktion oder Brauch des Nachtmahls," published in March or the beginning of April 1525, in Z, vol. 4, esp. pp. 19 and 21. For a study of the form of Zwingli's Eucharist, see Julius Schweizer, *Reformierte Abendmahlsgestaltung in der Schau Zwinglis* (Basel, n.d.).

53. "Ordnung der christlichen Kirche zu Zurich," in Z, 4:687-94; and "Christenlich ordnung und bruch der kilchen Zürich. 1535," in Z, 4:704-6. For a study of the development of Zwingli's eucharistic thought, see H. Wayne Pipkin, "The Positive Religious Values of Zwingli's Eucharistic Writings," in *Huldrych Zwingli, 1484-1531: A Legacy of Radical Reform*, ed. E. J. Furcha (ARC, 1985), pp. 107-43.

commemoration. It opened with a prayer calling the faithful to praise and thanksgiving for the gift of Jesus Christ, whose death was promised for all human salvation. The pastor then read the text of 1 Corinthians 11:20-29, which divided those who came to eat in faith from those whose lack of faith at the Eucharist would mean their damnation.[54] There followed the song of praise and thanksgiving. The pastor read John 6:47-63, from which Zwingli derived his conception of the meaning of the Supper. The entire congregation or the pastor recited the creed. The pastor prepared the congregation for Communion itself with a brief call to faith, then the Lord's Prayer and a second prayer, for God's help in the conduct of their lives.[55] Once the congregation had called upon God to enable them to live as Christians, whose very lives could bring others to acknowledge God's presence, the pastor reiterated the narrative of the Last Supper from 1 Corinthians 11:23-26: "For I received from the Lord what I also delivered to you, that the Lord Jesus on the night when he was betrayed took bread, and when he had given thanks, he broke it, and said, 'This is my body which is for you. Do this in remembrance of me.' In the same way also the cup, after supper, saying, 'This cup is the new covenant in my blood. Do this, as often as you drink it, in remembrance of me.' For as often as you eat this bread and drink the cup, you proclaim the Lord's death until he comes" (RSV). Then the minister or servers carried unleavened bread around to each of the congregation, from

54. "When you meet together, it is not the Lord's supper that you eat. For in eating, each one goes ahead with his own meal, and one is hungry and another is drunk. What! Do you not have houses to eat and drink in? Or do you despise the church of God and humiliate those who have nothing? What shall I say to you? Shall I commend you in this? No, I will not. For I received from the Lord what I also delivered to you, that the Lord Jesus on the night when he was betrayed took bread, and when he had given thanks, he broke it, and said, 'This is my body which is for you. Do this in remembrance of me.' In the same way also the cup, after supper, saying, 'This cup is the new covenant in my blood. Do this, as often as you drink it, in remembrance of me.' For as often as you eat this bread and drink the cup, you proclaim the Lord's death until he comes. Whoever, therefore, eats the bread or drinks the cup of the Lord in an unworthy manner will be guilty of profaning the body and blood of the Lord. Let a man examine himself, and so eat of the bread and drink of the cup. For any one who eats and drinks without discerning the body eats and drinks judgment upon himself" (RSV).

55. "O Lord, almighty God, who has made us through Your Spirit in the unity of faith into your one body, which body you have promised, we say praise and thanks to you for the good deed and free gift, that you have given your very own Son, our Lord, Jesus Christ, in death for our sin. Grant it to us that we do the same so truthfully that we do not show scorn to the undeceived truth with any hypocrisy or falsehood. Grant us also that we live so innocently, as your body, your kin, and children, that the faithless also learn to recognize your name and honor. Lord, protect us, that no one brings shame to your name and honor on account of our lives. Lord, increase faith in us in all ways, that is: trust in you, you who live and rule, God in eternity, Amen." "Aktion oder Brauch des Nachtmahls," in Z, 4:22.

which each took a morsel with his or her hands or asked the minister to give it to him or her. Once each had eaten her or his piece of bread, the other minister followed with the wine in a crude cup of wood or perhaps pewter, which was offered to each person. Once all had received the bread and wine, the "shepherd or pastor" began Psalm 113, a psalm of praise, again spoken alternately in the earlier version, spoken solely by the pastor in later versions. The service closed with the pastor's final thanksgiving and blessing.

Most Protestant services interweave prayers and psalms of thanksgiving in their Communion. In the sixteenth century all shared in the rejection of the medieval Mass as a reenactment of Christ's sacrifice on the cross. All held that one sacrifice — the moment of Christ's crucifixion and death — served for all time and for all who would believe in its efficacy. For all, "Eucharist" — the reception of bread and wine at the center of the service — was understood to be a meal of thanksgiving: for Christ's singular death for the sake of humankind, for the free and unmerited gift of salvation.

It is Zwingli's understanding of commemoration that sets his Eucharist apart. His conception of commemoration became the subject of debate. Luther confused it with a form of symbolism.[56] Calvin distanced himself from it, even as he incorporated some of Zwingli's understanding into his own service. Neither understood what Zwingli meant by commemoration or the nature of God's presence at the Eucharist, though Calvin came much closer than Luther. Zwingli's conception of the Eucharist was anchored in his conviction of the agency of the Holy Spirit and in his understanding of human cognition.[57] The

56. See, for example, "That These Words of Christ, 'This Is My Body,' etc., Still Stand Firm against the Fanatics, 1527," and "Confession concerning Christ's Supper, 1528," both translated by Robert H. Fischer, in *Luther's Works*, vol. 37, *Word and Sacrament III* (Philadelphia, 1961). The classic study of Zwingli and Luther's debate over the Eucharist, still unsurpassed, is Walther Köhler, *Zwingli und Luther: Ihr Streit über das Abendmahl nach seinen politischen und religiösen Beziehungen*, 2 vols. (Leipzig, 1924; Gütersloh, 1953). For a careful criticism of Köhler's Lutheran sympathies in this debate, as well as a summary of the development of Zwingli's eucharistic thought, see Locher, *Die Zwinglische Reformation*, chap. 15. Sec. 20, "The Lord's Supper," in "The Characteristic Features of Zwingli's Theology in Comparison with Luther and Calvin" (*Zwingli's Thought*, pp. 220-28), is an abbreviated translation of Locher's discussion in *Die Zwinglische Reformation*.

57. As we have seen, membership in the community of Christians brought education in the Word of God and in Christian ethics. That education had taught the people of Zürich to see God's agency in the world, to discern Christ in acts of brotherly love. In addition, Zwingli's own study of Greek had brought him into contact with Greek theological ideas. Most important among those was a different conception of "Spirit" as something at once intangible but acting *through* matter, the physical world. See Locher's important discussion of Zwingli's "pneumatology" in "The Characteristic Features of Zwingli's Theology in Comparison with Luther and Calvin," in *Zwingli's Thought*, pp. 178-80.

prayer at center in the Communion service invokes God's presence as Zwingli understood it: the Holy Spirit working *through* the faithful to help them live in accord with God's will. God's presence, in other words, was manifest in the ability of the people of Zürich to live as Christians. Commemoration for Zwingli, then, embraced the joyous acknowledgment and affirmation of God's agency not only throughout human history and in human salvation, as all Protestants held, but in the very ability of human beings to live as Christians each day. God was corporeally "present" for the people of Zürich, not in the bread and wine, as Luther insisted, but in their persons, insofar as they lived as faithful Christians.

At the nexus between Zwingli's understanding of commemoration and his understanding of human cognition was his idea of "sign" — it was, for him, the key to the Eucharist. As Zwingli argued against Luther, the bread and the wine are "signs" of the body and blood of Christ — they are not the thing itself, nor, on the other hand, the sterile, empty forms Luther claimed Zwingli was positing.[58] Zwingli's complex understanding of "sign" derived not from medieval scholastic notions of signs as conventions, but from humanist notions of language as historical and socially embedded. For Zwingli a "sign" interacted with human cognition. It was not some rigid symbol of fixed content, but inseparable from the mind that apprehended it, with all that mind's particular education and all the associations that mind brought to the "sign" — hence the central importance of education for Zwingli. Zwingli's understanding of commemoration is founded upon this conception of sign. The bread and the wine were signs whose content was articulated first by Christ himself at the Last Supper, then in the text of John 6. The content of those signs, in other words, was accessible only to those who could understand the words, the Word — the true meaning of which was learned over time and through the agency of the Holy Spirit — those faithful who heard in their souls the true content of the signs.

Communion was thus not merely an affirmation of the education in the Word, of the community "formed in faith." As Zwingli's debates with Luther revealed, it was a test of that education and that community. Only those who had heard the true content of the Word of God — who understood the meaning of Christ's words at the institution and of John's text — participated truly and fully in Communion. Only those, in other words, who had learned through a

58. Indeed, Zwingli's understanding of sign is the single greatest cause of his break with Luther over the Eucharist. See his two major treatises against Luther: "Amica exegesis, id est: expositio eucharisticae negocii ad Martinum Lutherum" (February 28, 1527) and "Daß diese Worte: 'Das ist mein Lieb,' etc. ewiglich den alten Sinn haben werden" (June 20, 1527), in Z, 5:548-758 and 795-977, respectively.

complex education in word, image, and act to comprehend the nature of God's presence in the world could understand the true nature of Christ's "presence" in the wine and bread.

When the people of Zürich came into their churches and stood before the simple table and the implements, that service marked more than a return to the simplicity of the original Last Supper. To those objects the people of Zürich brought an education that had sought to teach them how to "read" the "signs" of the bread and wine, to discern in them the specific nature of Christ's presence in the world, and to grasp their true content, the true meaning of those signs. Communion in Zürich "commemorated" the experience of God's presence. It commemorated that presence as it had been revealed in Christ's life and death, but not only that. Communion in Zürich also "commemorated," acknowledged and celebrated, God's presence as it was known, as agency, in the gestures of "neighbor" to "neighbor" and in the spoken Word that had become the lived Word. It commemorated a community of faith formed and informed by God.

Catechesis in Calvin's Geneva

Robert M. Kingdon

This paper will concentrate on the community of Geneva during the period of Calvin's own ministry. Geneva often served as a model for later Calvinist communities, and thus can reveal aspects of the entire movement. I am currently working, with a team of collaborators, on an edition of the registers of the Geneva consistory during the period of Calvin's own ministry.[1] These registers contain the weekly minutes of a semijudicial ecclesiastical body created at Calvin's insistence in 1541 as a mechanism to make sure that the entire population lived in a Christian manner, that Genevans not only accepted a new theology but also behaved as good Christians should. These registers provide an unusually rich and hitherto underused source of information on daily life in

---

1. We have prepared transcriptions of all twenty-one volumes for the period of Calvin's ministry (1541-64), and are now beginning a critical edition of these registers. Two volumes have been published: *Registres du Consistoire de Genève au temps de Calvin* 1, 1542-44, ed. Thomas A. Lambert and Isabella Watt, with the assistance of Jeffrey R. Watt, supervised by Robert M. Kingdon, Travaux d'Humanisme et Renaissance 305 (Geneva: Droz, 1996); vol. 2, 1545-46, ed. Thomas A. Lambert, Isabella Watt, and Wallace McDonald, supervised by Robert M. Kingdon, Travaux d'Humanisme et Renaissance 352 (Geneva: Droz, 2001), hereafter cited as *RConsistoire*. Vol. 1 has also been published in English translation (Grand Rapids: Eerdmans, 2000). See Lambert's introduction for a full description of how the consistory operated. For a less developed description in English, see Robert M. Kingdon, *Adultery and Divorce in Calvin's Geneva* (Cambridge: Harvard University Press, 1995), chap. 1. For an overview of Geneva in this period, see E. William Monter, *Calvin's Geneva* (New York: Wiley, 1967).

Copies of this paper were circulated in advance of publication and used by other scholars, including Barbara Pitkin, "Children and the Church in Calvin's Geneva," in *Calvin and the Church*, ed. David Foxgrover (Grand Rapids: CRC Product Services, 2002), pp. 144-64.

Geneva at a critical period of transition from Catholic to Protestant forms of religious behavior. They reveal much about the impact of the Reformation on the general population, including men and women, the literate and the illiterate, the cosmopolitan and the provincial. They provide information on the Catholic beliefs and practices Calvin and his associates were trying to suppress, and on the Protestant beliefs and practices they were trying to introduce.

The early years of the Protestant Reformation witnessed fundamental changes in the mechanisms for formation and education of a people of faith in Geneva. The most fundamental of these changes moved people from a Catholic reliance primarily on home instruction, particularly by mothers, to a Protestant insistence that catechism by professional clergymen supplement home instruction. Calvin and his fellow clergymen did not abandon home instruction. Indeed, they tried to strengthen it. But they insisted on a professional supplement in the form of catechism classes.

Prereform Geneva

Home instruction before the Reformation involved above all learning by memory a few prayers and the creed. The most basic expectations of Christians in Catholic Geneva were that they say these prayers and attend the Mass. They were expected to do many other things in addition, of course, but these were the most basic, the really fundamental expectations.

Attendance at the Mass may well have been required only once a year, the Easter obligation common to most of Catholic Europe. But people were clearly encouraged to attend more frequently, and those who were devout did. Masses were available every day of the week in seven different parish churches, in religious houses, and elsewhere. Attendance seems to have been significant. Nostalgia for the Mass appears fairly frequently among those summoned to the consistory to explain their religious behavior. It was often a problem for Calvin and his associates to explain why people should no longer attend the Mass, why the Mass and the Reformed Lord's Supper could not be regarded as interchangeable.

Of the prayers these Christians were expected to use in pre-Reformation Geneva, the most important were the Pater Noster and the Ave Maria.[2] The faithful were expected to commit them to memory and be able to repeat them on

2. There is a more extended report on prayer in Geneva before and after the Reformation, with examples drawn from the consistory registers, by Thomas A. Lambert, "Preaching, Praying, and Policing the Reform in Sixteenth-Century Geneva" (Ph.D. diss., University of Wisconsin–Madison, 1998; UMI no. 9819828), esp. chap. 10, "Popular Prayer in Reformation Geneva," pp. 393-479.

demand. They memorized them in Latin. These Christians were also expected to learn the *Credo* (Apostles' Creed) and, less frequently, the Ten Commandments. The *Credo* was also learned in Latin. The teaching of these basic texts seems to have occurred mostly in the home. Again and again when Genevans were called before the consistory in its early years, they were asked to recite their prayers. This was asked of them even when they had been summoned for entirely different reasons, for example, for sex offenses or sharp business practice. Again and again these Genevans would recite the Pater Noster and the Ave Maria, often adding the *Credo*. Again and again when an individual was asked where she or he had learned these prayers, the reply would be: at home, from my parents, from my mother and father, or from my mother, or from my father. Rarely would an individual say he or she had learned prayers from a priest or in church. One gets the impression of a wide and effective network of religious home instruction. One also gets the impression that mothers carried a particularly heavy responsibility for this instruction, often heavier than fathers. This was a type of instruction, furthermore, that did not require literacy. While literacy was almost certainly higher in Geneva than in the typical peasant villages of the period, it was nevertheless low by modern standards, and lower among women than men. Most of the women who were teaching their children to say these prayers were probably themselves illiterate, repeating texts they had carefully learned from their own mothers, reinforced by constant recitation of them at Mass.

There were, to be sure, schools in which more advanced instruction, including instruction in religion, was available to Genevans. The most important was a municipal college, established in the early fifteenth century with a generous gift from a wealthy local merchant named François de Versonnex in order to teach boys "grammar, logic, and other liberal arts." It was located next to the Franciscan Convent of the Rive, in the middle of the city. It cannot have been a very big operation. The building in which it was located was small, and its staff consisted of one to three teachers. The city government assumed some responsibility for the maintenance of the building and the salaries of the teachers, although there were continuing arguments as to whether the teachers were expected to live on their salaries alone and thus provide an education free to the students and open to all, or whether these teachers could charge fees from the families of those students who could afford to pay, perhaps limiting access. If they charged fees, furthermore, the question arose as to whether they were expected to share the take with the municipal government.[3]

---

3. For more on these early schools, see Henri Naef, *Les origines de la Réforme à Genève* (Geneva: Jullien; Paris: Droz, 1936), 1:278-99, and early chapters of *Le Collège de Genève, 1559-1959* (Geneva: Jullien, 1959).

In addition there seem to have been a number of private teaching masters who provided basic instruction as individuals or in small groups — in effect, small schools — in reading, writing, and perhaps elementary arithmetic to children from individual families willing to pay modest fees. Most of these children would have been boys of merchant or professional families. A few were girls, whose teachers were very likely female.[4] Religion was perhaps not a necessary part of this education, but it surely provided some part. There were also arrangements for training boys for the priesthood, in and around the cathedral church. This would have involved instruction in Latin, elementary theology, and liturgy. These students were supervised in the years before the Reformation by a Confraternity of the Innocents. It was also apparently possible for girls to get formal education in the convent of the Clare Sisters, located in the middle of the city.

None of these educational institutions offered really advanced instruction. Even though the city had received a license to establish a university back in 1365 from the emperor Charles IV, it had never done so. Genevans who wanted instruction on the university level had to go elsewhere, most commonly to Turin if they wished instruction in law, or to Paris if they wished instruction in the arts or theology, or to Montpellier if they wished to study medicine.

All of Geneva's schools provided some religious education. The basic text used in the college created by the Versonnex gift, for example, began with instruction in basic reading and moved on to teaching of the Pater Noster.[5] A set of school statutes for this college, adopted in 1502, provided that on feast days the rector was expected to provide for the older students a special public reading of passages from the Gospels, the Pauline Epistles, and the lives of the saints.[6] Every Sunday this rector was also expected to take the students together as a group to church to listen to a sermon.[7]

But formal education was certainly not obligatory in Geneva, and only small numbers of children were actually enrolled in the schools. Perhaps more of them were trained by the private masters, but we cannot be sure. Documentation on their activities is very thin indeed. It seems clear that the great majority of Genevans before the Reformation were expected to rely on home instruction to learn the rudiments of religious faith.

---

4. Liliane Mottu-Weber, "Les femmes dans la vie économique de Genève, XVIe-XVIIe siècles," *Bulletin, Société d'histoire et d'archéologie de Genève* 16 (1979): 391. I am indebted to Thomas A. Lambert for calling this reference to my attention.

5. Naef, *Origines*, 1:295 n. 2.

6. Naef, *Origines*, 1:282.

7. Charles Borgeaud, *Histoire de l'Université de Genève*, vol. 1, *L'Académie de Calvin, 1559-1578* (Geneva: Georg, 1900), 1:15-16.

Reform Geneva

The Protestant Reformation, when it finally did come to Geneva, was unusually abrupt and far-reaching. In fact, it can fairly be called a revolution, both in politics and in the church. The reigning prince bishop, who had been the titular ruler of Geneva, was forced to leave the city. So were agents of the duke of Savoy who had helped him govern the city. So were the canons of the cathedral chapter, and almost all the priests and religious of the city. Only one nun and a handful of priests, most of them poor chantry priests, remained. The nun was soon married and the priests were required to give up their jobs, not to say Mass any longer.[8] The members of the Catholic clergy who were exiled, together with their servants and other dependents, constituted a group of around one thousand people, about 10 percent of the entire population. They were, furthermore, among the most powerful, wealthiest, and best-educated part of the population. They had owned, both individually and as members of ecclesiastical bodies, a good percentage of all the property in the city. They had ruled the city of Geneva and the large diocese of which it was the headquarters, directed its church, provided much of the education, and provided most of the charity. They were replaced by immigrants, some from France, others from Italy, who in the end made up an even larger percentage of the population than those who left. Many of these immigrants were even wealthier and better educated than the people they replaced.

The most prominent of these immigrants, of course, was John Calvin. He was helped by about a dozen immigrant ministers, almost all of them highly educated, a number of them of noble birth. They were additionally helped by a small group of highly educated immigrant teachers. Only one or two of this cohort of religious leaders were native to Geneva. This handful of men together assumed responsibility for managing work that had been handled by dozens if not hundreds before the Reformation.[9]

After the Reformation the new regime's most basic expectations of ordinary Genevans were that they would attend sermons and say prayers. The sacrament of the Lord's Supper, which replaced the Mass, was no longer the central feature of a church service. It was, indeed, only offered four times a year. Instead a sermon delivered by a minister on salary from the city government, in

8. Gabriella Cahier-Buccelli, "Dans l'ombre de la Réforme: les membres de l'ancien clergé demeurés à Genève (1536-1558)," *Bulletin, Société d'histoire et d'archéologie de Genève* 18 (1987): 367-89.

9. On the revolutionary nature of the Genevan Reformation, see, inter alia, Robert M. Kingdon, "Calvin and the Government of Geneva," in *Calvinus Ecclesiae Genevensis Custos,* ed. Wilhelm H. Neuser (Frankfurt: Peter Lang, 1984), pp. 49-67.

form a commentary on a pericope from the Bible, became the central feature of a church service, and people were expected to listen to it. People called before the consistory were often asked whether they attended sermons, how often they attended them, who was the preacher they had last heard, what had been the subject of his sermon, upon which Bible verses had he commented. If they had trouble handling any of these questions, they were told to attend more sermons and to pay closer attention to them. If they protested that they had other responsibilities, including child care, they were instructed to set them aside. If they protested that they were hard of hearing, they were told to stand near the pulpit. If they protested that they had trouble understanding sermons, they were told to come more often, several times a week, once a day if necessary, so that they could become accustomed to listening closely, to become fully familiar with this method of instruction. Many were accused of revealing inattention by "murmuring" during sermons. A high percentage of those so accused were women, who had apparently been repeating prayers by rote as they had been accustomed to do during the Mass. They had never been expected to listen to a priest and were surely at first baffled and hurt by the consistory's reproaches.

Of the prayers Christians were now expected to know, the most important was clearly the Our Father, although knowledge of the Apostles' Creed was also expected, and occasionally of the Ten Commandments. Now the prayer had to be repeated in one's native language, or more precisely, one's maternal language. For most Genevans that meant the local patois, a dialect of Franco-Provençal, with a number of purely local usages. Prayers in Latin were unacceptable because it was felt, with some reason, that people did not understand them, could not explain in the simplest terms what they really meant. People asked to explain the sense of their Latin prayers before the consistory often gave up in confusion. The creed, as well, had to be recited in the maternal language rather than in Latin. These texts had to be committed to memory. It was unacceptable to read them from a book or piece of paper. Most people accepted this demand without protest and dutifully relearned these texts in their maternal language.

There was, on the other hand, some resistance to demands to drop certain traditional prayers. Prayers to the Virgin Mary and to the saints were unacceptable to the new Protestant leaders of Geneva, for theological reasons. They felt strongly that only God can answer prayer, that it does no good to ask someone else to intercede with God. Again and again members of the consistory had to explain to the faithful that it does no good to pray to the Virgin or to saints, that only a prayer directed to God alone can be efficacious.

Most Genevans were willing to abandon prayers to the saints. They dutifully accepted the argument that God does not listen to most intercessors. But many of them had difficulty abandoning prayers to the Virgin Mary. They might protest that they did not understand this particular prohibition. Would not the good Lord listen to his own mother?[10] They might anxiously inquire whether the Virgin would not be more likely to understand prayers from people faced with certain special problems, like a woman in labor before childbirth, or a man traveling in woods infested with robbers. In so doing they revealed in a significant way traditional beliefs about the value of intercessory prayer. One gets the impression that Marian devotion was deeply rooted in Geneva, more deeply rooted than devotion to local saints, as deeply rooted as reverence for the Mass.

When it came to teaching these new versions of prayer, however, this Calvinist community no longer relied solely on home instruction. While it certainly did not abolish home instruction, and in later years came to rely on it more heavily, it reserved to the church and its ordained ministers an important role in religious instruction. The consistory, to be sure, displayed frequent concern about home instruction. It reminded men who headed households that they had an obligation to provide religious instruction to the children in their homes. That included not only their own children, but also the young servants at work in most households of the middle class. In the more prosperous households the number of young servants could be quite substantial. The entire household was expected to gather together periodically to repeat prayers. It is my impression that the role of women was not emphasized as much as it had been in pre-Reformation Geneva, that the duty of supplying and supervising household religious instruction was much more clearly now a duty of fathers.

Home instruction, however, was not enough for Calvin and his associates. It was no longer the only vehicle for religious training but became complemented and supplemented and supported by the catechism classes that became a regular part of religious instruction. Calvin and his associates did not seem to trust the people of Geneva to teach the basics of Christianity to their children without assistance. They seemed to have believed that most parents were not well enough informed to teach their own children properly. They may also have feared that parents would continue to teach Catholic versions of these basics. Catechism classes were accordingly set up in each of the churches servicing the parishes into which the city was divided. The ministers assigned to each of these parish churches were expected to conduct these classes. This switch from home instruction alone to home instruction supplemented by parish catechism is probably the most basic change in religious education in Calvin's Geneva.

10. See the case of Janne Pertennaz, cross-examined at length on her opinions of the Virgin Mary and other matters in *RConsistoire*, 1:26-27 (fol. 13, April 4, 1542).

The Parish Community and Catechism

There were three parish churches remaining in Geneva after the Reformation. Four parishes had been abolished as the city reduced its physical size by razing suburbs and withdrawing the remaining population into an area protected by city walls. The city had also closed a number of convents with chapels attached to them that had been open to the general population. Thus worship was concentrated into fewer actual buildings. One of the remaining parish churches was Saint Peter, the former cathedral. It was located high on the hill that dominates the city, in a neighborhood in which the bishop and the cathedral canons who had once ruled Geneva had lived; many of the patrician bourgeois who now ruled the city and some wealthy recent Protestant immigrants settled here. Another was the parish church of the Madeleine (Magdalen), at the base of the hill, not far from the river Rhône that splits the city in two, in a quarter containing primarily the homes of small merchants and traders and the markets in which they sold their goods. The third was the parish church of Saint Gervais, across the river from the larger part of the city, in a quarter containing primarily the homes of artisans and other manual workers and the shops in which they worked.

A staff of several ministers was attached to each parish church and took turns handling a variety of duties. There were services every day of the week, early in the morning, and three services on Sunday. Sunday began with an early service, at daybreak — 6:00 or 7:00 A.M., depending on the season — intended in part for servants and others who had continuing duties during the day. There was a main service about 8:00 A.M., which most people were expected to attend, and an afternoon service at 3:00 P.M. In between these two later services, at noon, the catechism classes met. Every child was expected to attend catechism class in the parish in which his or her family lived.[11]

These classes were called catechisms because of the special method of instruction they used. It was a method that had been tried in earlier years; it preceded the Reformation. But it seems to have become really popular and widespread only with the Reformation. It involved a series of simple questions, put by a clergyman or other teacher, and set answers that could be committed to memory. It was a method that had proved to be an enormous success in Germany, where the catechisms drafted by Martin Luther had been published in

---

11. This schedule of services was prescribed by the ecclesiastical ordinances. There are a number of editions of them. Two easily available ones can be found in *Registres de la Compagnie des Pasteurs de Genève au temps de Calvin,* ed. Jean-François Bergier (Geneva: Droz, 1964), 1.5, and *Ioannis Calvini Opera quae supersunt omnia,* ed. Baum, Cunitz, and Reuss, 10:20-21.

hundreds of editions and had been widely adopted throughout Protestant Germany. It was a method that was widely adopted and adapted by Catholics, most notably by Peter Canisius, and reinforced by the decrees of the Council of Trent (1545-63) and other pieces of reform legislation. It was also the method adapted by Calvin for Geneva. In 1537, soon after his initial arrival, he had drafted his first catechism for the religious instruction of children. He then arranged for its publication. Use of this catechism may have been suspended in Geneva on the abrupt ejection of Calvin and his patron Farel in 1538. Calvin spent his years of exile in Strasbourg, as minister of a congregation of French refugees; there, in a larger and fully Protestant city, one that had gone further in developing Protestant institutions and practices than Geneva, he was in a position to learn a good deal more about the method of instruction by catechism. He even had the opportunity to do more work on his own version of the catechism for use within his new congregation.

When Calvin agreed to return to Geneva in 1541, he did so on two conditions. First he demanded that the city introduce genuine discipline by creating the institution that was to become the consistory. It would see that Genevans not only accepted true belief as he defined it but also behaved in a way that was truly Christian. After the government of Geneva accepted Calvin's conditions, he promptly set to work. His first step was to use his own considerable legal and political skills to draft and secure approval for a set of ecclesiastical ordinances, a kind of constitution for the Reformed church.[12] They created the consistory, a new semijudicial disciplinary institution. It was technically one of several committees of the city government, made up of elected elders and presided over by one of the four "syndics" or reigning magistrates of the city. But it was also a part of the church, since all the ministers were ex officio members. It began functioning within weeks, before the end of 1541, and Calvin immediately assumed a major role in its operations. He continued to participate actively in its deliberations, in fact, for the rest of his life. He also fought strenuously for its powers, above all the power to excommunicate and forgive sinners, without any right of review by the councils representing the entire population that ran the city government. When these sweeping powers were challenged in later years, he threatened to leave the city; after considerable turmoil, he won his way. Excommunication became a feared and effective sanction because it barred people not only from Communion but also from participation in other church rites and sacraments, such as baptism. An excommunicate, for example, could not act as godfather at the baptism of the child of a friend. After Calvin's triumph, excommunication seems also to have become a considerable impedi-

---

12. *Registres*, 1.1-13; *Calvini Opera*, 10:16-30.

ment to normal business and social life. In fact, it could even lead to banishment from the city. Most of those faced with this penalty made strenuous attempts to have it lifted — or they went into exile.

Calvin's second condition was that the city make a serious attempt to educate everyone in the true Christian faith by adopting and using the new method of catechism.[13] Calvin soon began drafting a catechism himself and had completed a full draft early in 1542.[14] The published catechisms were intended primarily to be guides to the teachers conducting the classes, but they could also be followed by students who were literate. They were divided into sets of questions put by a minister and answers expected of the children in attendance. The 1545 catechism was to be used over a period of fifty-five weeks, just over a year.[15] Only a half-dozen questions were discussed each week, an amount of material small enough to be committed to memory. The questions are divided into four main categories. A first category in most of these catechisms (though in second place in 1537), and easily the longest section, was about the faith. It contained a close examination of the Apostles' Creed, including an analysis of each succeeding phrase. It was obviously intended to lead to memorization of the creed. The second category in these editions (although first in 1537) concerned the law. It contained close examination of the Ten Commandments from the Old Testament, supplemented with the verses in the New Testament in which Jesus rephrased and summarized the law into two great commandments. Each is analyzed separately at considerable length, and in the end each child was obviously expected to be able to recite the Ten Commandments and the New Testament supplement by memory. A third category focused on prayer. After some general questions about the nature of prayer, about how it should always be directed to God alone rather than to saints, about how it should always be in the vernacular, and so on, this part of the catechism moves to an intensive examination of the Lord's Prayer, with close analysis of each phrase, again with the obvious expectation that everyone would commit it to memory. A final section — the only one that does not focus on a single text intended for memorization — was de-

13. This was Calvin's report in his address to his fellow ministers on his deathbed. See *Calvini Opera*, 9:891-94, for one version, and Monter, *Calvin's Geneva*, pp. 239-41, for another.

14. It seems to have been put to use immediately, even before publication. It was first published in 1545. Copies of Calvin's two published catechisms, of 1537 and 1545, are now very rare, although the second was published in several editions. Most of them seem to have been used up and thrown away. Scholars have, however, located copies of each and edited them for modern use and research.

15. For a good recent edition of this text, see Olivier Fatio, ed., *Confessions et catéchismes de la foi réformée*, Publications de la Faculté de Théologie de l'Université de Genève 11 (Geneva: Labor et Fides, 1986), pp. 25-110.

voted to the sacraments. It deals with the only rites recognized as sacraments by the Reformed, baptism and Communion. After the catechism proper, the 1545 edition also supplies texts of daily prayers and psalms suggested for use on waking, before and after meals, and before going to sleep.

The obvious intention of this catechism was to make sure that every child in the community could ultimately repeat from memory a set of basic summaries of the faith: the Apostles' Creed, the Ten Commandments with their New Testament supplement, the Lord's Prayer. Anyone who could do that was accepted as a member of the Christian community. At the end of a catechism cycle each child would be questioned individually by a minister and, if successful, then admitted to a first Communion.

This catechism remained in constant use in Geneva for the first generations following the Reformation, but it never won the wider acceptance within the entire Reformed movement achieved by other early innovations in religious ritual developed by Calvin for use in Geneva. The catechism that has won far wider use within the international Reformed community is the Heidelberg Catechism, drafted by several of Calvin's admirers in Germany twenty years later, in 1562. It is commonly attributed to Ursinus and Olevianus, the leaders of the change to a Calvinist version of Protestantism in the Rhenish Palatinate. A comparison of the two texts helps explain why Calvin's version was not used more widely.

Beyond its clear and useful main structure, the Geneva catechism is not particularly well organized. It was clearly slapped together in some haste. The questions to be asked by the ministers often turn into short explanations of a point of doctrine, with the student expected to answer only *"voire"* (truly), or *"c'est cela"* or *"il est ainsi"* (that's so), or with some other sign of assent. The answers expected of the children range from these simple statements of assent to rather long expositions of points of theology. That meant that the difficulty in using this catechism would vary considerably from one section to another and probably from one week to another for the average child. Calvin himself recognized that this catechism needed to be improved. On his deathbed, in his final remarks to his fellow ministers, he recalled the circumstances of its hasty composition and his regret at never having improved it.[16]

The Heidelberg Catechism, on the other hand, is much better suited to actual use in religious instruction. It asks real questions that are short and supplies measured and pertinent answers. It is more clearly and coherently organized. It again requires memorization of key texts, the Apostles' Creed, the Ten Commandments, and the Lord's Prayer, and provides explanations of each part

16. See above, n. 13.

of them. It is designed to be used over a period of fifty-two weeks, thus just one calendar year, not the rather awkward fifty-five weeks of the Geneva cate-chism.[17]

Attendance at catechism classes in Calvin's Geneva was not limited to children, particularly in the beginning when the Protestant regime was first being created. Adults who were judged religiously illiterate were also expected to attend. Again and again when the consistory discovered that an adult could not repeat the Our Father and the creed in French, he or she was told to attend catechism. A number of adults learned these basic texts from children, their own or others, since it was clear that children, through attendance at catechism, could often pick up this information more easily. Adults who were not able to recite from memory these basic texts were not permitted to receive Communion. Groups of them would be summoned before the consistory before each quarterly Communion service and asked to recite the Our Father and the creed. Those who could not were asked to keep trying to memorize these texts and temporarily denied Communion. They were often instructed to return to the consistory to prove that they had in fact now mastered these texts. Occasionally when the person summoned, typically an old and probably illiterate woman, seemed to be trying hard in good faith but simply could not master these texts, the consistory would relent and admit her to Communion anyway because she was at least trying and thus setting a good example to others. This is what happened to Myaz Richardet, for example, who appeared before the consistory in September, October, and December of 1542, and was finally allowed to participate in Christmas Communion.[18]

The use of catechism classes to instruct adults occurred primarily in the early years after the establishment of the Reformation, when the entire population was still learning what it meant to be Reformed. In later years it became less and less necessary. The percentage of people summoned who could say the Lord's Prayer and repeat the Apostles' Creed satisfactorily, the consistory discovered, was already fairly high in 1542, the first full year of these inquiries. These percentages were significantly higher in 1544. By 1562 the consistory no longer found it necessary to put questions about these matters to most of those summoned to appear before it.[19] By the time Calvin died in 1564, it could be assumed that most Genevans had received religious instruction in catechism

---

17. There are many editions of this catechism. I have used the one in Philip Schaff, *The Creeds of Christendom* (1877; reprint, Grand Rapids, 1966), 3:307-55, in both German and English; cf. Fatio, pp. 129-78, for a French text and some recent commentary.

18. *RConsistoire*, 1:121, 128, 149.

19. See Lambert, "Preaching, Praying, and Policing," pp. 408-19, for precise tabulations.

classes while they were children. Adult instruction at this elementary level was no longer necessary.

The basic instruction provided in catechism classes was reinforced by church services. The liturgical order of the weekly services, though identified as a sermon, involved more than the sermon, which was its most central element. It also included a cappella congregational singing of psalms from the Old Testament, led by a *chantre* or cantor. A good deal of effort was devoted by the leaders of the early Protestant church in Geneva to arranging for translations of the psalms into French and for composition of appropriate tunes. The final version adopted during Calvin's ministry included translations by Clément Marot, the French court poet, and Theodore Beza, the Calvinist theologian and churchman who was to become Calvin's successor as leader of the entire movement. It also included musical settings by Louis Bourgeois, *chantre* of the cathedral church of Saint Pierre, Claude Goudimel, and others. It was repeatedly printed and distributed throughout the French-speaking Protestant world and served as a basis for translations into other languages.

Even more important for our purposes, however, was the fact that these services involved congregational recitation of the Lord's Prayer and the creed. In some services the Lord's Prayer was even recited twice.[20] Constant participation in these services sealed the wording of these texts in the minds of everyone, both literate and illiterate. It reinforced and fixed the instruction originally received in catechism.

Consistory Oversight

At the most fundamental level, then, religious education in Calvin's Geneva involved three new institutions, each supplementing home instruction. The catechism classes taught the basics of the faith, primarily in the form of three basic texts, to children and adults alike. Church services fixed these basics in the minds of all. The consistory constantly oversaw the entire educational process. It put continuing pressure on the entire population to follow the new Protestant guidelines, particularly among adults who had been raised Catholic.

This system of education relied heavily on rote memory. This raises questions about how much meaning these texts held for the people who memorized

20. For a useful summary of the usual order of service, see the introduction to Jean Calvin, *Sermons sur les Livres de Jérémie et des Lamentations*, ed. Rodolph Peter, Supplementa Calviniana 6 (Neukirchen-Vluyn: Neukirchener Verlag des Erziehungsvereins, 1971), pp. xxv-xxxix, esp. the table on xxxiii.

them. It raises the possibility that the people of Calvin's Geneva, though they had won the right to be called Christians by memorizing the Lord's Prayer, the creed, and the Ten Commandments, had committed themselves only to purely mechanical exercises, that they did not need to understand what these texts really meant, that these texts had no real influence on their behavior. In short, these texts could have become mantras, held to have magical value simply in their repetition, without regard to their content. This danger occurred to Calvin himself. He felt that if the Lord's Prayer was used too frequently, it might come to be regarded as a kind of magical spell, like certain Latin prayers in common use among Catholics.[21] This was a reason he gave for not encouraging the repetition of the Lord's Prayer too frequently, specifically for not including its recital more than twice in a single church service.

Evidence from the consistory registers, however, argues persuasively against such a mechanical or magical usage. When a man or woman was summoned during the early years and asked why he or she had not received Communion during the last service, a frequent answer was "because I had hate in my heart" for a relative, a neighbor, or a business associate. The person questioned would explain that he or she could not in good conscience pray, as the Lord's Prayer requires, "forgive us our debts as we forgive our debtors," for she or he could not bring herself or himself to forgive specific acquaintances. In other words, these individuals remembered the terms of this most basic of all Christian prayers and took them seriously. Claude Vuarin, for example, refused to repeat the Lord's Prayer or attend Communion services because of his anger at others who had given false testimony against him. Claude Curtet similarly refused to repeat the Lord's Prayer or attend Communion because of a violent quarrel he had with his brother Jean over a joint business transaction that had gone sour. The widow of the innkeeper of the Bear Inn remained so angry at the man who killed her brother several years earlier that she varied the text of her version of the prayer. Instead of saying "Forgive us our debts as we forgive our debtors," she prayed the Lord to forgive her better than she could forgive the killer of her brother.[22]

---

21. Archives d'Etat de Genève, Registres du Conseil, vol. 44, fol. 268c (October 28, 1549): "Quant au Pater que l'on le dictz deux fois les dimenches deux fois [*sic*] a chascungs sermontz et aussi au cathezimes et que de faire autrement que cella seroit ung enchantement et ung charme comme aultresfois l'on disoyt *In principio erat verbum*." Quoted in Lambert, "Preaching, Praying, and Policing," p. 328 n. 111. Cf. the similar sentiment in the passage quoted in the *Calvini Opera*, 21:457, also for October 28, 1549.

22. These examples are all cited in Lambert, "Preaching, Praying, and Policing," pp. 453-54. They are taken from *RConsistoire*, 1:133-34 (fol. 68, October 26, 1542 — Vuarin); 48-49 (fol. 24, April 27, 1542 — Curtet); 2:267-68 (fol. 72v., August 5, 1546 — the widow).

The consistory took seriously such explanations. Rather than simply dismissing or disregarding them, it made sustained efforts to reconcile people who had serious disagreements, in order to enable them to repeat the Lord's Prayer in good conscience and thus receive Communion. The quarrel between Curtet and his brother, for example, festered for another year. When the brothers tried to have it settled through a civil suit, the city's governing council, in its capacity as chief city court, urged them to settle their disagreement between themselves. Finally in March of 1543, as plans were being made for Easter Communion, the two brothers appeared before the consistory. Jean Curtet said he was willing to do anything that *gens de bien,* people of standing and property, would do. Claude said he was now prepared to leave vengeance to God. They both had to listen to the ritual scoldings, involving quotations of relevant parts of Scripture, that were a standard part of these proceedings. Then they agreed to forgive each other and, to seal this agreement, touched each other "in sign of peace."[23]

These arrangements for reconciliation were not always tied this directly to the understanding of a prayer, but they became an important function of the consistory. Another striking case began at the initiative of a widow of a patrician family, Françoyse Tissot, who complained before the consistory that her illustrious son, Pierre, then treasurer of the republic, was neglecting her and letting his own brother run wild. The consistory called in Pierre and his wife for explanations, and eventually called in the other son as well. Pierre denied most of his mother's charges and intimated that she was simply becoming forgetful. He promised, however, to continue doing his best to take care of her and the rest of their family. After a number of consistory sessions, Françoyse finally agreed somewhat grudgingly to be reconciled with her son Pierre and his wife, "for the love of God and of the government."[24]

These reconciliations could become quite formal ceremonies. They might even be removed from the regular semiprivate sessions held before the consistory itself and attached to public church services, presided over by representatives of the consistory, often including Calvin himself.[25] A ceremony of this sort was clearly intended to make reconciliation certain and permanent by making it as public as possible. It was yet another way in which the consistory tried to make sure that Genevans lived in a truly Christian manner.

23. *RConsistoire,* 1:205-6 (fol. 101v., March 22, 1543).

24. *RConsistoire,* 1:266-67 (fols. 136-37, November 1, 1543).

25. For more on these ceremonies of reconciliation, see Robert M. Kingdon, "The Geneva Consistory in the Time of Calvin," in *Calvinism in Europe, 1540-1620,* ed. Andrew Pettegree, Alastair Duke, and Gillian Lewis (Cambridge: Cambridge University Press, 1994), pp. 26-33.

Reformed Education

Additional institutions were created to instruct Genevans who were capable of learning more, especially the minority who were literate. The formal pre-Reformation instruction in religion offered by distinctively Catholic institutions, of course, ceased. The municipal college established by the bequest of Versonnex had collapsed in the agitation leading up to the Reformation, and its building was no longer available. But the legislation creating the Protestant regime provided for the creation of a new college to take its place, located in the Franciscan Convent of the Rive, next door to the building for which Versonnex had paid. It remained a municipal elementary and secondary school but gained an entirely new staff. The first regent or director of the college was a man named Antoine Saunier, who doubled as a minister in the very earliest years after the Reformation, before Calvin had even arrived. He was paid a generous salary but was expected to share it with two bachelors who would assist him in the instruction. Soon after Calvin arrived in the city, he replaced Saunier as school director with Mathurin Cordier. This was a real coup, since Cordier had acquired a considerable reputation as one of Europe's most accomplished and widely respected teachers of students on the elementary level.

The program of instruction at the Collège de Rive was reorganized. Instruction was now more compartmentalized, with the student body broken down into seven classes. The seventh, or lowest, class is said to have attracted 280 students in 1541 — a surprisingly large number, given the amount of space in the former convent and the size of the staff. A considerable pent-up demand may have arisen in the turmoil between 1538 and 1541. Eighth and ninth classes were soon added, to provide education even more elementary than had traditionally been offered. The Franciscan convent proved to be too small, and additional space soon had to be found. A private house was purchased as an annex. Then space in other places scattered throughout the city was commandeered for use. All students were examined every year, and those who passed were promoted to the next higher class. The promotion ceremonies became public events of some importance. The curriculum continued to supply the basic training in the humanities typical of the period. Each textbook written for this school began with elementary instruction in learning the alphabet and reading, but then moved on to the Lord's Prayer, the Ten Commandments, and the creed.[26] The school day ended with a general assembly in which the entire stu-

---

26. On these textbooks, see Henri Delarue, "Les premiers manuels en usage au Collège de Genève," in *Le Collège de Genève, 1559-1959*, pp. 57-75, and particularly 60-61, on those that combined an introduction to reading with these religious texts.

dent body recited the Lord's Prayer, the creed, and the Ten Commandments. The school's program thus powerfully reinforced the religious instruction which almost all its students had first received in catechism.

There were also provisions from the early years for less formal instruction in religion for the literate. Arrangements were made to encourage public reading of the Bible. Every inn and tavern was required to keep on the premises a chained copy of the Bible, in the hope that literate visitors would not only read passages silently for their own edification but would also read passages aloud for the edification of others. Some innkeepers were called before the consistory to be reminded of this requirement.

The city of Geneva also sponsored public lectures on the Bible. They were intended for an even more sophisticated audience than the students in the Collège de Rive, people who were already well educated, most of them adults. They were an early substitute for the instruction on the university level that the city had not as yet provided. It was to deliver these advanced lectures that John Calvin had originally been hired. As an otherwise unidentified "Frenchman," hired on Farel's recommendation to give public lectures, he had been placed on the city's payroll only months after the city had formally decided to become Protestant in 1536. Calvin was apparently expected to explain to adult Genevans what they had done by turning Protestant, what were the new ideas to which they had committed themselves. He soon became more than a lecturer, and the lectures he had originally been hired to deliver now became sermons within church services. Only in 1541, on Calvin's return from a period of exile, did he officially assume a full range of pastoral responsibilities. When he returned, however, he never abandoned the lecturing for which he had been originally hired. He reported that immediately after his return in 1541 he resumed preaching on the Bible, and made a point of beginning at the very place at which he had been interrupted by his abrupt expulsion in 1538.[27] He continued these sermons to the end of his life.

He supplemented them with lectures in Latin he delivered in a chapel across an alley from the cathedral church, in a building that had belonged to a religious community and had served as one of Geneva's parish churches before the Reformation, now called the Auditoire de Calvin. In form both Calvin's sermons and lectures were commentaries on the Bible. He would select one book of the Bible each year, from either the Old Testament or the New, and then proceed by the *lectio continua* method to comment on each succeeding pericope. He often spoke without a written text. These sermons came to be so highly val-

---

27. See T. H. L. Parker, *Calvin's Preaching* (Louisville: Westminster/John Knox, 1992), p. 60, and the sources there cited.

ued, however, that the city hired secretaries to copy them down verbatim as Calvin spoke. Some of these copies were later edited for publication, several by Calvin himself. A number of them have never been published, yet still survive in the manuscript copies recorded by contemporary secretaries.[28]

These sermons and lectures attracted increasingly substantial audiences. The audiences, however, were not made up exclusively of ordinary Genevans. The sermons were in French and intended for the general population, but the lectures were in Latin and clearly intended for men of education. Many of those who listened to them were not Genevans at all, but members of the growing number of religious refugees who had flocked to Geneva to escape persecution at home and to acquaint themselves more fully with the Calvinist version of the faith. Many became ministers themselves, and before long missionaries back to their home countries. The great majority of the newcomers came from France, but significant numbers came from other countries.

Yet another institution designed to inform the educated was the *congregation,* a kind of adult Bible class. It was supervised by one of the licensed ministers, but laymen could, and often did, participate. The most celebrated session of this *congregation* was held in the fall of 1551, when Jerome Bolsec attacked Calvin's doctrine of predestination. That particular session was not supervised by Calvin himself but rather by his colleague Jean de St. André. The text assigned for discussion was John 8:47: "He who is of God hears the words of God; the reason why you do not hear them is that you are not of God" (RSV). Bolsec, a well-educated former Carmelite friar who had converted to Protestantism and now supported himself as a physician, primarily to the household of a refugee French nobleman, was a relative newcomer to the community. He retained an interest in theology and had gotten into arguments on theological issues with members of the corps of ministers. He used the occasion of this particular *congregation* to attack frontally Calvin's view of predestination, arguing that it made of God a tyrant like the pagan Jupiter. He supported his argument with a number of biblical allusions, and insisted that Calvin's version of predestination had distorted a doctrine taught by Augustine. Calvin rose to defend his position, astonishing the audience with the length and precision of his quotations from Augustine, no doubt from the anti-Pelagian tracts. The argument thus became a rather technical scholar's quarrel on the precise meaning of Augustine's teaching on predestination — hardly a debate the average Genevan could follow closely. But the spectacle of their religious leader being attacked by a newcomer was enough to provoke such

28. The editing of these sermons is one of a number of projects still facing experts on Calvin and his reformation. They are being published in a series titled the Supplementa Calviniana in Neukirchen-Vluyn by the Neukirchener Verlag des Erziehungsvereins, 1936-.

indignation that Bolsec was immediately thrown into jail, tried for misbelief, convicted, and banished from the city. A number of laymen who had expressed sympathy for Bolsec were rounded up, brought before the consistory, closely examined, and forced to recant. It is evident from their testimony that they could not follow the intricacies of the quarrel. But they had been impressed by Bolsec's good works, as a physician, and by the apparent erudition of his argument. And some of them at least had grasped the essence of his argument: that predestination as Calvin taught it can be seen to make of God an arbitrary tyrant. The very fact that relatively uneducated laymen and laywomen followed this debate and expressed opinions on it reveals that the impact of a *congregation* could extend well beyond the educated audience for which it was primarily intended.[29]

. Finally, toward the end of Calvin's ministry, the city established an academy, a school of higher education, the forerunner to the present University of Geneva. This created an institutional framework for pulling together all the educational activities developed in Geneva intended to provide instruction in the intricacies of Calvinist doctrine. It trained Calvinist ministers for the next several generations, not only for Geneva itself but also for the increasing number of other countries that followed Calvin's leadership. It featured improved instruction at the elementary level, as envisioned by Cordier. It folded into its curriculum the lectures Calvin had been giving since his first arrival in Geneva. It added instruction in disciplines never before offered in Geneva, most importantly biblical Greek and Hebrew, taught by newly appointed faculty members. Its rector was Theodore Beza, a brilliant young disciple of Calvin's, trained in law and the humanities, who had made an early reputation as a fine Latin poet. His knowledge of Greek may have exceeded Calvin's. He was to become Calvin's successor as moderator of the Reformed Church of Geneva and as the recognized intellectual leader of the entire branch of Protestantism that had come to look to Geneva for leadership.[30]

Conclusion

By the time of Calvin's death in 1564, Geneva had a complete and complex set of new institutions for instructing the local people in a new version of the Chris-

29. See Robert M. Kingdon, "Popular Reactions to the Debate between Bolsec and Calvin," in *Calvin: Erbe und Auftrag, Festschrift für Wilhelm Neuser zu seinem 65. Geburtstag,* ed. Willem van 't Spijker (Kampen: Kok, 1991), pp. 138-45, for more on this episode.

30. For a recent history of this institution, see Karin Maag, *Seminary or University? The Genevan Academy and Reformed Higher Education, 1560-1620,* St. Andrews Studies in Reformation History (Aldershot: Scolar, 1995).

tian faith. They were encouraged to keep up home instruction, now supplied with a number of supplements. For the entire population, both children and adults, there were weekly catechism classes, their lessons reinforced with religious services, several dozen a week. Public lectures, public theological discussions, eventually an entire academy were founded to train expert leaders for all these institutions, in Geneva and elsewhere. The consistory, an institution that monitored the entire process, made certain that it reached everyone in the community. These were the methods that Calvin's Geneva adopted to educate and form the population in the faith. For the first generations they seem to have been remarkably effective. People who did not want to accept them left, in considerable number. But even more were attracted by them and came, either for temporary visits or to settle permanently. Geneva became the model for an international religious movement of considerable reach and influence.

In later generations the role of the consistory in this process faded. It remained active and feared. Indeed, it reached an all-time peak in activity in the years right after Calvin's death. But it served less and less as an educational institution and more and more as an arbitrator of arguments and a guardian of public morals. And it became increasingly picky about the kind of behavior it expected of Genevans. People could be called in not only for actual sexual misbehavior but also for merely joking about sex. In 1568, for example, two men and a woman were excommunicated for "scandal and disrespect for the institution of marriage." Their crime: they had watched a groom the morning after his wedding cut a loaf of bread into pieces to show how many times he had had intercourse with his bride during their first night together.[31] By the seventeenth century, however, the Consistory of Geneva had become much less active than it had been at the height of the Reformation. Its records are much less detailed; it obviously summoned many fewer people; its sentences of excommunication were no longer so greatly feared.[32] This may well be testimony, however, to its success. By the report of all contemporaries, the texture of life in Geneva had changed radically. The lessons of the Calvinist Reformation had been internalized and were being automatically passed on by generations of devoted fathers, helped by generations of devoted catechists. The consistory was no longer necessary. The Reformation had succeeded.

31. Cited by E. William Monter in "The Consistory of Geneva, 1559-1569," *Bibliothèque d'Humanisme et Renaissance* 38 (1976): 483.

32. Monter, "The Consistory of Geneva," p. 484.

Ritual and Faith Formation
in Early Modern Catholic Europe

Philip M. Soergel

In 1754 the English Protestant revivalist George Whitefield came face-to-face with the religiosity of Catholic Europe, and as we might expect, despised what he saw. While sailing to the American colonies, his ship docked near Lisbon for more than a month. His visit came at Lent, and during a prolonged drought as well. Thus Whitefield observed daily processions clogging Lisbon's streets, not only for the penitential season but to place requests before God for relief from the drought. The revival preacher's visit came at a time when the great epoch historians traditionally have called the Counter-Reformation still cast a long influence over religious practice. During his visit to the Portuguese capital, Whitefield observed the full complement of rituals scholars have long associated with Counter-Reformation religion. The experience prompted apocalyptic outbursts, as the rites he witnessed seemed a confirmation that the "fullness of time" had come. At the same time, the preacher rejoiced in the great miracle of the Reformation, a miracle that had redeemed much of Europe from Roman idolatry.

One year later Whitefield's letters to his friends appeared in print at London and Boston.[1] Their criticism of Portuguese religion was not unrelieved. Whitefield did admire the sincerity of Lisbon's penitents and the grace of its preachers. But this sincerity and grace were directed to the service of a deceiving institution, the Roman Church, which did everything it could to foster what Whitefield called "dumb shew." To shock his readers, the preacher included de-

---

1. George Whitefield, *A brief account of some Lent and other extraordinary processions and ecclesiastical entertainments seen last year at Lisbon* (London and Boston, 1755); the texts are reprinted in *The Works of the Reverend George Whitefield, M.A.* (London, 1771), 3:73-80.

tailed descriptions of two religious processions. The first honored Francis of Assisi, and in it the faithful carried carved tableaux through Lisbon's streets. These scenes reminded onlookers of key events from Francis's life: the saint's abandonment of worldly riches; his reception of the stigmata; his rescue of people from a collapsing house at Madrid; his death, in which flowers sprang from his funeral bier; and finally his rescue of poor souls from purgatory. As the last scene approached, the assembled crowd clambered to touch knotted cords swaying from the saint's image.

Distasteful as such an exhibition was to Whitefield, he was even more horrified by a second procession later the same day. That evening, under the glow of moonlight, penitents dressed in white with "only holes . . . made for their eyes to peep out" began a march through the streets. Bound with heavy chains at their ankles, these flagellants made a "dismal rattling." Some carried "great stones on their backs, and others dead men's bones and skulls in their hands." Some bore large, heavy crosses, while others extended their arms in cruciform fashion. Still others carried bows "full of swords with the points downwards."[2] Whitefield took great pains to describe the individuality of these flagellants, including even a detailed record of the various ways they whipped themselves. Yet the responsibility for their bizarre behavior, he contended, was not their own. He blamed the Roman pope squarely for their actions.

For Whitefield Catholicism was a strange, mindless religion of displays — displays that ultimately kept the cult's laity in political and religious subjection. Having "sucked in and imbibed" superstition from their earliest youth, Catholics could offer no resistance to a life of bondage to the clergy and secular authorities. Judgments like Whitefield's were as common as the rain in Georgian England. As the English saw it, in those countries where Roman authority persisted, the laity habitually practiced an exotic collection of superstitious rites. These rites were encouraged, sometimes even foisted upon them, by pope and clergy, and they served to buttress not only the Roman Church's power but state authority as well.

Interpreting the "Counter-Reformation"

Like Whitefield, many twenty-first-century men and women retain a profound distaste for highly ritualized religious experience. The stylized beatings of masked flagellants appear as foreign, mysterious, and threatening. The crowds Whitefield observed struggling to touch cords hanging from a saintly image be-

---

2. *The Works of the Reverend George Whitefield*, 3:77-79.

speak a mentality that is archaically magical and superstitious. The true site for religion, a modern wisdom urges, is the interior space of heart and mind. Thus a sort of religious "evolutionism" continues to wage war on ritual as dead and archaic. This evolutionism, as Mary Douglas observed in *Natural Symbols,* "assumes that a rational, verbally explicit, personal commitment to God is self-evidently more evolved and better than its alleged contrary, formal ritualistic conformity."[3]

In this essay I want to avoid interpreting early modern Catholic rituals as formalistic or conformist and instead begin to peer behind the masks that have frequently obscured the mental world of groups like Lisbon's flagellants. The rites these groups practiced were typical of Catholic piety from the late sixteenth through the eighteenth century.[4] Many observers, though, continue to see that piety as a religious experience forged and created among clerical and political elites and subsequently imposed upon the laity. Certainly early modern Catholic regimes, like many of their Protestant counterparts, were often authoritarian; they aimed to control their subjects' religion in ways we find abhorrent. Yet even when the absolutist pretensions of Catholic rulers and the hierarchical structure of the early modern church are taken into account, Lisbon's flagellants, her crowds of pious spectators, cannot be robbed of creativity, discrimination, and agency. The early modern laity clearly favored some forms of ritual, even as they remained aloof from others. These preferences, then, can tell us a great deal about their perceptions of Christian truth during a turbulent period of the church's history. They speak as well to the problem we are striving to understand here: the sometimes conflicting, sometimes complementary patterns of formation, education, and indoctrination that emerge in textually based religions.

Before we can begin to understand the potent role rituals like Lisbon's processions played in the laity's attempts at forming their religion, we must take stock of the vast differences separating us from this early modern world. From the late sixteenth to the eighteenth centuries, religious belief and practices did not circulate in Europe in a free market. Missionary efforts may have converted a minority to particular religions, but most people were "cradle" Lutherans, Calvinists, or Catholics. And in many Protestant and Catholic states, secular and clerical officials aimed to define and cultivate their beliefs and practices in very specific, concrete ways. We cannot discriminate the degree to which the la-

---

3. Mary Douglas, *Natural Symbols: Explorations in Cosmology* (New York, 1973), p. 22.

4. I am not the first to make these observations. See esp. John O'Malley's remarks in "Catholic Reform," in *Reformation Europe: A Guide to Research,* ed. Steven Ozment (St. Louis, 1982), pp. 297-319; and more recently, those of Keith P. Luria in *Territories of Grace: Cultural Change in the Seventeenth-Century Diocese of Grenoble* (Berkeley, 1991).

ity retained power over their own religious formation without first taking stock of these attempts at control.

The century following 1550 has often been called an age of confessions, a characterization that emphasizes the clear battle lines that developed between the various post-Reformation religions.[5] Almost everywhere, religion coalesced around more clearly defined dogma, and secular and clerical authorities combined forces to insure doctrinal purity, to establish uniform religious practice, and to increase social and moral discipline among their subjects. Thus each of the major European confessions — Catholicism, Lutheranism, and Calvinism — came to share certain key structural elements, such as the emphasis on doctrine and discipline. At the same time, an increasingly differentiated ritual and cultural life helped foster new identities as parishioners came to think of themselves not just as Christians but as Catholics, Lutherans, or Calvinists.

Among Catholics, the process of creating a distinct identity was once said to begin with the Council of Trent (1545-63) and the Counter-Reformation it helped inspire. More recently, however, the chronology of Catholic reform has widened considerably to take account of the many serious devotional movements active within the church from the fifteenth to the eighteenth century. The Protestant reformations, in fact, were one product of this surge in lay piety and reforming zeal. Thus it would be inadequate to describe the renewal within the early modern Roman Catholic Church solely as a "Counter-Reformation," a pejorative term since it reduces the enormous spiritual creativity evident within the church to an essentially negative, anti-Protestant reaction. This "Catholic Reformation," to use a more appropriate phrase, consisted of both

5. German scholars in particular speak of the period as an era of "confessionalization." The theory of confessionalization is best summarized in the words of one of its most distinguished practitioners, Ernst Zeeden. Confessionalization is "the intellectual and organizational hardening of the diverging Christian confessions . . . into more or less stable church structures with their own doctrines, constitutions, and religious and moral styles." Quoted in Robert Bireley, S.J., "Early Modern Germany," in *Catholicism in Early Modern Europe: A Guide to Research*, ed. John O'Malley (St. Louis, 1988). That collection also contains a useful bibliography of confessionalization studies treating early modern Germany. In France and the Anglo-American world, historians have often spoken of the period in a similar, although slightly different vein. The era from the late sixteenth to the eighteenth century has often been characterized as one of "acculturation." Promoters of the "acculturation" thesis call attention to the dogged efforts of clerical elites to establish a more uniform doctrinal and sacramental Christianity. The works of Jean Delumeau, Philip Hoffman, and John Bossy are among the most widely known of this "acculturationist" school. See Jean Delumeau, *Catholicism between Luther and Voltaire: A New View of the Counter-Reformation* (London, 1977); and more recently, *Sin and Fear: The Emergence of a Western Guilt Culture, Thirteenth–Eighteenth Centuries* (New York, 1990); John Bossy, *Christianity in the West, 1400-1700* (London, 1985); and Philip T. Hoffman, *Church and Community in the Diocese of Lyon, 1500-1789* (New Haven, 1984).

negative elements of counterreform designed to combat Protestantism specifically and strains of long-term, positive, spiritual, and devotional renewal. Although we might insist on abandoning the term "Counter-Reformation" altogether, I rely on it in a limited sense: as a literary shorthand to describe the formulation of doctrinal and disciplinary reforms at the Council of Trent, and the processes through which those disciplines were established, altered, and sometimes ignored in the various Catholic states of Europe.[6]

The decrees that arose from the almost two decades of deliberations in the Italian city did contain a clear, forceful, and often negative response to Protestantism. And although those beliefs were not simply imposed on Catholics in the wake of Trent, they did serve as the definition for an official Catholicism for more than four centuries. In its insistence on a "formed" faith, the council drew perhaps the most important distinction between Catholic truth and the doctrines promoted by the emerging Protestant confessions. For the bishops, heads of religious orders, and ecclesiastical dignitaries who convened at Trent, faith was a necessary precursor — "the beginning, root, and foundation" — of a life that should be lived in grace. In contrast to the Protestant reformers, salvation and justification were defined not as one-time life events but as a lifelong process. And they required a constant infusion of divine grace working in concert with an individual's moral cooperation.[7]

This Catholic definition of salvation as a process arose from a radically different view of human nature from that of the Protestant reformers. For Luther the condition of human beings after the act of saving justification was like a "poor, wicked harlot" redeemed through marriage to the "rich and divine bridegroom Christ." Even after this stunning, highly improbable union, human beings retained all the wickedness that might accrue to a fallen woman.[8] In an age that seemed to glory in outpourings of such rhetoric, the pronouncements of Protestant reformers often made brilliant use of the "shock tactic." The long-debated formulations concerning sin and human nature that issued from Trent appear, by contrast, as a surprising model of charity and re-

---

6. The distinction between Catholic reform and Counter-Reformation is a venerable one, and present already in Hubert Jedin's monumental *History of the Council of Trent*, 5 vols. (New York, 1957-61).

7. Besides the lucid treatment of Jedin, short but judicious considerations of the council's doctrinal pronouncements can be found in the *New Catholic Encyclopedia* (New York, 1967), s.v. "Trent, Council of"; and the *Dictionnaire de Theologie Catholique* (Paris, 1923-50), s.v. "Trente, Concile de."

8. Martin Luther, *Tractatus de libertate christiana* (1520), in *D. Martin Luther's Werke. Kritische Gesamtausgabe* (Weimar, 1897), 7:55; ET, *The Freedom of a Christian*, in *Luther's Works*, trans. W. A. Lambert (Philadelphia, 1957), 31:352.

straint. Left untreated, sin held all the pernicious effects of a terminal condition. But for those who strove toward righteousness, their efforts might be met with a generous outpouring of divine aid. The fathers of Trent believed that sanctified perfection was still an earthly possibility, even if for most it remained a distant improbability. The Catholic life, then, should be a journey in pursuit of this ideal.

These were carefully reasoned and mediating positions, positions that the Tridentine fathers concluded could not be established without a disciplined and hierarchical church. Since the early Reformation a wisdom popular among many reform-minded elites within the Roman Church had in fact credited the appeal of Protestantism to the indiscipline and vices of the clergy. The notion was an ancient one shared by many medieval ecclesiastical reformers as well. If the church was to be purified in "head and members," the process of cleansing had to begin in the body's most vital, ruling parts. Trent's decrees consequently tried to address the clerical indiscipline it perceived had festered within the church, giving rise to the Protestant heresies. The council repeated older decrees forbidding the absence of bishops from their diocese. It stipulated expanded procedures for the licensing of preachers and required pastors and bishops to preach to their laity on Sundays and holy days. Trent envisioned as well a far-reaching seminary system that would train priests in theology, liturgy, and pastoral care, although the establishment of this ideal, like many of the council's decrees, lay at a point in the distant future for much of Catholic Europe.

Trent's most significant achievements, then, were to set new guidelines, and to reiterate old ones, through which clerical discipline might be established within the ecclesiastical framework of the church. Certainly the Tridentine fathers did not neglect lay religious practice. They articulated a detailed theology of the sacraments, tackled a number of thorny and long-standing issues that had surrounded the sacrament of marriage, and spoke to controversies that directly impinged on lay piety. They affirmed, for example, popular beliefs in the sacrificial character of the Mass, and they lent their approval to ancient extrasacramental customs and disciplines like the veneration of the saints, pilgrimages, and processions. In the later Middle Ages these had been an important source for a truly widespread surge in lay devotion; now Trent reaffirmed their vital role even as it tried to prune abuses, like the worst excesses of the indulgence trade, that had grown up around them.

Trent may have considered these important issues vital to lay religion, but we cannot conclude that lay religious practice was the council's central concern. The fathers directed the preponderance of their attention to administrative and disciplinary reforms of the clergy. The program they outlined was ambitious, and the clerical disciplines they prescribed were established neither quickly nor easily. In most places the Roman Church was forced to ally itself with secular powers to accomplish the reforms of the clergy Trent mandated, and state and diocesan authorities often greeted these decrees with lukewarm enthusiasm. Local conditions thus profoundly affected the establishment of the Tridentine program as various patterns of counterreform emerged in the numerous Catholic states of western Europe.[9]

Catholic Reform in Bavaria

Let us consider the Counter-Reformation in one European state, the duchy of Bavaria, a large and relatively powerful territory within the Holy Roman Empire. Bavaria has long been seen as typical of the extremes of censorship and prohibition that could emerge in the early modern Catholic state.[10] At the same time, Bavaria's richly visualistic and ritualized religion has often been treated as the logical outcome of the state's and church's efforts to control lay religious practice. The Bavarian state, in other words, has been credited with fostering a formal, ritualistic conformity like that Whitefield would attack in eighteenth-century Lisbon. Certainly the Bavarian state did throw its support behind certain rituals, but as we will see, it could not impose these on its subjects. Rather the devotional and ritual resurgence that occurred in Bavaria arose not primarily from the state's encouragement but from the laity's own demands. A closer look at the dynamics of lay, state, and clerical interaction in Bavaria, then, can help us refine our notions about the role state and clerical control exercised on early modern patterns of religious formation.

In Bavaria the Counter-Reformation arrived a full generation earlier than in most northern European states. In the years immediately following the conclusion of the Council of Trent, Bavaria's Duke Albrecht V (r. 1550-79) and his state and clerical officials pioneered a number of harsh and repressive measures designed to root out the territory's minority of Protestants. First threatened with fines, Protestants were, by 1570, forced to renounce their beliefs or face expulsion. During the century that followed a steadily intensifying stream of measures

9. The essays contained in *Catholicism in Early Modern Europe* summarize the enormous wealth of contemporary research on the complex patterns of Counter-Reformation.

10. Dieter Albrecht, "Gegenreformation und katholische Reform" and "Die Barockzeit," in *Handbuch der bayerischen Geschichte* 2 (Munich, 1988), pp. 268-94 and 714-35; Andreas Ludwig Veit and Ludwig Lenhart, *Kirche und Volksfrömmigkeit im Zeitalter des Barock* (Freiburg, 1956), passim; and R. Po-Chia Hsia, *Social Discipline in the Reformation: Central Europe (1550-1750)* (London, 1989), p. 41.

attempted to establish uniform Catholic beliefs and practices among Bavarian subjects. Booksellers, students, and merchants were all closely scrutinized, and state officials conducted frequent forays into the countryside, making unannounced house sweeps to unearth prohibited Protestant books. Ducal decrees, moreover, came to require regular attendance at Mass and confession. An ingenious system of ticketing, eventually adopted in other Catholic states, was developed to insure their compliance; each year Bavarians were to present their local officials with tickets they received when performing their sacramental duties.[11]

We do well, though, not to overemphasize the effectiveness of these measures. Early modern states, unlike their twenty-first-century counterparts, were frequently ill equipped to enforce the decrees they so often pronounced. Chronic administrative and fiscal weakness plagued most governments, and while at some times and places religious policies like these could be enforced with dogged determination, their administration was more often haphazard and piecemeal. Nevertheless, a distinct Catholic identity can be seen emerging in early modern Bavaria. But it was less the result of the state's prohibitions than we might imagine. The formation of a more self-conscious Catholic identity was as much the product of a rich ritual and devotional culture within the early modern church.

Lay Religious Practices

Even as the Bavarian state moved against its Protestant minorities at the end of the sixteenth century, a widespread resurgence of lay devotion also occurred. The state and clergy did not initiate this pious surge. Rather, Bavaria's dukes, their officials, and the territory's counterreforming clergy often appear to have been trying to rush ahead of it, moving to support and discipline the laity's desires for both new and time-honored forms of piety.

One of the first signs of this rise in lay devotion is evident in Bavaria's towns, where new confraternities quickly multiplied at the end of the sixteenth and beginning of the seventeenth centuries, satisfying a broad demand for an

---

11. The "prehistory" of the Counter-Reformation in Bavaria is treated in W. Götz, *Die bayrische Politik im ersten Jahrzehnt der Regierung Herzog Albrecht V von Bayern, 1550-1560* (Munich, 1896). The measures summarized here are treated in Dieter Breuer, *Geschichte der literarischen Zensur in Deutschland* (Heidelberg, 1982), pp. 39-42; Helmut Neumann, *Staatliche Bücherzensur und -aufsicht in Bayern von der Reformation bis zum Ausgang des 17. Jahrhunderts* (Heidelberg, 1977); K. Heigel, "Die Censur in Altbaiern," *Archiv für Geschichte des deutschen Buchhandels* 1 (1876): 5-32; Hans Rößler, *Geschichte und Strukturen der evangelischen Bewegung im Bistum Freising, 1520-1571* (Nürnberg, 1966), pp. 12-13.

associational piety. Part of a European-wide phenomenon, these early modern sodalities were different from the relatively autonomous confraternities of the later Middle Ages. Their male members bound themselves in ritual brotherhood, promising to perform good works and to meet regularly for prayer and devotions. In Bavaria these new organizations may have first appeared in the towns where counterreforming clerics worked. The first of the new brotherhoods appeared in the university town of Ingolstadt in 1577. The second formed a year later in the duchy's capital, Munich, where Bavaria's duke was the first to inscribe his name in the membership rolls. He encouraged members of his family and court to follow. As a consequence, Munich's new confraternity had a distinctly elite flavor during its first years. Soon, however, members of the town's guilds and professions clamored to join, and when they did, new brotherhoods multiplied to accommodate them. By 1600 a system of sodalities arranged along occupational lines was already taking shape in Munich and in other Bavarian towns.[12] In the short span of a generation, they had spread to almost every corner of the duchy.

The new organizations frequently embraced a militant piety. Many chose triumphant images of the Virgin as standards, and they imagined themselves as spiritual armies that might effect a Catholic reconquest of Europe. This victory, they reasoned, could not be accomplished without the purity of mind and body of each of the brotherhood's members. The search for spiritual perfection thus became enormously important in their devotional life, with prayer vigils, frequent penance, and ascetic regimens like the wearing of hair shirts and self-flagellation becoming important means of catharsis.

In several cases the confraternities dedicated themselves exclusively to the service of a local saint or a shrine patron. For example, Altötting, Bavaria's premier Marian pilgrimage site, benefited especially from rising confraternal devotion, becoming the site of a new Archconfraternity of the Altötting Madonna. The Bavarian Duke Wilhelm V (r. 1579-98) was himself the first to inscribe his name in the membership roll. Less than thirty years after its foundation the Altötting congregations claimed more than 6,200 members in their various constituent branches throughout Bavaria. In addition to meeting regularly for prayer and devotions, members were required to process to the shrine by foot once every four years. During the seventeenth century similar organizations developed at other Bavarian pilgrimage sites as well.[13] Many brotherhoods

---

12. Louis Chatellier, *The Europe of the Devout: The Catholic Reformation and the Formation of a New Society*, trans. Jean Birrell (Cambridge, 1989), p. 15.

13. The details concerning the Altötting pilgrimage confraternity are from Georg Schreiber, "Strukturwandel der Wallfahrt," *Wallfahrt und Volkstum in Geschichte und Leben:*

made public pilgrimages to local shrines or helped in the staging of urban processions.

Certainly the religious life of these pious brotherhoods should not be read as typical of all early modern Catholics. The confraternities, it is true, enrolled significant numbers of Bavaria's male subjects, but they were still comprised of self-selecting groups of the devout. A desire to achieve spiritual purity, to practice group devotions, to perform good works, and to counteract the perceived threat of Protestantism linked these associations' members. But though their devotion may have been more intense than that of many laypeople, broad sectors of the duchy's population practiced at least some of the same rituals the confraternities promoted. In particular, Bavarians of both genders and all social stations generally shared the congregations' affection for processions.

Like the devotional confraternities, state and clergy aimed to discipline these widely popular religious demonstrations. Their efforts to control, though, did not always have the desired effects. During the reign of Albrecht V, for instance, the state and clergy may have scored a success when they moved to expand the celebration of the feast of Corpus Christi, using its traditional procession to glorify the state and institutional church and to signal the authority of both over religion. Ducal decrees required state officials to march in the annual procession, and Bavaria's dukes undertook the provisioning of the festival on a lavish scale. These departures may have underscored the feast's function as a state ritual, but to the thousands who participated in the annual event, Corpus Christi's importance lay elsewhere.

With its dramatic living tableaux, Munich's Corpus Christi procession provided a forum through which local guilds and confraternities competed for civic honors and displayed their Catholic allegiance. Each year hundreds of costumed laypeople reenacted the key events of biblical history atop elaborate decorated floats that moved with the procession. In this way the town's laypeople involved themselves in a dramatic staging of the forces that had produced Christ's passion and instituted the ongoing sacrifice of the Eucharist. The intensity of their enterprise rose to baroque proportions during the early modern

---

Forschungen zur Volkskunde 16/17 (1934): 1-183, here esp. 29; and Maria-Angela König, *Weihegaben an U. L. Frau von Altötting* 2 (Munich, 1939), pp. 90-91. On the rise of these pilgrimage confraternities generally, see Chatellier, pp. 153-55; Ludwig Paulussen, "Marianische Kongregation," in *Lexikon für Theologie und Kirche,* ed. Michael Buchberger (Freiburg, 1930-38); Philipp Löffler, *Die marianischen Kongregationen in ihrem Wesen und ihrer Geschichte* (Freiburg, 1911); Josef Miller, "Die marianischen Kongregationen im 16. und 17. Jahrhundert: ihr Wesen und ihr marianischer Charakter," *Zeitschrift für katholische Theologie* 58 (1934): 83-109; Anna Coreth, "Die ersten Sodalitäten der Jesuiten in Österreich: Geistigkeit und Entwicklung," in *Spiritualtät aus dem 16. und 17. Jahrhundert: Jahrbuch für mystische Theologie* 9 (1965): 7-65.

period. As confraternities multiplied in Munich before and after 1600, for example, new groups demanded to be included in the historical procession. This desire for group participation was, in fact, the driving force behind the huge increase in the numbers who marched, an increase already evident in the last quarter of the sixteenth century. In 1574, for example, the participants in Munich's Corpus Christi cortege numbered 1,439, and in 1582, 3,082, while documents from the 1590s and 1600s suggest a subsequent steady enlargement.[14] Bavaria's dukes and their cadre of counterreforming state and clerical officials may have viewed Corpus Christi as a way to impose control, discipline, and uniformity on their subjects. Yet for Munich's inhabitants the feast plainly served a variety of social and religious purposes.

The duchy's townspeople may have concentrated their attention on producing ostentatious displays like these, but Bavaria was a profoundly rural region. None of its towns could exercise the influence over the surrounding countryside that the great international trading centers of the empire did. But in the territory's vast stretches of farmland and villages, a similar surge in lay devotion, evidenced in the steady multiplication of local pilgrimages, soon manifested itself as well. The custom of making processions to the graves, relics, and images of the saints was, it is true, an ancient way of garnering miraculous intercession and saintly protection. In the course of the Middle Ages Bavarians had created a panoply of sacred sites in the countryside and, by the fifteenth century, pilgrimage to many of these had grown amazingly popular.[15] The attacks of Protestant reformers in the half-century after 1520 had, however, caused many of these sites to decline, some even to disappear. Yet at the end of the sixteenth century, devotion to the saints began to make an undeniable comeback. In the seventeenth and eighteenth centuries this reflorescence would outstrip the popularity saints and their shrines had enjoyed in the later Middle Ages.

Bavaria's dukes and its state and clerical officials encouraged but did not

14. Alois Mitterwieser, *Geschichte der Fronleichnamsprozession in Bayern* (Munich, 1930), esp. pp. 36-37, and Sigmund Riezler, *Geschichte Baierns* 6 (Gotha, 1903), pp. 244ff. An easily accessible, if poetic, description of Munich's Corpus Christi procession is also in Michael Kunze's *High Road to the Stake: A Tale of Witchcraft* (Chicago, 1970), pp. 353-58.

15. Medieval developments in Bavaria are best summarized in Steven D. Sargent, "Religion and Society in Late Medieval Bavaria: The Cult of Saint Leonard, 1258-1500" (Ph.D. diss., University of Pennsylvania, 1982); Sargent, "Miracle Books and Pilgrimage Shrines in Late Medieval Bavaria," *Historical Reflections* 13 (1986): 455-71; Josef Staber, *Volksfrömmigkeit und Wallfahrtswesen des Spätmittelalters im Bistum Freising*, published as vol. 20, no. 1, of *Beiträge zur altbayerischen Kirchengeschichte* (1955); and Philip Soergel, *Wondrous in His Saints: Counter-Reformation Propaganda in Bavaria* (Berkeley, 1993), pp. 15-43.

summon forth this renewed devotion. The impetus behind the state's and the clergy's efforts to nurture pilgrimage and saintly devotion was clearly anti-Protestant. Since the earliest years of the Reformation, Protestants had waged war against the saints and their shrines. They had vehemently attacked the miracles the clergy promoted at these places as frauds or as products of a deceived religion of barter. In the last quarter of the sixteenth century the Catholic clergy in Bavaria began to work to rehabilitate the cult of the saints from these Protestant attacks. At Ingolstadt and Munich, for example, the counter-reforming clergy issued a number of apologetic and propagandistic works that outlined the spiritual benefits of pilgrimages, attempting to mold them into an expression of Catholic religiosity. The works that flowed from the Munich and Indolstadt presses ranged from "pilgrimage books," which related lore and miracles about shrine sites and their patrons, to imposing theological treatises like the voluminous *Procession Book* by a Jesuit, Jacob Gretser.[16] Works like these spoke most effectively to a cadre of literate lay and clerical devout who were striving to understand the deeper meanings and purposes of traditional religious practices. The ideas they frequently contained — that pilgrimage was a kind of everyman's spiritual exercise, that processions were an ancient, time-honored way to demonstrate humility before God and his saints — did not "trickle" down to animate all Bavarians' religion. In the countryside most people, even many clerics, were unable to read these defenses of traditional religious devotion.

To Bavaria's villagers state and clerical support for saintly pilgrimage would still have been obvious. It would have been manifest in the imposing processions of the territory's dukes, their court, and members of the counterreforming clergy to the duchy's most prominent shrines. The arrival of the counterreforming orders at pilgrimage churches throughout the countryside would also have demonstrated ecclesiastical sanction. But although the state and church lent active encouragement to the renewal of the cult of the saints, they remained relatively powerless to regulate just how, when, or where the laity exercised its devotion.

The case of the cult of Saint Benno at Munich, for example, exposes the limits of state and clerical control. In 1578 the Bavarian Duke Albrecht V imported the relics of a relatively obscure Saxon bishop, Saint Benno, to his capital, Munich. During the next century his descendants and Munich's clergy la-

---

16. These subjects are treated in greater detail in my *Wondrous in His Saints*. Gretser's monumental volume outlined every spiritual benefit that could derive from processions and every ascetic and devotional discipline that might be applied to them. Jakob Gretser, *De sacris et religiosis peregrinationibus* (Ingolstadt, 1606); German trans.: *Processionsbuch* (Ingolstadt, 1612).

bored long and hard to establish a devotion for Benno, a saint who had conveniently been the victim of Protestant iconoclastic attacks. Eventually installed in the town's parish church, the Frauenkirche, Benno's miraculous intercessions began to be broadcast enthusiastically by Munich's clergy. The Wittelsbach dukes, moreover, imagined Benno's relics as the focal point for a national shrine, a kind of Bavarian Saint Denis. They commissioned a splendid architectural frame to be built as the backdrop for his cult, and they even interred their own family members in a specially constructed mausoleum beneath Benno's remains. But all these exertions never succeeded in establishing the cult as anything more than a modest devotion visited by locals from in and around Munich.[17]

Time and again we see similar evidence of the degree to which the resurgence of pilgrimage occurred independently of state and church intentions. In the course of the seventeenth century, for instance, most of Bavaria's villages obligated themselves through perpetual vows to perform an annual circuit of processions to local holy places. Communities often named as many as ten or twelve local shrines they visited on Sundays and holy days, usually during the summer months. Although local priests certainly may have advised which shrines their communities should visit, these decisions were made by the villagers themselves. Laypeople were responsible for keeping alive the pilgrimage circuit annually, for undertaking the preparations for these journeys, and for ensuring that a respectably sizable contingent of their fellow villagers participated.[18] Throughout the seventeenth and eighteenth centuries the enthusiasm for these annual journeys was infectious — so much so that by 1700 the institutional church had begun to question their wisdom. At that time the Bavarian dioceses of Regensburg and Passau tried unsuccessfully to curb the annual processions. Many villages had filled up their summer months with so many pilgrimages that no one was left at home on Sundays and holy days to take part in the Mass.[19]

17. Robert Böck, "Die Verehrung des hl. Benno in München," *Bayerisches Jahrbuch für Volkskunde* (1958): 53-73. The monumental building program undertaken in support of Benno's cult is treated in Karin Berg, "Der Bennobogen der Münchner Frauenkirche: Geschichte, Rekonstruktion und Analyse der Frühbarocken Binnenchoranlage" (Ph.D. diss., University of Munich, 1979).

18. Hermann Hörger, "Dorfreligion und bäuerliche Mentalité im Wandel ihrer ideologischen Grundlagen," *Zeitschrift für bayerische Landesgeschichte* 40 (1977): 244-316, and Hörger, *Kirche, Dorfreligion und bäuerliche Gesellschaft. Strukturanalysen zur gesellschatsgebunden Religiösität ländlicher Unterschichten des 17. bis 19. Jahrhunderts augezeigt an bayerischen Beispielen*, pt. 1 (Munich, 1978).

19. See Walter Hartinger, "Die Wallfahrt Neukirchen bei hl. Blut," *Beiträge zur Geschichte des Bistums Regensburg* 5 (1971): 23-240, esp. 96.

By this and other accounts, the surge in saintly devotion in Bavaria was enormous. An inventory conducted during the 1960s within the modern state of Bavaria, for example, catalogued more than a thousand still-functioning pilgrimage sites; the vast majority of these cults first appeared, were reestablished, or grew dramatically in the early modern period.[20] Far from a static, unchanging dimension of lay religion, the processions undertaken to local shrines also displayed considerable development over time. In the later Middle Ages Marian devotion had begun to challenge and displace older cults of thaumaturgic saints. While saints' cults did not disappear in early modern Bavaria, the trend to an increased preeminence of the Virgin continued. Some older saints' and eucharistic cults even successfully transformed themselves into new Marian pilgrimages. These changes were not "clerically imposed," but rather they occurred in response to a new broadly shared piety that embraced Mary as the unquestioned leader of the celestial hierarchy.[21]

In the countryside new processional forms also appeared, forms that suggest a rising self-consciousness about the role that pilgrimage played in the laity's notions of Catholic identity. In the seventeenth century, for instance, Bavaria's villagers came increasingly to appropriate a traditional horse procession once practiced by the imperial nobility and medieval pilgrims. Known as an *Umritt,* such a procession had first been used by the medieval German emperors to mark the geographical bounds of their authority and to collect pledges of obedience from their subjects. At the very end of the Middle Ages, *Umritte* also emerged as a form of piety at shrines of the bleeding host. At these sites pilgrims revered eucharistic wafers miraculously preserved against the alleged desecration of Jews or heretics. A kind of metaphorical crusade, the *Umritt* celebrated Christ's victory in preserving his presence in the host against attack, even as it underscored the pilgrims' determination to protect the shrine in the present and future.[22] Early modern Bavarians came to practice these equine processions, not just at bleeding host shrines but at many saints' and Marian pilgrimages as well. The practice became extraordinarily popular. By 1756, for instance, more than seven thousand horsemen took part in the annual horse procession to the shrine at Scheyern, a procession that was only one in "a land that rejoiced exceedingly

20. Robert Böck, "Die Wallfahrtsinventarisation der bayerische Landesstelle für Volkskunde," *Bayerisches Jahrbuch für Volkskunde* (1960): 7-21.

21. See esp. Ludwig Hüttl, *Marianische Wallfahrten im süddeutsch-österreichischen Raum* (Vienna, 1986).

22. R. Schmid, "Königsumritt und Huldigung in ottonisch-salischer Zeit," *Vörträge und Forschungen* 6 (1961): 114ff.; Lionel Rothkrug, "Holy Shrines, Religious Dissonance, and Satan in the Origin of the German Reformation," *Historical Reflections* 14 (1987): 230-31.

in *Umritte*."[23] Like the militant piety male confraternities embraced, Bavaria's horseback pilgrims imagined themselves as an army, a spiritual army that demonstrated both its affection for the saints and its determination to protect them against heretics and unbelievers.

Brotherhoods of horseback pilgrims, like those of confraternal chambers, helped create foreign enemies. An *Umritt* or a Corpus Christi procession, in other words, inscribed a space of belief and practice and created a public forum in which early modern Catholics demonstrated their most fundamental religious assumptions against their Protestant neighbors. This hard-edged, often polemical strain of piety informed lay religion during the seventeenth and eighteenth centuries, manifest not only in harsh and repressive states like Bavaria but also in places where the counterreforming program of secular and clerical officials was far less severe.[24] Among Catholics, as among Protestants, rituals may have served as powerful media for social integration; at the same time, they were potent vehicles for religious and cultural differentiation. While a Corpus Christi procession served, in part, to set out a purified Catholic theology of the Eucharist against Lutherans and Calvinists, it also served to educate, teaching just how Catholics perceived the relationship between the Bible and their ritual praxis. The impetus came not just from the "top down," that is, from state and clerical elites to people, but from within the laity as well.

A history of religious formation in early modern Europe that failed to take stock of the brute force of state and clerical repression would perform an injustice. I have not denied those forces here. Instead I have insisted that in large areas of religious practice political and clerical elites and the laity converged, achieving consensus concerning the religious forms they believed were most suitable to their communities. At the Council of Trent the church's foremost theologians had defined the theology of redemption for Catholic life as consisting in process. That process was both a pilgrimage punctuated by sacraments and good works and a spiritual war waged perpetually against sin. When we

---

23. *Österreichischer Volkskundeatlas*, ed. Ernst Burgstaller and Adolf Helbok (Linz, 1959), map of *Umritte*. The figures for participants at Scheyern's *Umritt* are from Rudolf Kriss, *Die Wallfahrtsorte Europas* (Munich, 1950), pp. 55-56.

24. Several recent works on the history of the Counter-Reformation describe similar widely popular resurgences of pilgrimages and processions. See Keith P. Luria, *Territories of Grace: Cultural Change in the Seventeenth-Century Diocese of Grenoble* (Berkeley, 1991); Marc R. Forster, *The Counter-Reformation in the Villages: Religion and Reform in the Bishopric of Speyer, 1560-1720* (Ithaca, N.Y., 1992); and Trevor Johnson, "Blood, Tears, and Xavier Water: Jesuit Missionaries and Popular Religion in the Eighteenth-Century Upper Palatinate," in *Popular Religion in Germany and Central Europe, 1400-1800*, ed. Bob Scribner and Trevor Johnson (New York, 1996), pp. 183-202.

peer into the religious universe of the early modern Catholic town or its enveloping countryside, we see these metaphors springing continually and vividly to life. Thus the widespread surge in processions and pilgrimages evident in early modern Catholic Europe becomes far more than a mute and mindless subjection to state and clerical authority. That criticism, kept alive from Whitefield's day to our own, betrays at once a misunderstanding of the religious demonstrations of a Lisbon or a Munich. Behind the masks of Lisbon's penitents reposed convictions — convictions apparent in the steady conflation of older ritual forms and in the dynamic creation of new ones. In a Corpus Christi procession or a simple rural pilgrimage, the laity taught a faith they perceived as in need of constant nourishment through physical actions. And in bodily as well as verbal utterances they displayed a longing to perfect their fallen natures, even as they tried to remediate the effects sin produced in their communities.

Spiritual Direction as Christian Pedagogy

Lawrence S. Cunningham

It is perilous for a person to teach who has not been first seasoned by personal experience.

Amma Syncletica

Behind every saint stands another saint. That is the great tradition. I never learnt anything by my own old nose.

Baron Von Hugel

Christian education is, and has historically been, more than the education of the intellect alone. It is instead an education of both mind and heart, aiming to convert a person to a deeper existential grasp of faith. For that reason it is important to attend to those forms of Christian education which profess to enhance piety and foster spiritual growth. This essay will consider what has traditionally been called "spiritual direction," both as a historical tradition and as a contemporary practice. Spiritual direction is an ancient form of Christian instruction in which a mature Christian person aids another in the pursuit of Christian perfection by serving as a guide, counselor, or teacher. Such instruction may occur in many informal ways, ranging from the spiritual advice or support given by a friend or family member in a particular setting to the ordinary pastoral counseling tasks performed within the ecclesial community. This paper will focus on more formally recognized spiritual directors who, through actual appointment (e.g., as a novice master in a religious house or as a retreat director), by their personal charismatic or sacramental authority, or through the *cura pastoralis* of a minister in a parish, guide persons who seek a fuller or deeper life of Christian service, freedom from sinful dispositions, mastery of deep-rooted temptations against faith, and/or advancement in the life of prayer.

The ancient tradition of the spiritual guide envisions one person of proven religious experience helping another person overcome temptations against faith and also counseling him or her into a deeper life of prayer and the following of the gospel. This form of teaching involves, typically, someone teaching another either face-to-face or through other forms of exchange. The tradition of spiritual guidance, for example, has produced an enormous literature of letters. It may well involve confession, though not necessarily in the sacramental sense of the term. Such direction may be of short duration (e.g., through a novitiate year or at a certain trying period of life), or it may continue on a more or less long-term or permanent basis.

When we call spiritual direction a *tradition*, the term is not used loosely. As these pages hope to show, there are many instances where the lines of transmission from one spiritual director to another are quite clear and continuous, sometimes over generations. To cite but one example: early in this century the influential Anglican director-scholar Evelyn Underhill was directed by the Roman Catholic writer and director Baron Friedrich Von Hugel. Von Hugel, in turn, had sought the direction from the celebrated nineteenth-century Parisian priest Abbé Henri Huvelin, who had not only been a profoundly influential director at Paris in the previous century but had himself learned the art of spiritual guidance from a close study of seventeenth-century masters.[1] Huvelin taught in France the spiritual guidance techniques of the sixteenth-century Jesuit and Carmelite schools of spirituality.

The historical taxonomy of spiritual direction is very complex in the Christian tradition.[2] This paper can only suggest some models and their trajectories in order to provide a broad outline of the types and roles of the spiritual director, as a means of describing only one way Christians are instructed in aspects of their faith. It will not be possible to compare the role of the spiritual director in Christianity to those persons who have analogous functions (e.g., the sage, guru, or Zen master) in other religious traditions, even though such persons bear what Wittgenstein has called a "family resemblance."[3] This paper consid-

---

1. Huvelin's *Some Spiritual Guides of the Seventeenth Century* (ET, 1927) witnesses how close he did study them.

2. The most authoritative survey is "Direction, spirituelle," in *Dictionnaire de Spiritualité, ascetique et mystique* III (Paris: Beauschene, 1932-), pp. 530-47; also see "Direzione spirituale," in *Dizionario degli istituti spirituali* III (Rome: Paoline, 1973).

3. Comparative essays may be found in *Abba: Guides to Wholeness and Holiness East and West*, ed. John R. Sommerfeldt (Kalamazoo: Cistercian Publications, 1982); *Maitres et disciples*

ers a few typologies of spiritual direction and concludes with reflections on the recovery of spiritual direction outside the Roman Catholic and Orthodox traditions, and with some final notes on the contemporary situation in spiritual direction.

The Abba/Amma

One of the first examples of systematic spiritual direction can be found in the practices of the early desert ascetics, whose activities began in the early fourth century. The influential *Life of Antony*, written by Athanasius shortly after Antony's death in A.D. 356, reports that when Antony, in obedience to things he heard in the Gospel, decided to take up a life of withdrawal and prayer, he "sought out an old man who had lived the solitary life from his youth" and "emulated him in his goodness."[4] Antony was not joining a "religious order"; it would be anachronistic to think of him as a "monk." He simply took up the solitary life and, as it were, apprenticed himself to someone who would initiate him into this style of life. Antony desired to lead a "Gospel" life as he understood it, and found someone who could teach him how to do that.

After twenty years of solitary withdrawal *(anachoresis)*, Antony assumed a teaching role for those who came to seek him out, whether for the alleviation of their problems (14), to dispute with him like certain Greek philosophers (72), or to seek his advice, as in the case of the emperor Constantine and his sons (81). More to our subject, however, people came to Antony to find out how to lead the ascetic life (14-15). Those attracted to him recognized his charismatic authority as an "icon" of the Gospel. Indeed, Athanasius says he wrote his book so that "other persons might learn what the life of the monk ought to be," as well as for the "benefit of the pagans" (94).[5]

---

dans les traditions religieuses, ed. Michael Mestin (Paris: Cerf, 1990). I have attempted to sort out these "family resemblances" in "Sages, Wisdom, and the Catholic Tradition," *Warren Lecture Series in Catholic Studies* 27 (Tulsa: University of Tulsa Press, 1993). For a recent attempt at inculturating Christian spiritual direction in a multicultural context, see *Common Journey/ Different Paths: Spiritual Direction in Cross-Cultural Perspective,* ed. Susan Rakoczy (Maryknoll, N.Y.: Orbis, 1992).

4. *Life of Antony* 3. The standard translation is *Athanasius: The Life of Antony,* trans. Robert C. Gregg (New York: Paulist, 1980). Parenthetical references in the following text are to this source.

5. Readers of Augustine's *Confessions* will recall how influential the book was both in his own story and, earlier, in the lives of certain young intellectuals in Trier. On the impact of Athanasius's work on monasticism, see Graham Gould, "The Life of Antony and the Origins of Monasticism in Fourth Century Egypt," *Medieval History* 1 (1991): 12-22.

The Life of Antony provides two important clues about the role of the early monastic Abba (father) and Amma (mother) as spiritual directors. First, they served as masters/mistresses for those who wished to enter into the ascetic life, and second, they were recognized widely as holy persons to whom a broad range of persons might go for advice, consolation, prayer, or guidance on moral, spiritual, or other problems. In the collected literature of these desert ascetics gathered under the title "Sayings of the Desert Fathers" (Lat. *Verba Seniorum;* Gk. *Apophthegmata Patrum*), we find numerous examples of such direction given both to aspiring ascetics and to others who came for spiritual advice.[6] Most of this material appears in the form of short sayings, exempla, or brief reminiscences of what one Abba remembers another saying.

Among the desert ascetics, spiritual direction was given — or better, described — in an almost stereotypical way: The petitioner would approach the Abba/Amma and ask one of two questions, "Can you give me a Good Word?" or "What must I do?" The response was given in a pithy aphorism or, frequently, in a saying rooted in the Scriptures that the petitioner would take away to put into practice. Examples of these questions and answers abound in the literature; here are two chosen from many:

> A brother came to Scetis to visit Abba Moses and ask for a word. The old man said to him: "Go, sit in your cell, and your cell will teach you everything."[7]

> Some old men came to Abba Poemen and said to him: "When we see brothers dozing at the synaxis [i.e., the nightly liturgy], shall we rouse them so that they will be watchful?" He said to them, "For my part, when I see a brother dozing I put his head on my knee and let him rest."[8]

This literature and its derivatives reveal the beginnings of a more systematic vocabulary and practice. The petitioner might be encouraged to "manifest the heart" *(exagoreusis)* so that the Abba could better understand the impulses which hold a person back from "purity of heart," or aid him in that discernment *(diakrisis)* by which a person overcomes vice and grows in love of God. From the simple sayings of the desert fathers an entire monastic literature

---

6. The complicated history of the compilation, translation, and diffusion of these sayings need not detain us; for an excellent survey of recent scholarship, see Douglas Burton-Christie, *The Word in the Desert* (New York: Oxford University Press, 1993).

7. *The Sayings of the Desert Fathers: The Alphabetical Collection,* trans. Benedicta Ward (Kalamazoo: Cistercian Publications, 1975), p. 118. On the relationship of the Abba to his disciple, see Graham Gould, *The Desert Fathers on Monastic Community* (Oxford: Clarendon, 1993), pp. 27-83.

8. *Sayings,* p. 151.

would evolve, setting out the views that hold people back from "purity of heart" (the classic term for growth in grace) and the Gospel virtues that perfect them in their Christian life.[9]

Two historical trajectories in the subsequent history of the Christian spiritual tradition take their origins from these monastic beginnings. In the Christian East there is an unbroken tradition of the spiritual master or mistress, usually but not always found in monasteries, who serves as a spiritual guide for those who wish to be formed in the ascetic life or to whom others come for advice, counsel, or direction. In time there evolved the concept of the elder (Gk. *Geron*; Russ. *starets*), who retreated into a life of solitude for a long period and then, in the traditional formulation, "threw open the doors" to receive those who wished to come for direction. Readers of Fyodor Dostoyevsky's *The Brothers Karamazov* will remember the fictional starets, Father Zossima, based on an actual monk the author had met in 1873.[10] Contemporary Orthodox believers still visit the great monastic centers of Mount Athos, Saint Catherine's in the Sinai, the island of Patmos, or Zagorsk in Russia to seek the "good word" of the elders who dwell there. They are the contemporary progeny of a spiritual tradition in the Christian East that goes back to the desert monastic experience. They form what Kallistos Ware has called a "largely hidden . . . apostolic tradition of the spiritual fathers and mothers in each generation of the church — the succession of saints stretching from the apostolic age to our own day, which Symeon the New Theologian has called the 'golden Chain.'"[11]

In the West, by contrast, the charismatic spiritual director slowly became "institutionalized," first by the appointed position of "novice master" in monasteries and, beyond the cloister, by the slow evolution of the priest who functioned as a minister of sacramental confession. In the former case a young monastic was put under the care of an appointed elder who held office in the monastic community. The office of the novice master had a slow but steady evolution in Western monasticism. The *Rule of Benedict* stipulated only that an aspirant be put under a "senior chosen for his skill in saving souls,"[12] while the

---

9. The classic study of this development is Irenee Hausherr's *Spiritual Direction in the Early Christian East* (Kalamazoo: Cistercian Publications, 1990). The most important of the early books on this diagnosis of vice and virtue are Evagrius of Pontus's *Praktikos* and the *Institutes of John Cassian;* both works were written as a result of direct contact with the desert ascetics of Egypt. Cassian's work is directly dependent upon Evagrius.

10. Whether this was Father Ambrosy of Optino or Saint Tikhon of Zadonsk has been debated. See the range of opinions in *A Karamazov Companion,* ed. Victor Terras (Madison: University of Wisconsin Press, 1981), pp. 29-30.

11. From the introduction to Hausherr's volume cited above.

12. *Rule of Benedict* 58.6.

contemporary code of canon law mandates that everyone who enters religious life must spend at least a year under the guidance of an officially designated novice master/mistress.[13] The practice of confessing one's failings to another person was also regarded as a way of advancing in spiritual perfection; that one's sins were thereby also forgiven was widely believed. It was also widely accepted that such a confession could be made to someone who was not a priest. As late as the thirteenth century, Thomas Aquinas permitted sacramental confession to a layperson when a priest was not available.[14] Like monasticism itself, sacramental confession in the Western Church slowly became clericalized.[15] While individual spiritual direction was available through many venues, sacramental confession to a priest became more and more common as the way of spiritual direction for the majority of Catholics.[16] Frequently such counsel was given short shrift because of the increasing emphasis on the confessor as a judge of sin and his role as giving penances in response to confession of sin. Spiritual direction, then, remained a desideratum, but it had to be sought through ways other than monastic formation or sacramental confession.

The Soul Friend

The model of direction described above may be considered "vertical": a relationship in which disciples put themselves under the direction of masters/mistresses or penitents subject themselves to the scrutiny of a judge/confessor. Such a relationship was vertical merely because it depends on either the sacramental or the juridical authority of the director. In some cases, like that of the priest or novice director, it was both sacramental and juridical. In either case there was nothing informal or charismatic about the relationship. Another way of thinking about spiritual direction, however, is to consider a more "horizon-

13. Canons 646-653 of the new code of canon law (1983) deal with the novitiate and the role of the novice master.

14. In the "Supplementum" to the *Summa theologiae* Q 8.23. Thomas called such confession an imperfect sacrament. For a history of the sacrament and good bibliographies, see Kenan Osborne, *Reconciliation and Justification: The Sacrament and Its Theology* (New York: Paulist, 1990).

15. The evolution of sacramental confession is a highly complex and not fully understood historical issue, beyond our scope here.

16. As late as the 1960s, the entry "Spiritual Direction" for a standard reference work could say in its opening paragraph: "In Catholic theology, especially during the last two centuries, the term [i.e., spiritual direction] has usually been taken to mean the counselling of individuals within the framework of sacramental confession." See *New Catholic Encyclopedia* (Washington, D.C.: Catholic University of America, 1967), 4.887.

tal" model: a person seeks out a confidant for spiritual advice and/or instruction based on that person's purported spiritual experience or charismatic reputation.

In the Celtic tradition such a person is called a "soul friend" (Gaelic: *anamachara*). While it is true that the soul friend was often described in the Latin sources as a spiritual father *(pater spiritualis)* or a confessor *(confessor* or *pater confessionis)*, "soul friend" was in fact a broad term for any confidant who stayed with a person through the joys and travails of life, and to whom one would go for counsel and instruction. An old legend connected to the life of Saint Brigid has her telling a young man, whose *anamachara* had died, to go and "eat no more until you find a soul friend because a person without a soul friend is a body without a head."[17] The Celtic soul friend, whether man or woman, had a variety of functions in the Irish church. Like early Abbas/ Ammas, they were guides for those who sought out the monastic life and its ways. They also served as counselors for those outside the monastery, and they were found in both aristocratic and royal circles. The term "soul friend" was also employed to describe intense spiritual friendships between equals who encouraged each other in the Christian life.[18] The soul friend is also linked to the practice of confession and the performance (and mitigation) of the fierce penitential practices characteristic of Celtic spirituality. Some soul friends lived together for mutual support and sustenance, much as the desert ascetics occasionally did, in small communities like the monastic *skete* (hence the designation *syncellus,* one who "shared a cell").

This essay will use the model of the soul friend to treat spiritual direction in contexts different from, and later than, those found in the Celtic church. Though it derives from a monastic milieu, the term has been used in elastic ways that make it popular in our own time as a new paradigm for understanding spiritual direction. Some contemporary authors have attempted to sketch

---

17. Quoted in Diarmuid O'Laoghaire's "Soul-Friendship," in *Traditions of Spiritual Guidance,* ed. Lavinia Byrne (London: Chapman, 1990), p. 30. On the monastic setting of the soul friend, see Lisa Bitel, *Isle of the Saints: Monastic Settlement and Christian Community in Early Ireland* (Ithaca, N.Y.: Cornell University Press, 1990), pp. 92-94; and Edward C. Sellner, "A Common Dwelling: Soul Friendship in Early Celtic Monasticism," *Cistercian Studies Quarterly* 29, no. 1 (1994): 1-22. For a discussion of the origins of the Celtic concept of soul friend, see Nora Chadwick, *The Age of the Saints in the Early Celtic Church* (New York: Oxford University Press, 1961), and John McNeill, *The Celtic Church* (Chicago: University of Chicago Press, 1974).

18. I must resist an excursus on spiritual friendship as a mode of spiritual direction. For a good outline and bibliography, see Brian P. McGuire, *Friendship and Community: The Monastic Experience* (Kalamazoo: Cistercian Publications, 1988), and the discussion in Sharon Elkins, *Holy Women of Twelfth-Century England* (Chapel Hill: University of North Carolina Press, 1988), p. 38 and passim.

out how a person can, in a deeply personal and engaged fashion, help another as a teacher, mentor, guide, and sustainer along the way of Christian development, especially in the life of prayer and faith.[19] This recovery of the notion of the soul friend reminds us that, along with the work of the priest-confessor or the canonical religious master/mistress of novices, informal strategies undertaken by a wide variety of persons to aid others along the spiritual path have existed all through the Middle Ages and down to the present. While it would be impossible to sketch out a historical trajectory of such enterprises, it is possible to highlight two ways in which a person served as a spiritual guide for others. With no pretension to exhaustiveness, some examples make the point.

With the recovery of women's stories in the Middle Ages, we now see more clearly how women served as spiritual guides for other women (and in the case of some virtuosi, men), inside the cloister and beyond it. The polymath nun Hildegard of Bingen (1098-1179), judged purely by her letters, provided spiritual advice, gave counsel, solved theological and exegetical conundrums, urged penance, and demanded reform from a range of persons up to and including the pope.[20] The authority of Hildegard, and of others like her, derived not from an office but from her perceived spiritual charisma. It is clear that female religious virtuosi, empowered by their spiritual reputation, were frequently called on to serve as directors for others. Clare of Assisi (1198-1253), long before her fateful meeting with Francis of Assisi, formed part of a group of spiritually minded women (under the influence of Clare's own mother) whose lives were shaped by a style of life not unlike that of the Beguines. They developed their spirituality through mutual encouragement, relatively unencumbered by male supervision.[21] In the same vein, a century later Catherine of Siena (1347-80) led a life of intense devotion, first at home and then outside her home under the discipline of Dominican oblature. She cared for the sick, destitute, and dying in her native

---

19. Notably the work of the Anglican theologian Kenneth Leech, *Soul-Friend* (San Francisco: Harper, 1977). See also Tilden Edwards, *Spiritual Friend* (New York: Paulist, 1980); Alan W. Jones, *Exploring Spiritual Direction: An Essay on Christian Friendship* (New York: Seabury Press, 1982); Edward Cletus Sellner, *Mentoring: The Ministry of Spiritual Kinship* (Notre Dame, Ind.: Ave Maria, 1990).

20. Her letters, translated into English and based on a reliable text, are in the process of publication. Already published are *The Letters of Hildegard of Bingen*, ed. Joseph Baird and Radd Ehrman, vol. 1 (New York: Oxford University Press, 1994); vol. 2 (1998).

21. Clare's canonization process reveals that long before she took a religious habit she was part of an extended group living in her home, led by her own mother, which observed a prayer life and entered into "conversation" with Clare. See Ingrid Peterson, *Clare of Assisi: A Biographical Study* (Quincy, Ill.: Franciscan Press, 1993), pp. 91-98. The acts of the canonization process may be found in *Clare of Assisi: Early Documents*, ed. Regis Armstrong (New York: Paulist, 1988), pp. 125-83.

city. Regarded as a prophetic figure, this barely literate young woman was sought out frequently for advice and counsel. More to our point, she provided spiritual counsel to a small group of men and women who lived in community with her — her *bella brigata* (beautiful band), as she called them. In the last years of her life she composed (or maybe dictated) a long treatise on the spiritual life for the sake of her admirers and for the reform of the church.[22]

The early thirteenth-century rule for recluses, the *Ancrene Wisse,* written by men for women, explicitly stipulates: "Let no man ask your counsel or talk to you; advise only women."[23] Obviously these early recluses gave direction to women. One direct indication of this practice is Margery Kempe's observation that, in 1413, she visited Julian of Norwich, the author of the *Showings,* seeking her spiritual counsel. She then recorded some of the advice she received from the anchoress, who clearly had a reputation for direction.[24] Examples of this sort could be multiplied, but the basic point is this: women were directors for other women and sometimes for others.

That Hildegard of Bingen was a prolific letter writer is not exceptional; letter writing for spiritual direction was in fact a commonplace. There is a vast literature of spiritual direction in the form of letters or treatises. Sources from the patristic period down to the present day show experienced persons writing to others who consulted them for direction about the spiritual life. Many spiritual treatises that have come down to us from the Middle Ages began as letters written to give instruction toward advancement in the spiritual life. Consider as but one example the activities of Bernard of Clairvaux (1090-1153). Apart from the hundreds of letters which have come down to us, two of Bernard's most famous treatises began as extended letters to recipients seeking his counsel. *De consideratione* consists of five "books" he wrote to Pope Eugenius III, one of his former monks who had been recently elected to the papacy. Written over a span of time, it was both a treatise on the role of the papacy and an urgent reminder that the true end of a person, even a pope, was contemplation. Bernard's other treatise, *De diligendo Deo (On Loving God),* combines a letter written to a Roman curial figure with another letter originally written to a Carthusian who sought reflections on how truly to love God. Bernard's use of the epistolary for-

22. *The Dialogue of Saint Catherine of Siena,* ed. Suzanne Noffke, O.P. (New York: Paulist, 1980); see also Diana L. Villegas, "Discernment in Catherine of Siena," *Theological Studies* 58, no. 1 (1997): 19-38.

23. In *Anchoritic Spirituality,* ed. Anne Savage and Nicholas Watson (New York: Paulist, 1991), p. 75.

24. *The Book of Margery Kempe,* trans. W. Butler-Bowden (New York: Adair, 1944), pp. 33-34; see also Joan Nuth, *Wisdom's Daughter: The Theology of Julian of Norwich* (New York: Crossroad, 1991), p. 7.

mat has a lineage that goes back through Anselm of Canterbury to the letters on spiritual direction of Augustine and Jerome. The widespread custom of giving direction through letters, a persistent feature of Christian spiritual direction, has continued to the present day.[25]

The Golden Age of Spiritual Direction

The ancient tradition of spiritual direction took on a new urgency and earlier tendencies crystallized during the sixteenth and seventeenth centuries.[26] Either directly or indirectly, spiritual formation became an instrument of Catholic reform. Spiritual direction in this period was a pluriform phenomenon, which could be used to energize new religious orders and those who fell under their influence (e.g., the Jesuits); for the reform of an already existing religious order (the Spanish Carmelites); or for the spiritual advancement of laypeople who sought direction from an acknowledged spiritual master/mistress.

The Spiritual Exercises of Ignatius of Loyola (1491-1556), a slight work not meant to be read but experienced, developed out of Ignatius's own religious experiences and was steadily refined by him over the course of his life.[27] This manual aimed to conform the person who underwent the exercises to the life of Christ through a series of conversions that would make the exercitant a contemplative in action. The exercises are experienced in one of three ways: on a directed retreat in which a person goes through the "weeks" of the exercises in a time of prayer and meditation with regular consultation with a director; on one's own, utilizing some free time during the day; or on a retreat in which the director "preaches" to those who undertake the exercises. The full exercises de-

---

25. Modern and contemporary spiritual writers like Baron Von Hugel *(Letters to His Niece)*, Evelyn Underhill *(Collected Letters)*, C. S. Lewis *(Letters to Malcolm Chiefly on Prayer)*, and Thomas Merton *(The School of Charity: Letters on Spiritual Renewal and Spiritual Direction)* have used the letter as a powerful instrument for spiritual instruction; these writings have become, in turn, literary devotional classics.

26. For a survey of research and bibliography, see Massimo Marcocchi, "Spirituality in the Sixteenth and Seventeenth Centuries," in *Catholicism in Early Modern Europe: A Guide to Research,* ed. John O'Malley, S.J. (St. Louis: Center for Reformation Research, 1988), pp. 163-92; and the essay in *Christian Spirituality: Post-Reformation and Modern,* ed. Louis Dupré and Don E. Saliers (New York: Crossroad, 1989).

27. The best English version is *Ignatius of Loyola: The Spiritual Exercises and Selected Works,* ed. George Ganss (New York: Paulist, 1991). Most translations are based on the autograph version of 1544 done by a copyist and corrected by Ignatius; that version, and three early Latin translations, are to be found in *Sancti Ignatii de Loyola Exercitia Spiritualia,* Monumenta Historica Societatis Jesu 100 (Rome: Historical Institute of the Society of Jesus, 1969).

mand four weeks, but often they are preached in a more compressed form over a few days or a single week. The basic point is this: this conversion journey, rooted in the life and deeds of Christ, is done under the direction of one already experienced in this spiritual path. For Ignatius these exercises not only offered basic formation for the Jesuits, they were to become an instrument for creating committed Christians of both sexes, whether clerical, religious, or lay.

The retreat movement, inspired by the Ignatian model, has provided the modern church an intense experience for Christian education and formation carried out in a nonacademic, intense, focused, and spiritual manner. Not only can the modern retreat movement be traced back to the giving of the *Exercises*, but Ignatian practice shows how a spiritual director was expected to function. Joseph Tetlow, a contemporary Jesuit director, clearly distinguished the work of spiritual director from that of therapist or sacramental confessor: "In therapy you must mention whatever comes to your mind by way of free association, and deliberately holding back is what interferes with the healing process. In confession, you must tell a priest in detail what you have done or left undone contrary to your own conscience. In Ignatian spiritual direction, you choose what to tell your director about your experiences in prayer and silence, what you are doing and what you are desiring. Your director helps you to interpret those experiences."[28]

Ignatius desired all of his fellow Jesuits to be formed in the way of *The Spiritual Exercises*. He further envisioned the *Exercises* as an instrument for the development of those to whom his Society of Jesus would minister. This aspect of the Jesuit apostolate was so central to the Society that by 1599 the Roman Jesuits developed a Directorium to aid Jesuits in their task of taking people through the *Spiritual Exercises*. That same year the Jesuit general, Claudio Aquaviva, issued instructions on how Jesuits ought to give spiritual direction both in and outside the administration of the sacrament of penance. Much of the director's work was oriented toward aiding people in cooperating with the promptings of divine grace, thus to aid them in the battle against temptations, and to foreclose any penchant toward false quietistic mysticism. People were to discern the promptings of divine grace so that they might ultimately choose the greater good for the "greater glory of God."

It is hard to overestimate the genius and impact of Ignatian spirituality. The Jesuits were able to integrate this spiritual discipline within the larger apostolate of maintaining schools, parishes, and missions. Their intention was to provide intense spiritual direction, following a disciplined method of

28. Joseph A. Tetlow, *Ignatius of Loyola: Spiritual Exercises* (New York: Crossroad, 1992), p. 37.

prayer and formation, within the framework of traditional pastoral institutions. Ignatius "gave" the *Exercises* to his first companions who, in turn, gave them to theirs, and so on, down to the present day in a continuous line. The Jesuits themselves directed their students, parishioners, and others through the same exercises (often in a modified or partial form) as a means of evangelization and/or formation. In this fashion every Jesuit was both the subject of close spiritual direction and, when the opportunity arose, a purveyor of direction to others.

In the wake of the Protestant Reformation, spiritual direction also flourished in the sixteenth and seventeenth centuries as an instrument of Catholic reform. The great Spanish mystics Teresa of Ávila (1515-82) and John of the Cross (1542-91) devoted much of their energies to the spiritual direction of their fellow Carmelites in order to reform their convents and bring them to a higher life of prayer and contemplation. It is fair to say that all of John's writings are exercises in spiritual guidance.[29] John realized how crucial it is that a spiritual director be someone who has had spiritual experience, not a person who wishes to dominate, one who has a sense of discretion and judgment and is free from the desire to manipulate. In his *Living Flame of Love,* John locates the bad spiritual director ahead of Satan as a destroyer of souls. He describes such directors, dependent on book knowledge and guesswork, as one of the three "blind persons" (the other two being the devil and the soul's own pride) who will lead people astray.[30]

Teresa of Ávila received great aid from the spiritual directors who helped her understand her experiences of prayer. She also received bad advice, especially from those who had little experience in the life of graced prayer. One could argue that her own writings, especially her autobiography *(Mi Vida), The Way of Perfection,* and *The Interior Castle,* were composed for the precise purpose of helping other women, who lacked theological education (Teresa herself could not read Latin), to understand the ways of prayer. Her works, in short, were vernacular guides to supplement her own teachings. She wrote of her experiences with clinical detail so as — to paraphrase one of her finest interpreters — to help others avoid the pain she experienced at the hands of bad directors. In this enterprise Teresa's literary output is not unlike that of John of the Cross. Both were spiritual guides for those who sought perfection. Teresa's task was the more difficult, both because she had no formal theological education

29. It is worthwhile noting that John never uses the word "director" for his ministry. Frequently he talks about a guide *(guia)* or a spiritual master *(maestro espiritual).*

30. See John's long excursus on spiritual direction in *The Living Flame of Love,* in *The Collected Works of John of the Cross,* ed. Kieran Kavanaugh and Ottilo Rodriguez (Washington, D.C.: ICS, 1979).

and because she was a woman. These two facts alone brought her activities more than once to the attention of the Inquisition. Nonetheless, Teresa's teachings, as well as those of the Spanish Carmelite school in general, would have an enormous impact beyond the frontiers of Spain.[31]

The Carmelite practice of prayer and contemplation entered France through the establishment of Carmelite convents in the late sixteenth century. Their presence deeply influenced a whole century of French spiritual writers whose powerful writings were to impact not only the Catholic world but many persons in both the Orthodox and Protestant worlds. The "French School" (so named by Henri Bremond) put a strong emphasis on spiritual direction, whether that direction was given to those destined for the priesthood or religious life, or to devout laypersons who wished to learn about the path of perfection. Many of the great figures of the French School were themselves under the spiritual instruction of directors of both sexes.[32]

The use of spiritual direction as part of a general pastoral strategy is well exemplified in the life of Francis de Sales (1567-1622), who, despite a busy life as a reforming bishop of a large diocese, found time to give personal spiritual direction to a number of individuals. Like many of his predecessors, he provided most of his direction through notes and letters. Indeed, his now classic work *The Introduction to the Devout Life* (1608; amended and amplified in 1609) began as a series of letters written to a young woman who was a relative by marriage. While the *Introduction* draws from a large number of traditional sources, what is most interesting about this work (and perhaps a clue to its perennial popularity) is de Sales's conviction that the style of spiritual direction must be tailored to the specific vocation of the person who seeks instruction. He saw clearly that a monastic horarium was hardly appropriate for a layperson. As he put it: "Devotion must be exercised in different ways by the gentleman, the worker, the servant, the prince, the widow, the young girl and the married woman. Not only is this true, but the practice of devotion must be adapted to the strength, activities, and duties of each particular person. . . . It is

---

31. On the role of Teresa as a woman director, see Alison Weber, *Teresa of Avila and the Rhetoric of Feminity* (Princeton: Princeton University Press, 1990); Carole Slade, *St. Teresa of Avila: Author of a Heroic Life* (Berkeley: University of California Press, 1995); G. T. W. Ahlgren, *Teresa of Avila and the Politics of Sanctity* (Ithaca, N.Y.: Cornell University Press, 1996).

32. "Berulle is directed by Madeleine de Saint Joseph and the frail Catherine de Jesus; Pere Eudes by a woman of the people, Marie des Valles; . . . M. Olier by Agnes de Langeac together with Marie Rousseau and several others." In Henri Bremond's classic, *A Literary History of Religious Thought in France* (London: SPCK, 1936), 3.1-2. For a good survey of the French School, see *The French School of Spirituality*, ed. Raymond Deville (Pittsburgh: Duquesne University Press, 1994).

an error, or rather, a heresy, to wish to banish the devout life from the regiment of soldiers, the mechanic's shop, the court of princes, or the home of married people."[33]

This brief essay cannot treat all the ways post-Tridentine spirituality affected the early modern Catholic Church, but it can enumerate a few points. First, spiritual directors were legislated for religious houses of both sexes (confessors often functioned in this fashion), and as well for seminaries whose structures first took shape in this period. Second, with the rise of active congregations of women religious there developed close spiritual direction provided by the women who directed such congregations for the men who were their patrons or institutional founders. Such characterized the spiritual friendships between Teresa of Ávila and John of the Cross, Jane de Chantal and Francis de Sales, and Louise de Marillac and Vincent de Paul. Third, these teachings on prayer and the life of prayer created a demand for people who could guide such forms of prayer and meditation, which in turn provided new "schools" of spirituality embraced by both religious and laypeople. In the baroque period, some argue, schools of spirituality and treatises on prayer or direction would prove far more original than the work of systematic theologians. Finally, these exercises in the pedagogy of prayer were seen as instruments of church reform. They molded not only more worthy priests and religious (a leading concern of the Tridentine program) but devout laypersons who could be exemplars within the world. A strong emphasis on spiritual direction was essential to the vocation of the committed reformers. Cardinal de Bérulle loved to quote Gregory the Great's aphorism *Ars artium cura animarum* (The direction of souls is the art of all arts).[34]

Spiritual Direction and the Reformed Tradition

It should not surprise us that the work of the spiritual director was looked upon with some suspicion by the Reformers. After all, the idea of one person leading another into a deeper life of prayer smacked of the cloister and had too

33. Francis de Sales, *Introduction to the Devout Life*, trans. John K. Ryan (New York: Harper Torchbooks, 1966), p. 37. Note the use of the word "devotion." Terms like "spirituality" and, especially, "mysticism" did not come into common usage until this period, at least in the sense in which we use the words today; see Michel de Certeau, *The Mystic Fable* (Chicago: University of Chicago Press, 1992), 1:95-97. On the meaning of devotion, see Michael Buckley, "Seventeenth Century Spirituality: Three Figures," in *Christian Spirituality: Post-Reformation and Modern*, pp. 36-41.

34. *French School of Spirituality*, p. 166.

many connections with the practice of auricular confession. Moreover, many functions of the spiritual director found their outlet in the ordinary pastoral duties of the ministers in reformed churches. It would be otiose to point out that the vast correspondences (as well as many of the treatises) of the Reformers were devoted to individuals who sought out answers to questions about pious living and growth in Christian virtue. A now classic, if old, work argues that there was a tradition of spiritual direction from the time of the early Reformers down to the present, but that the context, methods, and vocabulary was different from that of Roman Catholic models.[35] There is a stream of literature devoted to the *cura animarum* which runs from sixteenth-century Reformers like Martin Bucer through the seventeenth-century Puritans and down to nineteenth-century works that run the gamut from Scottish Presbyterians to Quakers.[36] Pietist practices, with their emphasis on small Bible study conventicles and the practice of biblical admonition (think of Spener's *Pia Desideria* or the pastoral work of Count Zinzendorf), have strong analogies with spiritual direction.[37]

Due to their intense interest in leading a godly and devotional life, the seventeenth-century Puritans in America utilized various forms of close spiritual direction. Ministers were expected to consult regularly with their parishioners about the quality of their life of prayer. Further, in the words of a recent scholar:

> "Private conferences" — sessions with a mentor or spiritual director — were an expression of the membership of each believer in the covenant. Parents with children, masters with apprentices, teachers and Harvard tutors with students, older women with young women and girls — indeed, every church member — had a responsibility to care for the spiritual welfare of others. Ministers engaged in spiritual counselling as part of their calling, but they encouraged everyone to find a "spiritual friend" other than a minister with whom to confide and pray.[38]

35. Jean-Daniel Benoit, *Direction spirituelle et Protestantisme* (Paris, 1940). Benoit, however, writes much of Calvin and quickly elides to the nineteenth century, thus omitting the Lutheran, Pietist, and Quaker traditions.

36. Representative titles cited in Leech, pp. 84-88. Leech notes in particular the vast number of collected letters on the Christian life published in English in the seventeenth and eighteenth centuries. For an earlier collection one might begin with Martin Luther's *Letters of Spiritual Counsel*, in Library of Christian Classics, vol. 18 (Philadelphia: Westminster, 1956).

37. For selected texts see *Pietists: Selected Writings*, ed. Peter Erb (New York: Paulist, 1983), pp. 10-16. As Erb points out, many of the Pietists were deeply influenced by French quietists, a movement which evolved out of the French School of spirituality.

38. Charles Hambrick-Stowe, "Puritan Spirituality in America," in *Christian Spirituality: Post-Reformation and Modern*, p. 347.

It is among the Anglicans that we find the strongest emphasis on spiritual direction among churches of the sixteenth and seventeenth centuries. This was especially true in the seventeenth century when writers like George Herbert, Nicholas Ferrar, and Jeremy Taylor practiced a form of "classical" spiritual direction with an explicit awareness of Roman Catholic models and their limitations. As Taylor wrote in the preface to his 1660 *Doctor Dubitantium:* "Our needs remain and we cannot be well-supplied out of the Roman storehouse."[39] Martin Thornton has pointed out that there was hardly a published Anglican author in the seventeenth century who did not see spiritual guidance as an integral part of the pastoral duty of the clergy.[40]

As with many things, it was the Tractarian movement of the nineteenth century that rediscovered the riches of the Caroline divines of the seventeenth century. Even though there was a tendency among the Tractarians to rely heavily on French Catholic models of confessional practice (this was as true of a Catholic convert like Frederick Faber as of the Anglo-Catholic scholar Edward Bouverie Pusey), nonetheless there was an interest in the guidance of souls. In the twentieth century, apart from Evelyn Underhill, C. S. Lewis, Kenneth Leech, and others already mentioned, the most systematic thinker on the theology of and place for spiritual direction within the Anglican tradition has been Martin Thornton, whose work on spiritual guidance has been one of the most theologically sound and systematically developed of any work on the subject.[41]

Some Contemporary Trajectories

First, the intersection of direction and psychology. Spiritual direction involves a relationship between someone providing insight into the interior life and the reception of this advice by the person seeking direction. In a post-Freudian culture it does not take much effort to see how categories of spiritual direction could become psychologized both for good and for evil. At the same time, a spiritual director must have some sense about where his or her competency ends and the need for a professional psychologist begins.[42] Most contemporary

---

39. Cited in Leech, p. 79.

40. Martin Thornton, *English Spirituality* (London: SPCK, 1963), p. 273.

41. Martin Thornton, *Spiritual Direction: A Practical Introduction* (London: SPCK, 1984).

42. Two recent works which deal with these issues are Gerald G. May, *Care of Mind/Care of Spirit: Psychiatric Dimensions of Spiritual Direction* (San Francisco: Harper, 1982), and John J. Evoy, *A Psychological Handbook for Spiritual Directors* (Kansas City, Mo.: Sheed and Ward, 1988). On the difference between therapy and direction, see Lucy Bregman, "Psychotherapies," in *Spirituality and the Secular Quest*, ed. Peter Van Ness (New York: Crossroad, 1996), pp. 264-65.

writers warn directors against becoming amateur psychologists and, in the process, doing terrible harm to people who might require professional therapy and not spiritual direction.

Another profound question connected with spiritual direction concerns the danger of illicit or ignorant control by a "master" who counsels a disciple. Here the classical therapeutic doctrine of psychological "transference" becomes important, whether it be by the client or the director. In situations of transference there is always the further danger of manipulation or seduction.[43] We might recall here the consistent warnings of such spiritual masters as John of the Cross who well understood the dangers of a bad spiritual director. The lugubrious stories of spiritual manipulation found in our national media are a cautionary tale about how powerfully destructive a charismatic religious figure can be. As we noted earlier in this essay, quoting Joseph Tetlow, a distinction needs to be made between therapist and spiritual director, and that distinction should always be quite clearly recognized — even when, as is inevitable, psychological issues arise in the course of direction.

Second, spiritual direction as an ecumenical enterprise. Most of this essay has concentrated on spiritual direction within the broad Catholic or Orthodox tradition. There is an increased interest in Christian spirituality among evangelical and Reformed writers.[44] The Presbyterian writer Howard Rice, for instance, has argued that along with church discipline, corporate confession of sin within worship, and pastoral counseling there is an honored place in the Calvinist tradition for spiritual guidance done under the stipulated terms of the Second Helvetic Confession. It stated that any person who was "overwhelmed by sin" or perplexed by temptations should seek "counsel, guidance or comfort privately" either from a church minister or a "brother [sic] who is instructed in God's Law."[45] Rice stipu-

---

43. J. Strus sees this as a particular problem: "Direzione spirituale," in *Dizionario enciclopedio di spiritualitá* (Rome: Città Nuova Editrice, 1990), 1:803-5.

44. See, for example, the pertinent essays on Reformed, Lutheran, Wesleyan, and Holiness spiritualities in *Modern Christian Spirituality: Methodological and Historical Essays*, ed. Bradley C. Hanson, AAR Studies in Religion, ed. Lawrence S. Cunningham, vol. 62 (Atlanta: Scholars, 1990); M. Robert Mulholland, Jr., *Invitation to a Journey: A Road Map for Spiritual Formation* (Downers Grove, Ill.: InterVarsity, 1993); Bradley P. Holt, *Thirsty for God: A Brief History of Christian Spirituality* (Minneapolis: Augsburg, 1993); Howard Rice, "Spirituality and Discipline: A Reformed Perspective," *Christian Century* 109 (May 6, 1992): 486-88. Alister McGrath's *Evangelicalism and the Future of Christianity* (Downers Grove, Ill: InterVarsity, 1995) argues for the need for a well-developed spirituality from within the evangelical tradition, in order to obviate the need to draw from the Roman Catholic or Orthodox traditions so exclusively; to fill that need, see the same author's *Christian Spirituality* (Oxford: Blackwell, 1999).

45. Quoted in Howard Rice, "Consultation: Spiritual Guidance in the Reformed Tradition," in *Reformed Spirituality: An Introduction for Beginners* (Louisville: Westminster/John

lates guidelines for those who undertake spiritual direction: deep personal experience of the Christian faith, participation in worship, a disciplined life of personal prayer, some acuity with respect to human psychology, awareness of one's own limitations, some sense of the tradition of guidance, a sense of vocation, and the capacity to be honest with others.[46]

Precisely because Rice insists that a director have some knowledge of the tradition of direction, there will be an inevitable ecumenical nexus between those who engage in direction in the Reformed tradition and those masters/mistresses who work in other traditions. One can see those convergences simply by comparing the practical prescriptions of Rice (or others) with similar works written from within, say, the Roman Catholic tradition.[47] With the rise of ecumenical interest it is only natural that there should be a closer examination of the ways "individual guides and companions can help us to see ourselves in ways that we cannot see on our own."[48] This is not to dismiss varying emphases from within different traditions. There will inevitably be such differences since the diverse Christian traditions will have quite divergent theological anthropologies, sacramental theologies, and spiritualities.

Third, concern about the professionalization of spiritual direction. Beyond the perennial tradition of spiritual direction sketched out in this essay, there is, in the contemporary world, a gradual professionalization of spiritual direction as it becomes more common in churches and veers closer to the therapeutic culture in which we live.[49] Training programs, professional organizations (like Spiritual Directors International), a desire for certification, and the granting of graduate degrees in spiritual direction have raised a plethora of problems. What is the professional responsibility of such directors? To what degree are they answerable for their work in view of the litigious society in which they live? When does spiritual direction turn into amateur psychological therapy? What criteria are available to discern the value of esoteric trends (e.g., the popularity of Jungian categories in direction, the use of schemata like the Enneagram, or therapies derived from New Age practices) in spiritual direction? What about peer review and supervision? Will confidentiality between director and directee stand up in the courts in cases involving litigation either for

---

Knox, 1991), p. 120. Rice notes that spiritual guidance was very common among the Puritans in this country.

46. Rice, *Reformed Spirituality,* p. 146.

47. See Robert F. Morneau, *Spiritual Direction: Principles and Practices* (New York: Crossroad, 1992).

48. Holt, p. 20.

49. E. Brooks Holifield, *A History of Pastoral Care in America: From Salvation to Self-Realization* (Nashville: Abingdon, 1983). The subtitle of the book is very telling.

civil or criminal matters? Is it even possible to become a spiritual director through the academic certification route? These issues have now come to the fore and are beginning to be ventilated in the literature.[50]

Finally, one might object that spiritual direction is an elitist luxury open only to the more rarefied believers with the leisure to pursue such an endeavor as cultivation of the spiritual life. We even see the (obnoxious) practice of direction by fee. This objection, cast in a somewhat different form, was common among sixteenth-century Reformers who judged a good deal of Catholic devotional and mystic life as rooted in the theological errors coming out of monasticism.[51] Similar objections might also come from those who see spiritual direction in particular and the cultivation of the spiritual life in general as irrelevant to the larger issues of pastoral care, evangelization, and concern for the world.

Against such objections we should note that a large number of people who work with the very poor or in ministries like hospice care or shelters for the homeless have insisted on what is sometimes called "deep listening" or "listening with the heart" as a fundamental part of their vocations. In other words, such persons fully understand that if they are to avoid the trap of bringing support "from above" and intend, rather, to act in concerted solidarity, one of their most urgent tasks is to become listeners to those who frequently have no human person with whom they might share their fears, anxieties, and temptations to despair. In order to overcome the stereotype of the director as guru (implicit, perhaps, in the very word "director" or "master/mistress"), much of the writing coming, for example, from liberation theologies has attempted to recover the ancient tradition of the spiritual director as a listener, which is to say, a soul friend. All liberation theologians agree, for instance, that theology should come "from below" in the sense that it should be shaped in the context of actual events and experiences, especially those of the poor. This requires, in the first instance, listening to those voices. The concept of the director/guide as listener is hardly new. It is a precondition for manifestation of the heart, confession of sin, and a commonplace in spiritual ascesis.[52] It is, in fact, one of the most com-

50. I have gleaned some of the questions in my text from "Professionalism, Record Keeping, Legal Responsibilities: A Conversation with Robert J. Willis," *Presence: A International Journal of Spiritual Direction* 1, no. 1 (January 1995): 41-54.

51. On this issue see Heiko Oberman, "Simul Gemitus et Raptus: Luther and Mysticism," in *The Dawn of the Reformation* (Edinburgh: T. & T. Clark, 1986), pp. 126-54; Dennis Tamburello, *Union with Christ: John Calvin and the Mysticism of St. Bernard* (Louisville: Westminster/John Knox, 1994).

52. We might note, for example, that the ancient *Rule of Benedict* begins with the word *Ausculta* (Hear!). A hefty monograph would be possible on the theme of listening as a spiritual discipline.

mon tasks of any person in the pastoral ministry. It is worthwhile asking whether the opportunity to listen is not also an opportunity for spiritual guidance, since all the "counseling skills and techniques in the world will not make up for the lack of a 'listening heart.'"[53]

A Concluding Reflection

At the heart of my discussion is a small paradox. On the one hand, it is possible to discern a distinct ministry within the Christian tradition called spiritual direction. It is further possible to distinguish that ministry from that of teacher or preacher or priest or minister. No claim is made, however, that it is a significant motif in the pedagogical strategies of the historic Christian churches. Unlike preaching or teaching, after all, it is a "labor-intensive" enterprise involving one person with another person or very small groups of people. On the other hand, people in the most diverse situations within the church find themselves engaged in some form of spiritual direction, either on an ad hoc basis or for sustained periods. Like the desert ascetics, people of faith are often asked for a "good word" or queried, "What should I do?" Frequently those requests come either in the context of crisis or of spiritual or physical deprivation. Those who can provide an answer to such questions are, at the threshold, spiritual guides; which is to say, they are soul friends.

What the more formal kind of spiritual direction signifies is a readiness and aptitude to provide a good word (or a good ear!) on a consistent and fruitful basis as part of one's religious vocation. That consistency, more than any appointment or certification, is the hallmark of the authentic guide. Such a readiness develops only from the spiritual capacity to listen. After the Nazis closed his seminary at Finkenwalde, Dietrich Bonhoeffer wrote of his experiences in a book called *Gemeinsames Leben* (1939). A few lines in that work provide an appropriate coda for this paper:

> The first service that one owes to others in the fellowship consists in listening to them. . . . It is God's love for us that He not only gives us His Word but also lends us his ear. . . . Many people are looking for an ear that will listen. They

---

53. Carolyn Gratton, "Spiritual Direction," in *The New Dictionary of Catholic Spirituality*, ed. Michael Downey (Collegeville, Minn.: Liturgical Press/Glazier, 1993), p. 915. This article builds on the author's earlier book *The Art of Spiritual Guidance* (New York: Crossroad, 1992). See also Thomas N. Hart, *The Art of Christian Listening* (New York: Paulist, 1980); William A. Barry and William J. Connolly, *The Practice of Spiritual Direction* (New York: Seabury Press, 1982).

do not find it among Christians because these Christians are talking when they should be listening. . . . Christians have forgotten that the ministry of listening has been committed to them by Him who is himself the Great Listener and whose work we share. We should listen with the ears of God that we may speak the Word of God.[54]

When one attempts today to systematize the different forms of spiritual guidance in the various strains of the Christian tradition, it is almost reflexive to go back to the historical past to seek guideposts. Obviously the worldview of John of the Cross is not ours, but the shrewd insights that he and other spiritual masters and mistresses provide go beyond cultural limitations: be listeners; be prompted by the movements of grace; do not give in to delusions; do not manipulate; keep your eye on God and not on the director; and so on. Beyond that, contemporary spiritual guides "translate" time-honored phrases into a language with which we are able to resonate and from which we learn to grow. Older guides may have emphasized "abandonment" where we might speak of "risk"; we might see acedia as depression; and so on. This translation can be done if people have a nuanced sense of terminology and so avoid reductionism. In that sense spiritual direction is like the good householder of the Gospel who "brings forth old things and new." We learn from the old tradition not to bronze it but to make it malleable for the contemporary pilgrimage of faith.

54. Dietrich Bonhoeffer, *Life Together* (New York: Harper, 1954), quoted in *Writings on Spiritual Direction,* ed. Jerome Neufelder and Mary Coelho (New York: Seabury Press, 1982), pp. 86-87.

List of Contributors

John C. Cavadini is Associate Professor and Chair, Department of Theology, and Director of the Institute for Church Life at the University of Notre Dame.

Anne L. Clark is Associate Professor of Religion at the University of Vermont.

Lawrence S. Cunningham is John A. O'Brien Professor of Theology at the University of Notre Dame.

Joseph Goering is Professor of History at the University of Toronto.

Robert Goldenberg is Professor of History and Judaic Studies at the State University of New York at Stony Brook.

Stanley Samuel Harakas is Archbishop Iakovos Professor of Orthodox Theology, Emeritus (Holy Cross Greek Orthodox School of Theology), at Hellenic College.

Robert M. Kingdon is Emeritus Professor of History at the University of Wisconsin.

Blake Leyerle is Associate Professor of Theology at the University of Notre Dame.

Michael A. Signer is Abrams Professor of Jewish Thought and Culture in the Department of Theology at the University of Notre Dame.

Philip M. Soergel is Associate Professor in the Department of History at Arizona State University.

David C. Steinmetz is Amos Ragan Kearns Professor of the History of Christianity at the Divinity School at Duke University.

John Van Engen is Professor of Medieval History at the University of Notre Dame.

Lee Palmer Wandel is Professor of History at the University of Wisconsin in Madison.

Robert Louis Wilken is William R. Kenan Jr. Professor of the History of Christianity at the University of Virginia.

Elliot R. Wolfson is Abraham Lieberman Professor of Hebrew and Judaic Studies at New York University.